DULCINEA IN THE FACTORY

D0963908

A BOOK IN THE SERIES

COMPARATIVE AND INTERNATIONAL

WORKING-CLASS HISTORY

GENERAL EDITORS:

ANDREW GORDON, HARVARD UNIVERSITY

DANIEL JAMES, DUKE UNIVERSITY

ALEXANDER KEYSSAR, DUKE UNIVERSITY

DULCINEA IN THE FACTORY

Myths, Morals, Men, and Women

in Colombia's Industrial Experiment,

1905–1960

ANN FARNSWORTH-ALVEAR

DUKE UNIVERSITY PRESS

DURHAM AND LONDON, 2000

© 2000 Duke University Press. All rights reserved
Printed in the United States of America on acid-free paper ∞
Typeset in Trump Mediaeval by Keystone Typesetting, Inc.
Library of Congress Cataloging-in-Publication Data
appear on the last printed page of this book.

"¡Ta, ta!" dijo Sancho. "¿Que la hija de Lorenzo Corchuelo es la Señora Dulcinea del Toboso, llamada por otro nombre Aldonza Lorenzo?" "Esa es," dijo Don Quijote, "y es la que merece ser señora de todo el universo." "Bien la conozco," dijo Sancho, "y sé decir que tira tan bien una barra como el más forzudo zagal de todo el pueblo. ¡Vive el Dador, que es moza de chapa, hecha y derecha, y de pelo en pecho! . . . Pero, bien considerado, ¿qué se le ha de dar a la Señora Aldonza Lorenzo, digo, a la señora Dulcinea del Toboso, de que se le vayan a hincar de rodillas delante de ella los vencidos que vuestra merced le envía y ha de enviar? Porque podría ser que al tiempo que ellos llegasen estuviese ella rastrillando lino, o trillando en las eras, y ellos se corriesen de verla, y ella se riese y enfadase del presente."

"Ah, ha!" cried Sancho, "is the daughter of Lorenzo Corchuelo, whose other name is Aldonza Lorenzo, the same with the lady Dulcinea?" "Yes," answered the knight, "and she deserves to be lady of the whole universe." "I know her perfectly well, " said Sancho; "and this will venture to say, in her behalf, that she will pitch the bar, as well as e'er a lusty young fellow in the village. Bless the sender! She is a strapper, tall and hale [of] wind and limb. . . . But, when one considers the affair, what benefits can my lady Aldonza Lorenzo—I mean, my lady Dulcinea del Toboso, reap from your worship's sending, or having sent those, whom you overcome in battle, to fall upon their knees before her? Especially, as they might chance to come, at a time, when she is busy, carding flax or threshing corn; in which case, they would be ashamed to see her, and she laugh or be out of humor at their arrival."

Miguel de Cervantes, DON QUIJOTE, 1605,

trans. Tobias Smollett, 1755

CONTENTS

ILLUSTRATIONS

PREFACE

THIS BOOK EXPLORES two intertwined historical processes closely associated with worldwide modernity: the geographic expansion of factory production and the transformation of gender roles, whether real or potential, that is
implied by women's waged labor. As a history of the social relationships and
cultural understandings that shaped industrial work in a prosperous Latin
American city, it is meant as a corrective to overly simple generalizations
about "import-substitution industrialization" or "third world women workers." Wherever foreign or native entrepreneurs imported factory machines
from Europe and the United States, they also imported ideas and practices
associated with that machinery. Such ideas and practices were intermingled
with entrepreneurs' more or less self-conscious plans for remaking local economic relationships. In Colombia, for example, many early industrialists
saw themselves as social engineers. Yet factory owners nowhere controlled
the social and cultural activity by which industrialism was made local.
I begin by asking how people on the ground (and in the workrooms built
to house newly arrived machines) experienced, understood, and changed
the meaning of factory labor in the first half-century of Colombia's industrial experiment.

Although its name is now synonymous with drug trafficking and urban
violence, Medellín, capital of the Colombian province of Antioquia, once
enjoyed a very different reputation. If Bogotá, the country's capital, claimed
to be the "Athens" of South America, Medellín presented itself as the region's "Manchester," where local capital had transformed a mountain town
into the birthplace of an urbanized, industrial Colombia. Between 1905,
when the city's first cotton mill began production, and the early 1960s, when

Antioqueño industry was widely recognized as a pacesetter for Latin American manufacturing more generally, a compressed process of textile-led industrialization transformed the daily lives of hundreds of thousands of people. Medellín's mills became known for an intensely Catholic paternalism, by which the largest employers presented themselves as the moral guardians of female workers. Medellinense industrialists developed this disciplinary form only gradually, adopting it both in response to the direct possibility of labor activism and as a solution to what had become a vexed local dilemma: that the everyday reality of factories where women and men worked side by side contradicted deeply held beliefs about the immorality of sexual mixing.

This study traces the role of gender in shaping the way Colombian mill-owners solved a general problem of capitalist exploitation: how to ensure an element of consent in the relationship between those who labor for a wage and those who profit from the difference between labor's price and the price of labor's product. Nevertheless, my interest is in the idiosyncrasies of Antioquia's industrial history. Why did the chastity of female workers become the focal point of industrial discipline? Why, over time, were women then excluded from textile production? In the 1940s, when the workforce was evenly split between male and female workers, being seen dancing in the wrong part of town or wearing skirts considered "too short" would get a woman in trouble at work; getting pregnant would get her fired. By the 1950s, however, textile jobs were being redefined as "men's jobs," and the focus of work rules shifted. A disciplinary system that had centered on workers' gendered bodies gave way to one that revolved around the stopwatch of the industrial engineer. In the timing and shape of changing forms of factory control, the Medellín case has relevance for historians interested in the varied ways that gender has shaped industrial paternalism, Fordism, and neo-Taylorist management in different national contexts.

Beyond its comparative value, the story this book tells for Colombia provides evidence of the need to continue rethinking gender as an analytical category. In Medellín's mills, especially during the 1930s and 1940s, the difference between "good" and "bad" women was culturally as important as that between men and women. It underlay a moral code that shaped workingwomen's self-perceptions, as well as the self-perceptions of men who labored in mixed-sex workplaces, and it organized the local labor market almost as thoroughly as did the male/female distinction per se. Conceptually, the difference between the proper and improper behaviors of gendered subjects is generally understood as being dependent upon the cultural dichotomy of female versus male. I have instead attempted to understand the normative work of sexuality, by which a range of stereotypes are attached to gendered bodies, as being part of the process of gender differentiation itself. Although the reference in the title is to Don Quijote's fantasy that the village girl Aldonza is the chaste queen of his dreams, Dulcinea, one might point to more "modern" and less light-hearted examples: the "pure" white woman of racist fantasies, European reformers' images of the tubercular factory girl, or the hypersexualized images of *la mulata* in the Hispanic Caribbean and of African American men in the United States. This book is an examination of women's and men's experiences in a particular, and limited, set of work-places. Nevertheless, the richness of the sources available for Medellín has the potential to contribute to a range of discussions within feminist scholar-ship: about the instability of the term "women"; about the role of sexuality in shaping social hierarchies, such as class and race; and about the usefulness of historical approaches that focus on human subjectivity.

ACKNOWLEDGMENTS

MY FIRST DEBT IS to the many retired women and men who sat with me for long hours, sharing their memories of working lives spent in Medellín's textile mills. Whether they agreed to let another take their turn at the domino tables of the Asociación de Jubilados to answer questions for twenty or thirty minutes, or they invited me into their homes for hours of taped conversation, sometimes over various days, their willingness to talk to me provided me not only with "material" but also with inspiration. Special thanks are due those who immediately took an interest in my research, introducing me to friends and family members who might also agree to record their memories of mill-work. I am no less indebted to the retirees who simply made me think, even if by sending me away brusquely, as did a woman who pronounced: "I worked for thirty years, working is no fun. There's nothing else to say." Whether I have succeeded or failed to understand what retirees tried to communicate in our cross-generational conversations, I am grateful that I had an opportunity to listen.

My family in Medellín adopted my research as it adopted me, a long-lost *gringa* cousin. María Ester Sanín and Juan Guillermo Múnera contributed in a thousand ways, providing moral and material support from beginning to end. Not even they know how much their example has taught me about giving, about comradeship, and about how to do the seemingly impossible: be optimistic about Colombia's future. I owe a special debt to Jaime Sanín Echeverri and to the late José Sanín Echeverri, who explained Antioqueño expressions, laughed over my tapes, lent me the car, and vouched for me to factory archivists; I'm sorry to have known so jovial a grand-uncle for so short a time. My time in Medellín has also been made special by the kindness of Alejandro, Clarita, Elena, Eugenio, Fabio Andrés, Gerardo, María Helena, Lucrecia, Ignacio, Jesús, Juan Guillermo, Patricia, and Rodrigo; by my uncle José Alvear; and by the extended family of Jairo Alviar. In Bogotá, Ruth, Miriam, Fabiola, and Carlos Alviar Restrepo opened their hearts and homes. Their passionate interest in history has helped me appreciate the example set by my grandfather José. My most profound gratitude is reserved for my grandmother Ofelia, who simply *was* Colombia to me throughout my childhood— a Colombia of love.

Ana María Jaramillo has been an unwavering intellectual support and a true friend, sharing her own research material unstintingly. Many other Colombian scholars have aided me along the way. Thanks are due Alberto Mayor Mora, Ana María Bidegain, Argelia and Patricia Londoño, Catalina Reyes, Constanza Toro, Eduardo Sáenz Rovner, Diana Ceballos, Fabio Botero Herrera, Gloria Mercedes Arango, Juan José Echavarría, Jorge Bernal, Luis Javier Ortiz, Luz Gabriela Arango, María Claudia Saavedra, and Mauricio Archila Neira. Doing research in a city wracked by violence, I encountered only professionalism and courtesy. Edgar Moná and Gildardo Martínez facilitated my initial research at Fabricato; I thank also Ana María Bravo, Claudia Vélez, and Alvaro Murillo at that firm. The efforts of Orlando Ramírez, head archivist at Coltejer, and of Jairo Castrillón at Tejicondor, transformed an idea about personnel records into a viable research agenda. I must also thank Rodrigo Botero of Fatelares; Mariela Rios Madrid and the staff of the Archivo Histórico de Antioquia; Carolina Gil and the always helpful staff at the Fundación Antioqueña de Estudios Sociales; and Antonio Lopera at what was once the Patronato de Obreras. Numerous people associated with the Universidad de Antioquia helped me generously, including Jorge Pérez and Gloria Bermúdez. Gloria's skills as a librarian were a daily joy, but more so was her offer of friendship.

A Fulbright/Icetex Fellowship in 1990–91, together with financial support from Duke University and from the Andrew W. Mellon Foundation, allowed me to begin research; additional support from the Research Foundation of the University of Pennsylvania and from the Trustees' Council of Penn Women meant that I was able to complete my work in Medellín. At Duke, I benefited from the advice of Charles Bergquist, Carol Smith, Deborah Jakubs, Nancy Hewitt, John French, John TePaske, and William Reddy, who patiently read and commented on my work. While a graduate student, I also received invaluable guidance from Catherine LeGrande, Temma Kaplan, and participants in the Latin American Labor History conferences held at SUNY Stonybrook and at Duke. My intellectual debt to Daniel James, who directed my dissertation, will be evident to those who know his work; what may be less evident is a personal debt: his encouragement gave me the confidence to pursue a career as a historian.

This book has been substantially improved by the atmosphere of intellectual engagement provided by colleagues at the University of Pennsylvania; I wish to acknowledge a particular debt to Nancy Farriss, for her scholarly example and her warm friendship. Ann Matter, Barbara Savage, Tom Childers, Drew Faust, David Ludden, Lee Cassanelli, Lynn Lees, Michael Katz, Walter Licht, and Steve Feierman have been unfailingly supportive, as have Demie Kurz, Dina Siddiqi, Greg Urban, Lorrin Thomas, Marie Manrique, Julia Paley, Joan Bristol, Paja Faudree, Jorge Salessi, and Luz Marín. I would also like to acknowledge the practical help of Deborah Broadnax, Hannah Poole, Joan Plonski, and Valerie Riley. Christa Avampato, Carol Ou, Meredith Estrada, Ramón Marmolejos, and Romina Birnbaum helped in concrete ways. For his advice on the quantitative aspects of my research, I thank Mark Stern; heartfelt gratitude is also due Steve Pyne, whose help with regressions allowed me to avoid making several erroneous arguments I had initially attempted to make.

Whatever errors remain, of course, are my responsibility alone—a caveat that is doubly necessary in acknowledging the work of those who read the manuscript in its entirety: Barbara Hirshkowitz, Lynn Hunt, Marco Palacios, Michael Jiménez, Rebecca Karl, and the anonymous readers at Duke University Press. Their intelligence and gentle criticism, together with the professionalism of my editor at Duke, Valerie Millholland, greatly improved every aspect of the following chapters.

No amount of academic support, intellectual stimulation, or financial aid would have enabled me to finish this project without the nurturing I received from family and loving friends. Mary Ellen Curtin, Maria Cristina, Julie Cristol, Salvador DaSilva, María Rosa Funzi, Chris Pavsek, and Antonio Sungo have been loyally in my corner. Without the well of support I find in my father, George, and his wife, Cathy, in my siblings May, Mark, Isabel, and George, and in my mother, Pilar, I could not even have started to turn my research into a book. Nor would I have remained myself, through the process of writing, without the anchor of love I find, daily, in Rui DaSilva. His constant support, practical help, and boundless imagination have helped me work, certainly, but he has also helped me remember, from time to time, to stop working. With Kiamesso, whose arrival has coincided with the conclusion of this research project and the start of another, Rui gives me a reason to finish any book I start.

INTRODUCTION

You don't do wrong to the person who feeds you . . . it makes me mad whenever anyone does anything against Coltejer. I want all the best for Coltejer, all the best, because if it fails, I fail.—Ana Palacios de Montoya

I pray for Fabricato every day, because one was so poor and now one has this little house, because of the factory. Fabricato was very good and I pray to God every day for Fabricato, that it will succeed more and more and more.
—Celina Báez Amado

COLOMBIA'S FIRST INDUSTRIAL experiment is over. As retired textile worker Enrique López put it, commenting on a rumor that Rosellón, the mill where he worked for forty years, might be gutted and converted into middle-class apartments: "That's the end of that." The end of protective tariffs and governmental intervention to guarantee the profitability of nationally owned firms likely will not prove the end of Latin America's industrial dream, but the region has definitively abandoned import substitution as a model.[1] For the women and men who spent their working lives in the factories of Colombia's Aburrá Valley, located in central Antioquia and dominated by the city of Medellín, it is the end of an era.

In 1990–91, when I conducted the bulk of the research for this book, an illusory sense of permanence still clung to Medellín's big textile firms. Their company names—Fabricato, Tejicondor, and especially Coltejer, which owned Rosellón—had been household words throughout Colombia for more than seventy-five years. Retired workers pointed to the firms' expansion, and managerial personnel easily discussed plans to continue upgrading plant machinery. From a historian's perspective, the companies' sense of their own past was especially impressive. I found well-maintained collections of historical records, some of which had been transferred to microfilm, as well as carefully preserved antique looms, lists of "founding workers," and photographic displays documenting each company's early years.

By 1998 the illusion had been stripped away. At Fabricato, at the opposite end of the Aburrá Valley from Rosellón, I had spent months working with company records housed at the Patronato, which had been built as the "golden dream" of the firm's founder, Jorge Echavarría. Designed as a company-run

Map 1   Colombia and Latin America

Map 2   Antioquia and Colombia

recreation center and subsidized cafeteria, with an attached dormitory for women workers, it boasted welcoming gardens and a monument to Don Jorge. Even in 1991, with its sleeping rooms converted to offices, the Patronato stood as a reminder of a paternalistic company ethos. Workers still observed a moment of prayer, amplified by speakers mounted near their lunch tables. The addition of a carefully organized *sala histórica*, a one-room company museum, only cemented the role of the Patronato as the symbolic heart of a firm that was nearing the seventy-fifth anniversary of its founding in 1923. As that anniversary arrived, however, Fabricato was reeling from the impact of the Colombian *apertura*, or "opening," of 1990–94. Under President Cesar Gaviria, a corps of young, technically trained neoliberal reformers did away with protectionism and other import-substitution policies, and the textile companies lost their privileged position.[2] What had been long-running concerns, including high labor costs, indebtedness, and decades of inefficient practices at the managerial level, became acute problems.[3] Fabricato found itself insolvent, and the Patronato was transferred to one of the company's largest creditors: the state-run pension fund. Retired workers will still receive medical care in the spacious rooms of Don Jorge's "golden dream," now formally designated a historic building, but the company's current employees cannot be as confident about their own retirement years. Along with its one-time competitors Rosellón, Coltejer, and Tejicondor, Fabricato may soon need Celina's prayers.

From the perspective of elderly workers' memories, the neoliberal reforms that threaten "their" mills add insult to the ongoing injury of having watched Medellín almost self-destruct. When retirees sat down with me to tape-record their stories, they did so in a city in crisis. Bombings, drug-related assassinations, and gang warfare had become the stuff of everyday life in Medellín. In this context, the nostalgia that shapes retirees' memories has particular poignancy. Eighty-two-year-old María Elisa Alvarez, for example, lived in a neighborhood with enough of a reputation for violence that taxi drivers often refused to take me to her address. Aware that a young interviewer might not believe her, she raised her voice to insist that, "back then, Medellín was beautiful! beautiful!"[4] Another retired man of her generation, responding to a friend's comment that "people used to die of old age . . . but now, can you imagine, they die at seventeen or at twenty-two," said simply: "now, they don't die, they get killed."[5]

Many used the paternalistic management style of the Echavarría family as a symbol of everything that made "then" a better time than "now." "The industrialists of that time," emphasized Susana Osorio, "were not only very intelligent, very advanced, but also very human . . . think on it and you'll see: this was an *earthly paradise!*"[6] She and others of her generation know, however, that young Antioqueños will inherit a regional capital that has become an international watchword for homicide and drug-related crime.

Nostalgia is itself "historical." As a style of remembering, it is associated with modern secular culture and with rapid change in everyday technologies.[7] In the context of Medellín, the fact that retired textile workers idealize the industrial paternalism of the 1940s and 1950s is not simply a given—to be dismissed as an inherent part of their being old people telling stories about their youth. Rather, their nostalgia provides a starting point for questions about change over time.[8] It points to the way in which an imported form of organizing labor power, the factory, was transformed into an accepted, commonplace aspect of life in Medellín. In the early decades of this century, the cotton mills symbolized everything modern; they were visited, photographed, and talked about as manifestations of an industrial future—one that provoked as much anxiety as it did hope and pride. At the end of the century, their meaning has radically changed. Now the city's big factories represent a past, one that can sustain a nostalgic vision. Scholars tend to discuss Latin American import substitution in terms of its political-economic impact, asking whether it was right or wrong as a policy. This book instead asks how students of twentieth-century Latin America can begin to understand the uneven but still significant spread of industrialism in the region's urban centers. How can we grasp the meaning of factory work in the lives and memories of men and women like Ana, Celina, Enrique, and María Elisa?[9]

In answering these questions, the following chapters focus on the role of gender in structuring Antioqueños' engagement with industrialism. By using this term rather than the more common "industrialization," I mean to emphasize diffuse changes in attitudes and self-conceptions. Despite a rich historiographical literature that attends to cultural change in the broadest sense, policy makers, investors, and authors of survey texts tend to attach a narrowly technical meaning to industrialization, especially in third world contexts. In Colombia, the rhythms and hierarchies of factory work became culturally familiar (and familiar enough to be both consented to and pointedly resisted, at different historical conjunctures) in a complex process of interaction among capitalist entrepreneurs, social reformers, managers, and working-class women and men. I make two arguments about this process: first, that changing understandings of femininity and masculinity shaped the way all of these social actors understood the industrial workplace; second, that workingwomen in Medellín lived gender not as an opposition between female and male but rather as a normative field—marked by "proper" and "improper" ways of being female. The distance between chaste and unchaste behavior underlay a moral code that shaped workingwomen's self-perceptions, as well as the self-perceptions of men who labored in mixed-sex workplaces. Moreover, at least during the most intensely paternalistic period, the distinction between virgins and nonvirgins organized the industrial labor market almost as thoroughly as did the sexual division of labor.

Masculinization

Given the growth of women's labor history in the 1980s, and the dynamism of the field in the 1990s (as scholars have turned toward studying gender rather than "women"), the particularities of Medellín's textile industry will be of interest to readers familiar with other national contexts. During the twentieth century, Antioquia was transformed in precisely the way that local elites in many parts of the world hoped to transform their own regions. As wealthy entrepreneurs began importing looms rather than finished cloth, a bustling modern city replaced what had been an isolated mountain town. Wage workers began to be able to afford consumer goods undreamed of by a previous generation, and factories to meet their new needs sprang up alongside the textile mills and food-processing plants that had started the industrial boom. What makes the Medellín case unusual, from a comparative perspective, is the visibility of gender dynamics in the process of industrialization. The cloth factories employed a majority-female workforce in their early years but males almost exclusively by 1960. Gender relations in the city's industrial workplaces can be tracked through three distinct periods. Through about 1935, the mills were largely, although not exclusively, female spaces; in the late 1930s and through the 1940s they were mixed-sex, with women and men working side by side; but by the late 1950s men far outnumbered women.

Neither "gender" nor "factory work" remains a stable category over the course of the period 1900–1960; indeed it is a central contention of this study that each affected the social meaning of the other. In 1900–1935, when Medellín's mills were largely (although not exclusively) female workplaces, they were also relatively small enterprises, in which discipline required the presence of the owner or his direct representative. During this initial period, workers entered and left the mills relatively easily—to the frustration of owner-managers who found them "ungrateful" and difficult to control. By the early 1930s, weaving and spinning began to be seen less specifically as "women's work," and factory managers hired men in large numbers. Patterns of authority also began to change, as the mills became larger and owners delegated the task of keeping order. A series of politicized strikes in 1935–36 mark a turning point. After the strikes, Medellín's largest industrialists moved to consolidate a more bureaucratic paternalistic order, marked by extra-wage benefits and by a moralistic Catholicism. Virginity became almost a prerequisite for a woman's employment, as both married women and unmarried mothers were excluded from jobs at the big textile mills. At Col-

Table 1. Women and men employed in Colombian textiles, 1916–75

Year	Men	Women	Children	Total	% of Women
1916[a]	(166)	(623)		1,983	79
1923[b]	248	740		988	75
1926[c]	969	1,906	179	3,054	62
1929	986	1,943	189	3,118	62
1932	1,254	2,061	387	3,702	56
1938[d]	4,005	6,170		10,175	61
1940	7,104	8,041		15,145	53
1945	12,896	13,331		26,227	51
1951	7,528	6,788		14,316	47
—	—				
1967[e]	25,014	14,133		39,147	36
—	—				
1975	39,650	21,414		61,064	35

(a) This total includes those mills for which there are not separate figures for women and men; the percentage of women is calculated from the mills for which there are separate figures for women and men. *Informe de Hacienda, 1916,* as cited by Santiago Montenegro, "Breve historia de las principales empresas textileras," *Revista de extensión cultural (de la Universidad Nacional de Colombia, Seccional de Medellín)* 12 (July 1982), p. 62.

(b) This includes only those factories located in the Aburrá Valley. To the figures available in the *Anuario estadístico de Medellín, 1923,* I have added the available figures for Fabricato and for Montoya Hermanos y Cia. Luz Gabriela Arango, *Mujer, religión e industria: Fabricato 1923–1982* (Medellín: Universidad de Antioquia, 1991), p. 301; for Montoya, Inspector de Fábricas, Acta 1362, 10 April 1922, Archivo Histórica de Antioquia. See also Fernando Botero Herrera, *La industrialización de Antioquia: Génesis y consolidación, 1900–1930* (Medellín: CIE, 1985), p. 174.

(c) For 1926–33, see Santiago Montenegro, "La industria textil en Colombia, 1900–1945," *Desarrollo y sociedad* 8 (May 1982), p. 133. His figures are from the *Boletín de comercio e industria* for 1933.

(d) For 1938–65 (Census and Contraloria figures). See Dawn Keremitsis, "Latin American Women Workers in Transition: Sexual Division of the Labor Force in Mexico and Colombia in the Textile Industry," *The Americas* 40 (1984), p. 497.

(e) For 1967–75 (DANE figures). See Arango, p. 338.

tejer, Fabricato, and Rosellón, supervisory personnel (including the priests assigned to factory chapels) scrutinized workingwomen's dress and behavior—a woman who had either a lover or an illegitimate child had to conceal the fact. This period of rigid moral discipline was also a period of growth for the industry, and the absolute numbers of both women and men employed increased dramatically. The years 1936–53 thus mark a "golden era" for a particularly Antioqueño brand of welfare capitalism. By the mid-1950s, the mutually constituted meanings of gender and workplace discipline had shifted again. Men took over women's jobs, and the mills' labor control strategies shifted away from workers' "moral" comportment and toward a neo-Taylorist model of the work process, as explained in chapter 7.

Table 1 and figures 1 and 2 trace the transition from a female to a male

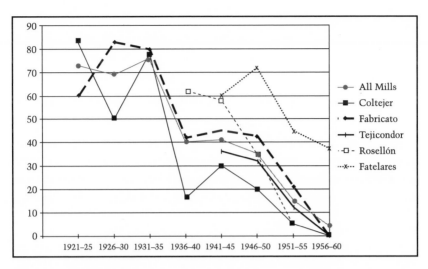

Figure 1   Percentage of new hires that were female, 1920–60. On sampling method, see Introduction, note 10.

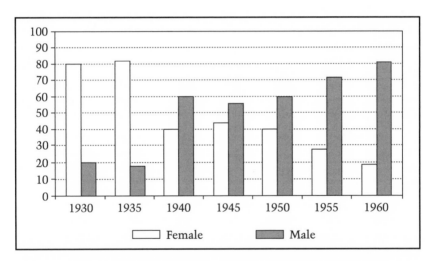

Figure 2   Relative percentages of female and male workers, measured by those present in the mills in a given year. On sampling method, see Introduction, note 10.

workforce, using both government statistics (table 1) and percentages calculated from a simple random sample of personnel files held by Medellín's large textile firms (figures 1 and 2).[10] In table 1, the masculinization of production jobs in the big Antioqueño mills is somewhat obscured, given that national statistics for the later period include smaller companies that produced readymade clothing as well as woven cloth—and garment work remained women's work. Nevertheless, the decline in women's employment is visible even at the level of such national statistics. The data from the personnel depart-ments of the five leading Antioqueño textile producers (figure 1) is clearer, although there are significant differences among firms. Midsized mills, for example, retained women longer and in higher numbers than larger mills. Fatelares, which appears as the anomalous case in figure 1, employed fewer than four hundred workers in 1960, when Coltejer and Fabricato each em-ployed more than five thousand. By the early 1990s, however, Fatelares's shop floor had become an almost all-male workplace, as were the weaving and spinning sheds of the other mills I visited. In sharp contrast to the mixed-sex world of textile work as I encountered it in retirees' memories and dusty personnel files, the production sheds and company-sponsored caf-eterias of all of Antioquia's big, now almost obsolete, textile plants were masculine spaces.

At the older and larger firms, the transition from female to male operatives took place in two discrete stages. Coltejer and Fabricato began hiring large numbers of men in the mid-1930s, especially in weaving. Where tending looms had been "women's work," it now became a job for both women and men—in part because of the introduction of automatic looms. The second and more definitive shift occurred in the 1950s. By 1960, mill managers had all but stopped hiring women; machine-tending in the textile mills, in spin-ning as much as in weaving, was redefined as "men's work." Figure 1 shows the shifts in firms' recruitment strategies, indicating both the initial switch from a majority-female to a mixed-sex workforce and the change in 1955–60, when the percentage of women among newly hired operatives dropped to almost zero. Figure 2, by contrast, traces the transition from female to male workers from the perspective of the shop floor. At no point did mill managers announce mass firings of female workers. Rather, a combination of normal labor turnover and overall growth allowed for a smooth transition. By 1960, most of the women remaining in the mills were older workers approaching retirement. As María Elisa remembered of a friend, who, she said, had been the last woman to weave at Tejicondor: "She [was] all by herself, by then it was only men."[11]

A range of other jobs within the mills were more durably sex-typed than weaving and spinning. Women never worked unloading and opening cotton bales, nor do they seem to have been employed on the dangerous carding machines known as "devils." Men predominated in the sizing section (en-gomadoras) and in loom-fixing. Dyeing, similarly, was a male preserve from the first installation of (imported) machinery for bleaching, coloring, and printing fabric. Drawing-in (pasa-lizos), on the other hand, remained largely female through the 1970s, and both managers and workers perceived it as a job that required "womanly" traits: deft hands and careful patience. Throughout 1936–70, in addition, the ranks of nonproduction workers ex-

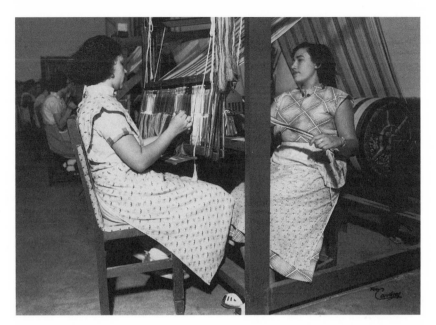

Female workers in the drawing-in section (*pasa-lizos*), Fabricato, 1955. Drawing-in remained largely female through the 1960s and 1970s. Photograph by Gabriel Carvajal. Courtesy of Fotos Carvajal.

Male worker in the dyeing and printing section (*tintorería y estampación*), Fabricato, 1955. Throughout Medellín's textile industry, from the initial decades, bleaching, dyeing, printing, "Sanfordization" and similar processes were the province of male workers exclusively. Photograph by Gabriel Carvajal. Courtesy of Fotos Carvajal.

Female worker in the finishing section (*acabados*), checking folded cloth, Fabricato, 1973. Photograph by J. Maillard. Courtesy of the International Labour Office. ILO Photograph V–Colombia–VT/ILO–72.

panded steadily, with ancillary positions tending to be sex segregated. Males were hired as plant watchmen, electricians, and groundskeepers, while females became office workers, cafeteria servers, and cleaners.[12]

Local explanations of the transition from female to male labor assume a strict economic rationality. The most commonly accepted argument involves state decision-making rather than decision-making at the level of the firm: that mill-owners stopped employing women when Colombian legislators required them to pay maternity leave. Yet protective legislation cannot be proven to have had any effect on factory owners' hiring policies. Such legislation dated from laws 53 and 197 of 1938, which granted eight weeks' paid leave, required employers to treat married and unmarried women equally, and expressly prohibited the widespread practice of simply firing any woman who became pregnant. Through the 1940s and early 1950s, however, mill managers routinely violated the 1938 legislation.[13] They also continued to employ large numbers of young women, despite laws 53 and 197. Nor is there any evidence that government officials suddenly began enforcing protective legislation in the 1950s, causing mill-owners to switch to employing males. Rather, the definitive shift toward an all-male workforce in the textile mills (1955–65) occurred without any change in the legal condition of women workers.

An argument based on protective legislation is also radically inconsistent with the social policies for which Antioqueño industrialists became famous. The large textile companies not only proclaimed a paternalistic philosophy but also led Colombian industry in the provision of extra-wage benefits. These were not firms that attempted to minimize total labor costs. Indeed, the transition to an all-male workforce happened as part of a shift toward employing heads of households. If industrialists' refusal to pay maternity benefits were based on an economic bottom-line, why would they have at the same time begun extending special benefits to married male workers, including prenatal benefits for workers' wives and free schooling for their children?[14]

Empirical problems bedevil a second widely accepted local explanation, that women evinced high levels of absenteeism and labor turnover. When pressed to explain why the factories had switched to male workers, retired women and men repeated an explanation that had circulated among managers and workers alike: "Women would get married and leave, but a man would be even more tied down [i.e., more tied to the job]."[15] Academic observers have tended to link this commonsensical explanation to changes on the shop floor. Both in 1935–40, when the large firms began importing automatic looms and again in 1955–65, with the adoption of the neo-Taylorist engineering, the shift toward male operatives happened with the introduction of new technologies of production. Where scholars have accepted the premise of female instability, the connection between masculinization and modernization has seemed to explain itself: more sophisticated production techniques required textile companies to invest more in training each operative, making men a better economic risk.[16]

In terms of time spent on the job, however, the statistical evidence is that men were as likely as women to leave after only a few years in the mills (figure 3). Women did leave their jobs at marriage (generally because mill managers required it), but this did not outweigh the fact that both women and men quit the mills for a wide range of reasons. Nor did women miss work more often than men, but rather the reverse (see figure 4). If labor turnover is measured from the perspective of long-term employees, who remained in their jobs while others came and went, the inadequacy of an argument based on female turnover rates is especially clear. Gradually, the textile firms succeeded in attracting and retaining a core of stable employees, but this was not a gender-specific group. Just as some men were willing to remain with one firm for much of their working life, so too were some women willing to do so (see table 2). Mill-owners' interest in reducing turnover cannot explain, by itself, the link between masculinization and increasing technical sophistication.

The argument that technological change in the industry required textile manufacturers to switch to male labor has a number of other weaknesses, as well. If higher levels of turnover made women more difficult to train, why

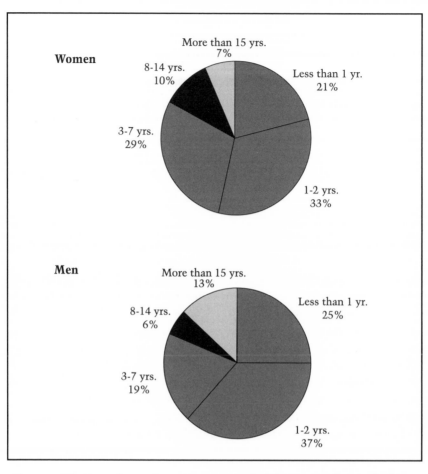

Figure 3 Women and men, by years spent on the job. On sampling method, see Introduction, note 10.

did Medellín's big employers not begin accepting married women? In a thorough study of Fabricato, the sociologist Luz Gabriela Arango argues that the mill's owners applied ideological rather than technical criteria to the question of women's work. Arango signals the difficulties that accompany any attempt to measure the relative "skill" required for different kinds of manual work, and she suggests that jobs at Fabricato became defined as "skilled work" because they were now jobs that men did, rather than vice versa. For Arango, the transition to a male workforce occurred as a diffuse effect of sexual discrimination: as textile jobs became more highly paid, they became jobs for heads-of-households, defined as male.[17]

Drawing on Arango's research, and on Anglo-American work on sex-

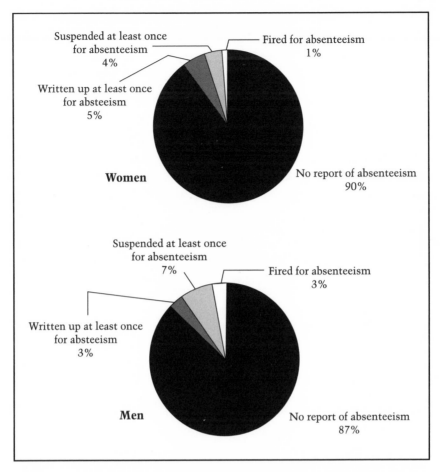

Figure 4 Women and men, by percentage noted as absent, whether that absence resulted in a written reprimand, suspension, or dismissal. On sampling method, see Introduction, note 10.

typing in industry, this book is premised on the idea that the changing gender pattern in Medellín's mills is a topic in cultural history—rather than simply an epiphenomenon of economic and technological change. A cultural approach need not subsume economics, technology, politics, or capitalist rationality to gender dynamics and representation. Nor does the notion of "cultural history" imply a divorce from "social history." As used by scholars today, "society" refers more to relations among sets of persons, and "culture" to relations among ideas, symbols, and linguistic signs, as these are used by groups of people, but neither concept has meaning without the other. The goal here is to examine change over time in Antioquia's industrial work-

Table 2. Percentage working in given year, who had been employed less than three years, or three, five, or ten or more years. On sampling method, see Introduction, note 10.

	1930		1935		1940	
	No.	%	No.	%	No.	%
Women						
Employed less than 3 years	7	87	12	71	13	59
Employed 3 or more years	1	13	5	29	9	41
Employed 5 or more years	1	13	3	18	4	18
Employed 10 or more years	1	0	0	0	2	9
Number in sample, for year given	8		17		22	
Men						
Employed less than 3 years	2	100	6	100	28	85
Employed 3 or more years	0	0	0	0	5	15
Employed 5 or more years	0	0	0	0	3	9
Employed 10 or more years	0	0	0	0	0	0
Number in sample, for year given	2		6		33	

places, with this change being understood as an interplay among economy, culture, and society at the local level.[18]

In Medellín, "women's work" became "men's work" as a result of four distinct, although interrelated, processes, each of which is explored in some detail in the following chapters. First, Medellín's textile industry was no marginal endeavor but rather the crowning achievement of Colombian policy makers' decision to use import substitution as a path to becoming an industrial nation. Medellín's textile capitalists found it in their interest to raise wages, thus strengthening their political claim on protectionist tariffs. In a subtler but no less powerful way, the self-image of Antioquia's emerging industrial elite—who saw themselves as modernizers of their country—predisposed them to raise real wages and to extend extra-wage benefits. Especially in the case of the different branches of the Echavarría family, owners of Coltejer and Fabricato, mill-owners' understanding of social-Catholic teachings led them to view the factory as a mechanism for preventing the spread of communist agitation in Colombia. Thus the slow transition to a family-wage system, premised on the employment of a specific type of male worker (sober, industrious, married, and culturally adapted to a modern consumer economy) was compatible with the political and economic position occupied by Medellinense industrialists.

Second, Antioquia's manufacturers were always part of an international textile industry. Like industrialists in a variety of other world regions, mill-owners in Medellín hired women or men to perform specific tasks in part because they imported ideas about what kind of operative "went with" the

1945		1950		1955		1960	
No.	%	No.	%	No.	%	No.	%
42	55	40	53	8	22	2	10
35	45	36	47	28	78	19	90
15	19	17	22	27	75	19	90
3	4	5	7	8	22	19	90
77		76		36		21	
65	70	65	58	44	48	25	29
28	30	47	42	48	52	62	71
13	14	27	24	41	45	49	56
2	2	7	6	10	11	31	36
93		112		92		87	

machines they bought abroad. The Fábrica de Bello, Antioquia's first cotton mill, was established with machinery purchased in Britain, and buying agent Pedro Nel Ospina visited mills with a majority-female workforce.[19] With others of their contemporaries who imported looms and spinning machines, Pedro Nel and his partner, Emilio Restrepo, seem to have simply assumed that they too would hire female operatives.[20] By the mid-1950s, however, Colombian manufacturers were importing different notions. Throughout the twentieth century, technological changes in Medellín's textile industry were changes that came from abroad, accompanied by a preformed gender ideology (whether or not local managers wholly adopted that ideology). As discussed in chapter 7, for example, textile engineers from the United States advised mill-owners in Antioquia to put men on spinning machines that had previously been operated by women.[21]

Third, a range of powerful local groups acted to influence gender relations in Medellín's textile mills. Antioquia's Catholic hierarchy and, more specifically, the Jesuits who worked to build a Catholic Social Action movement in Medellín, involved themselves in every aspect of the city's industrialization. Guided by the papal encyclical Rerum Novarum, churchmen worked to convince industrialists to adopt a paternalistic style of management as a guard against communism, and they created Catholic unions to guide the labor movement away from left-wing organizing efforts. From the beginning, Catholic activists also shaped the way Medellinenses discussed "the woman question." Priests and lay people established charitable institutions to tend to workingwomen's spiritual needs, promoted legislation to protect female industrial workers, and pushed Antioqueño industrialists to make proper moral conduct a condition of women's employment. Rather than pushing for women's exclusion from manufacturing jobs, Catholic reformers in Medellín helped establish disciplinary practices that defined some women as fit for well-paid jobs and others as unfit.

Fourth, the women who took jobs in Antioquia's early textile mills redefined the meaning of femaleness for themselves and for those who watched them enter and leave the new workplaces. If upper-class observers understood the mills to pose a danger to the proper relationship of males and females, it was in part because wage-earning women, in practice, were remaking the meaning of gender difference. In the end, I am less interested in gender as a set of rules and symbolic distinctions (between and *among* females and males) than in workingwomen and workingmen's subjective experience of the dichotomous norms of gender. My heart is with Aldonza Lorenzo and Sancho Panza, not with the unreal Dulcinea. My goal is to understand the way gender entered Medellín's mills by reconstructing not only the local discourse of "women's work" but also the shifts, instabilities, and contradictions of a cultural system in motion. What did sexual difference mean at the quotidian level of workplace relationships?

Freezing the frame at either the beginning or the end of the period 1905–1960 would underscore the contrast between the female world of Medellín's first industrial workshops and the largely male world that these same workshops became, but it would limit an observer's ability to understand *how* factory labor changed. Weaving and spinning did not simply go from being something done by women (and children of both sexes) to being something done by adult males. Along the way, textile work itself was transformed—as a result of the complex, interrelated processes summarized above. What had been a labor-intensive industry became capital-intensive. Factory workrooms went from being crowded places, in which co-workers were close enough to converse easily above the noise of manually operated machines, to being sparsely populated, with long rows of automated looms or spinning frames being tended by a single operative. One of the objectives of this book is to comprehend shifting gender patterns in Medellín's mills as a product of the connections and contradictions among the diverse factors structuring industrial work. Whether one were a woman or a man, doing factory work in Medellín meant occupying a constantly changing social location, one shaped by transactions that were at once international, national, regional, and local.

The Wages of Protectionism

Recent academic interest in the role of gender in shaping industrial development has focused on the growth of low-wage *maquiladora* plants, where female workers produce export products for a world market.[22] A word of caution may therefore be necessary. Any attempt to compare Antioqueño industrialism with more recent cases must begin by recognizing two key differences. First, Medellín's textile industry developed from a local capital base. Second, textile capitalists were able to set labor policies without much fear of price competition from either domestic or international producers, especially during the late 1940s and early 1950s, when industrialists exercised a powerful political influence in the country.

Their protected market gradually allowed Colombian firms to develop a "Fordist" model of industrial discipline, based on the provision of extensive extra-wage benefits, and—by the 1950s—the incorporation of the expensive supervisory methods of scientific management.[23] A second caution: although enthusiasm for what North Americans would label "welfare capitalism" (an enthusiasm rooted in Colombians' adaptation of European social-Catholic ideology) was evident in Antioquia from the beginnings of the industrial period, this is in no way comparable to the Fordist craze described by Mary Nolan for early-twentieth-century Germany.[24] I use the term in a general sense, to describe employers' interest in combining an older paternalistic tradition with the progressive adoption of imported technology, as well as their self-positioning as social engineers. Because Colombian manufacturers maintained wage-levels that allowed for workers' participation in a modern consumer economy, and because they cultivated employees' loyalty by providing health, recreation, and other benefits, workers' experiences in Medellín are roughly comparable to those of their counterparts in North American and European manufacturing in the twentieth century.

Additionally, Medellín fits a broad pattern within Latin American experiments with "welfare capitalism," loosely defined. Several cases of twentieth-century industrial development in the region share its main characteristics: a dependence on state protection; a local business environment dominated by relatively few firms; and wages higher than those offered by working-class jobs in nonindustrial sectors of the economy.[25] Latin American economies have been marked by the harshest human exploitation in various other areas: in *mini-* and *latifundio* agriculture, in the extraction of natural resources, and in the informal service economy of towns and big cities. Urban workers' experiences, especially in protected industries, cannot be taken as emblematic of Latin America's heterogeneous "working class." Nor can their experiences be understood by reference to a model of proletarianization drawn from England's industrial revolution in the late eighteenth and early nineteenth centuries.[26] In Antioquia, the big textile firms grew by exploiting Colombians in general, via the prices they commanded for their products and the aura of grandeur that clung to "modern" industry, not by impoverishing a local proletariat.

The protectionist tariffs that ensured a market for Antioqueño industry were always controversial at the national level. Journalists and politicians connected with competing economic sectors charged that middle- and low-income consumers were footing the bill for the rapid expansion of a few large firms. In response, Antioqueño industrialists invested in publicity campaigns that identified their own interests with those of the nation as a whole, as Eduardo Sáenz Rovner has documented. Through the Asociación Nacional de Industriales (ANDI), dominated by the Echavarrías and their allies, manufacturers promoted the idea that factory owners earned only modest profits and that the big companies' large base of small stockholders gave Colombian industry a "democratic" structure. They also played on anti-imperialist sentiment to accuse those who criticized high tariffs of playing into the hands of foreign interests, which would benefit the more if Colombia remained rural and nonindustrialized. The ANDI thus drew on early *dependista* ideas to make their point: they denounced the "international division of labor" and insinuated that the country's big coffee exporters, who argued against protectionist policies, did not have consumers' interests at heart so much as their own desire to protect a cozy relationship with the United States. In such arguments, the industrialists' trump card was the high-wage jobs they offered.

A representative piece of promotional material, aimed at young people, told the story of a cartoon protagonist named Juan. In a comic-strip format, Juan was introduced as "one of the many thousands of Colombians who had not learned to read or write." He lived "in great poverty," with no option other than rude agricultural work, until finding a factory job. The job changed his life. "At night, instead of drinking up his wages in *aquardiente*" (a clear cane brandy), Juan attended school, according to the cartoon. "Conversations with his co-workers made him understand that wearing shoes was necessary for good health," and he began to be seen by the company doctor. Along the way, Juan learned not only how to read but also how to use soap to wash himself and how to brush his teeth, according to the cartoon representation. Furthermore,

> when he went home to his *pueblo* on vacation, he was *a different person.* Everyone admired the progress he had made. . . . He explained to them that if it were not for national industry, there would be no good jobs in Colombia . . . Colombia would be condemned to the life of a primitive people.[27]

Juan, of course, was a fiction of industrialists' self-presentation as economic actors whose efforts served to improve the lives of all Colombians. Yet their desire to present themselves as civilizers of their country influenced employment policies at the country's largest firms. By the 1940s, managers at Medellín's largest mills did, in fact, offer night schools, distribute literature promoting bodily hygiene, provide free medical care, and require workers to wear shoes whether they wanted to or not. Many of the retired workers I interviewed would have recognized Juan. They remembered recently arrived *campesinos* who put on shoes and began to wear "city clothes" when they entered the textile mills, or they described their own younger selves in such terms. Like Juan, retirees described their old jobs as "good jobs." The oldest workers, who had entered the mills in the 1920s, had seen their real wages increase, over time, with the dramatic expansion of the textile industry. Those who had begun work in the 1940s, during the period of greatest expansion, remembered those years as "the good old days," when a person's wage-packet was large enough to allow one to save for a radio, television, or refrigerator. Elderly people expressed their awareness that a working life spent in the town they had grown up in, in domestic service in the city, or in manual labor outside the industrial sector, would not have allowed them to hope for the relative comfort they enjoyed as retirees of Antioquia's most powerful manufacturing firms. Implicitly, they compared their own working lives not only to those of their contemporaries who had not worked in industry (Juan's hometown friends, so to speak) but also to the working lives of a younger generation, for whom well-paid factory jobs were scarce.

From the perspective of comparative work in labor history, the Medellín case adds an unusual twist to discussions of "labor aristocracies" and of the way sexist and racist assumptions have privileged specific groups of white male workers.[28] The political-economic context of Antioqueño industry did create an enclave of well-paid workers, who enjoyed benefits that set them apart from other wage earners, but this was not a group defined primarily by racial or sexual difference. Nor did membership in one of Colombia's clientelistic, clan-like political parties significantly affect one's chances of getting a good job within the mills. "Fabricato had neither color nor politics" was the phrase retirees used to emphasize the difference between Antioqueño society, on the one hand, where skin tone and party affiliation did influence a person's opportunities, and the new factories, on the other hand, where neither had much weight. Exclusion along gender lines, moreover, happened only in stages, over a period of five decades. In the 1940s, as the publicists of the ANDI formulated their public relations strategy, women accounted for almost half of the workforce in the largest and most established branch of Colombian manufacturing: the textile mills of the Aburrá Valley. Our "Juan" had many female counterparts.

For women, as for men, what would have rung true in the ANDI's propaganda was the contrast between rural and urban opportunities, together with a second contrast between industrial work and work in less wealthy sectors of the urban economy. Reviewing the work of other economists, Juan José

Table 3. Real wages in Medellín's textile industry, based on female spinners' and weavers' earnings at Fabricato, 1925–50

Year	Real Wages, 1935 = 100	Year	Real Wages, 1935 = 100
1925	72	1938	87
1926	68	1939	150
1927	81	1940	162
1928	83	1941	166
1929	74	1942	138
1930	87	1943	143
1931	94	1944	124
1932	124	1945	123
1933	113	1946	129
1934	91	1947	126
1935	100	1948	125
1936	100	1949	135
1937	100	1950	130

Source: Juan José Echavarría, "External Shocks and Industrialization: Colombia, 1920–1950" (Ph.D. diss., Oxford University, 1989), p. 436.

Echavarría estimates a differential of 65 percent between what male day laborers earned in the countryside and the wage commanded by a manual construction worker in Bogotá.[29] Factory wages, doubly supported by higher labor productivity and by protectionist tariffs, were certainly higher; a differential of 100 percent seems conservative. Wages and working conditions for women doing manual work likely varied even more than men's, not only from countryside to city but also from live-in domestic service to hourly waged labor. Over time, even within the world of industrial and semi-industrial jobs, female wages in the textile mills gradually outstripped those offered by other kinds of urban workshops. In 1920, female weavers and spinners earned less than their counterparts in the local cigarette factories and about the same amount as women in other kinds of industrial workshops, including the city's coffee-packing plants, or *trilladoras.* By the 1940s, however, as industrialists began raising wages, women employed in textiles were earning almost twice as much as their counterparts in coffee packing, and between 15 and 50 percent more than women in the city's food-processing, cigarette, and beverage plants.[30] Women's earnings in the cotton mills also increased in real terms, almost doubling between 1925 and 1950 (see table 3). Additionally, the differential between women's and men's earnings in Colombian textile mills was small, when compared to figures from other textile-producing countries. According to a 1947 survey by the International Labour Office, women earned more than 80 percent of men's wages in Colombia and only two other countries.[31]

The retired women I met in Medellín knew that as lifelong female wage-earners they occupied an anomalous status in the wider society. With years of labor in the cotton mills, many (although not all) had bought their own homes and had ensured for themselves a modest retirement. Most told stories about boyfriends and remembered suitors, presenting the fact that they had not married as a decision they themselves had made—rather than as a product of factory rules against married women's employment.[32] The phrase I heard most often might be translated as "it wasn't right for me" (*no me convino*). Retired women discussed *why* getting married had not been right for them by tracing their own roles as breadwinners; other aspects of their choice remained in the background. Celina Báez Amado, for example, recalled what it meant to her to send money home, a theme she returned to several times in our conversations:

> Celina: I'd save five or ten little cents, to be able to send money home; that was happiness.
> Ann: Yes, to be able to help out.
> Celina: Now, right after I started there, Can I tell you this too? A loom-fixer, a guy . . . he tried hard for us to get married, [saying] that he'd keep on looking after my family. And I thought Hum! Hum! Nothing doing; they say yes, that they'll look after one's family—
> Ann: Yes,
> Celina: But when they're married then they don't . . . I had what was, my way of thinking, not because I didn't like men or anything like that.
> Ann: Did it make you sad not to get married?
> Celina: No, no, it was like happiness, Thanks to God! And I didn't think, in my way of thinking, about getting married but instead about looking after my family, looking after my brothers, looking after my mother.[33]

Celina's sister Gumercinda, with whom she shared the company-built house that a mortgage from Fabricato had helped them buy, used a similar phrase: "Marriage wasn't for us, thank God."[34] She too was acutely aware that dependence on a husband might have precluded the two things of which she and Celina were most proud: first, that they had raised and educated all of their nephews, and second, that they had scrimped and saved to improve slowly what had been a modest one-story row home but now boasted three well-appointed floors. Other women who had reached retirement in the mills, even if they did not enjoy the economic stability of the Báez sisters, shared Celina and Gumercinda's sense of achievement. From the perspective of old age, the prize of a stable pension or a house of one's own loomed large. Along with an earlier role as a support for parents or siblings, retired women valued their ability to provide for themselves in retirement. Remembering her desire for a job at Coltejer, Ana Palacios de Montoya (who used the nickname "Nena") put the two together, saying, "I lived with my father and with my mother, when I worked it was for them. I washed and ironed clothes in people's houses, that's how I started . . . I wanted a job in a company where I would have a retirement pension, and a company where I would earn more, and where I would be able to provide for them better."[35]

Nena's story diverged from the norm, in that she did marry. Shortly before retiring, she "secretly" wed her long-time lover and the father of the children whose existence she had successfully hidden from Coltejer; her compressed way of narrating this life adventure is presented in chapter 6. Even with that difference, however, the way Nena combined gratitude toward Coltejer with pride in her own achievement was common among the women I interviewed. Like Celina, she talked about the loyalty she felt for the company in the context of describing her retirement as something she had earned. In both women's narratives, home ownership and the right to a stable pension symbolize a working life well spent.

> Celina: Yes, and it's like they say, "a good marriage or a good bachelorhood" [bien casado o bien quedado]. Yes, thank God, I pretty much had no problems in the factory. No one had to say anything about me. I worked with all my heart and soul; I behaved myself well, so that they wouldn't fire me, maybe that's why they gave me this little house . . .
>
> Ann: And this house, was it let or rented to you?
>
> Celina: No, adjudicated. [And returning to the theme of the house after I had asked a set of different questions] . . . That was when Don Rudesindo Echavarría was alive, who was the general manager of the factory, a super person, he was super, and Don Jorge Echavarría, who I didn't know, who built the Patronato for the women workers,
>
> Ann: In 1934 or something like that,
>
> Celina: Yes . . . I remember that Don Rudesindo Echavarría came, shortly after the neighborhood was founded, he came with the Board of Directors to see this field, this here, these trees, and he was thinking about making a children's park for the whole neighborhood . . . for the workers' children. This was all, almost all—A lot of single women got houses adjudicated to them, but more than anything it was for the married men, who had families. . . . They bought their houses and brought their wives, while the single women brought their mothers—like happened with us. . . . And we live here happy; we have that stand of trees, we live well. . . . Fabricato built us the church, Fabricato gave us the parish house, the theater. . . . Like my mother used to say, I say it too, "I'm not leaving this house until they carry me out dead."
>
> A person's got their house, and for me it'll be eighteen years. And

when I had worked my thirty years they paid me, and so I'm here in this house, doing nothing and getting my little paychecks—so a person's got something to eat, right?[36]

Nena, similarly, evoked the paternalistic involvement of her former employers to underscore her own good judgment.

Nena: I saved little by little, eighty pesos a week, which was a lot of money at that time, and so there it was, I saved four thousand pesos in one year . . . and that's the way it was, so the year after that, I finished paying off the house [she is referring more to the lot, as this was a house that had to be rebuilt]. . . . It was falling down, that little house, but I thought—oh my, the illusions I had for that house. . . .

And so I picked up and started saving, saving and saving, and when I had, for that time it was a lot of money? When I had a set amount? . . . Well then, the engineer from the factory came [from Coltejer], and he told me how things were done except that they took me up there and they were going to finish two or three rooms for me but oh no, I had enough for more, saved. And also I asked him: "Doctor [referring to the engineer], would the company maybe make me a loan?" . . . And he said, "I think so"; and, yes, the company lent me seventeen thousand. . . .

Well, they built the whole thing, even the back room, back to the house behind.

Ann: Workers from the company?

Nena: No, they were friends of mine, but they were contracted by them [the company]. And so they came and they tore everything up, doing the work, and because I had so much saved? Well then when they had it all like that then I said, "Doctor, why don't you do me a budget of how much it will cost to do the plaster? . . . And to have it painted?" . . . And so when they had finished everything that house was swept clean and finished, and I even had furniture already bought, I had bought everything. . . . A Doctor came from over there, that was Doctor Toro [to her husband], Manuel María Toro, you remember, and the architect too, and he told me, "We came to give you a big hug and to congratulate you, because no one else, look, not even a man, no one else has been capable of getting a house finished and to the point where you get it back even swept clean . . ."

And so I finished paying that seventeen thousand that I owed them and then I said, "No, I have to start saving to finish the second story, so that when my old man is old, and me too—how nice it will be to be sitting there with him on the balcony." [Laughter.] Well, now we're retired. It's exactly the way I dreamed it would be, exactly the way I thought, that's how it turned out for me.[37]

Using memories like Celina's and Nena's as a starting point, this book interrogates the conditions for working-class women's access to "good jobs" in Medellín's cotton mill districts. My interest is not only in women's exclusion, over time, but also in their five decades of inclusion—an inclusion that was always problematic. How did female operatives, their male coworkers, and their employers negotiate a local remaking of the sexual division of labor? What did this negotiation hinge on, and what was the context in which it became undone?

Conceptual Approach

Class and gender are imperfect sociological abbreviations for complex human experiences. When used as a shorthand way of identifying social groups, both concepts tend to become impoverished. Often, scholarly and other observers understand each in terms of foundational categories: women, men, workers, peasants, capitalists. Locating social agents within a category (or multiple categories) is assumed to be a first step in knowing their desires and motivations and in understanding what guides (or what "should" guide) their actions in the world.[38] Categorization thus figures as a shortcut to understanding subjectivity. For two reasons, I have attempted to avoid an approach predicated on categorical identities. First, even in approaches that emphasize the problematic way that such categories come to have social significance, there is a danger of reifying the abstractions of class and gender—of assuming a neat congruence between our always provisional descriptions, on the one hand, and the constantly changing, multidimensional ways that people think and act in the world, on the other. Where scholars attempt to circumvent a reliance on categorization by instead exploring the creation of meaning in discourse, this danger remains—indeed it becomes perhaps harder to see how creativity, improvisation, and critical self-awareness figure in discursively constructed subjectivities. Second, beginning with seemingly discrete categories will undermine any attempt to explore the overlaps and divergences between class and gender—as systems of social hierarchy and as scholarly concepts with different genealogies. When economic relations and sexual difference are understood in terms of the bounded groups they are imagined to create, the male/female hierarchy either appears as "less important" than economic forms of stratification (meaning that women's experiences will be erased) or as analogous to class hierarchy (with the result being a feminist blindness to exploitative relations among women).

In this book, I focus on those aspects of class and gender that can be situated in a local context and can be traced, over time, at the level of social and cultural relationships. I am less interested in the construction of categories than in the way that people perceive themselves and act within a "relational setting" that connects them to others and shapes their everyday practices.[39]

My approach to class thus centers on the relationship (an "objective," economic relationship as well as a "subjective," interpersonal one) between those who worked for wages in Medellín's cotton mills, on the one hand, and those who either owned the mills or who managed them as the owners' direct representatives, on the other. Using the concept in this way is problematic. Given that class has multiple and interwoven definitions, any attempt to use the concept in an open-ended, noncategorical way will seem confusing to some readers. As a description of the exploitative economic relationship between those with access to capital and those with access to nothing but their labor power, class is rooted in Marx's analysis of what was new about the society produced by England's industrial revolution.[40] However, Marx's use of the term depends not only on what was observable in capitalist Europe but also on the political possibilities of industrial society— not only on what was present in a situation of proletarianization (class in itself) but also on what he believed to be incipient and as yet unrealized (class for itself). For many, the idea of class is therefore indissolubly bound to a teleological vision that is also Eurocentric and sexist: the notion that the industrial workers of advanced capitalist nations (imagined in this story as male) will be the heroes of a proletarian revolution. As a study of women and men on the periphery of industrialism, who never coalesced around a class-based political project, this book follows a long-term trend within labor history, one that has progressively distanced the field from any such teleology.

The problems raised by the teleological content of the class concept are connected to a wider set of conceptual difficulties stemming from the generally accepted division between objectivity and subjectivity. These cannot be overcome simply by jettisoning the notion of a foretold revolution. Understanding class as a relationship that is constituted *both* by human subjectivity and by the economic structures created by human society is a worthwhile analytic project only if it helps deconstruct the objective/subjective dichotomy. Economic "structures" are created and maintained by human action, which cannot be understood separately from cultural and psychological "structures." Nor are a person's thoughts and feelings over a lifetime ever wholly separable from the social and economic context for their personhood. In this connection, it is significant that the difference between "class in itself" and "class for itself," in Marx, is not the same as the difference between "objective" and "subjective" as these terms are commonly used. For Marx, class is interconnected with "culture" and "mode of life," even when the reference seems to be to "class in itself."[41] When discussed as a structure having "an independent existence," Marx's notion encompasses the multiple ways that individuals "find their conditions of existence predestined, and hence their position in life and their personal development assigned to them by their class" (*German Ideology*).[42]

Ira Katznelson's attempt to sort out the meanings of this "congested" term is helpful here. Working within a Marxist intellectual tradition, he separates class into four related parts or "levels": (1) the proletarianization of labor; (2) the social organization of workplaces, neighborhoods, and overall life patterns; (3) a group's shared dispositions or cultural understandings; and (4) collective action generalizing a class-based engagement in politics.[43] Aspects of subjectivity, understood in terms of the psychological and cultural dimensions of working-class life, are important to this second, third, and fourth levels, but a traditional notion of "class-consciousness" is required only for the fourth. As did E. P. Thompson before him, if not as gracefully, Katznelson emphasizes the importance of working people's understandings of self and society without subsuming this subjectivity to a model of "true" or "false" consciousness.

Throwing out the teleology of proletarian revolution is thus only a first step. A necessary second step involves jettisoning the assumption that the subjective dimension of class (whether or not this involves collective action) is a *reaction* to objective economic structures. Katznelson's formulation works against a straight teleological reading of labor history, but it remains within a base/superstructure model and thus makes objective class relations appear logically prior to subjective experience.[44] In this sense Thompson's work goes further, as the overall effect of his multilayered description is to demonstrate that the political and cultural aspects of class emerged simultaneously with the economic change associated with capitalist manufacturing—indeed were *part* of the way this change occurred. The subjective world of working-people's values and opinions, for Thompson, in no sense "follows" economic class: "The working class did not rise like the sun at an appointed time. It was present at its own making."[45]

With most contemporary work in working-class history, the present study implicitly argues against economic reductionism and for historically grounded cultural analysis. By now, however, the base/superstructure model has been so thoroughly overturned that it no longer provides even something to tilt against as we explore new approaches to class.[46] Instead, as William Sewell has argued, a range of interdisciplinary approaches are put forward by their practitioners as all-encompassing, all-powerful alternatives.[47] One result of the persuasiveness of recent work centering on language, power/knowledge, and the symbolic construction of communities has been to institutionalize poststructuralism as a methodological ultimatum in labor history. Seemingly, one must either accept or reject a focus on "discourse," defined broadly as the set of ideological and cultural processes by which meanings are produced in any society, or, more specifically, as the range of connections among "statements, texts, signs, and practices" that have meaning across dispersed sites of social activity.[48] It is not my intention to present this study as an easy synthesis between discursive analysis and more empiricist or materialist approaches. By focusing on class as a multidimensional relationship that can be situated in a time and place, rather than as a categorical identity, I hope to gain from the tensions among divergent approaches.

Aware that what I take as my subject, workers' gendered experiences in a rapidly changing industrial context, will appear differently when viewed through different conceptual lenses, I have attempted to explore (rather than artificially minimize) the distance between various possible configurations of the subject "workers' experiences." If experience is the discursive construction of subjectivity, then one has to ask what languages of selfhood were culturally available to those who worked in Medellín's factories (but for whom the identity "worker" may or may not have been significant). If the emphasis is placed not on the process of becoming-a-subject but on the way people (as linguistically and culturally constructed subjects) render meaningful events and relationships in their lives, the questions to be asked instead involve agency. Over time, how did working people in Medellín develop languages and political/cultural strategies that enabled them to "creatively reappropriate" some aspects of the world around them?[49] A focus on sensuous life experience, including pain and deprivation, as well as pleasure, will raise still other questions. Conceding the incompleteness of attempts discursively to "contain" the alternative subjectivities made possible by bodily sensation will allow an historian to ask what permeability, or conflict, existed between the world of discursive norms and the unspoken world of everyday bodily practice. Readers familiar with the diverse academic literature on subjectivity and experience will recognize in the present study an eclectic appropriation, and often a very partial one (in the twin senses of incomplete and tendentious), of seemingly incompatible theoretical work. Perhaps the most obvious presence will be Pierre Bourdieu. His writings on "doxa" have entered my thinking about class by way of their relevance to the argument this book makes about gender relations: that the difference between "good" and "bad" women (which itself had a meaning inflected by class hierarchy) structured Medellinenses' experiences of factory work as thoroughly as the male/female dichotomy.[50]

My working definition of gender follows most feminist writing in distinguishing between anatomical sex differences and the cultural dichotomies of male and female. My emphasis, however, is on the connection between gender and sexuality, once sexuality, too, is separated from anatomy. I understand gender to refer both to the social difference between femininity and masculinity *and* to the normative codes by which persons socialized as women or men are placed, and place themselves, vis-à-vis other women and other men. Neither of these two aspects of gender is logically prior to the other. One cannot usefully understand gender by first examining the social mechanisms that separate males from females, as hierarchically positioned "sexes," and only then sketching differences among women (or among men). Divisions between those who are "properly" or "improperly" feminine and those who are "properly" or "improperly" masculine are as much the work of the sex/gender system (in Gayle Rubin's phrase) as is the dichotomy between femaleness and maleness.[51] Femininity has social meaning not only because it defines a role for women that is different from that defined for men but also because the way a woman lives her femininity marks her social standing. That standing is determined relative to other women. Most obviously, wives and prostitutes are both emphatically recognized as "female," yet the difference between the two is fundamental to gender in many cultures.[52] Where the difference has salience, it does not simply mark off a distance between this good woman and that bad woman. Rather, it creates a normative field in which gender-specific practices function as signposts of personal, familial, or group status.

Feminist scholars investigating racially stratified societies have demonstrated this conclusively: intragender sexual norms (analytically distinct from the male/female dichotomy as such) are used to sustain the wider social hierarchies that rank persons, families, and behaviors. Ann Stoler's work on colonial Asia demonstrates that the difference between "native" concubines and European wives helped define and maintain racial boundaries.[53] Similarly, in her careful study of nineteenth-century Cuba, Verena Stolcke (formerly Martinez-Alier) describes the ideological overlap between whiteness and female chastity: a woman who could prove her sexual respectability was thereby able to claim a degree of "whiteness" that she would not otherwise be able to claim. Conversely, moral faults that made a white woman "ineligible for marriage within her own ethnic group" made her "eligible for marriage across the race barrier."[54] In the context of Cuban slavery, a family's honor depended on its success in controlling the sexual behavior of its female members, and honor had a racial definition. For the United States, Evelyn Brooks Higginbotham states the problem succinctly: "the exclusion of black women from the dominant society's definition of 'lady' said as much about sexuality as it did about class." Because they understood this, middle-class black women policed the public representation of their own sexuality as part of the struggle they waged against racism.[55] By defining gender as a normative field that not only distinguishes between females and males but also creates hierarchies among women and among men, I hope to apply the insights generated by such work on sexuality, gender, status, and race to Marxist-feminist debates about the relationship between gender and class. Despite a rich theoretical tradition of its own, feminist labor history has thus far benefited only tangentially from the reconceptualization of gender that is evident in scholarship focusing on the way racism is sexualized and on the historical legacy of "raced gender."[56]

The influence of Marxian concepts, centrally that of class, has had both negative and positive effects in attempts to formulate an analysis of gender oppression. Feminist activists who conceptualized gender by analogy to class gained an arresting set of metaphors but lost the ability to speak to the experiences of many working-class women. To say that women are oppressed by men as workers are oppressed by capitalists (or, in left discourse in the United States, where the analogy to race had its own history, to say that women are oppressed by men as blacks are oppressed by whites) is to dismiss class (and race) as these hierarchies operate among women. Such formulations left no room for addressing the fact of paid domestic service, for example, a central fact of women's lives in Latin America and most of the world.[57] Where feminists attempted to analyze sexism by reference to race and class, their analogies erased those women who were "also" wage workers or "also" subject to racism, as feminists engaged in antiracist and working-class struggles have pointed out again and again.[58] On the positive side, the intellectual link to Marxism and Marxian-influenced social science has meant that many feminist theorists assumed from the outset "the futility of posing the feminine 'problem' in abstract and universal terms," as the Argentine sociologist Elizabeth Jelín argued in 1974.[59]

Marxist-feminists, like Jelín, attempted to understand gender as it operated in class-stratified societies—rather than in abstraction from class—and in so doing they set the boundaries for a debate about sexism and capitalism that has profoundly shaped the work of labor historians interested in gender. As it developed in Anglo-American feminist writing, that debate centered on Heidi Hartmann's analysis of patriarchy and capitalism as separate but intertwined systems of domination. Hartmann insisted that patriarchy pre-dated capitalism and that across class lines men, as men, benefited from women's subordination. Thus Marx's analysis of capitalism could not serve feminists as an analysis of male domination and socialism would not solve women's problems. Gayle Rubin and others (drawing on Engels) had argued, and in a more sophisticated way than Hartmann, that sexism pre-dated the development of class societies based on the appropriation of labor power through the mechanisms of the market.[60] And the Brazilian sociologist Heilieth Saffioti had advanced an argument similar to Hartmann's "dual systems," although more rigidly Marxist. Yet Hartmann gained a wide scholarly readership, perhaps because she did not address the question of gender systems in general but rather focused her attention on the relationship between gender and class in the particular context of Anglo-American industrial society.

Hartmann's arguments, and the examples she used, set an agenda for feminist labor historians. Criticizing feminists and Marxists who presented women's role in reproducing proletarian families as a mechanism by which capitalists indirectly appropriated female labor, Hartmann acknowledged that women's unpaid labor in working-class homes benefited capitalist employers, but insisted that it also—and primarily—benefited working-class men, as men. Hartmann also pointed to male workers' role in restricting women's participation in the paid labor force. Capitalists had not by themselves decided upon "women's place" in the industrial order; rather, male workers had actively claimed better-paid jobs for themselves. For Hartmann, capitalism had created industrial society as a world in which specific social locations (proletarian, capitalist employer, member of a "reserve army of labor," person doing unwaged household work, etc.) stood in hierarchy to one another, as "empty places." Her point was that Marxists had no theoretical understanding of why women occupied specific positions and men others: "the categories of Marxism cannot tell us who will fill the empty places."[61] The concept of patriarchy, defined as a system in which men are dependent on one another (despite their hierarchical ordering) to maintain their control over women, provided a way of understanding why persons of a particular gender filled this or that "place" in capitalist society. Whether or not they used Hartmann's terminology, feminists of her generation began to reshape labor history by asking the questions she did: What kinds of gender relations obtained within working-class families and communities? To what extent had male unionists in different contexts built their own class identity on the exclusion of women from their workplaces and radical movements?

Hartmann's presentation of "dual systems" theory also generated a range of critiques, many of which presaged later developments in both feminist theory and labor history. First, as Anne Phillips and Barbara Taylor noted in a pioneering essay on "skill" as a gender-specific category, Hartmann's analysis reified both capitalism and patriarchy, presenting each as a stable and discrete "system." She failed to recognize capitalism as a historical development in no sense separable from the society that gave rise to it. In practice, they insisted, industrial capitalism had never created "empty places" but rather sex-specific places that were coded as either "female" or "male," with each designation being the result of concrete struggles between wage earners and employers.[62] Laura Lee Downs extends this critique of Hartmann in a recent comparative study of the French and British metalworking industries, in which she argues that gender has not been extrinsic to changes in the work process, something employers could "bring in" from outside their factories, but rather has been intrinsic to the organization of production—forming part of how capitalists, technicians, supervisors, and operatives thought about work. For Downs, separating patriarchy and capitalism will only impede feminist attempts to analyze "a structure of inequality that workers and employers alike understood and experienced as a seamless entity."[63]

A second, though related, set of debates concerns the usefulness of "patriarchy" as an idea and as a parallel category to "capitalism." Gayle Rubin and Gerda Lerner provide sophisticated discussions of the opposing positions in their most general form: that patriarchy should be used only in its narrowest meaning, to delineate societies in which females and junior males within lineage groups are subordinated to a male elder (Rubin), and that a broader definition provides feminists with a conceptual tool for understanding female subordination across cultures, without implying homogeneity (Lerner).[64] Whether or not they use the term "patriarchy," feminist labor historians have engaged a version of this question by asking whether or not male workers have consistently behaved as though they shared a "patriarchal" interest with their male employers. For Ruth Milkman, for example, analyses like Hartmann's "lapse into determinism."[65] She and other historians interested in how sex-typing developed in particular industries at particular moments have generally emphasized the heterogeneity of sex segregation, in contradistinction to the blanket approach taken by Hartmann.[66] Within Latin American studies, recent scholarship has emphasized variety: *machismo* no longer appears with a single, always predatory face, and "patriarchy" is beginning to be defined by the range of its forms.[67] In two decades of scholarly work, evidence has accumulated to suggest that sexual division and class exploitation are neither direct nor harmonious. Between gender and class there exist innumerable gaps and contradictions, too many for there to be anything like the tight fit implied by Hartmann's statement that the "mutual accommodation between patriarchy and capitalism has created a vicious circle for women."[68]

Through the 1980s and 1990s, feminist discussions of gender and class were also changed by the way poststructuralism changed the terms of the debate about social being and social consciousness, as summarized in the above discussion of the class concept in labor history. Where Hartmann had taken class to be a stable and analytically powerful concept and gender to be its undertheorized pair, recent work has tended to assume the precariousness of class. Joan Scott points out that Hartmann and other Marxist-feminists working in the 1970s struggled with a "self-imposed requirement": that the gender system be understood as having a "material base." Only then could it be paralleled to class.[69] Because Scott understands class itself as a product not of material relations but of cultural and linguistic categories, categories that are themselves shot through with evocations of gender and inequality, she does not see the two systems as parallel to one another but rather as mutually constitutive. As she frames it, in a reference to Gareth Stedman Jones, "If we look closely at the 'languages of class' of the nineteenth century we find they are built with, in terms of, sexual difference. . . . Gender becomes so implicated in concepts of class that there is no way to analyze one without the other."[70] Scott treats gender as both a process of differentiation that constructs female and male subjects in unequal relation to one another *and* as a powerful symbol for all differentiation and inequality. Scott's approach overlaps with other critiques of Hartmann, as summarized above, but she disallows the notion that women's and men's coherent identities provide a starting point for a unitary or synthetic theory of class and gender. Rather, Scott challenges precisely those concepts through which many feminist labor historians began to construct an alternative to Hartmann's "dual systems" methodology: "identity," "experience," and "agency."

The arguments made in this book grow out of and bear on this long-running debate about gender and class. I acknowledge the significance of each of these different strands of the feminist rethinking of dual systems theory. In Medellín, hierarchical notions of sexual difference were integral to the economic and technical decision-making that went on at the mills, from managers' choices about whom to hire, or what supervisory methods to adopt, to workers' decisions about whether to keep or quit their jobs. The local meanings acquired by the factory system (as a new wrinkle in the regional history of capitalism) can in no way be separated from changing local patterns of gender differentiation. Similarly, cautions against the seeming determinism of "patriarchy" are well taken, both because the factories created new opportunities for some women and because the local sexual division of labor was characterized by change rather than stability. Scott's attempts to envision what she calls a "non-foundational" history are helpful on still another front.[71] The trouble with Hartmann's model may stem less from her use of capitalism and patriarchy as analytical terms and more from her dependence on internally undifferentiated categories—"women," "men," "employers," "workers"—that she (and many of her critics) use descriptively rather than analytically.[72] Thus Scott suggests that the key to understanding gender and class as mutually constitutive is not to examine how the two come together in the life experiences of groups of people but rather to trace the discursive process by which specific categories of personhood are constituted and might then be said to "have" experiences.

Nevertheless, aspects of dual systems theory remain useful—no matter how dated the work it generated now appears. Recent scholarship has tended to emphasize the way class and gender are mutually constituted but to ignore instances in which they can be mutually contradictory. Downs, for example, conceptualizes class and gender as lived identities. From the perspective of people's everyday experiences, she insists on their seamlessness. Scott focuses on the interrelation of gender and class in symbolic relationships of power; she conceives of gender as a signifier of inequality that shapes and legitimizes the meaning of other forms of inequality, such as class.[73] Despite their sharp methodological differences, both share a tendency to overlook cultural processes that work to disarticulate gender from class. Without denying the gains made by labor historians' move away from Hartmann's model, which was founded on the presumed "separateness" of structures of domination, we run two risks if we concentrate on mutual coherence at the expense of seeing discontinuity among the relationships that mark out inequalities of class and gender. First, it becomes difficult to understand change over time, a problem Scott is aware of and attempts to address in her explication of a poststructuralist approach to gender.[74] Second, emphasizing the analytical inseparability of gender from other forms of domination works to obscure differences among women (and among men)—both in everyday social practice and in the symbolic construction of meaning.[75] Wealthy women are able to exploit the labor of poor women and poor men the world over precisely because their class status effects social relationships that transform a seemingly shared gender-based subordination of females to males. This remains true even if the economic superiority wealthy women share with men in their families derives from gendered assumptions. In no sense am I arguing that class relations and gender relations should be studied separately. Studying both requires attention to possibly radical contradictions among a variety of power relationships, as well as to the parasitic mutuality of structures of domination.

On the surface, the Medellín case seems to provide evidence for the argument that class and gender directly reinforce one another. Through the 1930s and 1940s, factory owners manipulated the value attached to chastity to buttress their own authority, and female operatives, who earned less, on average, than males, were subject to more stringent rules of behavior. Femaleness would thus seem to have compounded the subordinate status ascribed to workers. Yet my analysis supports an alternative reading. I focus on the tensions among the various relationships that marked out inequalities of class and gender in the lives of Medellinenses. My interest is in tracing changes in textile workplaces and in assessing the role of symbolic differences among women, as well as between women and men. From the perspective of workingwomen's self-representations, no "seamlessness" existed either at the level of capitalism and patriarchy as hierarchical ideologies or at the level of lived subjectivity.

Conclusion

In Medellín, women's jobs became men's jobs as part of the more general process by which industrialists secured a disciplined workforce. It did not happen because one sex was more easily trained or more compliant than the other but because of a conjuncture of social and cultural factors that were at once local and extra-local. This study focuses on the changes in workplace organization that accompanied the gradual masculinization of the mills, from the imposition of a rigid system of sexual controls during the period in which these were mixed-sex workplaces to the more technocratic procedures associated with the transition to an almost all-male workforce. Throughout, the shift from female to male labor appears not as an endpoint of analysis but rather as a beginning place for theorizing the relationships of power and inequality we call "class" and "gender."

The following chapters are structured to emphasize change over time. Chapter 1 provides an overview of the twentieth-century history of Medellín, assessing the city's role in the regional economy of Antioquia and its place in the development of a discourse of *Antioqueñidad*. It delineates the initial process of industrialization, led by the family-owned import houses that first invested in textile mills, and it provides a sketch of the experiences of the rural migrants who made up the majority of the textile workforce. Chapters 2 and 3 examine the period 1900–1935, in which most millworkers were women and girls. Chapter 2 traces the development of "the woman worker" as a discursive category, one that can be juxtaposed to workers' everyday actions and to their political practice in the region's first work stoppage, a month-long strike triggered by women's anger about sexual harassment by male supervisors. The third chapter focuses on workers' interactions with employers and co-workers in the early years of the industry, when it was relatively easy to get work at the mills and high levels of turnover were the norm.

The book's second half traces the rise and fall of an intensely paternalistic industrial system in the period 1935–60. Chapter 4 examines the citywide labor unrest of 1935–36, placing this in the context of national politics. I identify the strikes as a turning point for worker-management relations in the mills. Industrialists switched to a mixed-sex workforce, and the mid-1930s mark the beginning of a period in which mill discipline begins to center on the control of women workers' sexuality. Chapters 5 and 6 analyze this gender-based disciplinary system, both in its claims to total hegemonic control and in the everyday social practices that fissured that imagined totality. A final chapter describes the undoing of this disciplinary model during the transition to an all-male workforce in 1953–60. A paternalistic practice that centered on controlling workers' mixed-sex interaction was jettisoned in favor of a neo-Taylorist vision of discipline, although one that remained paternalistic in its endorsement of male workers' right to a family wage. In the book's conclusion, I return to the theoretical and historiographical contexts for this research to assess what the close reconstruction of human relationships in an idiosyncratic set of Latin American industrial workplaces may offer to the methodological rethinking currently underway in feminist studies, comparative labor history, and social/cultural history.

PART I. THE PLACE
OF FEMALE FACTORY LABOR
IN MEDELLÍN

ONE

Medellín,

1900–1960

IN 1947, *Life* magazine proclaimed Medellín a "capitalist paradise."[1] Stunning photographs by correspondent Dimitri Kessel presented a Medellín that seemed to cross the dream of Yankee-style entrepreneurship with an updated version of the El Dorado myth. This "South American showplace" was a city where "nearly everyone makes good money and lives well" and where, "unlike many parts of the civilized world, it is still possible to run a small stake into a fortune." In a departure from most English-language reporting about Latin America, the heroes of this story were the Medellinenses themselves. *Life* pointed to "their hard work, love of money, dazzling business talents, and universal prosperity," and the magazine concurred with a local belief that "if there is ever a 'second conquest of South America' it will come from Medellín."

The correspondent had clearly been shown around by the city's industrialists and their wives, and his visual essay, with its accompanying text, provides a glimpse of how the Medellinense elite presented themselves and their city to the outside world. Kessel's photographs emphasized the contrast between Medellín's "brisk modernity" and its "ancient piety." The gleaming new multistory buildings near the Parque de Berrío were juxtaposed with scenes that North Americans would find quaint: Catholic schoolboys dressed in the robes and round hats of seminarians, a hillside cross, a pretty girl receiving a suitor from her balcony. *Life*'s editors presented this as a wholesome contrast; Antioquia's prosperous capital combined the best of old and new. Catholic traditionalism protected family life from the incursions of modernity, as upper-class ladies were "great stay-at-homes" and young people's courting practices were closely chaperoned at all levels of society. Nevertheless, the visiting correspondent found the upper class a sophisticated lot, and he took pictures of businessmen meeting for drinks and of ladies joining one another to play cards at the country club. Other photographs celebrated the city's forward-looking industrialists, especially the Echavar-rías—whose gracious homes in the "El Poblado" sector prompted a comparison to "Philadelphia's Main Line."[2] The "spic-and-span buildings" of the cotton mills appeared too, with the aside that Medellín's factory workers were "docile, well-trained and well cared for," with unions under the tutelage of the local church hierarchy. Throughout, the article conformed closely to what the city's moneyed families believed about themselves and the city they took pride in. They had succeeded in transforming a remote Andean town into a modern city, and they had done so without social dislocation or class war.

Life offered a simple explanation of this new prosperity: after being land-locked for centuries, Medellín was now "opened to the world by air transport." Low freight rates meant that raw cotton could be flown in from the coast and finished goods flown out. Here, however, Kessel and the writers he worked with confused symptom with cause. Both Medellín's rush to assume a modern face and its thriving industry had begun in the days of mule-packs and railroads. In 1905, the region's first mechanized looms, and the Pelton waterwheel that was to power them, had been packed in over the same mountain trails that generations of traders had used to carry out gold and to bring in imported goods for sale to Antioquia's miners and farmers.[3] The machines arrived "in pieces," and each piece, including the waterwheel and the complicated gears and belts designed to distribute power to the looms, had to be laboriously cleaned, fixed, and put back together.[4] Despite the limits of geography, forty years before *Life* noted that "its 'discoverers' hail it as a capitalist paradise," Medellinenses were importing, building, and planning in ways that demonstrate that they thought of their town as an incipient modern center rather than as a backwater. Turn-of-the-century Medellín boasted a university (founded in 1871), an electrical plant (1897), streetlights (1898), and a regulated slaughterhouse (built between 1891 and 1911). Within a few more years, the city had the beginnings of a city-wide sewer system (1913) and a growing network of electric trolley cars (1919).[5] The purpose of this chapter is to place Antioquia's industrial boom in this urban context. Why did a generation of entrepreneurs begin importing machinery to this particular Colombian city? What was their relationship to city space? How did workers, most of whom arrived in Medellín from nearby rural hamlets, think about the urban world they shared with this entrepreneurial elite?

As did *Life*'s editors, I use Medellín as a shorthand term for the whole of the Aburrá Valley, including Bello, Envigado, and Itagüí, as well as the con-

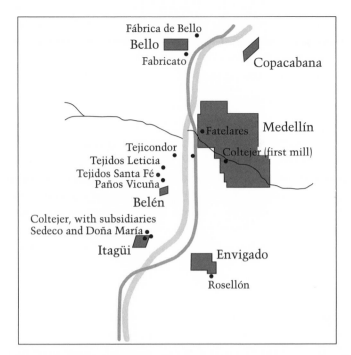

Map 3   The Aburrá Valley, showing principal textile manufacturers. Source: Adapted from James J. Parsons, *Antioqueño Colonization in Western Colombia*, rev. ed. (Berkeley: University of California Press, 1968), p. 175.

tiguous urban districts of América, Belén, Robledo, and El Poblado. Throughout the nineteenth and twentieth centuries, these communities have maintained a separate identity from Medellín itself, one rooted in their plazas and original churches. Nevertheless, the region's industrial development has worked to link the outlying towns tightly with downtown Medellín and to make them subordinate to the expanding city. Emilio Restrepo, for example, chose Bello as the site for his cotton mill, the first in the region, not because of any familial link to its inhabitants but because it offered easy access to Medellín and had a swift creek (for the waterwheel).[6] Although local people of all classes called his company Tejidos de Bello, he and his partners insisted on its legal name, Tejidos de Medellín.[7] Don Emilio commuted daily to Bello in a light, two-horse carriage, and he installed a telephone line that allowed him to confer quickly with overseers on days that business or leisure kept him in Medellín. Similarly, the investors who imported looms and spinning machines for Tejidos Rosellón, built in 1912 in Envigado, at the other end of the valley, thought of themselves as Medellinenses. Their decision to invest in Envigado was a purely economic calculation, aided by the local municipal council's willingness to exempt them from local taxes.[8]

By framing industrialization in terms of the urban history of the Aburrá Valley, rather than emphasizing the social mores of the Antioqueño region more generally, my approach departs somewhat from the existing historical literature. Colombianists have tended to debate Medellín's industrial development by agreeing or disagreeing about what made Antioqueños different from people from other parts of the country. Far less work has been done on the process by which Medellín's increasingly wealthy business elite began to set themselves and their city apart from small-town Antioquia itself. Because that process is so visible in the clannish world of the city's early manufacturing sector, I have moved away from the debates about *Antioqueñidad* that have characterized the literature in English and toward the urban history being done by Fernando Botero Herrera and other historians currently based in Medellín.[9]

Antioqueñidad

Medellín emerged as the economic center of the gold-mining province of Antioquia only slowly. Not until the early nineteenth century did it definitively supersede either Santa Fé de Antioquia, capital of the province throughout the colonial period and the city that exploited the gold of the rich lode-mine of Buriticá, or Rionegro, a merchant's town that held a strategic position along the trade routes linked to the Magdalena River. Founded in 1675, later than many comparable cities of Spanish America, Medellín developed as a food producer and commercial supplier for the spreading mining camps of the region, as gold prospectors followed the rivers and creeks in search of rich placers. Rather than depending on any single mining zone, Medellín was poised to profit from a regional market in foodstuffs and merchandise, which allowed it a gradual and sustained economic growth. Vis-à-vis other nearby trading towns, including Santa Rosa and Marinilla as well as Rionegro, Medellín's advantage was its fertile valley land. At fifteen hundred meters above sea level, the locality has a temperate climate, rich soils, and an abundant water supply that allow two harvests yearly of corn and beans, as well as a wider variety of secondary crops than either higher or lower altitudes.[10]

Relatively few researchers have explored the relationship between the Aburrá Valley and other Antioqueño subregions—either before or after Medellín was declared the provincial capital in 1826.[11] Rather, historians and social scientists have tended to identify Antioqueños, in general, with cultural traits that are in themselves taken to explain Medellín's extraordinary economic development in the late nineteenth and early twentieth centuries. Theories linking Medellín's prosperity to the existence of a specifically Antioqueño personality did not, of course, originate with academic work, but rather with the long-lived stereotypes of Colombian regionalism. In my experience, Bogotanos are still likely to characterize *paisas,* or Antioqueños, by reference to their alleged facility in business, their strict Catholicism, and their enormous, tightly knit families. In the Pacific Coast *departamento* (department) of the Chocó, long economically subordinated to Antioquia, *Antioqueñidad* has a negative meaning, with Chocoanos pointing more to the apparent greediness of their *paisa* neighbors than to their religiosity or love of family. In Antioquia itself, the stereotype has a distinctly positive intonation, even when economic ability is emphasized over the more noble aspects of the Antioqueño myth.[12] I remember, for example, an uncle of mine warning a fruitseller not to think she could cheat him, reminding her that "we are both *paisas.*"

Life presented the myth of *Antioqueñidad* in one of its more enduring guises, as a counterpart to the North American notions of Yankee frugality and ingenuity:

> Colombians in general amuse themselves with jests about Medellín's feverish commerciality and thriftiness, but the Medellinenses just keep right on going to bed early and working hard. They like to make money ... nowhere in South America is so little time wasted on a business deal. This sometimes results in jokes at Medellín's expense. There's the story, for instance, about a Medellín matron who got on a train with her maid and trousered son. When asked to pay full fare for the boy because he was wearing long pants, she argued that if the fare were based on the matter of pants she should ride for half price and her maid should ride for free. Far from being annoyed with this, the Medellinenses characteristically regard it as good publicity, like the old jokes in the U.S. about Ford cars.[13]

However much they embraced this Yankee-like image, Antioqueños have had a more complex attitude toward another aspect of the regional stereotype—in which *paisas* are taken to be either Jewish or "like Jews." Street-level characterizations of the Antioqueño as a shrewd moneymaker often have an implicitly anti-Semitic dimension, deriving from the persistent myth that *Conversos,* forcibly converted Spanish Jews, settled Antioquia in the colonial period. As Ann Twinam has shown, the association between Antioqueñidad and Jewishness developed and thrived between about 1850 and 1930, precisely in response to the region's economic expansion. There is considerable evidence that the myth is rooted in Colombian anti-Semitism but almost no evidence that it has any basis in fact.[14]

Antioqueño intellectuals, often anti-Semitic themselves, have had an ambivalent relationship to the charge of Jewishness, some embracing the notion, some emphatically rejecting it. Lifelong researcher Gabriel Arango Mejía mined genealogical records to prove conclusively that Antioqueño families did not have *Converso* antecedents, while writers who sought to promote a positive counterimage created their own ethnic myth, that of *la raza Antioqueña,* which finessed the question of Basque or Jewish presence in the past.[15] This *la raza Antioqueña* was described as one that had developed as a *mestizaje* among the diverse peoples brought to the region by the Spanish conquest, but whiteness was taken to predominate. The genetic and cultural contributions of Africans, in particular, were erased from most characterizations of *Antioqueñidad.* Unsurprisingly, *paisa* intellectuals relied on explicitly gendered imagery to construct this whitened narrative of regional identity. They described the region's women as fecund race mothers and their mountain-born sons as passionate adventurers, virile and "strong of arm," as well as good businessmen.[16] In the 1960s, these regional apologists provided a ready-made explanation for academics seeking to explain the region's unusual industrial development. Drawing on theories of economic change that split the world into "traditional" and "modernizing" societies, sociologists like Everett E. Hagen argued that inherited psychological traits predisposed Antioqueños to value hard work and entrepreneurship.[17] Other scholars quickly set about debunking Hagen and his followers, insisting that the accumulation of money capital and entrepreneurial experience in the region owed more to local economic history than to inborn personality traits. Yet the notion that Antioqueños are somehow different, and that this difference shapes their economic behavior, has died hard. Verbally, if not often in print, locals and outsiders seeking to understand the violent chaos of Medellín in the 1980s and 1990s have sometimes turned to this discourse of exceptionalism, suggesting that drug traffic in the region owes something to the proverbial *paisa* aptitude for making money or that the consumerism and family loyalties of young gang-members mark them as essentially Antioqueño.[18]

In sharp disagreement with such monocausal ethnic theories, economists and historians have pursued a different set of research questions, asking not what cultural propensities made Antioqueños different but rather what features of the regional economy allowed an industrial "takeoff" in the early 1900s. Here the debate has centered on mining and the trading systems associated with the expansion of small-scale gold extraction in the late eighteenth and early nineteenth centuries. For some, the region's broad-based prospecting economy, in which small producers with access to cash bought long-distance trade goods from a range of importers, facilitated the growth of an unusually dynamic commercial elite.[19] For others, the dramatic expansion of a smallholder coffee economy in the central *cordillera,* south of Antioquia proper but settled by Antioqueños, generated new markets for manufactured goods (first foreign, then domestic), as well as a mechanism for capital accumulation among processors and exporters and, at the national level, a definitive source of foreign currency.[20] Although the most persuasive explanations continue to be those that allow for multiple causation, recent monographic work has played down the importance of coffee and lent support to the argument that it was the merchant fortunes of Antioqueño importers that became the basis for capital investment in industry.[21]

By contrast, relatively little research has been done to extend or revise the work of the economic historian Luis Ospina Vásquez, whose 1955 study, *Industria y protección en Colombia*, examined Antioqueño industrialization within the context of a wider political debate about protectionism.[22] For Ospina Vásquez, industrialization in Antioquia, as elsewhere in Colombia, owed principally to state intervention and the fixing of tariffs that helped ensure the profitability of national factory production.[23] He explained the decision of rich Medellinenses to mount manufacturing enterprises more or less in passing: in the early 1900s, according to Ospina Vásquez, there was a great excitement for industrial ventures, and specific investors felt themselves likely to succeed.[24] Rather than occupying himself with *Antioqueñidad*, for which he had the greatest sympathy, Ospina Vásquez approached industrialization as a political problem.[25] He traced not only changes in the national economy before and during the shift to industry but also the ideological shift that led Colombian elites to abandon free trade for protectionism. While those who promoted ethnic theories and those who objected fiercely to such theories tended, equally, to present Antioqueño industrialization as a good thing, Ospina Vásquez expressed a critical uncertainty: "By now, it would be enormously difficult to go backwards; but we cannot say . . . why we have taken this road, where it leads, or whether it helps us or hurts us."[26]

Industry and Urbanism

As the next generation of economic historians reevaluate protectionist tariffs, as well as the debates over dependency and import substitution that characterized the 1960s and 1970s, they will likely focus on the dramatic process of urbanization that has remade Latin American societies over the course of the twentieth century. In 1870, 95 percent of Colombians lived in the countryside, a percentage that dropped rapidly in the 1910s and 1920s. Between 1938 and 1985, however, the relative weights of the rural and urban population reversed themselves: Colombia was 69 percent rural in 1938 but 69 percent urban by 1985, with the population increasingly concentrated in the largest cities.[27] Antioquia underwent the same transformation: 72 percent of the region's population still lived in rural areas in 1928 but only 34 percent did so in 1973, by which time industrial towns of the Aburrá Valley accounted for 49 percent of all Antioqueños.[28] A wide range of "push factors" fueled this change, including high levels of violence in the countryside, the inaccessibility of schools for rural children, and the direct economic pressure faced by *campesinos* unable to earn enough to feed their families. The "pull" of Medellín's urban economy was more specific, coming primarily from the opportunities for waged work generated by the city's textile-led industrialization.

Medellín's physical infrastructure expanded equally rapidly, accompanied by massive changes in the feel of city space. If an outsider had visited the city in 1899, with the first automobile to reach the city, and then returned in 1931, with the beginning of regular air service, she or he would have seen an almost unrecognizable downtown. After fifty years of planning and construction (1875–1931), Medellín had a grand just-finished cathedral, one of the largest brick buildings in the world, and, at the cathedral's entrance, a new central square. This was denominated "Bolívar Park" rather than "plaza," just as the city's Plaza Mayor had been renamed the Parque de Berrío (after the nineteenth-century Conservative politician Pedro Justo Berrío). That the two central squares were now "parks" rather than "plazas" underscored the separation between the landscaped focal points of the new city center, accented by imported statues and fountains, on the one hand, and the newly distinct Plazas de Mercado of Guayaquil and Florez, on the other. In contrast to the nineteenth-century pattern, by the early 1930s Medellín's banks and business offices were spatially separated from the small-scale buying and selling of hawkers and stall owners. Indeed, the city's elite pursued the modernization of the growing financial district near the Parque de Berrío with such zeal that many expressed relief when a series of fires destroyed most of the older buildings on the square.[29]

Throughout the early decades of the twentieth century, wealthy members of the city's powerful civic improvement association, the Sociedad de Mejoras Públicas (SMP), worked to modernize everything about Medellín. Streets were renamed, with indicators of only local significance, such as "El Guanábano" (the Guanábano tree) or "Los Huesos" (The Bones), being replaced by the proper names of heroes of national independence, revolutionary battles, or Latin American countries: "Bolívar," "Junín," "Perú." On these same streets, automobiles, trolleys, and bicycles began to displace horses, cattle, and mules—in no small part because the city's modernizing elite actively promoted a new vision of urban space. The SMP pushed the municipal council to require that goods and mail be transferred to carts or wagons outside the city, to ensure that mule-trains not be driven through the downtown area. At the same time, the association pressured landowners to put their city tracts to urban rather than rural uses. Coffee-exporter Eduardo Vásquez, for example, was asked to destroy plantings of *cañabrava* and plantains on city lots he owned, while livestock traders were warned that animals destined for market could no longer be herded or corralled in the streets.

Table 4.   Population of Medellín and of the Aburrá Valley, 1905–64

Year	Medellín	Aburrá Valley towns (including Medellín, Bello, Envigado, Itagüí)	Antioquia	% of Antioqueño population residing in Aburrá Valley
1905	59,800[1]		650,000[2]	
1912*	70,500[3]	84,400	741,000[4]	11
1922	(85,000)	(131,500)	(850,000)	(15)
1938*	168,300	202,370	1,188,600	17
1947	(253,900)	(347,000)	(1,382,900)	(25)
1951*	358,200	441,500	1,570,000	28
1964*	772,900	995,739	2,477,300	40
1973*	1,100,100	1,394,290	2,828,000	49

Asterisks denote census years; estimates given in parentheses; all figures rounded off to nearest hundred. Unless otherwise noted, figures are taken from the regional statistics reproduced in Anthony James Beninati, "Commerce, Manufacturing, and Population Redistribution in Medellín, Antioquia, 1880–1980: A Case Study of Colombian Urbanization" (Ph.D. diss., State University of New York at Stony Brook, 1982), pp. 158–59 and 165, or from the census figures and estimates compiled in Daniel Herrero, "Le développement industriel de Medellín, 1925–1965," in *Ville et commerce: Deux essais d'histoire hispano-américaine,* ed. Herrero and Bernard Kapp (Paris: Editions Klincksieck, 1974), p. 172.

1 Constanza Toro, "Medellín: Desarollo urbano, 1880–1950," in *Historia de Antioqua,* ed. Jorge Orlando Melo (Medellín: Suramericana de Seguros, 1988), p. 299.

2 James J. Parsons, *Antioqueño Colonization in Western Colombia,* rev. ed. (Berkeley: University of California Press, 1968), p. 103.

3 Toro, "Medellín," p. 299.

4 José Olinto Rueda, "Historia de la población de Colombia: 1880–2000," in *Nueva historía de Colombia,* 9 vols., ed. Alvaro Tirado Mejía (Bogotá: Planeta, 1989), vol. 5, p. 366.

Our returning visitor would have also seen evidence of the city's first wave of industrialization. Through the 1910s and early 1920s coffee-packing plants had sprung up all over Medellín. These semi-industrial workshops, called *trilladoras,* employed seven hundred women in 1916 and twice as many by 1924. In the same period, Medellinense entrepreneurs opened cigarette factories, cotton and woolens mills, candy and chocolate companies, breweries, bottling plants, a match factory, and smaller workshops making shoes, sacks, and ready-made apparel. Indeed, the new factories quickly became a kind of genteel tourist attraction, and not only out-of-towners but also the local upper class regularly went on factory tours. Beginning in 1905, the Bello mill set fixed visiting hours and began selling tickets at $20.00 pesos per person. Demand was high enough that Don Emilio Restrepo soon raised the price to $50.00 on Thursday afternoons and $100.00 at other times, with an additional charge for those who arrived without previous notice. (As a point of reference, operatives earned about $0.30 a day in 1916.[30])

From one end of the valley to the other, a perceptive visitor might have noticed that factory whistles and clocks now segmented the daylight hours

The Fabricato building, downtown Medellín, 1940s. In 1972, rival Coltejer erected a tall, needle-shaped building that has become Medellín's best-known landmark, continuing the textile firms' tradition of setting a modern tone for the city. Photograph by Francisco Mejía. Courtesy of the Fundación Antioqueña de Estudios Sociales.

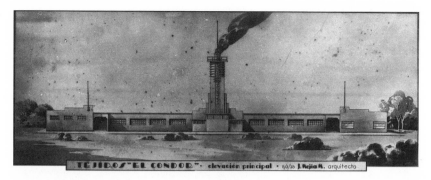

Architect's sketch of Tejicondor, 1935. Photograph by Francisco Mejía. Courtesy of the Fundación Antioqueña de Estudios Sociales.

of those who worked in or near the new establishments. As the SMP's board promoted the construction of outlying middle- and working-class neighborhoods, the city also began to have a distinct commuter rhythm. Workers and a growing class of professionals now moved in and out of the city center on trolley cars (which were transporting nine thousand passengers a day by the early 1920s) or in gasoline-powered trucks and buses. With smokestacks, trolley lines, and newly opened streets changing the city's physical shape, no one landing at the new airfield, as did *Life* photographer Dimitri Kessel, could fail to see what SMP members so consciously attempted to make visible: that this was a booming modern city.[31]

Medellín's Mill-Owners

The *Life* piece focused on Carlos Echavarría, the city's most successful industrialist and president of Coltejer. Kessel photographed him with his family, at home, and in Coltejer's cafeteria, eating the same subsidized lunch provided to workers. His siblings' mansions were also pictured, beneath a descriptive headline, "The Rich: Live in Gracious Style, are Intricately Interrelated." Whatever their prejudices about Latin Americans, *Life*'s readers found enough familiar references to recognize this as an upper-class family in U.S. terms. Carlos had attended Columbia University and played on the football team, his daughter was enrolled at a private boarding school in New York, and his prized dog (also photographed), a brindle boxer, was a "Madison Square Garden Champion." Several generations of Echavarrías also studied or lived abroad for more directly practical reasons, to staff the New York office of the family's coffee-exporting firm, to receive technical training in textile production, or, in one case, to spend five months as a worker at Burlington Mills, rotating through each department as a way to learn the busi-

Monument to Don Jorge Echavarría, being unveiled by his widow in a ceremony at Fabricato, 29 June 1944. Photographer unknown, reproduction by Fernando Garcés and Foto Garcés. Courtesy of Fabricato.

ness.[32] For although *Life* presented their lives as effortless and refined, the Echavarrías were a family that expected its members to work hard.

Figure 5 sketches the Echavarría clan and their relationship to both Coltejer and Fabricato, over three generations, without attempting to trace the family's involvement in business ventures apart from textiles. Carlos's great-grandfather Rudesindo Echavarría Muñoz had made his fortune selling foreign manufactures, primarily cloth, in the Antioqueño mountains. His sons Rudesindo and Alejandro, with their long-time partner Vincente Villa, diversified the family's interests, acquiring shares in a range of local firms and several powerful banks. (Alejandro served as president of the Banco Hipotecario de Medellín and cofounded the Banco Alemán Antioqueño.) In partnership with Villa, who had married into the family, the Echavarrías also controlled Medellín's electric utility, which they sold to the city in 1918. By that time, Coltejer consumed half of the electricity generated by the company, and the fact that all of Medellín depended for its energy on a company that favored one factory had given rise to widespread resentment, including mob gatherings at Alejandro's home.

Coltejer was incorporated in 1907, as a joint venture of R. Echavarría and Compañía and Alejandro Echavarría e Hijos. According to Rudesindo's son Enrique, they had begun with the idea of installing a handful of English

Rudesindo Echavarría Muñoz = Rosa Isaza Pérez
R. Echavarría e hijo

Rudesindo (1854–1897)
(marries María Josefa Echavarría)

Alejandro (1859–1928)
(marries Ana Josefa Misas)

Echavarría & Compañía
(operates with this name during 1897–1902)

R. Echavarría & Compañía
Fabricato

Pablo	Jorge
Alberto	Ana
Ramón	Lucía
Enrique	Jaime
Rudesindo	——

Alejandro Echavarría & hijos
Coltejer

Gabriel	Guillermo
Sofía	Alejandro
Germán	Diego
Margarita	Rosa
Luisa	Carlos J.

Pablo: Involved in local politics and road-building. Married his cousin Sofía. Partner in **Fabricato** but withdrew in 1934 to aid his sons in founding the hosiery firm **Fatesa** (later bought by **Coltejer**), having sent his son to the USA to learn hose production.

Alberto: Founding partner in **Fabricato**.

Ramón: Worked with his uncle at **Coltejer;** gerente of **Fabricato**, 1924-42.

Rudesindo: Worked at **Coltejer,** then gerente of **Fabricato**, 1944-49 and in 1957.

Enrique: Gerente of Medellín's only electrical plant, controlled by the Echavarrías and by Vincente B. Villa until it was acquired by the municipality in 1918. Gerente of **Fabricato**, 1921-23. Author of several books of memoirs and a history of the local textile industry.

Jaime: Gerente of **Fabricato**, 1942-44, also closely connected to **Tejidos de Bello** and **Tejidos Santa Fé.**

Sofía: Married her cousin Pablo after attending finishing school in New York. A respected society matron, she founded the city's symphony.

Ana: Married to Vincente B. Villa, partner to the Echavarrías. Son Luis joined the family business as a chemical engineer at **Fabricato** and as gerente of **Pantex.**

Lucía: After Ana's death, Lucía married Vincente. Well-known society matron, active in local Red Cross.

Jorge: Administrator of **Fabricato**, 1923-34, after having overseen **Coltejer** in his early twenties. Lived in the United States for extended periods and was the brother charged with purchasing looms and spinning machines for **Fabricato**. Married to Isabel Restrepo, niece of Emilio Restrepo (**Fábrica de Bello**).

Alejandro: Co-founder of **Pepalfa.**

Gabriel: Partner in **Coltejer;** involved with numerous Medellín firms; co-founder of **Pepalfa.**

Guillermo: Married one of Don Emilio's nieces, Angela Restrepo, sister to his cousin Jorge's wife Isabel.

Germán: Gerente of **Coltejer**, 1928-35.

Margarita: Married John Uribe, owner of woolen goods firm **Paños Vicuña,** which then merged with **Paños Santa Fé,** a company briefly owned by **Fabricato**. Uribe was also a partner in **Indulana,** another woolens mill that merged with **Paños Vicuña.** Son Diego took over the company, and served on **Coltejer's** board as had his father. Another son, Hernán, also joined the company.

Luisa: Married same John Uribe, after Margarita's death.

Rosa: Married Gustavo Uribe, John's brother. Her son Rodrigo was Gerente of **Coltejer,** 1961-74.

Carlos: **Coltejer's** best known Gerente (1940-61), who greatly expanded the company. Powerful in Colombian financial circles throughout this period. Married to Elena Olarte Restrepo, sister of his brother Gemán's wife, Lucía Olarte Restrepo.

Figure 5   The Echavarrías of Coltejer and Fabricato. Source: Alfonso Mejía Robledo, *Vidas y empresas de Antioquía* (Medellín: Imprenta Departamental de Antioquia, 1952). See also Mary Roldán, "Genesis and evolution of *La Violencia* in Antioquia, Colombia (1900–1953)" (Ph.D. diss., Harvard University, 1992), pp. 541–43.

looms in a corner of Alejandro's large coffee-packing plant. Quickly, however, they decided instead to buy enough looms to compete with the Fábrica de Bello. Indeed, Enrique claimed that they had openly copied the Bello mill; he and an architect had toured the inside after buying the tickets that Don Emilio sold to Saturday gawkers. Coltejer's inauguration in 1909 was itself a public relations coup: the country's president set the machines in motion via a telegraph-operated switch in Bogotá, and local notables gathered at the mill to hear speeches and to toast the new company's success. Coltejer grew rapidly, expanding its machine stock from 30 to 141 looms by 1916, by which time more than three hundred people worked at the mill. The firm concentrated on flat woven cottons, but it also produced knit goods and, after 1912, began installing spinning machinery to supply its looms.

Coltejer became a joint-stock company in 1914, but the Echavarrías were careful to preserve their position as the company's largest shareholders. Through the 1960s, even as the textile giant was becoming one of the most widely held companies in Latin America, with tens of thousands of Antioqueño shareholders, many of them middle- and working-class people who owned no other stock, Coltejer continued to be run as a family firm. When Carlos took over in 1940, he was following the pattern established in the company's earliest years. His father, Alejandro, had served as the company's first president and as general administrator of the mill. His elder cousins, Ramón, Jorge, and Rudesindo, had rotated through as managers; and a cousin from another side of the family, Eduardo Echavarría, had worked his way up from the position of a mid-level employee to become general supervisor.[33]

By 1923, sixteen years after helping their cousins found Coltejer, Rudesindo's sons were ready to apply the experience they had gained with their uncle Alejandro to a firm of their own (see figure 5). Although other investors joined them in establishing Fabricato, the new company quickly became an Echavarría enterprise. From its first day, which included speeches by the president of the republic and a general blessing by the archbishop, who consecrated the factory to the Sacred Heart of Jesus, Fabricato was the country's most modern industrial installation. The new mill boasted automatic rather than manual looms, a full complement of the most advanced spinning machines available, and the unparalleled benefit of a track connection to the Antioquia Railroad. A weaver on the new looms could tend up to twenty machines at a time, while weavers at close-by Fábrica de Bello, with machinery that was now twenty years old, could not manage more than one manual loom each.[34] Fabricato's monthly production, 140,000 yards in 1923 and nearly double that by 1926, rivaled that of mills with twice as many employees.[35]

Yet Fabricato spent more per worker than other firms, offering better wages and more comprehensive nonwage benefits. Jorge Echavarría, general manager from the mill's inauguration until his fatal illness in 1933, seems to have seen in Fabricato an opportunity to pursue his passionately held belief that an enlightened industrialist could make a well-run factory a model for society at large. Drawing on the principles of Catholic Social Action, Don Jorge from the beginning presented Fabricato as a different kind of workplace. After the champagne and speeches of Fabricato's first day, for example, he had sent the workers on an all-day excursion, by train, to see the national industrial exposition in Medellín. Rooted in the social encyclicals of Leo XIII, and in lay movements before and after his papacy, Catholic Social Action preached both that workers should humbly defer to their superiors and that these superiors should take it upon themselves to better workers' lives. Don Jorge, as workers called him, insisted on absolute obedience and personal loyalty. A staunch Conservative and anticommunist, he sympathized with European Fascism and despised the "Bolshevism" of Antioqueño Liberals, who, he thought, let their party be guided by a leftist minority of "reds and priest-baiters." With many other Colombian Catholics of his generation, he believed that only the church could point society toward a "Third Way," between the class antagonism of unbridled capitalism and the antireligious, anticapitalist appeal of socialism.

Jorge disagreed profoundly with his uncle's methods at Coltejer, where low wages, Jorge noted in his diary, "are fomenting class hatred—a grave error on Alejandro's part!!"[36] Within a few years of opening Fabricato, by contrast, Jorge started night classes for operatives, opened a small kiosk for snacks and occasional evening parties, gave paid vacations, and adopted a policy of spontaneously raising wages when food prices went up. His approach, and his social-Catholic rhetoric, prefigured the paternalistic practice that would later come to define Antioqueño industry.[37] At Coltejer, no less than at Fabricato, the younger Echavarría brothers worked to make Jorge's right-wing Catholicism the guiding principle of Antioqueño manufacturing. By the early 1940s, as outlined in chapter 6, all of the city's mills offered generous benefit plans, including paid vacations, subsidized cafeterias, continuing education, schooling for male workers' children, and company-funded recreational activities.

Indeed, the Echavarrías' paternalism and their reputation for generosity and charitable action extended far beyond their mills. With many other upper-class Medellinenses, the sons and daughters of the Echavarrías were often fervently Catholic, and good works were thus a public expression of their faith. Nor could they have avoided philanthropy. "La high," as members of the city's aspiring middle class called the new industrial elite, expected its members to donate money and time to hospitals, orphanages, homes for single mothers, housing projects, and urban improvement projects. The projects of the SMP and the San Vincente de Paul society provided a sort of social register visible in the layout of the city. Bolívar Park, for example, had been

Table 5. Principal textile firms, Aburrá Valley, 1920–60

Full Name	Local Name	Year Founded (year began production)	Primary Owners
Cía Antioqueña de Tejidos, later Cía de Tejidos de Medellín	Fábrica de Bello	1902 (1905)	Restrepo Callejas family, and Eduardo Vásquez
Cía Colombiana de Tejidos	Coltejer	1907	Echavarría family
Fábrica de Hilados y Tejidos del Hato	Fabricato	1920 (1923)	Echavarría family
Cía de Tejidos Rosellón (w/Tejidos Hernández)	Rosellón	1915	Medina family
Tejidos el Cóndor	Tejicondor	1935	Varied stockholders; by 1940, Grace involved
Fábrica Textil de los Andes	Fatelares	1890s/ 1939[2]	Montoya and Arango families
Tejidos Leticía	Telsa	1934	Rabinovich family

Sources: Luz Gabriela Arango, *Mujer, religión e industria: Fabricato 1923–1982* (Medellín: Universidad de Antioquia, 1991); Fernando Botero Herrera, *La industrialización de Antioquia: Génesis y consolidación, 1900–1930* (Medellín: CIE, 1985); Enrique Echavarría, *Historia de los textiles en Antioquia* (Medellín: Tip. Bedout, 1943); James Parsons, *Antioqueño Colonization in Colombia*, 1st and 2d eds. (Berkeley: University of California Press, 1968 and 1985); F. Gómez Martínez and Arturo Puerta, *Biografía económica de las industrias de Antioquia* (Medellín: Editorial Bedout, 1945); Alfonso Mejía Robledo, *Vidas y empresas de Antioquia* (Medellín: Imprenta Departamental de Antioquia, 1951); and Coltejer, *Balances e informes*, 1944 and first semester 1958, Archivo Coltejer.

built around a fountain donated by Alejandro Echavarría. In 1923, his fountain was moved to the San Vincente de Paul hospital, which he founded, and a statue of Bolívar, the purchase of which was arranged by his nephew Pablo, took its place at the center of the park. Echavarría women, especially Sofía and Lucía, held positions of influence and prestige in the upper-class world of Medellín's charities and nonprofit institutions. They also organized annual religious celebrations for workers and their families, apart from their expected role as godmothers and ladies bountiful for their husbands' and brothers' employees.

Fabricato, as the Echavarrías' second mill, established the clan as among the most powerful of Medellín's emerging industrialists, but the Echavarrías did not achieve undisputed preeminence until the boom years of the World War II era. Through the 1920s and 1930s, Coltejer and Fabricato competed with both larger and smaller textile producers in the Aburrá Valley, many of

Primary Product	No. of Workers in 1920[1]	% Female	No. of Workers in 1940 *period of rapid growth: (1940/46)	% Female	No. of Workers in 1960	% Female
Cheap, durable cottons	510	78				
Cottons (varied)	300	83	1,300 (1,300/6,000)		7300 (in 1958)	12
Cottons (varied)	134 (in 1924)	63	1,700 (1,700/5,000)	67	5240 (in 1965)	13
Cottons (varied)	380 (in 1922)	76	1,290			
Cottons (varied)	—	—	2,000 (1946 figure)		2,200	
Cayuba products, later bedspreads, towels	42	43	350 (1946 figure)	80	330	
Woolens	—	—	300	majority	900	

1 A severe financial crisis in late 1920 led factory owners briefly to lay off large numbers of workers; figures given are for the months preceding the crisis. From manuscript Actas de Visita by Antioquia's factory inspector, held at the Archivo Histórico de Antioquia.

2 Fatelares grew out of an earlier (1891) workshop which had been reorganized as Tejidos La Constancia in 1932; in 1943 the firm bought Tejidos Albión. Echavarría, pp. 50–52.

which were controlled by family-owned commercial houses like those of the Echavarrías, as shown in tables 5 and 6. Don Emilio's brothers and cousins, as Hijos de Fernando Restrepo y Compañía, owned the area's largest mill, the Fábrica de Bello, with only one nonrelative, the wealthy coffee-exporter Eduardo Vásquez, holding a significant number of shares. In the early 1920s, observers betting on Medellín's fledgling textile industry might as easily have picked the Restrepos as the Echavarrías, or they might have gambled on the Medina brothers, whose Tejidos de Rosellón had just bought out Tejidos Hernández and a second small mill. In addition to Rosellón, which produced flat woven cottons (as did Coltejer, Fabricato, and the Fábrica de Bello), the Medinas owned Tejidos Medina and Tejidos Unión (knit goods), as well as the hosiery mill Calcetería Helios. In woolens, similarly, Medellín's manufacturers were often family-owned businesses. As indicated in figure 5, the Uribes founded Paños Vicuña and ran it among themselves: All five brothers

Table 6. Comparison of mills in the Aburrá Valley, 1922

Name	Primary Owners' Family Name	Capitalized at: (pesos)	Monthly Production
Coltejer	Echavarría	623,670.00	150,000 yds
Fabricato	Echavarría	800,000.00	not yet operating
Rosellón, w/Tejidos Hernández	Medina	1,026,470.00	168,000 yds
Fábrica de Bello	Restrepo Callejas	(in 1916) 500,000.00	150,000 yds
Tejidos El Sucre (Antioqueña de Tejidos)	(Various investors)	200,000.00	
Tejidos Medina	Medina	44,000.00	
Tejidos Unión	Medina		
Montoya y Hermanos	Montoya		
Carlos Montoya	Montoya		

Sources: Fernando Botero Herrera, *La industrialización de Antioquia: Génesis y consolidación, 1900–1930* (Medellín: CIE, 1985), and Medellín, *Anuario estádistico* (1922), pp. 96–100. Data on work hours are extracted from the factory inspector's manuscript Actas (Archivo Histórico de Antioquia) and from the *Anuario Estádistico* of 1921, p. 77.
1 Figures for male and female wages at Tejidos de Bello are an estimate based on "Lista del jornal diario," Copiador 1919/20; Recibo de seguro pagado por la muerte de Ana Luisa Arango, Copiador 1927,

worked in the firm, and father John remained the *gerente,* or company president, until it merged with two woolens mills linked to Fabricato, at which point his son Diego took the helm.

A competing woolens mill, Tejidos Leticia, or Telsa, was the only important textile producer to be founded by immigrants rather than Antioqueños, but it, too, was run as a family firm. Producing blankets and thick woolens, Telsa was the project of the Rabinoviches, a Russian Jewish family that had arrived in Colombia in the late 1920s. Workers seem to have interacted with the "Rabinos," as retired operatives called them, in much the same way as with the Medinas and Echavarrías, judging from oral interviews, but Medellín's elite families never accepted them as equals. Nor did Tejidos Leticia ever emerge as a competitor to the huge conglomerates that Fabricato and Coltejer became.

The only local cotton manufacturer to approach the Echavarrías' mills in productive capacity, Tejicondor, did so only briefly, and only by depending on foreign capital. Begun by a group of local investors, rather than a family group, Tejicondor in 1940 allied itself with W. R. Grace, a North American investment firm—to the anger of Antioquia's manufacturing elite, which prided itself on a process of industrialization that began with and remained controlled by local capital. Apart from its competitors' resentment, however,

Hours of Work	Women	Men	Total Workers	Female Wages (pesos)	Male Wages (pesos)
10	240	60	300	.35–.80	.50–2.70
—	—	—	—	—	—
9½ and 10	290	90	380	.52	1.15
10	400	110	510	.10–.55	.25–2.20[1]
9½	30	15	45	.60	1.50
9	20	10	30	.20–.80	.60–1.80[2]
10	27	3	30	.35–.50	.40–.60[3]
9	18	24	42	.25–.45	.60–1.20[4]
10	15	5	20	.45–1.00	.30–1.60[5]

p. 306; and Acta 367, 11 Nov. 1921, Libro de Actas del Inspector de Fábricas, Signatura 8932, Archivo Histórico de Antioquia (AHA).

2 Estimate based on Acta 1637, 14 Oct. 1922, S. 8935, AHA.

3 Acta 1147, 15 Sept. 1921, S. 8933, AHA.

4 Estimate based on Acta 760, 26 July 1920, S. 8928; and 1681, 14 Nov. 1922, S. 8935, AHA.

5 Acta 789, 14 Aug. 1920, S. 8928, and 2001, 11 July 1923, S. 8937, AHA.

Tejicondor found itself stymied by its foreign partner when decisions had to be made quickly, and the company failed to keep pace with Fabricato and Coltejer.[38]

With a series of expansions and mergers in the 1940s, financed by emissions of new stock and by high profits, the Echavarrías' first-place position among Antioquia's industrial families was firmly established. In the three years between 1 January 1947 and 31 December 1949, for example, Coltejer and Fabricato reported net earnings of 178 and 289 percent, respectively. Together, they accounted for half of all textile goods produced in Antioquia, with Coltejer alone controlling 40 percent of capital investment in the region's most developed industrial sector.[39] The Echavarrías' two firms were now not mills but incipient conglomerates. Fabricato bought out the Fábrica de Bello in 1939 and Tejidos Santa Fé (woolens) in 1942; the company then used John Uribe's mills to expand still further, as mentioned. In 1944, the firm took the unprecedented step of entering into a cooperative venture with the U.S. manufacturer Burlington Mills to mount a capital-intensive synthetics plant (Textiles Panamericanos, or Pantex). Fabricato went on to acquire the Compañía Colombiana de Hilados, Tejidos Monserrate (in Bogotá), and two plants in Barranquilla.[40] For its part, Coltejer more than doubled its productive capacity in the early 1940s, purchasing the Medinas' mill, Roselló n, and Colombia's first rayon plant, Sedeco. The company also built a new plant on a plot of thirty-five square blocks in Itagüí, which became Coltejer's headquarters. The development of Coltejer's manufacturing subsidiaries, among them Textiles Rionegro, Furesa, Industrial de Yuca, and Polímeros Colombianos, is too complex to chronicle here.[41] Continuing this pace of growth in the 1950s, by 1960 Coltejer was one of Latin America's largest textile producers, measuring itself not against other Colombian firms but against its counterparts in other countries.

Medellín and *La Violencia*

The decade of the 1940s, when Medellín's textile industry boomed, saw the explosion of a bloody internal war between loyalists of Colombia's two mass political parties; the long conflict is known in Colombia simply as *la Violencia*, "the Violence." Through the early 1950s, which figure here as years in which textile capitalists experimented with new management forms and poured money into extra-wage benefits, Colombians were learning to live with widespread disorder, rampant banditry, and terrifying massacres. As Mary Roldán notes, this made for a surreal separation: "Just as individuals were organizing into armed popular groups . . . [and] refugees fleeing violence began their arduous exodus from their towns of residence, the president of the National Association of Industrialists (ANDI) could coolly declare that Colombia's economy had never been better."[42]

The best-known symbol of these years is the "Bogotazo," 9 April 1948, when crowds destroyed downtown Bogotá in anger at the assassination of Jorge Eliécer Gaitán, a brilliant political maverick who threatened the top-down structure of Colombian partisan politics. Yet the "Bogotazo" is only the tip of the iceberg; it does not capture the historical multiplicity of *la Violencia*. From one perspective, the Violence was a pitched battle between Liberal and Conservative civilians, with rightist priests fueling the conflict by exhorting Conservatives to fight a holy war against the Liberal Party—which they identified with international Communism, immorality, and the destruction of the Catholic faith. From another, it was an open war between the Colombian armed forces and guerrilla armies of Liberals, who used the vast southern grasslands as their base. From a third perspective, small farmers and other *campesinos* were killing one another in fights that sprang less from ideological abstractions and more from local contests over land and resources. Through the 1950s, small bands of armed partisans, thieves, and adventurers operated with impunity in vast areas of the Colombian countryside—at once enmeshed in such existing local contests and acting to spark new conflicts.[43] Whatever perspective one chooses, however, Colombia's *Violencia* was largely a rural war. The cities remained controlled by rich men and politicians who may have opposed or condoned the murderous activities of rural partisans but who in either case endeavored to keep this war away from their own homes.[44]

Roldán's work provides a more precise mapping of the social geography of la Violencia in midcentury Antioquia. It is not that the region suffered less in the countrywide conflagration but rather that a set of subregional divisions shaped the character of the bloodletting. Of the more than one hundred thousand Antioqueños displaced by violence and the perhaps twenty-six thousand killed, in the short span of 1946–53 (figures that place Antioquia third among Colombian departments in the number of victims of la Violencia), the majority came from those municipalities furthest from Medellín. Roldán demonstrates that traditional elites were able to check partisan violence within Antioquia's economic heart, the towns surrounding the booming Aburrá Valley and the southwestern coffee-producing municipalities, which together constituted a zone of economic integration. This was also a zone of relative cultural homogeneity, viewed as the geographic "core" of Antioqueñidad. Elite control was not unchallenged, and the aspirations of an emerging group of young career politicians, especially within the governing Conservative Party, helped fuel diverse episodes of violence even in those municipalities most tightly linked to Medellín's growing economy. Yet bipartisan economic networks and even the clientelistic party structure itself ensured that traditional authority figures were able to "manage" the violence in central and southwestern Antioquia. It was not partisan antagonism as such but rather the economic, political, and cultural difference between this zone of elite control, centering on Medellín, and the Antioqueño periphery (including the most violent municipalities of Cañasgordas, Dabeiba, Puerto Berrío, and Urrao) that determined the form of la Violencia in Antioquia. The peripheral municipalities, marked by ongoing contests for economic and political control and inhabited by people that the central authorities neither respected nor felt pledged to protect, bore the brunt of the death and destruction of the late 1940s and early 1950s. This spatial dynamic helps explain the surreal peacefulness of Medellín's textile workplaces in this period of civil war. Located in Medellín and recruiting the bulk of their workers from within central Antioquia, the mills were protected social locations—buffered from la Violencia by their privileged place within the Antioqueño economy and the regional political imaginary.[45]

In keeping with Roldán's argument that traditional elite actors worked to limit la Violencia within their zone of influence, the Echavarrías can be seen to have consciously excluded partisan violence from the mills. The family was strongly pro-Conservative, yet they allowed no partisan activism in the factories and offices of Fabricato, Rosellón, and Coltejer. Retired workers who identified themselves as Liberals, and those who were staunch Conser-

vatives, agreed that no one asked prospective workers their political affiliation. Nor, they said, did their employers ever attempt to tell workers how to
vote. Both were business as usual in many rural areas, and Medellinense
industrialists do seem to have tacitly condoned violence in the far-flung
municipalities where they owned ranches, but they disallowed such coer-
cion in the city they were so committed to modernizing.[46] The Echavarrías
worked closely with clerics, primarily Jesuits, to set up Catholic unions and
thus ensure that their plants were protected from any independent organizing, and they actively promoted the same fervent Catholicism that the Conservative Party claimed as its own. Yet they seem to have stopped short of
overt Conservative propaganda, and workers insisted that the mills were
islands of nonpartisanship, where productivity was more important than any
person's political loyalty. Only during 1957, when the Echavarrías joined
other members of the ANDI to launch a manufacturers' strike against the
short-lived military government of Rojas Pinilla, were overt politics permitted to interfere with shop-floor rhythms at Fabricato and Coltejer.[47]

The Echavarrías' unwillingness to permit partisan politics to disrupt production should not be confused with blanket neutrality. Antioqueño Conservatives were profoundly divided, first because party officials in small towns
resented the overweening power of Medellín, and second, because Conservative businessmen favored economic and social stability over the risks of
ideological warfare. Industrialists were pragmatic. They might ally themselves with Conservatives on the far right, but their political commitment
was to a technocratic bipartisan model of government (exemplified by the
moderate Conservative Mariano Ospina Pérez and by the rightist Liberal
Carlos Lleras Restrepo). A stable, technically competent government controlled by wealthy elites would allow them to negotiate protectionist tariffs
and an economic policy favorable to importers of capital goods; it would also
guarantee social stability in a way that mass violence against Liberals (supported by the far right of the industrialists' own party) could not do.[48]

Within the sectarian divisions of the Conservative Party, this vision meant
that industrialists might ally themselves with Laureano Gómez when it
served them to do so, but their most steadfast support was reserved for Ospina Pérez. *Ospinista* Conservatives valued elite consensus and preferred
negotiating with upper-class Liberals to exhorting poor and rural Conservatives to take up arms against the opposite party. *Laureanistas* had a more
thoroughgoing ideological vision, that of transforming the Colombian Conservative Party into a vehicle for building a corporatist state, as Franco had
done in Spain. The two factions were sometimes locked in conflict and
sometimes closely aligned against the Liberals (who were themselves split
into opposing camps), but the difference in their political styles can be
clearly seen in the Echavarrías' reputation for keeping partisan violence out

Table 7. Percentage of textile workers, by place of birth

Year	Medellín	Antioqueño districts other than Medellín	Other Colombian departments
1916	50.0	49.8	0.2
1920	45.2	53.4	1.4
1924	35.2	62.6	2.2
1928	28.1	71.4	0.44

Source: Fernando Botero Herrera, La industrialización de Antioquia: Génesis y consolidación, 1900–1930 (Medellín: CIE, 1985), p. 156, based on Medellín's Anuarios estadísticos, which include separate information for textiles only before 1929.

of the mills. In keeping with an oligarchic political sensibility, the Echavarrías could present Fabricato and Coltejer as oases of calm, exemplars of the usefulness of paternalism and persuasion as opposed to the participatory idiom of more radical political styles.

Antioqueño industrialists' commitment to paternalism may also have reflected a split in the regional church, as Roldán has suggested.[49] While Monsignor Miguel Angel Builes, bishop of the provincial town of Santa Rosa de Osos, fought a propaganda war against the "atheistic and anti-Christian communism" that he saw in Colombian Liberalism, Jesuits in Medellín committed themselves to heading off Liberals and socialists by preempting their appeal. Rather than fight the threat of "communism" with fire, they sought to extinguish it by supporting protective legislation for workers, organizing pro-Catholic trade unions, and preaching that employers should use their profits to raise workers' standard of living.[50] Within the church, as within the traditional party structures, patterns of authority in Medellín tended toward conciliation and cohesion rather than toward radicalism of left or right.

The Country in the People

Understanding of the economic place of Medellín within Antioquia, both as a "showplace" of a modernizing elite and as the center of a powerful subregion constituted by the central towns near the Aburrá Valley and the southwestern coffee-producing municipios, is only a first step. Placing the city's new industrial workplaces within the broader social and cultural geography of Antioquia further requires an examination of rural-urban migration from the perspective of workers themselves. Most of the people I interviewed had been born on farms or in Antioquia's small mountain towns, reflecting the general population of mill-workers. As early as 1928, migrants outnumbered the locally born, especially in textile jobs, with new arrivals coming from country districts near Medellín rather than from other Colombian departments (see table 7 and map 4). More than any other set of nonwork

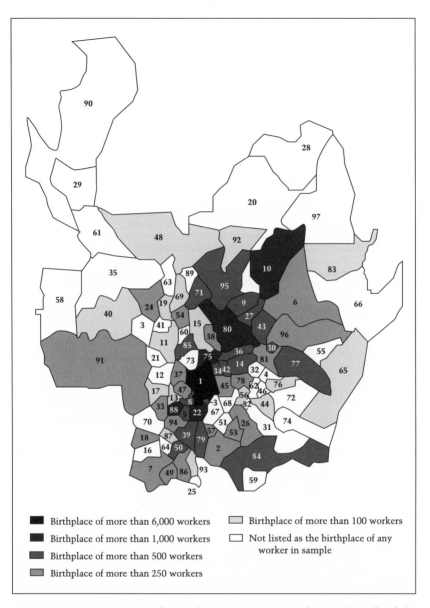

Map 4 Antioquia's municípalities, showing migration to the textile mills of the Aburrá Valley, 1905–1960. Shaded areas indicate birthplace of number of workers given in legend. Source: Author's sample of personnel records, as detailed above (Introduction, note 10).

| | Population in 1938 | | | | | Population in 1938 | | |
Municipality	No. in Sample	Men	Women	Total	Municipality	No. in Sample	Men	Women	Total
1 Aburrá Valley	150	91062	111308	202370	50 Jericó	11	8824	9281	18105
2 Abejorral	7	13407	14161	27568	51 La Ceja	12	4614	5501	10115
3 Abriaqui	0	216	190	406	52 La Estrella	14	2601	3152	5753
4 Alejandria	0	1291	1394	2685	53 La Unión	5	2081	2223	4304
5 Amagá	13	5301	5732	11033	54 Liborina	4	4079	4701	8780
6 Amalfi	5	5877	5726	11603	55 Maceo	1			9608
7 Andes	5	13433	14101	27534	56 Marinilla	2	6736	7171	13907
8 Angelópolis	8	2449	2487	4936	57 Montebello	6	3832	4055	7887
9 Angostura	9	4597	5158	9755	58 Murindó	0	686	639	1325
10 Anorí	38	4229	4118	8347	59 Nariño	0	4379	4683	9062
11 Antioquia	3	6190	6835	13025	60 Olaya	1	1339	1222	2561
12 Anzá	1	2476	2544	5020	61 Pavorandocito	0	300	273	573
13 Armenia	3	3418	3490	6908	62 Peñol	1	4099	4844	8943
14 Barbosa	14	6250	6553	12803	63 Peque	0	2713	2854	5567
15 Belmira	2	2361	2602	4963	64 Pueblorrico	5			10431
16 Betania	1	4732	5112	9844	65 Puerto Berrío	2	10532	7527	18059
17 Betulia	2	5084	5444	10528	66 Remedios	0	4123	2852	6975
18 Bolívar	5	8017	8269	16286	67 Retiro	15	2958	3144	6102
19 Buriticá	1	3012	3115	6127	68 Rionegro	15	8277	9568	17845
20 Cáceres	0	1517	1074	2591	69 Sabanalarga	2	2319	2491	4810
21 Caicedo	1	2047	2098	4172	70 Salgar	1	8035	8064	16099
22 Caldas	28			8626	71 San Andrés	10	3814	4127	7941
23 Campamento	2	3513	3357	6870	72 San Carlos	0	4143	4112	8255
24 Cañasgordas	5	7044	7451	14495	73 San Jerónimo	0	3633	3915	7548
25 Caramanta	0	4335	4331	8666	74 San Luis	0	1821	1541	3362
26 Carmen de Viboral	8	6846	7305	14151	75 San Pedro	25	3029	3196	6225
					76 San Rafael	3	3503	3311	6814
27 Carolina	11	3509	4096	7605	77 San Roque	12	8958	8090	17048
28 Caucasia	0			5480	78 San Vicente	7	5104	5506	10610
29 Chigorodó	0	242	232	474	79 Santa Bárbara	9	8383	8969	17352
30 Cisneros	9	3635	4454	8089	80 Santa Rosa de Osos	16	9946	11281	21227
31 Cocorná	0	8301	7521	15822					
32 Concepcíon	1	1914	2319	4233	81 Santo Domingo	6	5755	6468	12223
33 Concordia	8	6716	7057	13773	82 Santuario	1	5266	5769	11035
34 Copacabana	13	3532	4107	7639	83 Segovia	3	4112	2833	6915
35 Dabeiba	0	8198	7320	15518	84 Sonsón	14	15767	17847	33614
36 Don Matías	14	2769	2975	5744	85 Sopetrán	12	5799	6424	12223
37 Ebéjico	4	5662	5820	11482	86 Támesis	6	8560	9338	17898
38 Entrerríos	5	1867	1976	3843	87 Tarso	2	3791	3497	7288
39 Fredonia	14	12840	13309	26149	88 Titiribí	20	6843	7590	14433
40 Frontino	2	8192	8351	16543	89 Toledo	0	2279	2594	4873
41 Giraldo	1	1379	1442	2821	90 Turbo	0	5460	5029	10489
42 Girardota	13	4062	4772	8834	91 Urrao	6	9363	9793	19156
43 Gómez Plata	9	3578	3806	7384	92 Valdivia	2	4742	4305	9047
44 Granada	2	5054	5260	10314	93 Valparaíso	3	3478	3593	7071
45 Guarne	8	3770	4241	8011	94 Venecia	4	5515	5617	11132
46 Guatapé	0	1949	2005	3954	95 Yarumal	13	11327	13165	24492
47 Heliconia	5	2986	3113	6099	96 Yolombó	7	12445	11445	23888
48 Ituango	3	10152	10414	20566	97 Zaragoza	0	3290	1650	4940
49 Jardín	4	4917	5326	10243					

experiences, their country backgrounds—inflected by the daily religiosity that marked family life in central and southwestern Antioquia—shaped mill-workers' sense of themselves. When the publicists of the ANDI concocted "Juan" as a fictional worker whose move to the city was a move to prosperity, they did so via a simplistic set of oppositions (between country and city, ignorance and knowledge, backwardness and progress). Oral history provides a means of tracing what such ideological oppositions mean in workers' lives. It also fleshes out the evidence offered by city and factory statistics, by answering questions they cannot: How did a person get a job in the mills? What changed, and what did not, when rural people became urban workers?

In reconstructing the experiences of rural migrants, the memories of the minority of mill-workers who grew up in Bello, Envigado, or Medellín provide an initial point of reference. People who had grown up near the mills remembered getting hired in informal, spur-of-the-moment ways. Antonio Pineda, for example, said that he had been playing marbles with friends near the Fábrica de Bello when Don Emilio drove up in a horse-drawn carriage: "He got down from the carriage and right then the marbles rolled out, and he said to me, 'Aren't you ashamed of yourself? So big, and playing marbles? Avemaría! Come get a job.' "[51] As a thirteen-year-old raised in Bello, Antonio knew Don Emilio and knew the mill. His father worked in the boiler room—when he wasn't drinking—according to Antonio. And family lore had it that his mother had secretly gotten herself hired there when she was a young girl; after only six hours, however, his grandfather had found out and gone to get her. Susana Osorio, similarly, said that she had accompanied a friend who was taking a lunch pail to her father at Rosellón; on a whim, the two fourteen-year-old girls had asked a manager to give them work, and he had agreed. Estanislao Bedoya had been walking home from school and had stopped to ask a group of people standing at Coltejer's gate what they were doing. Next thing he knew, said Estanislao, the manager had put him to work cleaning machinery. As had been true for others I interviewed, the only difficulty he recalled was that of convincing his parents to let him return the next day.[52]

Rural migrants, however, were less familiar with the city and its opportunities. For some, getting a job had been easy, while others described it as an anxiety-filled experience. If hands were short, mill managers asked employees to recruit their friends or relatives. If a mill had all the workers it needed, however, a person might wait outside the gate every day for three months before being hired. In either case, it made a difference whether prospective workers knew someone at the mill who might put in a good word for them. María Cristina Restrepo, for example, said that a group of people from her small town had gone to work at Fabricato. They arranged jobs for her brothers, who then helped her get a position in spinning. The hard part, she said, was getting permission from her brothers, who did not want her to work: "I was dying of envy, I guess it was envy, watching the girls that went up to work. And so I asked them to let me go to work, and them saying no." What changed her brothers' minds was the attitude of Fabricato's administrator, who convinced them to let her visit the mill and who made sure that she did not have to wait with other job-seekers in the street outside the mill gate.[53]

For Concha Bohórquez, who had also worked at Fabricato, having to ask cousins and friends to help was more traumatic. She had grown up in the coffee-growing town of Pueblorrico, but had come to the city after her father died. Her sister and brother-in-law, according to Concha, had wanted for themselves everything her father had left them, and they had made her life impossible:

> I didn't do anything but cry. . . . Should I tell you what I brought with me? From the farm? A little paper bag, like the ones you used to see a lot, with string handles, and in it I had—some little shoes for the house and a dress. Nothing else. One or two dresses and what I was wearing, that's all I brought from home![54]

After praying to Jesus and promising that she would make a pilgrimage to a shrine in the town of Girardota, in Antioquia, said Concha, she managed to locate some cousins of hers who lived in Bello and worked at Fabricato. Nearly fifty years later, she still felt the sting of their rejection:

> Concha: I had two cousins there [at the mill], and neither one wanted to put in a word for me.
> Ann: And why didn't they want to put in a word for you?
> Concha: Ah, I don't know . . . they were ashamed of me, you know. Because I was more black [más negra], and I was a country-bumpkin [muy montañera yo], and, well [laughs] . . . Until one when he said, or I said to him, "all right, I want to know if you're going to help me get a job at Fabricato or not." And so he said, "yes, okay, I'll wait for you tomorrow at seven A.M." I went there to wait at seven A.M., supposedly to get me the pass—at seven A.M., right, and at eleven A.M. he still hadn't show up!
> Ann: Oh no!
> Concha: I could've smacked him! . . . And later he said, "Were you there at the gate?" And I said, "You don't need to know, what for? I won't beg you any more, that's the last time." . . . I was really hurt, by that.

She had also tried with two friends, Concha related, whom she knew from Pueblorrico. Catching them one day as they left the mill, she had asked them to help. But, she said, they had a brother who was a priest and they thought themselves above her. "Not a chance," Concha remembered them saying, "we're not going to help anyone . . . all you get is them embarrassing you and maybe losing your job too." Hurt by their attitude of superiority, Concha took a job sewing shirts by the piece, where the hours were flexible enough to allow her to continue to spend the mornings waiting at Fabricato's main gate. Finally, a woman who worked with her on shirts discovered what was making her so unhappy. As Concha remembered it, the woman helped her immediately: "She says to me, 'Eh! Avemaría! Aren't you a silly little fool, why didn't you tell me?" Within a week, Concha concluded, her new co-worker had arranged a job for her. As she told the story, with a dash of self-deprecating humor that was uniquely hers, it was a moral fable that underscored Concha's self-representation as an independent woman who had made her own way in the world.[55]

Her account points to the complex and sometimes contradictory layers of differentiation that shaped working people's self-perceptions and their perceptions of others. After her description of the snubs she had received, for example, Concha added that the manager who hired her at Fabricato had asked her for recommendations and had tested her to be sure she could read and write. As she put it, "they were sick and tired of taking in illiterates." That was why, she said, Fabricato had been forced to establish a night school: "to teach everyone . . . they were taking in people that were such *campesinos!* . . . They'd come in with *alpargatas* [a kind of sandal worn by rural Colombians], with a *mochila* [a woven bag] slung over their shoulder, and they'd be *whistling!*"[56] In the light of retrospect, Concha laughed indulgently at the figure cut by newly arrived migrants. Over time, she had perhaps come to share, or to have fun with, the images that shaped city dwellers' understandings of the differences between country and city, or of the differences between agricultural work and a "new" employment like machine-tending.

The color consciousness that Concha felt in her cousins' unwillingness to associate with her, similarly, was undoubtedly widespread among Antioqueños but is not, for that, the easier to analyze in interpersonal terms. Documentary evidence on the racial composition of the early textile workforce is slight. Photographs of newly hired workers, kept in company archives, establish that mill-workers varied widely in skin tone and in facial features. Yet they provide no evidence about how a person's appearance would have fit into social-cum-racial categories of the time. More suggestive are the written comments on personnel forms, some of which included spaces for noting the shade of a person's skin, their hair texture, or even whether their nose and lips were "wide" or "thin." However, this information seems not to have been a part of how jobs were assigned within the mill. More likely, recordkeepers' obsession with "identifying features" reflected the racially conscious discourse of the national system of *cédulas* (identity cards).[57]

In interviews with me, a fair-skinned person who was at once *gringa* and part of a Medellinense family of doctors and lawyers, retirees who referred to themselves as "black" insisted that racial discrimination—evident elsewhere in Medellín—had found no home in the mills. María Clara Henao, for example, said, "Look, I'm black [*yo soy negra*] and I was accepted very well there, I had no problem." "No, no, no," she insisted, "this thing about color. . . . Fabricato had no color [i.e., had no color prejudice], I don't think that Fabricato ever had color or politics."[58] Her claim that Fabricato's managers did not pander to the color prejudice that sometimes surfaced among employees is attested to by an incident in 1939. The coach of Fabricato's female basketball team wrote the factory's administrator that most of the players briefly quit the company team because they would not play with Amalia Ospina, "whom they did not like because of her color and humble position." He would not take Amalia off the team, however, and within a few days the women had come back. The team lurched forward to lose several more games—while Amalia was snapped up by another team to play in a national tournament.[59] Indeed, the fact that mill-owners recognized no racial boundaries among those they hired (or the existence of a community story that they recognized none), may have made it easier for darker-skinned Antioqueños like Concha to articulate the racism she felt at a familial and interpersonal level.

Concha tried so hard to get into Fabricato (or the Fábrica de Bello, where she also went to wait at the gate with other job-seekers) because she saw millwork as far preferable to the majority of other jobs a country girl might get in Medellín. Among the women I interviewed, there was general agreement that textile jobs were clean and respectable and that people were treated well in the mills. Most often, they compared factory work to domestic service, widely perceived as undesirable. María Elisa Alvarez, for example, explained that she had disliked working as a maid and so looked for a chance to ask for work at a factory. In 1929, after a year in the city, she had taken advantage of the opportunity offered by an errand to pass by Coltejer:

María Elisa: I couldn't work in people's houses!
Ann: And, yes, why not?
María Elisa: No. How can I explain? There was a house where I was treated, just beautifully! . . . but, no, I have to live where I can . . . in a place I like; it was like, "this isn't for me, I don't know, I'm used to going outside, to go somewhere in the morning and leave in the afternoon."
Ann: And, and how was it that you got hired at Coltejer?

María Elisa: Okay, it was simple. One day they sent me to buy some green beans on Colombia street, there was a place there, with beautiful garden crops, beautiful vegetables, and so I went in; I went to Coltejer, barefoot.

Ann: But there weren't a lot of people that worked there barefoot?

María Elisa: Yes, there were always people that worked barefoot, but no, I didn't go in to work barefoot. I went in wearing shoes. But that day I did go in, to ask for work, and the one that received me was Don Eduardo. . . . Then they sent me to have a medical exam, he was really nice, I remember, Doctor Bernal. He examined my teeth and he said, "So, I guess you haven't had any illnesses in your life?" And I said, "No Doctor," because you know that all I'd had was typhoid and smallpox . . . but he didn't ask me anything else, so I didn't tell him anything else.[60]

María Elisa's direct way of narrating her memories provides an unusual glimpse of the social relations that shaped life in early-twentieth-century Antioquia, and the five-hour interview we recorded together is a source I return to throughout the following chapters. María Elisa was seventeen when she went to work at Coltejer, making her typical of female textile workers hired in the 1920s and 1930s.[61] She had been raised on her family's farm near Ebéjico. It was good land, María Elisa said, with fields for pasturage, sugarcane, and tobacco. Her father had died young, however, and the family could not survive on the farm. "I could see our hunger, see it on the walls," María Elisa remembered, her voice agitated. The townspeople, she said, had helped them by buying whatever she and her sisters took to sell in Ebéjico, but she had hated the humiliation:

María Elisa: We worked a lot in the house, tobacco, jellies, everything. Huy! Thank God for rich people! Everything we were selling, whatever we were making, they'd buy it from us, to help us. Finally one day, with all of us ill, I was the healthy one . . . I was eleven years old, I said to my sister María, "María, let's go somewhere!" And she said: "Where are we going to go? You're worthless, you can't do anything!"

Ann: Why did she say that? Because you were small?

María Elisa: [As if speaking to her sister,] "somewhere else I'd work at anything, not here." I told her, "Because I die of *shame* . . . I'll take a basket of sorted tobacco into town, to sell in the stores . . . but it's not because I'm not embarrassed, it does make me ashamed." [Assuming her sister's voice,] "why does it make you ashamed? . . . because the Arredondo girls will see you!" And I said, "Yes, that's why; somewhere else, I'll do hauling, I'll do anything—but not here." So, one day she told me, "well we're going to go to Heliconia, but you're going to have to pick coffee." [And I said,] "I'll do whatever I have to! [*Lo que me toque!*] I told you, I'll do whatever I have to!"[62]

In Heliconia, María Elisa and her two sisters worked on a coffee hacienda, doing the rough labor of an export crop: weeding the coffee trees, working the harvest, preparing the beans, and filling and weighing sacks for export. They stayed there until one of the sisters, Anita, got married. María Elisa was sixteen at the time, and she remembered that she had missed Anita so badly that she wanted to go anywhere else. With her older sister, María, she left the hacienda to try her hand in the city.

A regular car service ran from San Antonio del Prado, a town near Heliconia, to Medellín, María Elisa said, but they came on foot; it was only a day's walk. She captured the difference between rural life and the city, as her younger self had felt it, by describing what she had felt the first time she took Communion in Medellín:

> María Elisa: The first church I went in was San Ignacio Church . . . my first Communion in Medellín was at that church. . . .
> Ann: What did one feel, the first time you took Communion in the city?
> María Elisa: The first Communion, the first time one took Communion in the city? Well, you thanked God that you were now far away from that kind of work, that was so rough, where you got rained on, here you would not get rained on . . . here you could begin to live differently. You would have your feet covered and, well, what else? You'd be better dressed. You felt happy, I felt happy to be here in Medellín.[63]

Other retired people shared María Elisa's way of phrasing the difference between agricultural work and a job as a weaver or spinner. As Eugenio Márquez put it, "there, you are working in the sun and the rain, all day, exposed to mosquitos . . . the change was good. Despite the noise [in the mills], which you felt, and the air, which was strange: with so much dust and heat."[64] Because I relied on retirees for my interviewing, such accounts cannot be taken as representative of all workers' views. Those who quit after only a few months, for example, may have included some who preferred agricultural work to machine-tending. Yet retirees' memories are persuasive: María Elisa knew the bodily exhaustion of waged agricultural work.

Her sense that wearing shoes, as city people did, and dressing neatly on a daily basis indicated one's own betterment also reflected broadly based cultural assumptions. These can be read in the way Antioqueño mill-workers used the verb *progresar* (to make progress), by which they meant to become more educated, more socially cultivated, or more able to afford the consumer goods offered by a modernizing economy. One man used the word to describe his decision not to follow his father into mule-driving; a woman to explain why her parents allowed her to travel to Bello to look for work. Various retirees applied *progresar* to on-the-job training that then allowed them to be promoted to better paying positions, and one woman used it to describe the way she and her siblings saved together to purchase a refrigerator for the factory-built house they shared.[65] *Progresar* thus meant to "make something of oneself," and it required increasing the distance between oneself and everything associated with the rough toil of farming.

Yet rural life held positive associations as well, and rural migrants contrasted the "healthiness" of country life and the moral strictness with which they had been raised to the ambiguities of city practices. In interviews, they emphasized their parents' unshakable religious convictions and the family-based practice of daily prayer: these were the hallmarks of a country childhood. Most said that they had been raised to recite the Hail Mary and the Rosary both morning and evening, but that factory labor had made it impossible to continue such time-consuming practices. As María Elisa remembered,

At home, we prayed the Rosary every day . . . and the Ave Maria was early in the morning. My mother would wake us up at dawn, and before she sent us out she made us, we prayed the Ave Maria, and she made the sign of the cross—and each one would take a little gourd and run off to the creek! . . . And we kept that routine, always it was the Rosary, afterwards we didn't pray the Rosary in the mornings, but just at night— but we *always* prayed the Ave Maria in the mornings. . . . Here in Medellín it was very different; I'd get up and rush to Communion . . . yes, in the church [in the neighborhood], and then to work.[66]

Like María Elisa, Concha had come to the city alone and had lived in rented rooms. She too set the religious observances she had been raised with against those she had kept up as a young adult. In response to a question about whether her daily religious practice had changed or remained the same when she left her small town, Concha told a story about a conversation she remembered having with a priest in Bello:

I have continued the prayers; the Rosary not much, I didn't used to pray the Rosary much, but I never missed a mass—or all the other pious practices. If I could go, I went. All of it; it went on about the same.

Not really the same, no, because when I was with my father I prayed a lot. I thought—one day I asked a priest, "Look Father," like that, just talking, not in confession or anything . . . "Look Father, when you were little, a kid, well, young, and you prayed a lot, a lot . . . and when you're older you stop praying so much, God recognizes it, he remembers that you used to really pray, right?" And I told him, "Look Father, it's that I almost don't pray anymore; I don't have time to pray or to do anything. I used to keep Sundays so holy, but now I have to wash and iron my few clothes, because I don't have time during the week."

And he said, "Nooo—that's fanaticism. Go ahead and do your washing on Sundays, and go to mass if you have time, of course. But praying? Pray as much as you can, no more . . . back then, you just didn't have any other diversion except for praying!"[67]

Those who made the move to Bello, Envigado, or Medellín with their family told different stories, but they too described a difference between the devotional practices of rural and urban dwellers. Most often, this was a difference they presented by contrasting their parents' styles of prayer with their own. Ofelia Uribe, for example, was only six when her father brought the family to Bello, where he and her older brothers got jobs at Fabricato. She remembered early mornings as "a martyrdom," with her mother waking the family up with shouted prayers, until her brothers insisted that factory work made them too tired to be awakened at four o'clock in the morning. Raising her voice, Ofelia imitated her mother: *"El ángel del señor anunció a María por obra y gracia del Espíritu Santo!"* (The Angel of God spoke unto Mary, by the grace of the Holy Spirit!) The children were expected to shout back "Ave Maria!" she said, "but *loudly*, I can't shout it here, but . . ."

And if you didn't shout back "Amén!" she'd come and pull off the covers, [saying], "You've got enough energy to dance around all the live-long day but not enough energy to pay homage to our Lord!" No, it was terrible! The Ave Maria at four in the morning!

Well, finally the boys were tired of it, and they said: "Mamá, we went to bed very tired, look Mamá, we went to bed very tired, pray your Ave Maria by yourself, okay? And pray for us, but don't wake us up Mamá, because we're too tired." And so my Papá said, "yes, they're right."[68]

Ofelia insisted, however, that other aspects of the family's religious observation continued without change. The evening Rosary never disappeared from their lives, she said; "never, never, never, never." With other retirees, Ofelia also remembered the elaborate preparations with which urban working-class families celebrated the day of the Holy Cross, as well as the ceremonies associated with Easter and with children's First Communions. Daily patterns of worship changed, but the intense religious practice of the Antioqueño countryside continued to be a part of mill-workers' lives. And, as discussed in later chapters, that religiosity intersected with the religious vision of employers like the Echavarrías, who used the cross-class devotional practices of Catholicism to ground the unusually paternalistic labor regime they adopted in the period 1936–50.

Conclusion

The location of Medellín within Antioquia, as part of the prosperous central zone of this Colombian department, and within *Antioqueñidad,* as a cultural and political discourse, is key to the way social and economic change happened in this Colombian city. Three aspects of the local past are directly relevant to the process of industrialization under study. First, the development of a local economy based on manufacturing occurred as part of a self-conscious project of modernization launched by the Medellinense elite in the first few decades of the twentieth century. Second, local patterns of capital accumulation were based on consanguinity, and Medellín's big textile producers were family firms. Third, Antioqueño industrialization can only be understood in the context of rural-urban migration. The move from the farms and small towns of central and southwestern Antioquia profoundly shaped workers' sense of themselves. This is especially evident in retirees' memories of their parents' lives and values, and in their descriptions of the religious practices of their childhoods and young-adult years.

From employers' perspectives, rural-urban migration might be cause for concern at a general level, but it was also palpable evidence of their modernizing efforts. By the 1940s, the city's wealthiest families presided over a city rather than an overgrown mountain town. Workers, too, shared in a discourse of progress that valorized the city over the country and factory work over agricultural work. Retirees' memories hint at the distance between the self-perceptions of those at the top of the urban hierarchy, who looked upon the city as a "paradise" of their own making, and the self-perceptions of those who worked Medellín's new factories, but this was not an unbridgeable distance. In María Elisa's remembered conversations with Don Eduardo and the doctor at Coltejer, or Antonio's memory of Don Emilio stopping a children's game of marbles to invite him to work at the Bello cotton mill, we hear echoes of the multiple ways owners and workers communicated with one another in Medellín. Chapters 2, 3, and 4 explore the vagaries of this cross-class interaction. How did industrial entrepreneurs and other members of the urban upper class perceive this expanding population of urban workers— a population that was at first largely female? How did the young women and men who sought work in the mills understand their own relationship to bosses, mill-owners, and one another? What began to change in Medellinenses' social and cultural interaction as the factories became familiar fixtures in the city?

TWO

The Making of *La Mujer Obrera*,
1910–20

WHEN MARÍA ELISA ALVAREZ arrived in Medellín at age sixteen, she had spent five years doing manual labor on a coffee plantation. Earlier, as a child, she had sold cured tobacco, sweets, and produce on the streets of her hometown. Once in the city, María Elisa worked for a year as a domestic servant, before being hired by Eduardo Echavarría at Coltejer. Less than a year later, she left Coltejer and went to work at a small dyeing shop, very briefly, and then at the Juan de Dios Hospital. "I was never one to go looking for family; I'd rather go along on my own, taking care of myself," she said, explaining that she always managed to find work easily in Medellín. From the hospital, where she had assisted the nurses and learned to wash bedridden patients, María Elisa went to work for a wealthy family, caring for their invalid son. When she became frustrated with the son's rudeness toward her, she returned for a few months to Coltejer. Shortly thereafter, María Elisa applied for a job at the newly opened Tejicondor, where she stayed until reaching retirement age.[1]

Judging from María Elisa's complicated work history, working-class women approached millwork as one of a variety of options for earning wages in Medellín. Her story provides a useful corrective to the category of *la mujer obrera* ("the woman worker") as that category functioned in early-twentieth-century Medellín. Discursively, *la mujer obrera* was defined by a series of erasures and exclusions. These can be traced in quantitative sources from the 1910s and 1920s, in the operation of local institutions, and in texts produced by Medellinenses who took *la mujer obrera* as their subject. Of the six jobs that María Elisa took in Medellín, for example, only three (Coltejer, Tejicondor, and the dyeing shop) would have been included in the annual reports on women workers issued by the municipal government. Appearing in statistical yearbooks from 1916 through the 1940s, these reports included a careful accounting of the number of women employed in the city's industrial workshops and of their hours, wages, towns of origin, ages, and civil status. Women working outside the new factories literally did not "count." Similarly, before beginning at Coltejer, María Elisa could not have sought a subsidized meal or dormitory bed at the "Patronato de Obreras," a charity that served women employed in Medellín's industrial workshops but excluded maids, waitresses, laundresses, and informally trained nurses. Nor could she have sought redress for wages gone unpaid, or for a breach of local labor law, at the city office of the "Policía de Fábricas" (factory inspection)—the one departmental office charged with protecting female wage-earners—except during her employment at Coltejer and Tejicondor. Nevertheless, the existence of statistical reports, charities, and a city agency exclusively focused on female factory workers is in itself an excellent starting point for a history of "the woman worker" as a fictive category that had long-term effects in Medellín.

This chapter examines the local definition of this category by examining three moments in which *la mujer obrera* made a dramatic appearance: in the founding of the Patronato de Obreras (1912); in the creation of the Office of Factory Inspection (1918); and in press reports of the industry's first strike (1920), in which women at the Fábrica de Bello demanded shorter hours, a wage increase, the right to wear shoes to work, and the dismissal of three sexually abusive foremen. Two arguments are developed that have resonance beyond Medellín. The first is that a discursive invention such as *la mujer obrera* may be demonstrably a fiction and yet be undeniably "real" in its historical effects, as historians influenced by poststructuralism have demonstrated for other national and regional contexts. In the Aburrá Valley, Catholic reformers, society ladies, government officials, and journalists who fancied themselves muckrakers drew on an international discourse about female labor to create a stereotyped image of the Antioqueña factory girl as a sexually vulnerable being in need of moral protection. The "woman worker" became a cypher within a reform-minded narrative of titillation, sexual danger, and uncertain rescue. That narrative had staying power, and the rhetoric and practice of reformers in the 1910s and 1920s became integral aspects of mill discipline by the 1940s. The second argument developed here is methodological: for the work of a historian, discourse analysis is necessarily incomplete. Reconstructing a fictional character such as *la mujer obrera* is a first step, but our understanding of her place—even her place within the world of discourse—requires asking questions about her nonfictional sisters. How did living, breathing female factory workers interact with churchmen, almsgivers, data collectors, and city inspectors? In what ways did the discursive figure of *la mujer obrera* overlap with or diverge from their life experiences?

Given that women had always worked in and near Medellín, as servants, agricultural laborers, gold-panners, artisanal producers, and the like, the seemingly sudden appearance of "women workers" as a discursive category requires some explanation. Even the existence, by the early 1910s, of coffee-packing plants (*trilladoras*) that employed hundreds of women did not provoke the level of public concern occasioned by the spectacle of women in industrial workshops. *Trilladoras* were neither foreign nor closely associated with progress. Mechanized factories, on the other hand, symbolized a new era. They were visited, photographed, and talked about as manifestations of an industrial future—one that provoked as much anxiety as it did hope and pride in Antioquia's progress. Protecting the city's *obreras* and controlling their behavior offered Medellinenses a way to protect and control the future.[2]

In Medellín, however, this was an imported future, and knowledge about the social impact of industrialization (and about the "woman worker") was very often imported knowledge. Debates in Europe and the United States provided rhetorical categories and ready-made images.[3] Having read about mass strikes in Europe and the United States, Colombian Liberals and Conservatives wrote about the need to ensure that such conflicts did not erupt at home.[4] For their part, Socialists relied on a double rhetoric of "dark, satanic mills," on the one hand, and evocations of a revolutionary proletariat, on the other, with each set of images being equally odd in the local context.

The bulk of the rhetoric about industry and the "social question" that circulated in Medellín in the 1910s and 1920s derived from an international Catholic discourse about industrialization. Colombian advocates of Catholic Social Action worked to make the church the intermediary between labor and capital. They translated and paraphrased texts about a "Third Way," in which neither avaricious capitalism nor irreligious socialism would prevail but rather a corporatist project of class cooperation. And they explicitly opposed mixed-sex workplaces, as had Pope Leo XIII, because of the inevitable moral risks of such mixing. Following the international church, Catholic reformers in Colombia focused more attention on women who worked in factories than on women doing other kinds of wage labor.[5] As a writer in the newspaper of Catholic Social Action in Medellín, *El Social*, put it, "the *obrera* of the factory . . . is the one that most properly bears the name of *obrera*." "The factory is woman's enemy," he continued, emphasizing the contrast between femininity and the sordid world of work:

> Enemy of her body and of her soul; exhauster of her health and poisoner of her virtue. The work [is] rough or urgent or hard or intense; the environment unhealthy. . . . the almost inevitable mix of women with

men, and what is worse, the dependence on them; finally, like a dark backdrop for so many stains, the lowness of the wage: these make the *obrera* of the factory a woman of misery, compelled to languish physically and morally.[6]

Such rhetoric differed little from that produced by nineteenth-century reformers in France or England.[7] Nor did it claim to be about local class relations. Rather, such pronouncements aimed to separate one abstraction, "the woman worker," from another, more dangerous one: "the working class." As a reformist trope, an *obrera* was not defined so much by her anomalous status as a female wage-earner as by the instability of her virtue, threatened by her exposure to dangerous men and by her own unformed character.

Colombian Socialists, left-wing Liberals, and even some Conservatives represented *la mujer obrera* in similar ways. Writers for Medellín's Socialist paper, *El Luchador*, imagined women workers as "fugitive butterflies . . . kept prisoners in the unyielding nets of the factory" or as "bustling bees, who have to work ten or twelve hours to be able to bring a crust of bread to their mouths and to cover their bodies with a rag." Even before the 1920 strike brought the question of sexual intimidation to the attention of Medellín's reading public, *El Luchador*, like *El Social*, was warning its readers about the sexual danger faced by women in the mills. Not only were *obreras* "made to work like *machos* but paid like slaves," at jobs that required "rough and intense" labor, but also they were perhaps forced "to submit themselves to the mistreatment of an overseer."[8]

The predominant theme was one of beauty despoiled and innocence destroyed, hence the colorful but defenseless winged creatures. Drawing on romantic convention, references to women's exposed bodies, poverty, and sexual endangerment linked pity to femaleness. In flowery language reminiscent of Jorge Isaacs famous novel, *María*, for example, an essayist for *El Luchador* described the terrible fate to which the mills exposed Medellín's *obreras*:

> When I met Flor María, she bloomed with her twenty years. She was beautiful, of a regal beauty . . . [as were] her tresses of hair. Her intensely black eyes seemed magnificent gems. . . . More than all this, she was as good as an angel and as sweet as a child.[9]

On the death of her loving father, however, Flor María was forced to go out to work: "She left the nest of her past joys and delivered her weak and fragile body to the hard labor of the factory." The writer concluded his description with a melodramatic warning: "Not long ago she crossed my path. She laughed like a mad woman. Her eyes no longer shone. . . . Poor Flor María!" Although this essay appeared in the Socialist press, the same story of innocence lost to the factory appeared in a 1948 novel by Medellín Conservative Jaime Sanín Echeverri, which describes the transformation of Helena, a farmer's daughter who loses her virginity while working at Coltejer and becomes, by the end of the novel, a sophisticated woman of loose morals.[10] Emanating from distinct political positions, such descriptions were indistinguishable in their characterization of *la mujer obrera*: she existed only as a trope of helplessness within a pre-scripted story.

The Patronato: Ladies and *Obreras*

The Patronato de Obreras acted out this narrative of presumed danger at the level of Medellín's public institutions. Founded in 1912 by young ladies from the city's better families, its paternalistic vision paralleled that of ladies' reform societies elsewhere: to uplift workingwomen with moral lessons, intercede with their employers where necessary, teach hygiene and housewifely skills, and protect them from the perils of city life. Yet the Patronato was less a reform society than an arm of Catholic Social Action; Father Gabriel Lizardi, a Jesuit, guided the young ladies' meetings and decisions, while nuns oversaw the day-to-day details of managing the projects developed by the board of directors.

While Catholic Social Action directed its male-oriented reading groups and mutual societies toward temperance and anticommunist organizing, the Patronato sought to protect women workers' femininity, chastity, and piety by teaching them the inestimable value of these. With financial help from the Echavarrías and others, the institution began with two soup kitchens, one in the southeastern neighborhoods above the city center, near Coltejer, and one below the Parque Berrío, closer to the train station. From the beginning, however, the soup kitchens were intended to attract women to the Sunday lectures that were Patronato's central project. These lectures ranked as "first and most important" among the activities of the institution, according to the mission statement outlined at the ladies' first meeting. Attending them would "enlighten [the *obreras'*] souls, teaching them to know God, to love him and serve him with the exact and faithful fulfillment of their duties."[11] Within a year, the ladies on the Patronato's board of directors began limiting access to the soup kitchens to those *obreras* who could prove they had attended that week's lecture.[12] As the Patronato expanded, growing to include a dormitory, training workshops, and a full curriculum of classes "appropriate" to workingwomen, attendance at Sunday lectures remained obligatory. The ladies of the board stuck to their central strategy of moral exhortation; whatever else they undertook to do, they continued to believe that providing *obreras* with sermons of moral guidance would improve their lives.

Lecture topics were general homilies: "Faith," "Hope," "Hygiene," "Luxury," "Mutuality," "Saving."[13] Or they were admonishments specific to women workers: "the practice of purity," "the manner in which one should behave during the days of Carnival," and "the modesty which one should maintain in the streets and workshops."[14] Between 1914 and 1918, attendance at the lectures ranged from 20 to 250, with somewhat more than 100 women generally in attendance. The society women who founded the Patronato defined their potential audience as *obreras*, using the same criteria that city officials used: women working in the *trilladoras*, textile mills, cigarette factories, and other manufacturing plants in and near Medellín. Given that city officials counted more than two thousand *obreras* in 1917, the Patronato seems to have had a normal participation rate of 5 to 10 percent of the city's female operatives.[15]

This percentage rate may seem high for a voluntary, religiously based organization, but it is too low to account for the weight of the Patronato de Obreras in the public memory of Medellín. Constantly evoked as a part of the local history of industrialization, the Patronato has significance beyond that of a sponsor of Sunday lectures. What is most often remembered and what tends to appear in photographic retrospectives of the city are not the lectures but rather the Patronato's dormitory and classrooms. By literally separating women workers and by concentrating on safeguarding their chastity, the dormitory gave physical form to the gender-based discourse of paternalistic concern that was beginning to define wealthy Medellinenses' feelings about industrialism. In later decades, for example, the larger factories imitated the Patronato: Fabricato started its own cafeteria and dormitory (called the Patronato of Fabricato), Coltejer opted for a cafeteria and learning/recreation rooms, and Rosellón maintained a live-in house for *obreras* from the countryside. Each of these firms also sponsored the kind of country outings and spiritual exercises originally undertaken by the Patronato. The Patronato occupies a central place in public representations of early industrial Medellín for two reasons: it established a model for later practice at the company level, and it set out an image of the ideal *obrera*, defined by her modest demeanor and chastity, that held sway in Medellín for forty years.

To the governing board, the institution's directors (always priests) stressed the virtue of ladies helping *obreras*, their less fortunate sisters. To the *obreras*, the lectures and activities directed them to be ladies within their condition as *obreras*. Classes included not only workaday skills like ironing, coffee sorting (with coffee and sorting tables supplied by a *trilladora*), and tobacco preparation (courtesy of a tobacco firm), but also refinements like "Spanish language," "arithmetic" "spelling and hand-writing," and "embroidery, lace-making, and artificial flowers."[16] The board also provided genteel entertainments: a pianola with fifty rolls of music, movies that met with church

Patronato de Obreras, 1918. Photograph by Benjamín de la Calle. Courtesy of the Fundación Antioqueña de Estudios Sociales.

approval, and frequent country outings, where the young ladies of the board would "sing, dance, and play with the *obreras.*"[17] By association with the young ladies of the board, as well as by physical separation from men, the Patronato made palpable the discursive distance between "workers" and "women workers."[18] Women workers could not easily claim inclusion in the masculine categories of "rough but honest toil" or "the dignity of Christian labor," but urban pastimes (like railway outings) and a measure of ladylike hobbies, together with demonstrated chastity, afforded them a specifically female kind of social standing. Femininity thus allowed for ambiguity in class status, where women workers were concerned, but that ambiguity depended on the maintenance of gender-specific behavioral norms. A man could claim respect by working hard and being honest, but this would not be enough for a woman; to maintain the distinction between *mujer obrera* and *mujer pública* (prostitute) she had also to follow myriad unwritten rules of feminine behavior, rules that were symbolically indexed by class. Teaching *obreras* to be ladylike, and to preserve their reputations, was entirely consistent with the institution's mission of "saving" them from possible degradation.

The Patronato's directors explicitly sought to ensure that chastity be the key index of a woman worker's value. This required combating other systems of ranking—one's racial appearance, where one worked, or the circumstances of one's birth could not be allowed to interfere with an order based on piety and feminine good behavior. The problem arose early on, as part of the ladies' attempts to define their goals; extending charity to the city's *obreras* meant deciding who fit that category and who did not. In 1915, the *señorita presidenta* of the board, Leonor Escobar, voiced her opinion that neither "servants nor the daughters of servants" should be admitted and that "there should exist a certain selection by caste and color." Other members of the board objected, but their objections themselves point to the tension between class and caste in industrializing Medellín. In opposing Escobar's proposal, board members maintained that the Patronato should accept those "who today work in the factories, without special distinction by social class," their reason being that "we believe that the constitution of our society today does not lend itself to such marked distinctions, given the race mixing which exists and the natural tendency of the servant class to want to improve their position."[19]

Social "class," servanthood, and race (defined by physical appearance and lineage), appear here as overlapping concepts; the board members do not separate race and occupational caste from class so much as they combine them by assuming their fluidity among working people. Upper-class society in Medellín was distinctly white and distinctly racist throughout this period. Membership in social clubs, access to elite educational institutions, the likelihood of receiving social invitations, whom one might be eligible to marry: all of these contained a racial index. Therefore, it was not that board members made no "marked distinctions" but rather that they saw no reason to make them among *obreras*, who shared a status as factory workers and whom they assumed to be racially mixed. Where the new category of *"obrera"* would intersect with other forms of differentiation among women was a volatile question. Escobar resigned as president, while the Jesuit director pleaded with the other young ladies to remain on the board.[20]

Fair-skinned and better-off workers, convinced of their social superiority, perceived the Patronato's openness as a snub. A year after Escobar's resignation, for example, members of the board of directors discussed their difficulty in attracting certain groups of *obreras*, especially seamstresses, shoe workers, and typesetters. It owed, they decided, "to the quite lowly personnel received by some of the industrialists, especially the Señores Echavarrías," and they recognized that "the *Obreras* of better education and family may feel themselves slighted."[21] "Education" or "family," in this context, functioned as code words for racial appearance. Indeed, color prejudice sometimes operated within working-class families, as suggested by Concha Bohórquez's memories of her cousins' unwillingness to associate with her. Yet the euphemisms were important: by the 1910s, neither the local church hierarchy nor most spokespersons for good society would condone overt racism.[22] Looking at Medellín's *obreras,* employers and upper-class reform-ers insisted on what they understood as a "modern" approach to race, admit-ting no color distinction, although they did not require that tolerance from their class equals. In microcosm, the difficulties of the young ladies on the Patronato's board suggest the way Colombian class discourse elided racial distinctions only among those groups subject to definition from above.

In rejecting Escobar's ideas, the board members and their Jesuit director articulated chastity as an alternative hierarchy. Given the difficulty of mak-ing racial distinctions, they argued, "It seems rational that the Patronato accept things as they are in society and that it make no distinction among the personnel of the factories, except solely in regard to moral conduct, which must be required to be excellent."[23] With this, they discussed the "necessity" of keeping themselves informed of the *obreras'* conduct, and they wondered aloud if it were possible to maintain a "detailed book of all that is known of what the *obreras* have done, not only those belonging to the Patronato but also of all the women working in the factories." The board particularly wanted to control the behavior of those who did attend lectures, but they regularly despaired of the exertion required to "persuade" even these women that they had a special duty to "stand out in the factories for their good conduct and for the practice of Christian virtues." Where they could exert more control the board members did, by refusing to recommend for place-ment any woman with a less than perfect record of moral behavior.[24]

Although hesitantly raised and quickly dismissed, neither Escobar's quib-bles nor the unworkable idea of a grand book of good and bad behavior were incidental to how a public discourse about women workers developed in Medellín. Rather, the board's conversations map the outlines of *la mujer obrera* as a local symbol. The Jesuit director and the other ladies of the board recognized, with Escobar, that servant-women fell into a different category, given that they focused their efforts exclusively on factory women. Where Escobar saw a caste, in that a servant-woman's daughter would inherit some stigma, they saw a position one might move in or out of over time. If a servant got work in a factory, as María Elisa had done, then to the ladies of the board, she became an *obrera.* The gap between the public perception of *obreras* and other types of urban women is instructive. The "woman worker" was not presumed to be sexually promiscuous as were stereotypes of *la negra* or of washerwomen, nor de-sexed, as were the flapper or *mujer-hombre* of decadent new fashion.[25] Rather, the "woman worker" was taken to be woe-fully ignorant and sexually vulnerable, easily led astray by more worldly *compañeras* or by dishonorable males. The Patronato's chief projects fol-lowed logically from this image: to provide a carefully monitored dormitory for *obreras* new to the city, to deliver moral instruction via long lectures on the workers' only unsupervised day, and to keep "bad girls" out of the mills.

The ladies' concern to monitor women's behavior suggests the divergence between the Catholic reformers' ideas about industrial discipline and those of the industrialists. In the 1910s and 1920s factory owners had not yet adopted the rigid moral system that later would be taken for granted in the city's largest firms. Whatever the wishes of the Patronato, for example, the industrialists hired women without regard to their moral conduct, at least in the early years. Reformers set out to change that, exerting pressure not only on the *obreras* but also on the mill-owners. They pushed industrialists to make piety and rules of chastity a part of mill discipline, and they sought paths into the mills, the better to enforce that vision.

Factory-sponsored spiritual exercises, for example, were initiated and planned by the Patronato until the late 1920s, when most of the mills began directly contracting priests to provide yearly spiritual exercises.[26] Before then, the ladies of the board and the director would either go to a mill or host a mass and celebration at the Patronato's chapel in that company's name.[27] The ladies organized the exercises themselves, asking only that factory owners provide some incentive to their workers to attend. In 1918, for example, the Patronato's board circulated a letter celebrating the Echavarrías' promise to pay a one-peso bonus to each *obrera* attending Coltejer's spiritual exercises and encouraging other mills to follow suit.[28] The exercises could be elaborate, involving religious lectures, confession, mass, and celebrations with food-stuffs and prizes. Like Sunday activities at the Patronato, these factory-sponsored rituals were performances aimed simultaneously at various audiences. They showed *obreras* how to behave themselves to be good women and good workers, but they also allowed the Patronato's director to meet with factory owners and demonstrate to them the utility of joining hands with Catholic Social Action. Making this sort of inroad into the mills helped garner support for the reformist vision of aggressively Catholic workplaces; building good relationships with industrialists also generated donations, as the Patronato's board members often discussed among themselves.[29]

As part of his goal of "forming a league of frequent communion among the *obreras*," the Jesuit director asked the board to help him compile a list, with addresses and supervisors' names, of all the factories and workshops that employed women. He planned "to visit each of them personally, one by one, with the aim of meeting the employees . . . [and] knowing the spiritual and temporal needs of this strata."[30] This plan of regular visits, of literally going into the mills, seems to have been the seed for the Patronato's only real foray into the arena of formal politics. In 1917–18, the ladies of the board joined prominent Jesuits and other Catholic reformers in pressing the Departmental Assembly to pass an ordinance on "Factory Policing and the Regulation of Work." The proposed ordinance would appoint a factory inspector to do precisely what the director of the Patronato had suggested—visit every mill employing women, and with the same end: to give reformers an entrance into the new workplaces and a voice in their organization.

Factory Policing

Ordinance 25 of 1918 was a flagship project for Catholic Social Action in Medellín. Drafted and tirelessly promoted by Francisco de Paula Pérez, an influential jurist and Conservative politician, it laid out the political and philosophical platform of Catholic reformers: only by curbing employers' excesses and intervening with protective legislation would Colombia prevent terrible class conflict. Arguing before the legislative assembly, Pérez warned his colleagues against ignoring problems which, unresolved, would lead to "inevitable social commotion," and he defended the ordinance as one that would "protect home and family."[31] Repeatedly, warnings about Bolshevism or about Mexican-style social upheaval joined arguments that were explicitly about gender.[32] Women workers' special vulnerability provided reformers with an unassailable framework for making a variety of assertions, and the moral imperative to protect *la mujer obrera* served them as a fallback position. When the proposed ordinance was defeated in 1917, for example, *El Social* admonished the legislators that they had not voted against social guarantees so much as against morality. As the paper put it, "an *obrera*'s health is precious . . . an *obrera*'s morality is still more precious."[33]

This language of sexual protection predominated throughout the campaign that guaranteed the passage of the ordinance. "It is imperative," insisted Pérez,

> that the policing gaze penetrate to the factories, to the end that places of work not become places of seduction or places fomenting lamentable deviancy. It is indispensable that young women have purposeful support, so that in giving themselves over to their labors do not hazard their virtue, so that in weaving productive pieces for the commercial market they do not also weave their lives' dishonor.[34]

By focusing on virginity and on the dangerous anomaly of women "giving themselves" to labor, Pérez reproduced the terms of debate that he and others had laid out in Medellín's Catholic press.[35] As part of the campaign for the ordinance, for example, *El Social* had run a long series of articles with the title "¡*Pobres Obreras!*" The writer urged his readers to descend, via his text, "to the abyss of the working classes." In that hell, he argued, they would discover women in need of protection and guidance—women who should be seen separately from working-class men.

In the black and fathomless abyss of the proletariat, it is not the *obreros* that inspire in me the most compassion. In it is another group that inspires in me pity much more profound, if that were possible.

It is the *obreras!*

It is the *obreras* that share all the miseries of the *obreros*, that suffer all the misfortunes that they do, and . . . some more. (Ellipses in original).[36]

The extra misfortunes faced by women workers were not, of course, described as a question of extra labor (additional chores at home, sewing, etc.) but rather as the danger of their falling prey to seduction and vice. As in Europe, Medellín's reform-minded writers linked the threatening moral dissolution of women workers to their presumed physical debilitation, intertwining the two in an image of quintessential vulnerability. "If statistics could be compiled of the souls and bodies that the factories send to the tomb!" despaired *El Social*'s polemicist, "who would not be horrified to see the funeral procession of so many consumed bodies . . . of so many souls fallen from the work-room to sin or even vice?"[37] Physical weakness and sexual vulnerability came together in evocations of "the white slave trade" as a particular danger to women workers.[38] Drawing on European texts, Colombian reformers also associated women workers with mill children who "have lost their health . . . and who, by living among adult workers, easily lose their innocence and even their shame."[39]

This logic, that child workers—most of them girls—suffered not only from working long hours but also from indiscriminate exposure to adults, mirrored the arguments for protecting women workers. *La mujer obrera* needed protection not only from unscrupulous administrators but also against the pernicious influence of co-workers (female as well as male), who might be foul mouthed, flirtatious, intemperate, or too frivolous. The first article of the proposed ordinance required that any factory employing women and men together also employ matrons, or *vigilantas*, "to guard respectfulness and morality."[40] That requirement became a central focus of enforcement for the "Office of Factory Inspection" created when the bill became law in 1918. After one of his first "acts of visitation," for example, Inspector Joaquín Emilio Jaramillo wrote to the administrator of Tejidos Hernández, to insist that he "admonish the lady or matron in charge of vigilance, to the end that she not neglect her delicate function even for a moment [and] not be absent from the factory in any hour that the personnel is at work."[41]

In 1920, when Jaramillo was replaced by the more zealous Daniel Vélez, such warnings became common.[42] Vélez demanded that the larger mills hire more *vigilantas* and that these should have no other duties aside from moral observation.[43] Concerned that they be effective as well as present, he denounced lax *vigilantas*, quantifying his zeal in stilted, technocratic reports to the Departmental Assembly. In 1924, for example, Vélez reported that "the dismissal of various matrons who have neglected to comply with their duties has been solicited and obtained; the number of those who have suffered such punishment is that of five: 5."[44]

In identifying the *vigilanta* requirement as the first goal in "policing" the factories, the inspectors remained faithful to the central premise of the ordinance, that sexual mixing made the factories dangerous. Their remedy involved not only observation by *vigilantas* but, more specifically, the imposition of silence in mixed-sex workrooms, as described in chapter 6. Vélez complained whenever he heard conversations among workers while performing his "acts of visitation," and he praised those mills with rules against talking. These were "sanctuaries" of labor.[45]

Vélez did not stop at general demands for silence and moral oversight. He took industrialists to task for not complying with other articles of the 1918 ordinance, which restricted child labor, established sanitation codes, and set limits to the accepted practice of fining workers for errors. He also worked vigorously to get male workers fired if they disrespected a female co-worker. Where he succeeded, this too was quantified for the Departmental Assembly; in 1922, for example, Vélez obtained the dismissal of twelve employees and supervisors "for moral faults and unmerited treatment of the personnel."[46] For Vélez, "moral faults" were a broad category. These included cases of "seduction" and "concupiscence," in which women brought criminal charges against co-workers or supervisors, as well as everyday kinds of infractions that reveal more about the inspector's totalizing vision of *la moral* than about his efforts to protect women workers from abuse.

Like the ladies of the Patronato, Inspector Vélez brought a distinctly bourgeois notion of *la moral* to the mills. He urged administrators to dismiss male workers who talked too much with female co-workers or who allowed themselves "inconvenient expressions" in mixed company.[47] In one case, he complained that a technician had offended a group of *obreras* by calling them "mares, tramps and other apostrophes."[48] At another mill the inspector was outraged that women workers should be exposed to a loom-fixer's intemperate odor:

> He presents himself in the workrooms with that sickness known as a hang-over and the obreras, some of whom are even *from very good families,* find it necessary, because of their poverty, to suffer the nauseous breath of said individual. (Emphasis added.)[49]

The inspector's tendency to lump together, under the rubric of "morality," everything from mixed-sex conversation to bad breath to rape, points to the coercive aspects of his approach to protecting women workers. Women did, in fact, demand protection—but they pursued that demand without necessarily conforming to the inspector's and the Patronato's ideal of quiet, lady-like *obreras*. If, for example, women from "good families" were shocked by a foul-mouthed man, the inspector's own words imply that many of the mill's *obreras* might not have been so shocked. His focus is on guarding poor women against bad influences and bad company, as much as against harassment. Vélez's logic paralleled that of the Patronato. *La mujer obrera* had to be protected not only from men "who 'like to fish in turbid water,'" as one official direly warned, but also from her own impressionable nature.[50]

This is not to imply that either the inspector or the ladies of the Patronato were part of an elitist conspiracy to constrain workingwomen's otherwise unconstrained sexuality. First and most obviously, numerous other social forces worked to shape workingwomen's sexual behavior. Second, the evidence suggests that reformers' obsession with *la mujer obrera* was not with her as a being-in-the-world but as a romanticized abstraction of poverty, sexual danger, and bodily weakness. Because reformers focused more on a "social type" than on actual *obreras*, interpreting their actions as essentially or only coercive would oversimplify the case. Their attempts to "protect" virginal and threatened *obreras* had a range of effects in the lives of women who may not have defined themselves either as virgins or as women in dire danger.

Nonfictional *Obreras*

The inspector, Antioquia's legislators, and the ladies of the Patronato pursued actions based on an understanding of *obreras'* sexual vulnerability that was paternalistic and condescending by definition. Nevertheless, their vision intersected with workingwomen's daily lives. Sexual attacks, disrespectful supervisors, lewd co-workers: these linked reformers' arguments to women's daily experiences. Indeed, the points at which reformist rhetoric echoed working-class women's complaints may have provided a seal of "authenticity" necessary to the reformers' success. By denouncing a lecherous foreman, for example, the inspector may have said publicly, from a position of power, some of the things that workingwomen discussed among themselves—even as the act of his speaking "for them" publicly erased women's own actions. Hence the double character of paternalistic projects like the Office of Factory Inspection and the Patronato. They provided real aid and articulated worries that resonated in workingwomen's lives, but they also pursued remedies—like silence in the workrooms—that must have seemed ridiculous to a good proportion of mill-workers, male and female.

The inspector's efforts to have abusive supervisors fired addressed one of the most serious problems faced by female factory workers—one not confronted by their male co-workers. In 1922, Vélez demanded that the manager of Tejidos de Rosellón fire a male worker who "had tried to corrupt an *obrera,* the fact being proven with sworn declarations."[51] The following year he (unsuccessfully) sought redress for Laura Rosa Sánchez, who declared that one Luís Angel, the administrator of Tejidos Unión, "had ruined her while she was working in the factory." According to the inspector, "Twenty-nine days ago she gave birth in the hospital and is dying of hunger with the baby girl— she's 18 and a bit years old. He gave her $2.00 [pesos] a week . . . they say he's got two in the factory that he's ruined."[52]

Vélez knew about Sánchez's case, and about others, because other women told him about her. Even without approaching the inspector directly, female millhands could circulate rumors that would reach his ear. Given Vélez's reputation as a stickler and a man willing to argue publicly with mill-owners (as he did at Tejidos Unión), one suspects that the inspector was not simply inventing it when he reported what workingwomen in a given mill "said" about their male supervisors.[53] Women workers ignored the inspector's arguments for the moral value of silence, and seem to have cared little for the *vigilantas,* but here was a point of convergence between the moralizing project of Catholic reformers and female mill-workers' own efforts to shape the moral world of the factory.

What got lost in this rhetoric of protection, however, was workingwomen's own involvement as moral agents. To the inspector, the important actors in ensuring that *obreras* were respected at work were few: the ladies of the Patronato, those industrialists who made their mills "sanctuaries of labor," and himself. Like notes made at the Patronato's board meetings, his reports and letters make no mention of women's own capacity to demand respect. Instead, the inspector stressed the depth of his penetrating gaze, representing women as passive objects of his concern. As he wrote to the Departmental Assembly in 1926,

> I am pleased to manifest to you that during this year . . . not one of the *obreras* was dishonored in a factory building, neither by an employee [white-collar] nor by a worker. An official must carry out multiple inquiries . . . and through interposed persons, to succeed in obtaining such a result in the matter of morality.[54]

As a fiction of passivity and danger, *la mujer obrera* erased workingwomen's ability to act as persons in the world. It was an idealized stereotype, but one that was never fully detached from the material fact of *obreras* who talked in the workrooms, went to *carnaval,* and trooped through the town's streets—whether to the plaza or to church. The points of overlap between the discursive category of *la mujer obrera* and breathing, moving *obreras* were points of instability. Paternalistic reformers required the visible object of women workers as a group; only the presence of *obreras* justified an over-blown discourse about them. But they could also "push back," in Sherry Ortner's phrase, against the unreality of the evolving discourse about them.[55]

The Patronato's charitable efforts are the best example of both this instability, or "pushing back," and reformers' incentive to erase it. Despite the sanitized public image they worked to project, the ladies of the board had to contend with frequent disciplinary infractions in the dormitory, including noise and "bad behavior."[56] Among themselves, they complained of the young women's absenteeism, "uselessness," "rebelliousness," and thievery.[57] The board also faced the almost insurmountable problem that relatively few *obreras* responded to their offers of moral guidance. As mentioned above, the *señoritas* attempted to drum up attendance at the Sunday lectures by allowing only those who had been present to eat at the Patronato's soup kitchen. They also conferred with the *vigilantas* of various mills, asking them to encourage women to attend. When these strategies failed, they tried gentle bribery. According to the minutes from a 1915 board meeting, "Seeing that the *obreras* of two factories have refused to attend the monthly meetings and that some, for senseless reasons, do not wish to belong to the Patronato, the board resolved to stimulate them with some cajolery."[58]

Building on earlier schemes of raffling off prizes at the Sunday lectures and of giving away clothes that board members had tired of, the board set up a system of tokens or *vales*. Women received a *vale* for each lecture they attended. These could be saved up and exchanged at the Patronato for a variety of consumer goods: dresses, yards of cloth, and so forth.[59] The board then decided to "open a kind of store or bazaar," in which *obreras* would receive a 10 percent discount if paying cash and a 20 percent discount if they brought *vales*.[60] Accepting that the women would still come sporadically, the ladies distributed *vales* only one Sunday each month.[61] Attendance still fluctuated drastically, and the board continued to experiment with country outings, special entertainments for regular attendees, and prizes for those who hadn't missed a Sunday in a given period.[62] But the *vale* system worked well. Indeed, it worked so well that they could hardly keep up with the demand, and spending on clothes and cloth and other goods began to strain the Patronato's budget.[63] On one Sunday in 1924, for example, attendance reached a high-water mark: 150 prizes were raffled off and 1,000 *vales* distributed. If all of those who collected *vales* were in fact *obreras* by the definition that city statisticians used, then the Patronato's board had achieved a participation rate of almost a third.

The existence of *obreras* who spent part of their Sunday at the Patronato because they hoped to win a prize or accumulate tokens for a dress was erased in local representations of the institution. Such frivolity fit only awkwardly with the Patronato's public portrayals of *la mujer obrera* as an op-pressed soul, "exposed to abandonment, to employers' immeasurable exploi-tation, and, what is more troubling, exposed also to moral degradation."[64] Among themselves, however, the young ladies of the board accepted that women workers might find Patronato activities dull. In 1923, the acting president urged the board to "rid the [Sunday] circles of their certain sim-ilarity to a pensioners' home," warning that *obreras* wouldn't come if they didn't find at the Patronato "the necessary freedom." She also complained of the "monotony" of life at the Patronato-run dormitory, suggesting an aware-ness that workingwomen living in rented rooms had alternative pastimes.[65] Yet board members became exasperated with the *obreras'* inconstancy, and the tone of their discussions about how to "stimulate" interest suggests that they viewed the problem as one of women's resistance to their project. *Obreras'* reasons for not coming were "senseless," their own expectations minimal. The women had only "to comply with this simple duty . . . to attend punctually the third Sunday of the month."[66] In frustration, the board repeatedly coupled cajolery with chastisement, deciding to limit this or that party or picnic outing to those women who'd been regular in their atten-dance—using such extras in the same way that they used the soup kitchens.[67] The board members' annoyance, however, reveals little about working wom-en's attitudes toward them; a historian cannot label workers' noncompliance as "resistance" only because upper-class actors saw it as such.

The ladies' difficulties in convincing workingwomen to attend gatherings at the Patronato demonstrate neither that the latter disavowed a paternalis-tic approach nor that they disagreed with Catholic reformers' notions of proper feminine behavior. Rather, workingwomen's noncompliance suggests simply that the Patronato looked different from within the frame of working-class practice than it did from within the bounded world of elite discourse. Similarly, the fact that women reported abusive supervisors to the inspector reveals not that they shared his ideas about how their working environments should be controlled but rather that his office provided a strategic resource. Such evidence points to the materiality of fictions like that of *la mujer obrera*, which created, from one perspective, a way to get free dresses and, from another, a way to get oneself fired for behaving improperly. Yet it also points to the difference between the fictive category of the "woman worker" and the everyday practice of nonfictional workingwomen. For the ladies of the Patronato, for the inspector, and certainly for factory owners and man-agers, *obreras* in the flesh were sometimes too lively to seem downtrodden and too capable in their own defense to seem in need of rescue. Despite its being "acted out" at the level of city institutions, the narrative fiction of *la mujer obrera* as a being defined by her sexual vulnerability and her need for protection was never complete unto itself; it existed in uncertain relationship to the public fact of visible workingwomen who behaved in a wide variety of ways.

Quixotic *Caballeros*, Virile *Señoritas*, and "Human Flowers"

In February of 1920, the women employed by Emilio Restrepo at the Fábrica de Bello surprised everyone, including Don Emilio, by declaring themselves on strike. After a decade of press representations of pitiable women workers, literate Medellinenses were unprepared for the possibility that *obreras* might act on their own behalf rather than passively accepting charity and moral instruction. Reporters tended to be at once charmed and condescending. As one described the scene for a Medellín paper, *El Correo Liberal*:

> Armed with sticks and stones, the girls went up resolved to take the pants off those of the opposite sex who attempted to go to work. They sang cheerfully, raising high on a pole the fundamental insignia of their sex, some skirts, as I understand to put them on the first *obrero* who tried to go in to work.
> Mr. Editor: Excuse me if today I don't report as usual. This is charming. In my job as a reporter I never imagined such a thing as a strike of 500 *señoritas*.[68]

From the first day of the month-long work stoppage, Bello's female workers radically expanded local observers' understandings of what "a strike" might be. They used gender strategically, shaming male strikebreakers with direct sexual taunts and accusing them of not being proper men. The striking women also made an unexpected demand, for the dismissal of three overseers, Manuel de Jesús Velásquez, Teódulo Velásquez, and Jesús María Monsalve, whom the workers nicknamed "Taguiaca." Their action generated a wave of public support, from Medellinenses across the political spectrum. Liberal newspapers reported the strike in great detail, in part because it gave them a chance indirectly to embarrass leading Conservatives, including the departmental governor, Pedro Nel Ospina, who was one of Don Emilio's business partners. In the end, however, the governor intervened personally to settle the strike. With the involvement of the archbishop and a group of influential Jesuits, including Father Lizardi of the Patronato, he forced Don Emilio to accede to the women's demands.[69]

Reconstructing the women's public action requires combining reports in Liberal and Socialist newspapers with a sparse archival record that includes letters exchanged by wealthy Conservatives. What emerges is a bifurcated story. On the one hand, the strikers' flamboyant gestures and their stamina—in staying out more than four weeks—turned the rhetorical tables. Unlike a speech about *obreras* made at the Patronato, or an editorial for or against protective legislation, any set of observations about the Bello strike required a recognition of workingwomen's agency. However condescending their attitude, those who wrote about the strike could not describe events on the ground without recording what strikers said and did.[70] On the other hand, the stereotyped image of *la mujer obrera*, by now a well-established trope in Medellín, had real force. Newspaper reports oscillated between representing the strikers as valiant and forceful *señoritas*, whose actions forced onlookers to think differently about women's capacity (one columnist went so far as to compare them to suffragettes), and depicting them as downtrodden waifs desperately in need of male protection.

Rhetorically, what united the two halves of newspapermen's portrayals of the striking women was the position occupied by male workers in their printed reports. Don Emilio employed between 360 and 420 women and girls, and between 110 and 175 men and boys, according to municipal statistics compiled by the factory inspector. The majority of male workers supported the strike, and a few men played leading roles. Nevertheless, male strikers found themselves erased in almost every public description of events in Bello. This became a strike of "500 *señoritas*," who were opposed in their claims not only by the company but also by cowardly strikebreakers, identified as "18 individuals of the masculine sex." Male reporters wrote as though they themselves were the only sympathetic men present and as though it were incumbent on them and on their readers to support the female strikers. Conservative officials and churchmen similarly ignored the working-class men involved. They involved themselves on the strikers' behalf because these were young women who figured locally as "damsels in distress" rather than as working-class activists. By ignoring male strikers, elite observers effectively extended the discourse associated with stereotyped images of *la mujer obrera*. They continued to understand the seemingly new category of "women workers" as a category defined by its distance from "the working class," figured as masculine, unstable, and possibly threatening.

Although the country had seen its first strike—or the first action by wage workers using the word "strike"—only in 1910, Colombian workers mounted at least thirty-three strikes between January of 1919 and February of 1920. Four of these took place in Medellín.[71] Nationally and locally, by the time workers at the Fábrica de Bello declared their own, strikes had become a familiar part of debates about class, politics, the state of the economy, and the maintenance of social order. Significantly, however, Liberal reporters left such debates aside in their coverage of Bello. Instead, they filed anecdotal, serialized stories reminiscent of novels and travel diaries. The correspondent for *El Correo Liberal*, for example, began by expressing his surprise that anything so interesting could happen in small-town Antioquia. As he put it, "the peaceful town of Bello . . . that seems more like an ox stretched out in pasture land, grazing, than the capital of a municipality, is today a theater of happenings. You heard me: happenings, in Bello."[72] Signing himself "el curioso impertinente," a reference to a character sketched in *Don Quijote*, a writer for *El Espectador* described town personalities and the physical setting, while at the same time presenting readers with engaging descriptions of his own emotions.[73] Translatable as "the curious and impertinent one" or "Mr. Curious and Impertinent," the reporter's chosen byline fit the tone of his articles. At the end of a day with the strikers, he wrote,

> I undertake the return to the Station between the fire of a burning sun and the yellow dust of the road. At every step I turn my eyes back toward the factory and my enthusiastic and sentimental young man's heart flies to those hundreds of little women. . . . A hoarse whistle-blast from the locomotive warns me that hurrying is useless; the smoke draws a black pencil-stroke between the green of the fields and the blue of the skies. Outfitting myself with a horse, and at a stretched-out gallop, I quickly breathe the heavy air of the capital [Medellín].[74]

Celebrating the fact that poor women, with nothing more to their names than "a good provision of rebellion and dignity," would have "the gallant and fertile madness" to confront their employer, "el curioso impertinente" declared himself on their side. "The virility of these girls," he wrote, "submissive slaves until yesterday, attracts me, fascinates me. I'd break a thousand pens, if I knew how to fence with pens, in their defense."[75]

Reporters' rhetorical fancy inspired them to create a heroine, a Joan of Arc leading this army of "*mujercitas.*" They found her in Betsabé Espinal, "a very pretty, very upright girl, who they say is most dexterous at her weaving job." Espinal was the subject of flowery descriptions, interviews, and lyric poems in both the Liberal and Socialist papers.[76] *El Luchador* (a Socialist paper) compared her to a goddess, an abject victim, a rebelling slave. She was luminous and sexual:

> As Betsabé spoke, erect atop a stool which served her as a tribunal, her brilliant black eyes darted over the multitude . . . lightning bolts of rage and flashes of just indignation. As her lungs swelled, giving a rhythmic motion to her bosom, it seemed that her heart was fighting to force its way out of her chest.[77]

With a flattering photograph, they published an interview with Espinal and painted a sentimental picture of her devotion to her aging mother, who was "crazy—perhaps from hunger" and whose "double suffering" she could never earn enough to lessen.[78] Although Espinal herself offered the names of other strike leaders, including Adelina González and Teresa Tamayo, who had

The Fábrica de Bello, 1910. Photograph by Rafael Mesa. Courtesy of the Fundación Antioqueña de Estudios Sociales.

initiated the work stoppage after presenting a formal petition to the manager, Espinal was the only woman to whom reporters attached any individual agency.[79] Her example corroborated the public vision of the strike as "a fight between a weakness that petitions with justice and an obstinate strength that refuses to yield."[80]

The gendered metaphor of female weakness before an inflexible force became a titillating narrative of sexual implication. Taking it upon himself to investigate the justice of the women's charges, "el curioso" launched "a general interrogation" with a group of *obreras*.[81] They asserted that Manuel de Jesús Velásquez was the most notorious offender: he had fired a boy who had seen him calling women into his office alone; he favored certain girls; he punished and forced the retirement of those who would not "give in to his presumptions." Our reporter insisted on details, asking questions and demanding verifiable cases, and he reproduced the conversation for his readers, complete with suggestive ellipses:

—He threatened a certain *señorita* with a fine if she left the workroom [. . .] she stayed alone with [him] and . . .
—And . . .
—Yes, it is known for certain. Poor thing [. . .]
—This is not enough for me [. . .] I need someone to be more concrete, someone to confirm if it is possible. Knowing looks. Vacillations. Blushes.

—He,—ventures one girl finally—he put my niece in the Home for Repentant Women [Casa de Arrepentidas].......... (Ellipses in brackets are added; others appear in the original.)[82]

The women's youth, and their status as unmarried virgins, ensured the effectiveness of their pointed humiliation of male strikebreakers. With the Socialists at *El Luchador*, Mr. Curious and Impertinent and the other pro-Liberal writers at *El Espectador* and *El Correo Liberal* presented the strikers as *"chicas"* and *"chinquillas"* to whom positive masculine adjectives could be applied. They were "gallant" (*gallardas*), "heroic and virile" (*heroicas y viriles*), and "manly" (*varoniles*). Readers learned that the striking women possessed "manly hearts" (*corazones de varón*) and that they had set an example for the "cowardly men" (*cobardes* and *hombres miedosos*) working at the mill. Nevertheless, the strikers remained unthreatening "little women" (*mujercitas*), whom reporters described in feminine terms. Readers encountered the strikers as "pretty girls" (*muchachas bonitas*), who shouted *Vivas* but did so from "dainty lips" (*boquitas de mujer*).[83] Even as they publicly ridiculed male strikebreakers, reporters emphasized the femininity of these "human flowers," as in *El Luchador*'s description of the strikers' morning routine during the strike's second week:

—Girls, make way—says the gentleman Mayor to the *obreras* grouped at the factory gate—so that the workers can enter.
—Of course Don Gabriel. With pleasure.
—Let's make way girls, so that the LADIES can go to work.
The path was made. And eighteen MEN, one by one, filed through that double row of human flowers, pretty girls who watched them . . . with pity. (Emphasis and ellipses in original.)[84]

Rather than making the strikers seem unwomanly or abnormal, reporters' representations played on the sympathetic, carnivalesque possibilities of gender inversion. These valiant girls were behaving "like men" because of a temporary lapse not on their part but on the part of their male counterparts, the *obreros* who had failed to behave as men should. Reporters presented this as an upside-down situation that only real men could put right. The editors of *El Correo Liberal* and *El Espectador* invoked the strikers' "natural weakness," to encourage readers to send money and moral support, and they hosted a fundraising meeting attended by gentlemen (*caballeros*) "of the highest social representation."[85] The city's Socialist paper, *El Luchador* (*The Fighter*) expressed the same sentiments in a workerist idiom, appealing to readers to defend "these indomitable women" in page after page of fiery polemic:

For these proud and rebellious slaves, vagabonds from the dungeon of Don Emilio Restrepo [the mill's owner], where their souls were outraged and where every minute, every hour that passed was a danger to their virtue and their honor. . . . For these masculine females who, when the vacillating *men* fell back one step . . . went forward twenty . . . every one of the *Luchadores* has an immense heart with which to love them and a strong arm to defend them.[86]

For both Socialist *luchadores* and Liberal *caballeros,* defending femininity was a matter of masculine honor; the gender inversion of striking women denouncing vacillating men elicited expressions of solidarity from male observers determined to right this "world upside down."

Racist and orientalist language played a supporting role in marking the distinction between honorable and dishonorable males. Such language may come from *A Hundred and One Nights* in its expurgated Spanish translation, a book that was widely read in Antioquia's coffee towns in this period.[87] Manuel de Jesús was labeled a "Sultán" and a "Nabab," and one fervent writer celebrated the striking women as "these purest of virgins, fugitives from the harem."[88] Physical descriptions of him and the other supervisors hinged on racial identifications: "el curioso impertinente," for example, depicted Manuel de Jesús as "more than dark" and as having "large lips," and a writer in *El Luchador* referred to Teódulo as "the forgotten Indian."[89] Such language extended the references made by strikers, who called the supervisors *negros lambones* (snitching blacks.) The exact meaning of *negro* (or *indio*) in this context is elusive, as the word has a discursive instability in Colombia. In working-class language it need not have been meant literally. The strikers themselves were racially very mixed, as Emilio Restrepo, like other Medellinense industrialists in this period, employed both women and men without regard for local color prejudice. In reporters' hands, however, such references helped make gentlemen's support for the strikers a defense of their racial honor as well as of their gender. *El Espectador* sounded this theme in references to "the noble and gentlemanly tradition that inspired Don Quijote," evocations of "the Latin soul," and calls to defend the striking women "if anything is left of our noble Castilian blood."[90] By casting the foremen as "Sultans," "Nababs," or "Black Chiefs" working for a "White Chief" (*Caciques Negros* vs. *el Cacique Blanco*), reporters positioned themselves as the women's rescuers.[91] With the villains clearly marked as dishonorable, and the "damsels in distress" positioned as having been abandoned by those men closest to them, male observers were able to convert unsettling images of masculine females into props for a familiar and reassuring script of chivalry.

Reading against the grain of newspaper reports and wealthy men's letters to one another, a different narrative can be pieced together—one in which the women's ways of ridiculing male strikebreakers form one part of a larger set of public gestures by the women and men who struck the Bello mill. On Saturday, 8 February, a group of women and men had presented Don Emilio with a petition demanding not only the foremen's dismissal but also a 40 percent wage increase. Reportedly, he had offered to consider giving a smaller increase to certain workers, but had refused to discuss firing his top employees.[92] Workers had begun organizing and planning their action, but "complete order" was observed at the mill on Sunday and Monday; not until Wednesday, 12 February, did Betsabé Espinal and others declare the strike. By then, workers' demands had expanded to include the provision of a lunch break, a shorter workday, and the suspension of an odd rule against women workers' wearing shoes inside the mill.[93] Don Emilio apparently claimed that he had prohibited shoes only to prevent conflict between the women who could afford to wear them every day and those who could not.[94] Workers, however, remembered that he had thought that the women's shoes would ruin the mill's floor.[95]

The sticking point was Don Emilio's unwillingness to fire his on-site managers, especially Teódulo and Taguiaca (Manuel de Jesús seems to have left the mill early in the strike, although newspaper reports are unclear on this point). A first round of negotiations broke down because workers refused to accept a settlement that included the 40 percent increase and a provision that hours would be reduced to nine hours, fifty minutes (as at the Coltejer mill across town) but that stopped short of committing Don Emilio to dismissing the supervisors.[96] The company had agreed only to listen to those women willing to present "concrete charges" before the proper authorities. Apparently through the intervention of the archbishop and Father Lizardi, Teódulo and Taguiaca then offered to resign, allowing Don Emilio to save face.[97] Within a few days of his accepting their resignations, the strikers went back to work—with a shorter day, a substantial pay increase, and a promise of scheduled breaks for breakfast and lunch.[98] In reference to wearing or not wearing shoes, the company agreed that "on this point, the *obreras* can act as they see fit."[99]

On the first day of the strike, women who supported the workers' petition seem to have argued publicly not only with male strikebreakers but also with female co-workers who threatened to go into work.[100] Although all reports agreed that the strikers successfully convinced other women to stay out, a somewhat different picture begins to emerge than that painted by reporters, who wrote as though the strikers were all female and their opponents all male. If somewhere between 110 and 175 men and boys worked at the mill, then a hundred or more men either stayed home or themselves came out to mock those males whom the women made look ridiculous. Even if reporters wrote almost nothing about the male strikers, one can speculate: Were some men present when the women and girls waved their skirts at male strike-breakers? If so, would they have been likely to find the sexual ridicule funny, to think only that it was a good tactic, or to join those who criticized the women for "not behaving like *señoritas*," as Espinal told a reporter that some Bello residents were saying?[101]

Only occasionally are there inclusions in the press coverage which suggest the possibility that female and male strikers worked together to shut down the Bello mill. "El curioso impertinente," for example, knew that Don Emilio was convinced that a Belgian technician, Fransisco Charpiot, had acted as an outside agitator. Reproducing a street conversation with a group of strikers, in the informal style of his reports from Bello, "el curioso" noted not only Charpiot's alleged involvement but also the presence of male strikers, whom he had not previously mentioned:

—Do you know . . . that the dyer, Francisco Charpiot, was fired from the factory today because he figures as the director of the strike?
—Him director of the strike? When! And you say he's been thrown out? Fine, we won't go back to the factory if he doesn't go back. . . . We won't go back—*affirm the men*.[102]

Don Emilio fired Charpiot immediately after the strike, along with a small group of male and female strike leaders, including Betsabé.[103] He might have gotten leaders' names from any number of sources, including the Socialist paper. Mixed in with *El Luchador*'s flowery rhetoric about these virginal "human flowers" was the text of the minutes of the strikers' first meeting, at which both women and men had played prominent roles. "With the attendance of the majority of the *obreros* and *obreras*," the strikers had elected a president, Antonio Quintero, a vice president, Benjamín Jaramillo, and a secretary, Manuel Osorio. They had also designated two formal representatives, charged with speaking for "both sexes" (*para ambos sexos*): "Rubén Hernández for the men" (*para los obreros*) and "*señorita* Betsabé Espinal for the women" (*para las obreras*). Quintero's name also appeared alongside Espinal's on a telegram sent to *El Luchador*, by which the strikers expressed their appreciation of a "monumental, much applauded speech" by the pro-Socialist Liberal Benedicto Uribe. Indeed, the difference between this telegram and a letter sent by "*las huelguistas*" to *El Espectador*, which had a much larger daily circulation, suggests that Espinal, Quintero, and other strike leaders were conscious of the image they presented to reporters. The one ended with a rousing "Socialismo Triumfante," the other with a plea that struck the editors for its "ingenuousness, beauty and valor": "Señor . . . señor we beg you, at all costs, have these men removed so that we [are supervised by] persons of dignity."[104]

What difference does it make that the women who hoisted skirts on poles to ridicule male strikebreakers did so as part of a movement that many men supported? Why should it matter that their action was part of a larger set of strike activities—including drafting a petition, attending strike meetings, and sending telegrams to supporters? By constructing an alternative narrative to that offered by Medellinense reporters, I am not attempting to settle the very local question of "what really happened." Rather, it is the distance between their melodramatic story of brave-hearted virgins and outraged *caballeros* and my skeptical rewriting that allows for a historical analysis of the women's activism. In the reporters' narration, shaped by a local discourse centering on *la mujer obrera*, the women's public action appears as "an unexpected act of valor" by downtrodden beings, who "had been suffering mistreatment, with awful pay and with the constant danger of perdition, almost without seeing the sun's light during the week."[105] Their ritualized shaming of the men who failed to support them seems, in this light, to be a celebration of the momentary power of this "feminine insurrection." Reporters used the raised skirts to further the story they wanted to tell about women abandoned by men and thus forced (temporarily) to take on a male role themselves. If, however, the women who struck the Bello mill had male allies, with whom they planned the strike, their protest seems less a reaction to terrible circumstance and more an act of self-assertion. It is not that they had no men to protect them but rather that they decided to protect themselves and publicly to join male co-workers in a discussion about what should change in Bello. Their act of derision then appears as carnival-style vulgarity, a way of marking out the difference between proper and improper male behavior. In this sense, hoisting skirts on a pole is akin to a range of well-known codes, especially in Southern European and Latin American cultures, that work to signal the cuckold's status as an emasculated fool.

As a symbolic gesture, however, the effectiveness of the women's mockery of male strikebreakers derived precisely from its multilayered meaning. A male onlooker might laugh at other men who found themselves insulted, by women, for being "like women." A feminist might wince for the same reason—that the strikers seem to be derogating their own gender by using femininity as a form of insult.[106] Yet a less literal reading is also possible, in that threatening to taking off men's pants may stand as a symbolic transvestism. The strikers figuratively took off their own skirts (waving above them on poles). The implied sexual reversal of the cuckold is relevant here, as perhaps the most threatening aspect of their ridicule was simply that these young women were loudly having fun at men's expense.

The ability to have ribald fun, of course, was not normally associated with the stereotype of *la mujer obrera*. Even if Medellinense reporters used a light-hearted tone, their prose had the overall effect of constraining the strikers to the position of downtrodden "poor ones" (pobres). Because they portrayed the striking women as having been abandoned by men of their class, the reporters' story became one in which a group of valiant maidens required the protection of caballeros in their attempts to fend off the sexual attacks of dishonorable males. The reporters' narration erased not only the involvement of male strikers but also the prosaic fact that these virgins negotiated for shorter hours, higher piece-rates, and a lunch break. If the strike was about female honor, then working women defined it more broadly than did the middle-class men who penned romanticized descriptions and pressed churchmen and politicians to speed negotiations with Don Emilio.

As with the difference between la mujer obrera as she appeared in speeches made at the Patronato and the workingwomen who showed up there in the hopes of collecting enough vales to buy a bolt of cloth or a dress, I would use the terms "fictional" and "nonfictional" rather than "imaginary" and "real." The fictional females of reporters' imagination had a reality of their own. Indeed, the image of virginal working girls needing the protection of chivalrous males had more staying power in Medellín and Bello than did the image of feisty female strikers. Decades after the 1920 strike, local people took it for granted that women in the factories required sexual protection— and that the factories themselves should provide it. By the 1950s, the Bello strike would have seemed an anomaly to most residents. Mill-owners were known to be absolutely strict about moral controls, and it would be hard for a person who did not remember 1920 to believe that Don Emilio had not fired the three men immediately. The very fact of a strike, too, would seem an oddity, as Antioquia's textile factories were understood to be places where workers simply did not strike. Interviewing retired textile workers in the 1990s, I found that most did not believe me that anyone had struck Don Emilio's mill in 1920. The only person I interviewed who remembered it herself categorically denied that it had been about anything but wages.[107] For Bello residents, the strike clashed too strongly with what they knew of their town's history: that the mill-owners had built a paternalistic domain in which proper moral comportment had been as important as the work itself. If you had wanted to keep your job, retirees said, you had to observe la moral. A young woman's virtue had been safe at work, as safe as if she were in her parents' front parlor. By 1990, the strict regulations that had governed factory work in the 1940s and 1950s were what people understood as "the past" in Bello, not the world of Don Emilio's mill. Community memory thus included chaste girls and protective males but tended to forget times when young women that had not behaved like señoritas.

Conclusion

Wealthy Medellinenses had begun to see their city transformed by imported machinery, which young women—sometimes working alongside men—were hired to operate. Spurred by this unsettling spectacle, groups of reformers acted to establish a framework for class and gender relations that would limit the cultural impact of industrialization. Under Jesuit direction, young society ladies founded the Patronato de Obreras—intended to protect migrant girls from the perils of city and factory life. Churchmen, legislators, and supporters of the Patronato then institutionalized their vision in the Office of Factory Inspection, charged with "policing" mixed-sex workshops. Both the Patronato and the office of the inspector depended upon the stereotyped image of *la mujer obrera* to justify their approach to a population supposedly defined by its sexual vulnerability. Symbolically, both separated working-women from workingmen by presenting feminine virtue as something to be protected and policed, as a form of social capital available to women irrespective of their class position.

In practice, the normative femininity promoted by Catholic reformers both overlapped with and conflicted with working-class women's own sense of themselves in the world. Working in a factory did make one sexually vulnerable, and poor women often sought help at the Patronato and in the Office of Factory Inspection. Nevertheless, workingwomen's attitudes and behaviors diverged from those of the almsgivers and reformers intent on their protection. Female wage-earners seem to have either cooperated with or ignored the factory inspector, as they chose. At the Patronato, the ladies found that their largest obstacle was neither fundraising nor the city's resident population of rogues but rather factory girls' simple indifference. Exasperated, they resorted to bribery, wooing young *obreras* with the offer of ribbons, pretty fabrics, and even their own used dresses. The 1920 strike is perhaps the best example of workingwomen's independence from *la mujer obrera* as a discursive category. Although it was precisely the pity and outrage of reform-minded observers that ensured their victory, the strikers' own actions were radically complex. Where the Patronato, for example, separated *obreras'* spiritual and moral needs from their material needs, the strikers joined the two. Wanting Taguiaca and Teódulo fired, from their perspective, was inseparable from wanting shorter hours, less unreasonable work rules, and a raise. Nor, from the strikers' perspective, was it wholly necessary to be ladylike in making their demands.

Rather than present *la mujer obrera* as an irrelevancy, I have emphasized her importance in Medellín. Over time, the discourse created by reformers associated with Catholic Social Action became a cornerstone of mill discipline. As workingwomen came to be understood as abject figures in a melodramatic narrative of sexual danger and rescue, mill-owners began to imagine their own role in more explicitly "protective" terms. By the 1940s, as we shall see, industrialists turned toward a paternalistic disciplinary vision, one that was explicitly anticommunist and that centered on the protection of female workers' virginity. The seeds of their project of seemingly total control had been sown in the 1910s and 1920s. Before jumping ahead to that later period, however, the evidence that the lives of nonfictional workingwomen conformed but little to the trope of passivity and helplessness that was *la mujer obrera* deserves more exploration. Chapter 3 is straightforwardly an attempt to trace, from the bottom up, female and male workers' everyday experiences in the early decades of Antioqueño industrialization.

THREE

New Workers, New Workplaces,

1905–35

ENRIQUE ECHAVARRÍA REMEMBERED Emilio Restrepo as an entrepreneur, an eccentric oddball, and an autocrat in labor relations. Reminiscing in the early 1940s, the younger man described Don Emilio's management style with the phrase "*el que manda, manda*" (the boss is the boss, period). Referring to Don Emilio, Echavarría insisted that "in his time there were no strikes."[1] Echavarría's memory, of course, was faulty—although he accurately represents wealthy Medellinenses' long-standing tendency to imagine the first decades of the city's industrial development as a halcyon era of strict rules and unquestioning obedience. Don Emilio had confronted not only the 1920 strike, in which workers had the upper hand, but also a wide range of everyday forms of workplace negotiation, from mumbled complaints to instances of open insubordination, that required his direct intervention.

Using factory records, including notes made by Don Emilio and by Eduardo Echavarría, Enrique's cousin and Coltejer's manager, as well as workers' memories of their earliest years in the mills, this chapter explores the fluidity of work relations in Medellín's first industrial workshops. Only after about 1935–36, when left-wing unionism seemed a possibility in Medellín, did the city's big industrialists move to adopt the system of bureaucratic paternalism they perfected in the 1940s. By the time Don Enrique penned his reflections on a time gone by, the big mills were places in which clear, printed rules governed even small details of workers' behavior (especially female workers' behavior) and layers of supervisory personnel separated an operative from the mill-owner and his family. What he likely remembered most clearly about Don Emilio's time and his own years as a young manager was the direct, unmediated way that discipline had been decided on the shop floor. There had been few wholly inflexible rules, as owner-managers tended to make them up as they went along. What Echavarría perhaps forgot, or chose not to include in his *History of Textiles in Antioquia,* was the fact that workers had also enjoyed a fair amount of leeway to make things up as they went, given that the new mills competed for hands.

Proletarianization in Medellín was not a contest over workers' control of the labor process. The factory model arrived in Colombia after a Euro-American process of deskilling and after the bulk of the work involved in textile production had been mechanized. By the 1910s, spinning and weaving on mass-produced machinery did not require artisanal knowledge—knowledge that was, at any rate, scarce in Antioquia. The region had been consuming imported cloth for generations. From the perspective of those born in turn-of-the-century Medellín, and migrants who arrived in the regional capital to work in the newly built mills, proletarianization instead involved something more ephemeral: the emotional quality of work relations. Raymond Williams would have labeled this the "structure of feeling" associated with millwork; Pierre Bourdieu might call it an aspect of Antioqueños' changing "habitus." Without attempting to apply a precise definition to an imprecise set of behaviors and attitudes, my interest is in reconstructing workers' ways of interacting with those who supervised them, and their ways of interacting with one another, in the first twenty-five years of Antioqueño industrialization.

In this period, the mills were simply new. Workers, supervisors, and factory owners did not yet have agreed-on rules of interaction for factory work, despite the efforts of Catholic reformers to codify an approach to the problem of managing mixed-sex shops. Within the spaces defined by mechanized textile production, women and men continued to behave in ways familiar to them. Through the 1930s, factory work retained both the personalistic, family-based patterns of class hierarchy in rural Antioquia and the social ambiguity associated with the urban public plaza.

Compared to factories in Europe, the United States, Mexico, and Brazil in the same period, Colombian mills were small. Through the 1920s and 1930s, the largest companies employed only about four hundred people, overseen by one or two supervisors and two or three female *vigilantas.* Often, the *gerente,* or chairman of the board, served also as a mill's daily administrator. Work discipline was a product of constant face-to-face encounters, and where these involved the *gerente,* they were encounters across deeply scored lines of class and familial status. At Fabricato, for example, discipline happened not only across the line separating an *obrera* from a middling supervisor (an *empleado*) but also, and daily, across the line separating an *obrera* from a son of Rudesindo Echavarría—someone likely to travel to London or New York, to patronize a country club, or to meet the country's president.

Such face-to-face discipline involved a kind of intimate knowledge. Both persons usually had some mediating understanding of the other's family, where a person worshiped, or where she or he traveled on vacations. Older retired workers remember the communication of such knowledge with relish. They recall that when they came looking for work the *gerente* mentioned that he had known their father, that they brought a letter from the town priest, known to the *gerente*, or that a friend or relative had performed domestic service for the *gerente*'s family. This sort of personal knowledge (real or invented) helped establish connections across class lines, connections that could be used in varying kinds of power-laden conversations. For example, when Eduardo Echavarría hired María Elisa Alvarez at Coltejer in 1929, he asked about her parents and then joked with her about the priest in her neighborhood of Medellín:

> María Elisa: He asked me for a recommendation, a recommendation— and I said, "ah, I'll just ask Father Rodríguez." And he said, "yes," he said, "the eternal father, like you all call him," and I said "yes, the eternal father [*el padre eterno*]."
> Ann: And, and, I don't understand, "the eternal father?" [Laughter.]
> María Elisa: Want to know why they called him the eternal father? Because he would kneel and when he was consecrating, you would just lose hope—that he would ever lower the chalice or lower the, the wafer . . . he just stayed there and stayed there. [Laughter.][2]

In María Elisa's telling, Don Eduardo's familiarity with her church and with a neighborhood standing joke eased the tension of asking for work. It was part of how the young Echavarría cultivated a personal relationship with each worker and part of how he and María Elisa spoke across class lines.

Displaying knowledge of workers' neighborhoods and nonwork time could either soften the edge of the *gerente*'s authority or sharpen it, depending on how such knowledge was deployed in cross-class exchanges. When María Elisa asked for a raise, she said, Don Eduardo told her what he likely told everyone, that it was just more money that she'd waste buying coconut candies from the women who sold snacks in the streets around the factory:

> So one day I just told Don Eduardo: "Don Eduardo, why don't you do me a favor and give me a raise?" He said: "¡*Descarada!* [Cheeky girl!], you're earning thirty [cents], and you want thirty-five!" And so I said, "Of course! And if you'll pay me my forty? . . . like I was earning at the [coffee] farm, *pues*, that was a lot better." So he said: "Why'd you come here then?" and I told him: "Well, Don Eduardo, because, I'm going to tell you the truth. Because—" And he said, "Why?" "Because I wasn't born for the pack-saddle [*enjalma*]." And he said: "So what were you

born for?" "For the riding saddle [*silla*]." He burst out laughing and said, "Just like that you can just say things." And I told him, "Well that's how it's said where I come from, I wasn't born for burden but for riding."

And he says, "Yes, to ride on top in the saddle, fine" [pausing and changing to a lower tone], "but I can't give you a raise." And he says to me: "Look, it's just to buy goodies and coconut candy from that *Señora* who's so filthy [*cochina*]." And so I said: "What?" I said, "I don't eat anything in the street, Don Eduardo . . ."

"Ah," I said, and I started taking off [my apron] and I got it and folded it and rolled it up. He says, "What are you doing?" [And I said,] "I'm leaving, Don Eduardo."[3]

As she told the story, María Elisa had turned the tables of the conversation by making the administrator laugh at a country aphorism. She then gave herself the last word, at least in memory, by producing knowledge about a connection between their families, transforming this story about his denying her a raise into a story about mutual respect. As she continued,

María Elisa: "I'm going, Don Eduardo; it pains me in my soul, because I have a fondness for this factory." "You do?" I said: "Yes, I have a fondness for all of you [the Echavarrías] ever since I saw your farm in Heliconia, but I'm going. Ever since then I've been fond of all of you because you had trust in us." And, "Why did we trust in your family?" "Because my nephews always carried the money-packet to pay the workers . . . and the overseer [*mayordomo*] always said 'there's not a cent missing Doña Calixta [a reference to Elisa's mother]. . . .' Since then we've known your family, Don Eduardo."

Ann: I don't understand—

María Elisa: That was the conversation I had with Don Eduardo when I left.[4]

María Elisa recounted their conversation carefully, switching into a sort of verbal transcription. Whether or not she changed that transcript in the telling, she had guarded the memory in a way that Don Eduardo likely did not. Such remembered conversations with the boss are an important part of how retired workers in Medellín communicated nostalgia for a better time and a better city. Factory owners appear in such stories as "very human," as retiree Susana Osorio put it, persons who may have been superior in rank or wealth but whom one knew. María Elisa provides a script in which the young Echavarría pauses to ask questions, drawing out her story of his family's indebtedness to the uprightness of her mother and nephews. More than explaining why she left the mill, her recounting evokes a personal connection not severed by her decision to walk off the job. The conversation with Don Eduardo, which she repeated elsewhere in the interview, also formed part of María Elisa's larger narrative of pride and self-sufficiency. As she put it, "I had a defect: I asked for a raise—and then, if I didn't get it—I would leave." María Elisa recounts the incident as she preferred to remember it, but her remembered conversation with Don Eduardo nevertheless suggests the way that Antioqueños felt that they "knew" one another across the hierarchies of class.[5] This sort of knowledge—a shared store of regional proverbs, being able to place a person's family, a sense of what sort of familiarity could be introduced in a given conversation—was exactly what industrialists would try to hold on to as the factories got larger and the relationships between owners and workers became more institutionalized.

El que Manda, Manda

If "the boss is the boss, period" misleads as a description of the relationship between owner-managers and the operatives they hired, it is nevertheless wholly accurate as a phrase to describe the industrialists' attitude toward protective legislation, the 1918 ordinance, and the efforts of the factory inspector. Inspector Daniel Vélez regularly complained that factory owners did not even pretend to heed him. In visit after visit to the Bello mill, for example, he found children under ten in the workrooms and ten-to-fifteen-year-olds working more than eight hours a day, in violation of the 1918 ordinance.[6] Hygiene was perpetually substandard and the bathrooms stank, according to the inspector—who had some oddly "modern" ideas about ventilation. (He insisted, for example, that the trees around the mill be chopped down to allow air to circulate.) Exasperated, Vélez fumed that "this is the only firm in which they pay no attention at all to the observations of the undersigned, and it seems that they do not even do him the honor of reading his reports."[7] As he had during the 1920 strike, Don Emilio seems to have simply ignored charges of illegality and poor working conditions. Vélez concluded that "[Don Emilio] believes that complying or not complying . . . is a matter of his personal preference."[8]

Other industrialists may have read Vélez's reports and listened respectfully, but they too ignored the inspector. At Coltejer, Vélez recorded the general administrator's response to a reminder that the company was legally required to extend life insurance to its workers (law 37 of 1921): "the *Señor Gerente* [Alejandro Echavarría] had told him that, for now, they would abstain from complying with said legislation."[9] Like Emilio Restrepo, Coltejer and other firms also seem to have "abstained" from complying with child labor laws, judging by the inspector's frequent written "reminders" about the law and his suggestions that this or that administrator check on workers that just might "result to be less than ten years old."[10] Medellín's mill-owning families were not, as yet, making any serious attempt to present themselves as benevolent employers or guardians of class harmony.

Vélez had the most trouble when it came to enforcing the only article of the 1918 ordinance that directly addressed contemporary disciplinary practice: the provision that a worker's weekly pay could not be docked by more than 10 percent. Workers commonly paid fines for wasting materials, producing imperfect cloth, arriving late, or leaving work at odd hours, and their employers claimed to have no other way to monitor production and enforce attendance. The administrator of Tejidos Unión, for example, refused to remove a notice he had posted to inform workers that those who failed to return after the lunch hour would forfeit their morning's wages. Although Vélez informed him that nonpayment of wages was illegal, the administrator maintained that nothing else worked. Like owner-managers at other firms, he ridiculed Vélez: "If it is the case that the Señor Inspector will guarantee that the factory receives an indemnity for their behavior . . . and if he sets it down in his *actas* that abuses and violations of the ordinances are also committed against the factory [by the workers] . . . then I will remove the notice and begin turning to the factory inspector for everything having to do with the *obreras*."[11] Despite mill-owners' objections, however, Vélez launched a personal crusade against fines; his *Actas de Visita* demonstrate both his fervor and the limited effectiveness of his position as a "policer" of the factories. At Bello, he got nowhere for the first several years. During almost every visit, Vélez complained that Restrepo levied fines that were "illegal and anti-Christian," such as a posted fine of $0.25 for lateness or absenteeism (when workers earned between $0.21 and $0.70).[12] Even when he noted some improvement, it was with biting sarcasm: "[Fines] have been reduced a bit, no doubt because now the wages they pay allow for no further reduction without the shame of having the workers working *ad-honorem*."[13] At Coltejer everything was done civilly, but Vélez had no more confidence that the manager paid any attention. When faced with *obreras'* complaints about illegal fines, on the one hand, and Eduardo Echavarría's book of receipts, on the other, Vélez wrote only that "the inspector's office can do nothing so as long as nothing is proved; the rest falls to the tribunal of the administrator's conscience."[14]

With persuasion his only real weapon, Inspector Vélez wrote endlessly about fines in the reports that mill administrators had to sign. He liberally dispensed advice, telling factory administrators how much more effective it would be simply to fire unsatisfactory workers and praising those who limited their use of fines. After an inspection of the factory of Tejidos Montoya Hermanos, for example, Vélez reported:

The *Señor* Administrator has become persuaded that in order to conserve discipline, the better and more correct system is that of changing

bad employees and stimulating good ones, rather than appealing continually to the hateful system of diminishing a worker's scarce wages . . .
with fines, of which the company itself is both judge and recipient.[15]

Vélez misinterpreted mill-owners' practice, however. Rather than indicating a despotic control over workers, the prevalence of fines derived from
mill-owners' lack of control. From the perspective of Medellín's early industrialists, Vélez's advice, that unsatisfactory employees simply be replaced,
was unrealistic. The mills were generally short-handed, and workers knew
it. In November of 1924, for example, Jorge Echavarría complained in his
diary that "the personnel are talking and lazing around [haciendo perro]," but
that he felt he should say nothing, "out of fear that they'll go to the factory on
the hill [Fábrica de Bello]."[16]

Keenly aware of the difficulty of maintaining their authority in face-to-
face confrontations, owner-managers sometimes simply avoided them. In
1912, for example, Emilio Restrepo complained to church officials about
Bello's parish priest, Father López, who had reportedly delivered a sermon
accusing the mill's supervisors of treating women workers "like dogs." Restrepo admitted that he wasn't sure exactly what the priest had said, but he
feared that asking too many questions might just make things worse. "I did
not want to investigate among the workers," he explained, "so as not to call
more attention to the matter among the weavers."[17] He was the gerente of
the Fábrica de Bello, with the authority to dismiss anyone who looked
askance at his questions, but Don Emilio curtailed his own behavior rather
than risk fueling discontent.

Father López nevertheless had succeeded in irritating Don Emilio. Their
mutual dislike seems to have flared in a dispute that seems almost a carica-
ture of the symbolic struggle for local authority between a town priest and a
brash, industrializing entrepreneur. They fought over the church clock. Don
Emilio sent a foreman to ask the priest to reset it, since the Bello clock, the
primary timepiece for most of the town's population, was fifteen minutes
ahead of Medellín's. According to Don Emilio, Father López responded angrily, telling the messenger that "his boss should let the poor obreras out
early, and not make them work so late for such a miserable salary."[18] As he
did later with Inspector Vélez, Don Emilio objected forcefully to such meddling. Complaining to the priest's superiors, he had Father López reassigned.

Learning by Doing

In August 1912, a few months before the incident with Father López, Don
Emilio's son Eusebio received an education in the quotidian, personalistic
negotiations on which both supervisors and workers understood hierarchy to

depend. With Don Emilio away on a business trip to Paris, Eusebio found himself in charge of daily operations at the Bello mill. In a long letter to his father (after a trying week), Eusebio demonstrated that he understood the destabilizing potential inherent in a range of workplace events, from a conflict between supervisors to cheating among piece-rate workers to the tense moments after a shop-floor accident.

First, he reported that the supervisors had continued fighting among themselves (as they had been doing well before Don Emilio departed). William Fiddies, an English loom-fixer, joined Teódulo Velásquez and Jesús Monsalve in a shared enmity for Miguel Solvés, a technician from Spain and supervisor of one of the workrooms.[19] Eusebio wrote to his father that Solvés was now doing nothing to enforce discipline in his section. He passed the day reading novels and newspapers, letting the workers do what they liked, according to Velásquez and Monsalve, and he did this with the express intention of getting back at the other supervisors by ensuring that the operatives would resent anybody who did make them work.[20] In a small workplace, discipline was easily fragmented: workers knew about supervisors' fights (especially in the case of Fiddies and Solvés, who nearly came to blows in the mill). One suspects that they found the supervisors' disagreements funny and that they took sides. Eusebio certainly had been well-enough trained by his father to know that obvious personality conflicts would destabilize a system of control that depended on face-to-face discipline.

Eusebio's second problem developed from this conflict among the supervisors. Teódulo charged that Solvés had not been checking the pay sheets. The bobbin-winders were being paid as though they had wound 150 to 200 bobbins daily when, in fact, they were winding only about 120. This Eusebio "investigated," as he explained to his father, finding that one of Solvés's assistants, nicknamed "Coco," had worked with the bobbin-winders to subvert the piece-rate system. Unnoticed by Solvés, Coco had worked out a scheme by which the bobbin-winders received the same wages from week to week, wages that reflected their pay sheet but not what they'd actually produced. Eusebio was particularly concerned by the hint of class consciousness associated with the fraud. As he reported to his father,

> I also discovered that Coco had told the girls on his machine that if I reduced their wages the best thing to do would be to go home for a few days, so that I'd have to call them and increase their salaries. Immediately upon hearing this I began making inquiries, in which I spent more than a week, and I am sure that it was true.

Eusebio cut the bobbin-winders' pay rates and fired Coco, incensing Solvés. "Just as I expected," Eusebio wrote his father, Solvés "reproached me severely . . . [saying], 'that poor fool, how could he have any idea what a strike is!'" According to Solvés, the charge against Coco was an "injustice" and Eusebio "would be sorry"; the one who should be punished was Teódulo, an employee the like of whom Solvés had never seen, who was responsible for "things that couldn't be tolerated." Then, in what was likely a fairly public confrontation, Solvés either quit or was fired (Eusebio didn't seem certain which). As Eusebio justified it to his father,

> This man [Solvés] was becoming more and more intolerable and even dangerous every day. He was a real socialist who would not let a single worker be reprimanded or let go; he was always on their side, instigating that their wages be raised and allowing things that should not be permitted in the factory.

The micropolitics of what "should not be permitted in the factory" can be partially traced here, as can the rudimentary disciplinary structures of a still-new system of workplace control. In part, the trouble with Solvés was about money; he publicly hinted that operatives were underpaid and he failed to police the piece-rate system in his part of the mill. Paying workers for what they had individually produced was key to the disciplinary system Don Emilio had imported at such expense. What is more suggestive is the fact that Coco would not have been found out so quickly if Teódulo had not been looking for a complaint against Solvés. All of Medellín's early mills relied on piece-rate systems that involved simple, easily reset counters and easily forged pay sheets. How often did groups of workers find ways around the piece-rates?

Alarmed by the rumor that the bobbin-winders might try to withhold their labor and by the level of tension among the supervisors, Eusebio feared workers' anger over Solvés's leaving. The day after his confrontation with the Spaniard, "fearing some disorder on the *obreras*' part," Eusebio got up at four in the morning to be in Bello before six.

> I went up and down the looms in the old workroom, talking to the *obreras* so that they would be more careful in the future and also to see the expressions on their faces. One or two of the bad *obreras* Solvés had tolerated made a face at me or said as I passed by, "Don Miguel was such a dear."

His careful precautions, including a telephone call to other supervisors the night before and a worker assembly later in the day, testify to Eusebio's consciousness of the fragility of his own authority.[21] It was, for example, worth reporting to his father that a few women had looked askance at him or muttered as he passed.

The better to prove to his father that he had, in fact, reestablished his authority, Eusebio included a final description of a strained moment on the shop floor. Either later that same day or the following day, a boy suffered a grisly (but not uncommon) accident at the bobbin-winding machine.[22] He reached in to straighten a thread, and the machine crushed three fingers on his right hand, two of which had to be amputated at the knuckle. His sisters "sobbed and cried out," but, added Eusebio, "despite this accident, there was no disorder at all." Of course, Eusebio's fears of worker unrest are recorded only because he wrote them down. If Don Emilio were in the mill, such moments of tension would have passed without written record. Yet these and other everyday incidents undoubtedly became part of an oral accounting of remembered wrongs, at least for a time. The other foremen's role in Solvés's firing; the accumulated memory of accidents; even a priest's willingness to confront Don Emilio—these formed part of the prehistory of the 1920 strike.

Se Creen Necesaria

Owner-managers were cautious about the interpersonal relationships on which discipline depended, in part because they were so often vulnerable to workers' whims. Just as Jorge Echavarría, at Fabricato, had refrained from saying anything to workers he saw "lazing around," Eusebio commented on but did not dismiss the "bad *obreras*" that he thought had been wrongly "tolerated" by Solvés. In the first few decades of Medellín's industrialization, factory owners were almost constantly short-handed. Eduardo Echavarría's experiences at Coltejer amply demonstrate the way workers' easy mobility frustrated his ideas of what should and should not "be permitted in the factory." Again and again, Don Eduardo noted in his personnel log the names of workers who "*se creen necesaria*" (think themselves necessary). Of one Margarita Hoyos he wrote, "for some time now she has had a bad attitude, bad attendance, and has been talking back—she took advantage of our necessity because of the lack of workers—*Ungrateful*." Yet he had not fired her; when Margarita left the mill it was because she quit in anger after being reprimanded for refusing to teach an apprentice.[23] When he was pressed for operatives, the administrator also rehired workers he had previously dismissed or who had a record of bad behavior, such as Teresa Montoya, whom he had fired for being "*grosera y respondona*" (given to rude language and back-talk) but whom Echavarría rehired when she returned a few years later.[24] At Fabricato, a fifteen-year-old who left in September of 1930 "was lazy, dirty, a liar," according to the manager who rehired him six months later. A twenty-nine-year-old woman who had already been fired once before, "for being rude and for using filthy language to the *vigilanta*," was also taken back.[25]

Through the 1920s and early 1930s, mill-owners and administrators tended

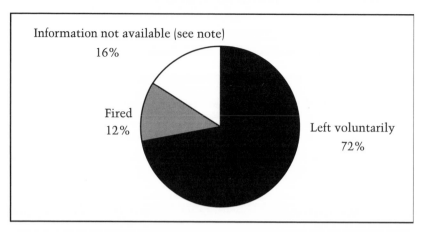

Figure 6 Relative percentages of persons who left voluntarily and who were fired, Coltejer, 1918–34. Note: From a sample of 144 of the 1,446 records contained in Coltejer's personnel log, held at the *hemeroteca* of Coltejer, in Itagüí, taking every tenth record after a random start. No information is available for those still employed at the mill in 1934, although it should be noted that more than three quarters of this group had begun their employment after 1930 and nearly a quarter had worked at the mill less than a year.

to overlook moral lapses, as well. When Ana Montoya quit her job at Coltejer in 1934, Echavarría noted that there were doubts about her "moral conduct" and that she'd had a child; yet his doubts had not automatically entailed her dismissal. Sometimes he hired a "fallen woman" (*una perdida*) out of pity, as with Evangelina Mesa—who then ran off with a mechanic, according to his notes. Another woman left without giving him enough time to train someone else, and Echavarría noted simply that "she was a girlfriend of Ramón Tejada, who was married." This Ramón he dismissed a few months later, "because he went to jail for not fulfilling his matrimonial duties." The administrator added that, "he's very much a womanizer and was always chasing after women in the factory."[26] Nevertheless, Ramón's bad reputation had not led to his firing until he was carted off to jail, indicating that Coltejer applied standards more lax than those of the city police. Ten years later, by the mid-1940s, the inverse would be true.[27]

The ease with which people could change jobs irked Don Eduardo enough that he expended effort to trace people who left. If he found out that they were working at another factory, especially after having sent word that they would be out just a few days, he wrote down where they had gone, together with comments on their "ingratitude."[28] As part of the same effort, Echavarría also tried to discover why workers quit his mill, and here his logbook allows a fine-grained reconstruction.

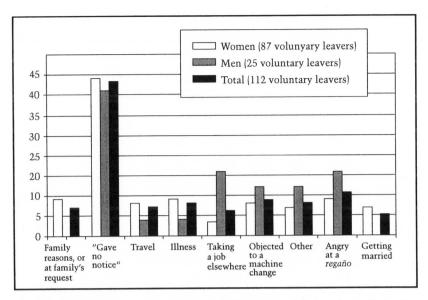

Figure 7 Workers' reasons for quitting, as a percentage of those voluntarily leaving Coltejer, 1918–34. See note on Figure 6, this volume.

As shown in figures 6 and 7, people were far more likely to quit than to be fired, a pattern that held true over time. Especially in the 1910s and 1920s, as the Coltejer log demonstrates, workers left the mills for a wide range of reasons. Most often, people gave no notice, and mill owners or managers had no clear idea why they left. "*Salió sin avisar*" (left without giving notice) is Echavarría's most common category, although it is one that disappears from personnel records in later years. Employers became more rigid about hiring workers who had left their own or another mill without warning, and, by the mid-1930s, workers had an incentive to give formal notice, since doing so made them eligible for severance pay. In the 1940s and 1950s, workers may also have been less likely to quit without lining up another job, since getting work in Medellín gradually became a more complex process over time. In 1920, leaving Coltejer meant quitting a job one had gotten by standing at the mill gate when word had it that hands were needed. The manager had picked you, asked one or two questions, and sent you to learn the job from another operative.[29] Twenty-five years later it meant quitting a job that one had gotten after producing various documents (a medical exam, a record of baptism, a certificate of military service if one were a man, etc.) and after serving a probationary training period.

In 1918–34, after those who "left without giving notice," Echavarría's most common descriptions were of workers who quit because they objected to a machine change (9 percent of the total) or because of a reprimand (11 percent of the total). Carmen Morales, for example, "left hot under the collar because of a rebuke"; Luis López quit rather than pay a fine; and Rubén Berrío walked out after being rebuked on the job, confirming Don Eduardo's opinion that he was "spoiled and of an uppity, back-talking character."[30] As seen in figure 7, males were more likely to storm out. They may have been quicker to anger, but it may also be that workers who perceived themselves as adults practiced more restraint, as female workers were older, on average, than males. Or more subterfuge: male workers almost never quit because they "were sick," nor did they tell the manager that they were needed at home. Females did both with regularity.[31]

As did those who left after a *regaño* (reprimand) they considered unjust, workers who left after being reassigned to a task they disliked challenged a fundamental principle of the factory model: that operatives were inter-changeable and that their positioning within the machinery of production was a manager's prerogative. Eloisa Echeverri left when switched to weaving drill, Ana Gómez when assigned to plaids, another woman when ordered onto the twisting frame.[32] Others quit when taken off contract work and put on a daily wage, or they left rather than teach apprentices, who slowed them down and reduced their earnings. One even took out her anger on the ma-chine she had been moved to, damaging it "out of malice," according to the administrator's note.[33] Some nonmachine jobs were considered humiliating or kids' work: Rosa Betancur quit rather than sweep, maintaining that "she wouldn't let herself be put down anymore." Another young man "gave notice that he was quitting because he now wore long pants and was embarrassed to distribute bobbins."[34] As in confrontations about who would or would not be publicly scolded, workers' sense of self-respect and of how to maintain the respect of others could contradict the logic of factory hierarchy.

Quitting seems to have been a time when rules of deference evaporated, sometimes with the easy laughter that María Elisa remembered as she de-scribed informing Eduardo Echavarría that she would leave if he didn't raise her pay, sometimes with scorn. Workers commonly insulted *vigilantas*, su-pervisors, even the head administrator, on their way out the door. They called their putative superiors *lambon* or *lambona* (tattletale), *mentiroso* (liar), *canalla* (thug), and, when fines were involved, *ladrón* (thief).[35] Colte-jer's administrator also recorded stronger epithets: María Flórez called the *vigilanta* an "H.P." (*Hijeputa* or *Hija de Puta*, translatable as "daughter of a whore").[36] More commonly, the administrator described workers' speech without transcribing their words. Otilia Quiros Montoya, for example, "con-ducted herself badly on leaving, insulting people *como una mujer cual-quiera, grosera*" (foully, like a fishwife).[37]

Echavarría relied on a shorthand set of categories, and his notes impede any attempt to understand workers' thoughts and feelings. Where workers used language or a tone inappropriate for cross-class communication, for example, he labeled it *grosería* or *altanería*. Only where he provides additional description can a historian gain a sense of what that inappropriateness entailed and thus what the administrator's words might mean. *Altanería*, for example, translates as "haughtiness" or "arrogance," and he used it to describe a woman who talked back to a foreman, saying "that if Don Eduardo reprimanded her she'd answer him back too."[38] Another woman answered the administrator "*groseramente y con altanería*" when she said "that I wasn't her father and couldn't scold her."[39] *Altanero* seems to have resonated a bit as "uppity" would in the United States; it may have fit a racial stereotype in some loose way, as "*sambo altanero*" (or "*samba altanera*") appears several times in Coltejer's personnel log.[40]

Grosería can mean simply disrespect or inappropriateness, as when the administrator writes that a worker "answered badly" or "was fired for being *grosera* with the lady director, [and was] a bad worker, lazy and badly behaved."[41] Or it can mean vulgarity: Ernestina Rios, for example, used *palabras groseras* (rude words) in talking back to the supervisor and had "a very dirty mouth." If men used coarse language as often as women, Echavarría was less likely to note it; he was more likely to cite women for *grosería* than he was men. Female vulgarity contravened not only factory hierarchies but also the wider behavioral norms that made workplace discipline possible at all. One suspects that a man's coarse talk may have provoked general laughter, while a woman's likely shocked some of her co-workers as much as it annoyed managers. At Fabricato, for example, a sixteen-year-old girl was fired and labeled a *corrompida* (corrupted woman) because, according to the manager, "her way of talking caused a scandal in the workroom."[42]

Managers' descriptions make it difficult to assess what a worker said or felt or *who* she would have offended with certain words, but personnel records also provide glimpses of workers' actions that "speak louder" than words. Violence against superiors, in the microcosm of the factory as in more dramatic historical moments, could not be contained by Echavarría's shorthand phrases; he was forced to describe what workers actually did. Alejandrina Mejía, "who was fired for talking back and being uppity," according to her logbook entry, "waited for [the *vigilanta*] at the corner this afternoon to beat her."[43] Angela Ríos, "fired for being troublesome, disobedient, chattery, and insufferable," similarly held the *vigilanta* accountable after work hours: "She behaved loutishly as she waited for the *Señora Vigilanta* and beat her and roughed her up in the middle of the street."[44]

Less often, violence against supervisors occurred within the workplace. In October of 1935, a twenty-one-year-old woman working at Fabricato was suspended for a week "for having mistreated a *vigilanta*"; furious, "she said that she would quit for good—after that she punched the *vigilanta* . . . three times right there in the workroom."[45] At Coltejer, Eduardo Arango attacked a foreman: "He shouted at him and threatened him with a knife in the work-room, causing a huge commotion."[46] However rarely such physical attacks may have occurred, their defiant signal was probably amplified by the next day's gossip and remembered as shop-floor lore. Violence against supervisors existed on a continuum with the back-talk, *altanería*, and daily quittings recorded by Coltejer's factory administrator. What happened in a given con-frontation was accompanied by an awareness of what might have happened next or what had happened last week or last year. Whether noted beside a person's name or told and retold as the week's best gossip, actions along that continuum reminded workers and managers of the instability of familiar, personalistic relations of power.

Nonwork

Any confrontation with an overseer involved everyone else in the mill, espe-cially in this early period, when machines were close together. Although the mills were loud and dusty, they were also crowded, relative to later decades. Doing factory work meant being in close proximity to persons outside one's family circle for most of the day, and more than the "vertical" relationship to a mill-owner or administrator, it was this "horizontal" relationship to large numbers of other women and men that made a mill job different from other kinds of employment in Medellín.

Colored by workers' laughter, friendships, animosities, flirtations, and public fights, the everyday social interchange of millwork had the feel of *la calle* (the street) as opposed to *la casa* (the household). As part of the diffuse "structure of feeling" associated with Medellín's early factories, workplace sociability cannot be understood either as a form of resistance to the fac-tory model or as an accommodation to it. Where loyalty to one another con-flicted with a manager's authority, horizontal relationships involved soli-darity; where co-workers shared only animosity, their interaction had an opposite meaning.

At Coltejer, for example, women and men occasionally acted on their anger about a fine or *regaño* by convincing a friend or sibling to quit with them. Otilia Posada and two friends were reprimanded for absenteeism, "and they made an agreement, all three of them, not to come back."[47] María Fer-nandez, similarly, quit because Echavarría fired her best friend.[48] Just as often, however, workers left not in solidarity with a friend but in anger at a disliked co-worker, as did Dolores Vélez, who "quarreled with her *com-pañera* and quit."[49] And Don Eduardo regularly dismissed workers not for poor performance but for fighting with other operatives: Carmen Ramírez was "fired for fighting and insulting another *obrera*," with a note that she was "badly behaved and wild and foul mouthed."[50] Workplace fights might also be continued after work, as in the case of Gabriela and Ligia Posada, who were fired after they had waited outside the mill, together with their mother, to revenge themselves on women who had complained about their behavior to Echavarría.[51]

Between friendships and animosities that turned nasty, like that between the Posada sisters and their detractors, lay an indeterminate field of sociability and horseplay. A worker named María Rendón, for example, stuffed cotton waste into a companion's lunch bucket; Amalia Toro hid yarn from a workmate; Lucila Mejía stole somebody's hat; and Cruz Uribe sprayed water at other *obreras*.[52] Boys also tussled and fooled around: a bobbin-carrier at Fabricato "tied up" a workmate, and various others received suspensions for hitting each other with bobbins.[53] Nor were low-level overseers like the *vigilantas* exempt from tricks and boisterous play: someone might throw a cone or shuttle as they passed, or make them the butt of a joke, as Ana de Jesús Puerta did by hiding her *vigilanta*'s shoes.[54] Focusing on the indeterminacy of this sort of rough-and-tumble fun, the German historian Alf Lüdtke discusses the continual social exchange of the shop floor as a medium of self-assertion, or *Eigensinn* (self-reliance or self-expression). *Eigensinn*, for Lüdtke, operates in moments of violent physicality, horseplay, and verbal exchange; these create an autonomous cultural space within a factory's walls.[55] Indeed, "work culture" may be entirely the wrong phrase, as the shop retained a feeling of the street precisely in its moments of nonwork: when a person ignored the task to which they had been assigned and took time out to play, make a friend, or defend herself against an enemy.

The point is not that stealing a workmate's hat, or punching her, contravened industrial discipline but rather that industrialism was occasionally irrelevant even in a factory workshop. In the fluidity of these first decades, Antioqueño workers did not so much "resist" industrialism as they recreated, at work, forms of sociability that had little to do with factories.[56] This was as true of their interactions with putative superiors as of their exchanges with one another. Conflicts between workers and supervisors, like those among co-workers, were embedded in an everyday sociability that included boisterousness and truculence along with deference to the rich. During the 1940s, when employers set out to remake work culture in the image of the patriarchal household, and definitively to separate *la fábrica* from *la calle*, they targeted exactly this source of indiscipline and instability: the street-like quarrelsomeness and rough play that marked millwork in the initial years of the industry.

Conclusion

Medellín's industrialists imported the factory model, its machines and floor plans, supervisors and technicians, but this did not by itself create the "feel" of industrialism in face-to-face exchanges. Antioquia's first factory workshops were informal, even chaotic spaces by comparison to the structured, bureaucratic workplaces they later became. Through the 1930s, rules about hiring and firing varied according to the need for hands. For their part, workers came and went as they pleased, knowing that jobs were easily come by. In this sense, María Elisa's story about leaving Don Eduardo's employ is representative.

The city's early textile factories were small, relative to the huge workplaces that Coltejer and Fabricato became by the late 1940s. Through the mills' first decades, 1905–35, interaction between mill-owners and mill-workers was shaped by the familiarity of daily exchanges. Work relations turned on the direct interchange between very wealthy men, accustomed to dictating the behavior of others, and newly urban wage-workers, most of them young and female, who enjoyed an unprecedented level of mobility. The combination made the disciplinary relationship between a mill-owner and a mill-worker more akin to that between a domestic servant and a person of wealth than to that between a machine operator and the head of a large manufacturing corporation, such as Coltejer or Fabricato in later decades.

Two things separated factories from other kinds of urban employment, especially for women, who formed the majority of the workforce throughout this period. First, industrialists' sense of authority, their sense that "the boss is the boss" (*el que manda, manda*), was necessarily tempered by workers' ability to quit a job they disliked. Given a seller's market for labor power, the first generation of mill-owners put up with levels of indiscipline that would not be tolerated by their sons. Second, the new workshops were places where hundreds of young women spent long days together, and with young men. Through the 1920s and early 1930s, the behaviors and patterns of mixed-sex social exchange that workers took into the mills reflected the boisterousness associated with *la calle* (the street).

What had been normal in the new workplaces of the 1910s and 1920s came under attack with the intense politicization of the "social question" in the 1930s. From the perspective of everyday interactions on the shop floor, Medellín's mills changed dramatically in 1935–40. This change had three aspects. First, local industrialists responded to the electoral defeat of the Conservative Party and the rise of a left-leaning union movement by becoming fiercely anticommunist, especially after the mass strikes discussed in chapter 4. In the period 1936–53, the Echavarrías and other mill-owners together adopted a strategy of benevolently bureaucratic paternalism, designed to "inoculate" their workers against unionization. Second, Catholic reformers succeeded in their effort to convince mill-owners to make chastity and proper comportment a condition of female employment, so much so that the Echavarrías of Fabricato adopted the model of the Jesuit-inspired Patronato as their own. Third, operatives' ways of interacting with co-workers, no less than their behavior toward putative superiors, began to be more closely monitored. By the 1940s, fines—which had been meant to reflect the value of merchandise damaged by poor work—were replaced by suspensions, as Inspector Vélez had urged industrialists to do. The change went further, however, as industrialists moved to tighten their control over work relations; far more than in the 1910s and 1920s, operatives began to be suspended for a range of things unrelated to the quality of their work, from fighting to flirting to using foul language. Chapters 5, 6, and 7 examine these three aspects of the process by which industrial discipline was effectively consolidated in Medellín.

PART II. THE MAKING
AND UNMAKING OF *LA MORAL*

FOUR
Strikes,
1935–36

I FOUND NO VIBRANT community memory of Medellín's textile strikes. Almost nobody outside the university believed that women had struck the Bello mill, and several retired workers (too young to remember 1920) categorically denied it as a possibility.[1] At the Retired Workers' Association, where old unionists gathered daily to play dominoes and meet friends, people described the strikes of the 1960s without reference to the 1930s, although several of their number remembered both. When I did interview people who remembered the strikes at Coltejer in 1935 and at Rosellón in 1936, their memories surprised young relatives who listened as we spoke. Most didn't mention the strikes until I asked, and many then used my questions to reemphasize their own loyalty to the company, often with a comment such as: "I was there when the strike happened, but I didn't participate . . . there's no reason to go against the person who feeds you."[2] Those who had participated, or who sympathized with strikers' goals, described their actions with deep ambivalence. My purpose in this chapter is to understand the strikes of 1935–36 from within this ambivalence.

For Colombianists, the fact that workers struck and took to the streets "even in Medellín" is a measure of the intensity of the social crisis that shook Colombian society in the 1930s.[3] Because strikes in Antioquia's textile sector did not result in the unionization of the mills, they seem anomalous, understandable by reference to a national labor history involving transportation workers, *petroleros*, and artisans but unconnected to the local history of Medellín's politically quiescent textile workers. Mill-owners, of course, saw the strikes in these terms exactly, as an aberration caused by outside agitators, or by the populist experiments of President Alfonso López Pumarejo.

Elected in 1934, López Pumarejo rhetorically declared a "Revolution on the March" while pursuing a Roosevelt-style platform of reform. Understanding what striking meant in the local context therefore requires an exploration of how electoral politics entered the subjective world of Medellinense workers. Yet the role of party politics fades when the textile strikes are analyzed from the perspective of workplace relationships. In the strikers' lists of demands, which invariably included complaints about workplace superiors, and in retirees' memories of strikes, which turn on personal stories of cross-class interaction, the conflicts of 1935–36 emerge as an extension of the fluid interpersonal world of the shop floor.

What did the act of striking mean in the context of López's populist experiment, and what did it mean to workers like those described in early personnel records: often insubordinate, quick to leave a job when offended, and likely to feel that they knew the factory owner personally? What did striking later come to mean for workers who remained at the mills long enough to enjoy the paternalistic benefits with which industrialists countered the threat of labor radicalism? The better to answer such questions of subjectivity, this chapter begins and ends with two personal narratives. Both are stories told by retired textile workers about their earlier selves, and both suggest that in workplaces marked by face-to-face relationships of power, joining a strike involved a personal kind of insubordination. In addition to strikers' demands, which appear in press reports and government documents, the memories recounted by María Elisa Alvarez and Enrique López demonstrate that labor conflicts were also conflicts over the emotional tenor of class relationships.

María Elisa's Story: *Pedreas* and Partisan Politics

Although she quit Coltejer because Eduardo Echavarría had refused to give her a raise, and although she insisted, in general, that "I had a defect: I asked for a raise—and then, if I didn't get it—I would leave," María Elisa had been horrified by the 1935 strike.[4] She sympathized with the strikers, saying that they only wanted better pay, but she insisted that "the Coltejer strike, it was *bastante cruda* [raw or rough], it was bitter." Most clearly, María Elisa recalled the way the strikers transformed the neighborhood streets in 1935. "¡*Corrillos en las esquinas!*" she exclaimed, remembering. "Gangs of girls on the corners with their rock-piles, ready to run . . . gangs of girls and guys, something one never saw in the factories."[5]

I had not asked María Elisa about the 1935 strike; rather, she had raised it, as a negative example, in the context of a discussion about the late 1950s. I asked her what she had thought of Tejicondor workers' attempt to unionize.

Her reply indicated that mine was the wrong question or a naive one: "No, *señorita*, at that time there wasn't much talk of unions." Instead, she immediately shifted our conversation backward in time, to 1935.

> María Elisa: Unions weren't well thought of, and many people didn't like them because of the rock-throwing that went on.
> Ann: Sorry, what? Rock-throwing?
> María Elisa: Look, they'd go after the companies or whatever it was, with rocks—*rocks*. There was a strike at Coltejer where they went after the company with rocks—they'd wait for the girls to come out, after work . . . they'd grab them and dunk them in the creek.
> Ann: Who?
> María Elisa: The other *obreras* that were on strike. . . . The ones that weren't with the strike, the ones who were with the company, they'd dunk them, they were *wicked* to them.[6]

Such public aggressiveness, especially by women, had etched the strike in her mind. Other women, too, focused on the rock throwing to express their disdain for these early strikes. Of the Rosellón strike in 1936, for example, Cristina Monsalve said: "It scared me, it scared me because, those people, so *out of control*, and the way they threw rocks and everything?" (*Esa gente, tan alborotada, y ¿cómo tiraban de piedra y todo?*)[7] There's no English word for *alborotado*; it means disorderly, out of control, or riotous. Because it also connotes a vulgar person, the female form, *alborotada*, captures perfectly the censure with which workers who strove to be proper women viewed the spectacle of their barefoot *compañeras* throwing rocks in the street. The censure was also rooted in physical fear; striking men might not beat women who sought to enter, but women like María Elisa and Cristina knew that female strikers would attack them.

Yet María Elisa, at least, told a complex, even contradictory story. For example, she recounted one *pedrea* (incident of rock-throwing) that didn't seem to have upset her, instead she remembered it as hilariously funny. At the tail end of our conversation about the 1935 strike, I asked her if she had heard of María Cano, the famous Communist orator. "*Ay sí!* María Cano, a wonderful woman," she responded, beginning a second story about rock throwing. Introducing María Cano with a double gesture, she described her as "one of the strike agitators; always with the workers" and as the attractive "daughter of Don Fidel Cano," who had also vacationed in María Elisa's hometown. (Fidel Cano was a prominent newspaperman and one of Medellín's most influential men, although María was in fact the daughter of one of his less wealthy cousins, Rodolfo Cano, an educator.[8])

"She was a little taller than you," María Elisa said, "with a pretty figure—

she didn't have a pretty face . . . [but] she, the way she walked was *so pretty.*" She and some friends had gone to hear María Cano speak, María Elisa remembered,

> during a strike . . . or a demonstration—in the Parque Berrío, no in the Plaza de Bolívar . . . and I went, of course I went to the demonstration, *pues,* knowing she was going to be there.
>
> Even if they called me a communist, I didn't care. Because I went to see, but what happened? They threw rocks at her, she had to get down, she went in and hid in an entrance-way. . . .
>
> And so there was this *señora* coming down Caracas street, carrying, like a, maybe a tray, covered with a white cloth. [Chuckles.] She was coming down and we were going up [away from the demonstration], but of course we were laughing, laughing because we'd all had to run. So we were going along and laughing and here comes the *señora* and she says, "What happened honey? Is the strike over?" and I said, "no, it's not over yet, we left 'cause they're throwing lots of rocks—" and [she says], "That's where I'm going, to throw rocks, 'cause they're throwing rocks at María Cano and I'm going to get them for throwing rocks at María Cano. . . ." And we kept going and she went toward the park. But look, we were dying of laughter, dying of laughter because of her. [Laughter.][9]

Not only was it all funny, but María Elisa also described herself as a participant—in the rally if not in the rock-throwing. The joke turns on the very urban juxtaposition of a gendered, petit bourgeois style with street rowdiness—the woman carries her rocks on a cloth-covered tray. That the exchange took place on the way to the plaza, figuratively *en la calle*, helps María Elisa tell it in a light-hearted way. The rock-throwing here does not reflect on the factory or contradict other stories she was interested to tell: about the moral atmosphere at Coltejer, the nastiness of the 1935 strike, or about her and her sisters' conformity to proper feminine norms.[10] Nevertheless, María Elisa described this incident with relish. Throughout our long interviews, she negotiated a line between presenting herself as having been shy, almost over-modest, and slipping in stories that pointed to an earlier rebelliousness and a street-smart confidence gained from having come to the city as an orphan who had to fend for herself.[11]

In María Elisa's story, as in almost all representations of María Cano, the orator embodies the gender tensions of the 1920s: between womanly decorum and outrageousness, femininity and radicalism. María Cano spoke at mass rallies, published erotic poetry, lived openly with her *compañero*, the Communist writer and orator Ignacio Torres Giraldo.[12] Like Mexico's Tina Modotti or Brazil's Patrícia Galvão, she mocked sexual norms while engaging in class-based political organizing.[13] In the small-town world of Medellín, however, she was also always "forgiven," being seen as a woman whose politics sprang from a passionate nature but who never lost the aura being a well-educated girl from a good family. María Elisa, for example, took pains to insist that she'd seen María Cano go to mass:

> She wasn't like they always said, no. Well, I say she went to mass because I was coming out and she was coming down too, well she was also in mass. I saw her there with this beautiful dress, I remember that dress so well, it was light-colored, with pretty sleeves like this, long sleeves was the fashion then, and heels? Serious heels! . . . and a pretty hat, sort of to the side, with a little veil.[14]

Here the dress serves as a complex symbol, allowing María Elisa to identify herself with María Cano's good taste and breeding, even as her story evokes one of city life's most common, and most gender-specific "injuries of class": working-class women's sensitivity to the fact that they will never have the clothing upper-class women wear.[15] María Elisa's descriptions of María Cano's good figure and lovely clothes soften the radicalism of the "revolutionary flower of labor," as the orator was known.

Still, María Cano had been a public Communist and María Elisa had gone to hear her speak. If our shared laughter at the incongruity of her younger self running away from the *pedrea* only to bump into this *señora* shaped the way she recounted the anecdote, it was also rooted in political memories. After finishing the story, Elisa expanded on its political aspect, explaining that "we were Socialist Liberals" and bringing our discussion of María Cano back to the labor activism of later years (the strikes of the early 1960s), with which we'd begun. "I have a work-mate, at Tejicondor . . . and I call her 'María Cano,'" she said, explaining that this had been a younger woman who always supported strikes and who was "a unionist—someone who knows about [labor] laws." María Elisa unequivocally praised both María Cano and the friend she likened to the orator, along with other *sindicalistas*, even as she distanced herself from strikes in either period and matter-of-factly described crossing the picket lines her friend had helped organize. Significantly, she used Liberalism and electoral politics to bridge the distance between these two ways of narrating her feelings about labor activism in the past.

Like most other retired workers, María Elisa presented the question as one of tactics: "*se le saca más a la empresa por las buenas que por las malas*" (you'll get more from the company by staying on their good side). She took this view, María Elisa explained, not only because of her loyalty to the company but also because one had to be realistic about workers' political chances:

> It's just stupid *señorita*, I'd always tell them: "Look kids, there's something important. Since the government isn't going to support poor folks?

We'll get blistered. It's a lot of blisters that we end up with, so don't fight if the government doesn't support us, don't fight, if the day comes that the unions have maybe some support from the government, but now we don't have it. Don't fight now!

Honestly, I was never against the factory, never, never. I could never be against the factory.[16]

In concluding a discussion of the Coltejer strike with a reference to strikers' lack of political support, María Elisa again counterposed 1935 and the early 1960s. In 1935 unionists *did* have governmental support—more than they had before or since. A self-described Liberal would likely have heard it said that López had supported the Coltejer strike in 1935, or that his administration strengthened the workers' hand. Yet multiple tensions pull María Elisa's narrative in different directions. Some of that tension derives from the class dynamics of the interview itself: a *señorita* arrives asking questions about both María Cano and Don Eduardo Echavarría. What does such a person want to hear? But because other retired women responded to the same *señorita* in a huge variety of ways, María Elisa's ambivalence cannot be seen as a function of my presence. If María Elisa left President López out of her descriptions of the Coltejer strike in 1935, despite the fact that his intervention helped workers win, it may have been because class-based organizing conflicted in fundamental ways with her understanding of politics as a set of linkages that crossed class lines.

María Elisa, for example, was "born Liberal." One's political affiliation, in her view, emerged in early childhood—a product of both family examples and one's deepest self. Her narrative explanation of how she became a Liberal began with her maternal grandparents, both Liberals, and it was a complicated story, reminiscent of García Márquez. While her grandfather was off fighting in one of the country's nineteenth-century civil wars, María Elisa said, her grandmother and a cousin had prayed so much for a Liberal victory that God punished both of them with Conservative children, one of whom later became María Elisa's mother:

> They kneeled down to beg for curses on the Conservatives because they'd been left all alone and they were pregnant with their first children, both of them. And that's when they had a pair of babies, both of them born Conservative, but the children of Liberal parents.[17]

The babies were thus second cousins; they also grew up and married one another. Thus María Elisa's mother, born Conservative, married her Conservative cousin. She was widowed young, however, and when she remarried, she made the mistake of choosing a Liberal. The children all followed their father. María Elisa said of herself that she was her mother's "punishment," just as her mother had been a punishment to her grandmother. Her Liberalism was a preordained disposition. Significantly, her understanding of where Colombian party affiliations "come from" (as believable as any explanations historians have offered), involves a strikingly gender-neutral view of political identities: two decades before women were granted suffrage. If a child in the womb can be identified as Liberal or Conservative, even in retrospect, then inclusion in party politics is hardly the province of those eligible to vote.

Communicating this way of thinking about politics required some dexterity, given the assumptions that I, as the interviewer, brought to our conversation:

> Ann: And how did you make the decision to become a Liberal?
> María Elisa: No, I was born, and ever since I was little I heard my father talking about the Liberals, with his friends, about who was president . . . and I was listening and what stuck in my mind was the word *liberal*, not the word *conservative* but the word *liberal*. [*Se me grabó la palabra* liberal, *no la* conservadora *sino la palabra* liberal.]

Her way of framing the answer to my question, along with her genealogical explanations, will be familiar to all students of Colombian politics. What is less familiar, because less studied, is the evidence her story provides about what such loyalties meant for urban working-class life (especially in the 1930s), for workingwomen, and for labor politics.

María Elisa faithfully attended Liberal Party rallies—"I never missed them!"—but she also was enthusiastic about the religious processions and "demonstrations" that the Conservative owners of Coltejer, the Echavarrías, had encouraged workers to attend. She used the same word for these as for the Liberal and Socialist rallies she attended (*manifestaciones* or "demonstrations"), adding that the company-sponsored ones were "very proper," without any rocks thrown. In describing these different sorts of street demonstrations, María Elisa was always very specific about which plazas and which streets they had occupied, but she remembered few details about what was being demanded or defended. Rallies and processions were events in themselves in a way that a strike could not be. No matter how many rocks were thrown, a Liberal rally, or a Socialist one with María Cano in attendance, was acceptable in a way that strikers' rock-throwing was not. María Elisa's politics allowed her to imagine herself "upwards," out of her status as a *pobre* or a female or a factory worker and into an exciting, cross-class urban world. For country-raised girls like María Elisa, street gatherings offered hugely varied possibilities for female behavior, only some of which appealed to her. María Cano's presence offset the rowdiness of a crowd, making rock-throwing simply part of an accepted style of urban politics. When street-style politics interfered with her sense of a valued connection to the Echavarrías, however, as in the 1935 strike, gender roles helped María Elisa express what was "wrong" with the public aggressiveness of strikes.

María Elisa's memories suggest that the cross-class legitimacy of the Liberal Party, or even of "Socialism," may have been an important part of how Medellín's workers thought about politics and labor activism. Two points of tension emerge from the way she recounts her stories about the *corrillos* of girls with rocks, about María Cano, and about the Liberal Party: first, the city demarcated places and times for appropriate political engagement. María Elisa felt one way about her and her friends' attendance at mixed-class rallies in downtown plazas (even pro-Communist rallies) and another way about the spectacle of strikers in the streets near the mill. A second point of tension is the Liberal Party itself. For María Elisa, attending Liberal political rallies was an expression of the cross-class partisan loyalty she was "born to feel" rather than of her interest in promoting a formal political platform. That a Liberal president intervened in favor of the Coltejer strikers thus did not change the fact that striking clashed with traditional forms of political behavior. While other workers, male and female, may have approached politics, rallies, and strikes very differently, María Elisa's way of describing her younger self provides a starting place for thinking about class and political culture in 1930s Medellín.

Liberalism and the "Revolution on the March"

Germán Colmenares captures the intensity of the change in Colombian political life by suggesting that the country came "late" to the twentieth century; only in the 1920s did new social groups begin to stake claims and nineteenth-century political forms begin to give way.[18] The key moment of change was 1930, when the Conservative Party lost its first presidential election in almost fifty years. They lost because Conservatives split their votes between two rival factions and because the Colombian church hierarchy, which generally arbitrated such divisions, failed to provide definitive support to one or the other.[19] The larger reason for the ruling party's collapse, however, was the economic and social crisis of the late 1920s. The national economy had expanded dramatically between 1922 and 1928. Coffee prices nearly doubled in four years, while annual exports of the unroasted bean rose from one-half million bags in 1900–1910 to more than two million in the early 1920s to three million in 1930. Measured in dollars, coffee exports rose from sixty-four million in 1922–24 to one hundred and twelve million in 1925–29.[20] This enormous expansion coincided with the successful negotiation of a settlement with the United States, which agreed to pay Colombia twenty-five million dollars in indemnity for the loss of Panama. With its growing export volume and this sudden injection of cash, the country's credit possibilities ballooned, especially given the prevailing financial climate of giddy speculation. The Colombian government was able to borrow as never before, more than tripling its debt between 1922 and 1928.[21] This money was spent on a long-overdue modernization of the country's transport system, which expanded the export economy but also sparked a dramatic inflationary spiral. Enormous public works projects meant that wages rose quickly, but prices also rose, especially for urban rents and foodstuffs.[22] The economic scene was further complicated by fiscal disarray in the provinces, which themselves borrowed money abroad.[23] By 1928, when Colombian politicians were finding borrowed money harder to come by, both urban and rural workers would be hit hard by the contraction of this "debtor's prosperity," as it was labeled by the young opposition leader López Pumarejo.

Debt-led or no, the economic expansion increased workers' powers of negotiation. Public works employing thousands of men, plus the huge demand for rural workers, increased the mobility of huge numbers of poor Colombians. By the mid-1920s, workers were in a position to demand that their wages keep pace with rising prices. Led by railroad and river-transport workers, incipient unions launched record numbers of strikes and *pliegos de peticiones* (formal demands for negotiation).[24] Strikers drew on the oratory and organizing talents of Communist leaders, and it was in these years that Raul E. Mahecha, Ignacio Torres Giraldo, and María Cano became legendary figures for the Colombian left.[25] The radicalism of transport workers and wage laborers in the foreign-owned oil and banana enclaves, especially, panicked Conservative President Abadía Méndez (1926–30) and his minister of war, Ignacio Rengifo. Increasingly, they turned toward intransigence and army intervention. In 1928, the Abadía administration faced its most serious challenge: a prolonged banana workers' strike against the United Fruit Company. The army's response, of course, has been immortalized by García Márquez in *One Hundred Years of Solitude*. Even without an accurate count of the dead, the massacre of the banana workers was a political juggernaut: it launched the populist career of a young Liberal named Jorge Eliécer Gaitán and radicalized a generation of left-leaning workers and intellectuals.[26]

Coming at the tail end of this economic instability and intense social conflict, the 1929 crash was a late last straw for the internally divided Conservative Party. Nor did the economic downturn help Colombian Liberals in the inevitably perilous business of assuming power after so long as an opposition party. The transition was eased by the bipartisan political strategy of elite Liberals, headed by Enrique Olaya Herrera, who won the presidency in 1930. Olaya had been a cabinet minister and then special ambassador to Chile under the dissident Conservative Carlos E. Restrepo and no less than ambassador to Washington under Abadía.[27] But people at the lower levels of the party were less likely to have either the experience to step into official positions or the willingness to cooperate with the Conservatives who still controlled many aspects of public life—especially at the municipal level. Violent confrontations marked the transition in several country towns. By 1932, however, when Colombians of all political persuasions rallied to Olaya during a border conflict with Peru, the Liberal president enjoyed an undisputed legitimacy.

Olaya represented only one part of a remarkably heterogeneous party. Precisely because they had spent so long in the opposition, Colombian Liberals had been able to graft new ideas onto the ideological stem of *laissez-faire* orthodoxy: hence a label like Elisa's, "*éramos liberales socialistas.*" By 1930, the mainstream of the party supported state intervention in the economy, and upper-class Liberals, at least, cared but little for the old arguments about centralism, anticlericalism, or who had been at fault in the last civil war. This is not to say that the Liberal Party became less partisan; on the contrary, its years in the minority had if anything strengthened what Richard Stoller calls the "emotional power" and "*mística*" of party identification among Liberals.[28] Like the cross-class Conservative Party, Colombian Liberalism included workers, peasants, small merchants, bankers, and *latifundistas.* Unlike the Conservatives, however, Liberals also included a smattering of young people with revolutionary notions, gleaned from the Mexican revolution and Haya de la Torre's Alianza Popular Revolucionaria Americana (APRA) as well as cooler heads who were convinced that only redistributive policies could prevent a social revolution—a conviction shared by some Conservatives. Colombia's most famous dissident Liberal, Jorge Eliécer Gaitán, personified this eclecticism; through the 1930s and early 1940s, he led a diverse populist movement with a rhetoric that blended a creative reading of Marx with calls for moral reform. As Alvaro Tirado Mejía argues, this heterogeneity had strengthened Liberalism as a standpoint of opposition but created profound contradictions for a ruling party. The genius of López Pumarejo, Olaya's successor, was that he used the party's contradictions to govern.[29]

While his predecessor had attempted a bipartisan government, staying close to the political center, López proved himself willing to alienate Conservatives and even centrist Liberals. Olaya had undertaken reformist measures, such as the eight-hour day and workers' right to organize, and had done so within a reformist discourse. López arguably did less for workers than had his predecessor, in the sense that he advanced no sweeping new labor legislation, but he nevertheless made radical, pro-labor rhetoric a centerpiece of his first administration (1934–38).[30] Influenced by Lázaro Cárdenas's emerging institutional revolution and by Roosevelt's "New Deal," he declared a "Revolution on the March." The change López envisioned involved a range of top-down reforms: closing loopholes in the tax system, lessening church control of public education, and pursuing a limited land reform. López also pushed for changes in the constitution, to abolish literacy requirements for voting, for example, and to allow for more state intervention in the economy.[31] From the perspective of politicized workers and smallholders, however, what set López apart was primarily what he did *not* do, as David Bushnell succinctly puts it.[32] He did not use the state's coercive power to resolve strikes in favor of employers and large landowners, and he did not favor company unions over independent, even Communist ones. López also distinguished between governmental involvement and personal involvement, and his most significant action on behalf of workers was his willingness to involve himself in strike negotiations *por cuenta personal*, as an individual rather than as the president.[33]

Across Colombia, workers took López at his word, and they launched a record number of strikes during his "revolution."[34] In two symbolic conflicts early in his term, the president delivered on his promises: he helped settle a strike by the historically militant workers of the La Dorada railway, and he sent his minister of war to the banana zone—not to repress the strikers but to represent them in negotiations with United Fruit.[35] López also welcomed Gaitán back into the Liberal fold after the latter's failed electoral experiments with his splinter party, the Revolutionary Left National Union (UNIR).[36] López thus undertook an alliance with organized labor and the country's polyglot left, although the Colombian Socialists and Communists pursued López more than vice versa. He had little to lose in this partnership, as rightist Liberals and Conservatives had already begun to consolidate an anticommunist, anti-*Lopista* opposition.

Medellín's first large textile strikes thus happened as part of an intensely political wave of labor activism. In March of 1935, a bipartisan group of large landowners launched a short-lived rightist party—in an explicit attack on the president's policies.[37] The mainstream Conservative Party began to step up its attacks on the president, sketching the political conflict as a religious war and refusing to concede the legitimacy of either the current administration or the reformed constitution. International tensions shaped the arguments, as Colombian newspapers reported on the Spanish Civil War and European Fascism. By 1936, the political lines were drawn. On the first of May, López welcomed demonstrating workers and allowed Communist and Socialist leaders to address a workers' demonstration from the balcony of the presidential palace in Bogotá. For their part, following the Soviet line, the Colombian Communist Party declared a "popular front," using the slogan "With López, against the Reaction."[38] This larger confrontation became mixed with local grievances in the strikes at Coltejer and Rosellón, both of which involved Communists. To Antioqueño industrialists, *Lopismo* seemed inseparable from the threat of left-wing unions; the national climate, in turn, made all worker activism necessarily partisan. In a Conservative stronghold like Medellín, any strike in 1935–36 carried higher political stakes than before or since. A city-wide strike, such as the Coltejer conflict became, was even more disruptive of traditional political forms.

Coltejer, 1935

During the first wave of labor activism associated with López's "Revolution on the March," workers at Coltejer drew up a *pliego de peticiones.* Arguing that Coltejer paid lower wages than its competitors, the workers asked for an increase of 50 percent for workers earning less than one peso a day, 30 percent for those earning more than one peso, and 20 percent for workers paid more than two pesos a day. Many of their other demands derived from existing labor legislation. The *pliego* called on the company formally to recognize the union and to agree not to fire unionists. Workers also wanted paid vacations, more job stability, and severance pay—in conformity with a law passed the year before.[39] Such demands have a generic quality; they read like *pliegos de peticiones* presented at other factories and in other kinds of workplaces in this period. Yet the Coltejer *pliego* also included a few specific, everyday grievances. If a worker were late, he or she was generally not allowed in until the next scheduled break and so lost a morning's wages; the strikers demanded that the gate be kept open a few minutes later on rainy days—that there be some degree of human flexibility. They also wanted time for breakfast and a different plant doctor; along with the wage increase, this last point became one of the most difficult obstacles to a settlement.[40]

In late May 1935 a delegation "composed of two men and three women" from the newly created Spinners' and Weavers' Union of Antioquia (Sindicato de Trabajadores de Hilados y Tejidos de Antioquia) presented their *pliego* to López's national labor inspector, on his official visit to Medellín.[41] The national inspector helped mediate two weeks of inconclusive negotiations, after which the workers delivered an ultimatum: either Coltejer's owners settled within twenty-four hours or the company would see its first strike. Meanwhile, they consolidated their support among other city unions. Painters, masons, tailors, trolley drivers, typesetters, and electrical workers, among others, called for a boycott of Coltejer's products and promised financial support.[42] By 14 June, when five hundred workers walked off Coltejer's early shift, they could negotiate from a position of power. President López supported their strike, and they had enough local backing to paralyze the city. These outside sources of strength made the 1935 strike different from anything Antioquia's industrialists had seen.

On the strike's second day, unions across the city began calling their members to daily rallies. Medellín's recently formed Union Assembly organized a system of daily morning meetings to keep unionists informed of the negotiations with Coltejer, and assembly delegates declared a general strike for

19 June. Beginning on 18 June, electrical workers shut off the city's power between six A.M. and six P.M., effectively extending the work stoppage to every shop using municipal power. Electrical service would be restored, they announced, only if negotiations began to progress more smoothly.[43] The demands being negotiated were still those of Coltejer's strikers, but the movement had become much larger than their original *pliego de peticiones*. Although it appears anomalous in the history of Medellín's textile industry, the strike thus fits directly into a history of left-wing unionism in Colombia; it helped define the group of unions that became the Fedeta, or Federación de Trabajadores de Antioquia.[44] Coltejer's workers won most of their demands, but the strike's more important outcome was the consolidation of a citywide labor movement—a movement that quickly lost its toehold in the textile mills.

The involvement of such combative unions and the spreading general strike ensured government intervention. On the strike's third day, Antioquia's government secretary closed the mill by decree, and both he and the national labor inspector involved themselves in negotiations. President López stayed informed by telephone, and by 18 June he had sent his war minister and the minister of industry to Medellín.[45] In addition to the city police, the departmental guard was called out, and a cavalry corps was dispatched from a regiment stationed at Rionegro.[46] The next day, the governor outlawed public meetings and demonstrations. But López maintained the neutral, and thus pro-labor, position he had taken in other conflicts.[47] As at Ciénaga a few months previously, his cabinet ministers arrived in Medellín as mediators, not enforcers of the status quo ante.

With the factory closed, the strikers no longer faced the threat of strikebreakers, but the movement remained concentrated in the first shift and workers on all shifts had divided loyalties. Thus the closing helped the strikers, who enjoyed more solidarity from the municipal unions than from within Coltejer. The strike's first two days, especially, had seen constant clashes between strikers and *esquiroles*, just as Elisa remembered. Judging from the lists of names published in the city's papers, female and male strikers participated about equally in the daily struggles between those who wanted to enter the mill and those who came to picket. Dozens of women's names were taken down by police and reporters, who denounced them as troublemakers.[48] Inés Valencia, Albertina Guerra, and Elisa Flórez, for example, were threatened "with being cuffed and taken into custody" if they continued to propagandize among those still working.

Yet no women sat on the strike committee and none seem to have attended any of the negotiations. Additionally, female municipal employees may not have participated in the solidarity strikes. A work stoppage planned by the telephone workers' union, for example, failed because female operators stayed at the switchboards.[49] Certainly, reporters treated the Coltejer action as a "male" strike, referring to the workers with the masculine *obreros* and leaving aside the portraiture by which they had so vividly represented Betsabé Espinal in 1920. In their *pliego* and in public statements, strike leaders often did the same, and none of their demands addressed needs specific to women.[50] The contrast to the Bello strike could not have been more marked. What had changed since 1920?

Most obviously, by 1935, many more men now worked in mills like Coltejer (see table 1 and figures 1 and 2, above). Gender divisions within the factory were no longer those of male supervisors/technicians and female subordinates. Male weavers and spinners worked alongside women and often earned comparable wages. Nor had those observers concerned with Medellín's "social question" continued to define these as female workplaces. Where Medellín's factory inspector had previously been charged with protecting "morality" above all, by the 1930s his job focused on keeping yearly statistics and assessing employers' compliance with labor legislation. With the appointment of Juan Vallejo in 1934, for example, the inspector's reports dropped a previously obligatory paragraph reporting whether or not any *obrera*'s honor had been compromised. This was part of a larger discursive shift. Politicians and newspaper columnists now tended to use the international language of "modern industry," speaking about unions, strikes, wages, and workers' benefits, rather than about the impending breakdown of the family or the insalubriousness of factories. Just as reporters told the story of the 1920 strike through a transcendental moral narrative, of female victimization and lapsed chivalry, so they narrated the 1935 strike as a secular conflict between labor and capital. In each case, the discursive frame erased key aspects of the event, irrespective of reporters' political leanings.[51] At Coltejer in 1935, newspapermen found no charming *"señoritas"* on strike, but rather women marked by the grittiness of street confrontations and inseparable from *"la clase obrera"* as a category.

By making the strike a process of negotiation within "the association of labor and capital," the Liberal press, particularly, muted workers' claims. *El Diario,* for example, represented the dominant faction of Antioqueño Liberalism and supported the governor's mediation; the editors supported the workers' demand for better wages, but denounced the solidarity strikes. They also dismissed the Coltejer workers' noneconomic demands, including their insistence on a different plant doctor and on having time for breakfast.[52] As in 1920, however, the strikers were only partially constrained by reporters' way of telling their story. Although company president Germán Echavarría refused to dismiss the plant doctor, he was forced to compromise, and the company agreed to hire an assistant doctor. According to the settlement, workers "will be able to choose . . . between the current doctor and the assistant."[53] Facing the same demand a few months later, Rosellón's managers would also adopt this formula. Coltejer workers won union recognition, a promise that the company would set up formal grievance procedures, and a guarantee of legally required benefits, such as eight days of paid vacation and the right to severance pay. They also gained an assurance that, when it rained, the gatekeepers would allow "several minutes for workers to enter." The wage settlement, too, came fairly close to the strikers' demands; Coltejer would establish a base wage of $0.45 pesos for apprentices, workers earning less than one peso would receive a 30 percent increase, those between one and two pesos would receive 20 percent, and those over two pesos would receive 15 percent.

The Coltejer strikers had won because of the city workers' solidarity; by themselves, they could not hope to enforce compliance, nor were they able to build on the settlement to solidify their support on the shop floor. Six months later, for example, the Coltejer union called a work stoppage to follow up on the June settlement and to support the Rosellón strikers; without city employees' support, it failed miserably.[54] Ironically, the Coltejer workers' triumphant strike may have left them organizationally weaker, by 1936, than workers at Rosellón, whose strike was declared illegal and who enjoyed no solidarity strikes. What the Rosellón strikers did have, however, was internal cohesion and more involvement by female operatives.

Rosellón, 1936

In part because their strike was led by Communists and declared illegal, Rosellón workers enjoyed none of the solidarity that the Coltejer strikers had; they had stepped a bit outside the umbrella of *Lopista* politics. The all-male unions that had helped workers at Coltejer win their demands stayed away from Rosellón; on the ground, this meant that the strikers relied on women. At Rosellón, female strikers led delegations to ask the city's butchers for donations of meat, organized a communal kitchen, sold flowers to raise money for the strike, and got arrested.[55] They also served on the union's board, and two women, Rosa Estrada and Camila Madrid, were elected as union spokespersons.[56] Even if only because the strike leaders (still predominately male) needed all the help they could get, strikers at Rosellón cooperated across gender lines more effectively than had the union activists at Coltejer.

The *pliego de peticiones* that began the strike included a demand that almost certainly came from the women workers: for the dismissal of two widely disliked *vigilantas*, Carmen Pareja and Cleofe Henao. Charged with maintaining order and policing the mill's moral atmosphere, the *vigilantas* supervised the female employees. More than fifty years later, regardless of

whether or not they had supported the strike, the women I interviewed remembered Cleofe. Exclaimed Cristina Monsalve, "Cleofe Henao . . . Avemaría! What a *vigilanta*, you hear? They all hated her! . . . She was a real stool
pigeon, she'd tell on you for anything."[57] According to another woman, "she
was one of the ones that would suspend you for the most insignificant
things . . . there could be some cotton on the floor, or spilled, just for that. She
was really mean; we all had a lot of respect for her, or to put it better, fear."[58]

Other points on the workers' petition were similarly concrete, rooted in
everyday complaints. After their first demand, for the reinstatement of José
Guió, president of their newly formed union, the strikers wanted toilets in
the dyeing section; extra pay for night work and for the time it took to clean
and ignite the boilers; half-pay for time lost by mechanical breakdowns; and
the guarantee that they'd receive their pay each Saturday. Other demands
included permission to keep bobbins at the foot of the spinning machines
during the night shift and either lower prices or better quality merchandise
in the company store. As at Coltejer, Rosellón workers wanted a half-hour
for breakfast, more vacation time, and the replacement of the plant doctor.
They were minutely specific about wage increases, as well. Not only did they
outline a sliding percentage increase favoring the lowest paid workers but
they also detailed a specific list of raises for those on piece-rates:

> For workers in spinning, an increase of five *centavos* ($0.05) for every ten
> numbers marked by the counter . . . for bobbin workers, an increase of
> twenty *centavos* ($0.20) for every one hundred, including the colored
> ones . . . for workers on the automatic bobbin-winders, an increase of
> fifty *centavos* for every thousand, [etc.].[59]

Compared to the Coltejer workers' *pliego de peticiones*, these read less
like labor statutes and more like grievances from below.[60] This difference of
emphasis owed not to women's more central involvement but to Communist organizing. As Gilberto Mejía describes it in his memoirs, the party had
only a tenuous connection to the Coltejer strike committee; at Rosellón,
however, Communists organized the union and party recruits led the strike
movement.[61] Through December of 1935, Mejía and a fellow party member,
Jaime Clark, had organized street meetings outside the mill, talking to workers and linking their complaints to the need for a union. His fiery speeches
and Jaime's quickly printed flyers were convincing, Mejía recalls, precisely
because they had listened: "before talking, we would find out, *pues*, about
their problems in the factory, their needs, their pains, and we'd put together
our intervention based on these things."[62] Although they joined López in a
one-sided "popular front," Colombian Communists like Mejía sought to mobilize and politicize workers against the legal structures of a state dominated
by two oligarchical parties. They emphasized workers' everyday grievances

more than legal niceties. Caught by a technical infraction of the legal code, at least according to the governor's office, the Rosellón strike was quickly declared illegal. Along with union president José Guió, Mejía spent most of it in jail.

But no clear line separated a legal from an illegal strike, just as none divided Liberal workers from Communist recruits. With López risking his presidency on this thin ground of overlap, the Rosellón strike lent itself to Liberal political maneuvering. From Bogotá, Gaitán announced his opinion that the strike was legal, while Antioquia's governor turned its illegality to political advantage: attacking Communist organizers while intervening on the workers' behalf. As an appointee put it,

> the governor chose to declare the strike illegal . . . to more efficiently control the professional agitators and clear them away from the healthy part of the workers' movement, that sincerely aspired, and rightfully, to improve their working conditions.[63]

Thus it was an instrumental illegality, and the governor worked to ensure that the workers won concessions nevertheless. When the company attempted a lockout, he interceded personally—meeting with workers at "El Guáimaro" (a well-known large tree) and serving as a mediator in the final negotiations. *El Diario* backed the governor, running anticommunist editorials but professing sympathy with the workers' "reasonable" aspirations. Envigado's city council supported the strikers more forcefully, sending council members to the negotiations and publicly announcing the municipality's intention to employ workers fired by the company.[64] In the end, both sides claimed victory; the strikers because they successfully negotiated a few points and the company because "we made some wage concessions but sustained our point of view with respect to the factory's internal organization."[65]

The Rosellón workers won less than they had hoped, but their gains were more than symbolic. They had wanted a 40 percent increase for the lowest paid workers and 25 percent for those earning between one and two pesos, for example, and received increases of 12 and 8 percent, respectively. Workers on piece-rates won raises within that range, as well as a promise that "the company will post contract rates in visible places . . . to the end that workers be able to rectify their accounts." Of their other demands, the strikers gained a 25 percent bonus for night work; extra pay for cleaning and igniting the boilers; bathrooms in the dyeing section; a half-hour for breakfast; and an assurance that workers would get paid on Saturdays. The company refused the strikers' request for a guaranteed number of vacation days that could be taken at a worker's discretion, granting only to continue to honor traditional rest days: Holy Thursday and Friday, the first of May, a week at Christmas, and standard patriotic holidays. The strikers also won a pledge that the company would not fire any worker for participating in the union, a pledge they proved unable to enforce.[66]

Rosellón's managers refused to fire either the administrator or the doctor, conceding only to move the *vigilantas* Carmen and Cleofe to different jobs in another part of the mill, with the promise that "the company will impede them from exercising reprisals."[67] Consistently, Medellín's textile industrialists proved themselves more willing to negotiate wages than the removal of supervisors. At Bello in 1920, for example, Emilio Restrepo quickly granted the strikers wage increases and other concessions but had to be pressured by Governor Ospina before he agreed to dismiss Velásquez and Monsalve. Nor is it clear that either actually left the mill: Teódulo Velásquez, at least, appears on an employee list for 1933.[68] Workers at Rosellón had themselves declared a brief work stoppage in February 1920, unsuccessfully demanding "the expulsion of the current administrator."[69] They made the same demand, more forcefully, during a three-day strike in 1929. That conflict ended with a negotiated solution, with the company agreeing to raise wages and to provide free medical services, but the *gerente* insisted that the strike settlement include the following apology: "The undersigned delegates . . . expressly declare that there was no real motive for the work stoppage . . . and that by the same token they retract the charges that had been improperly formulated against the administrator."[70]

As they would six years later, the members of Rosellón's board of directors categorically opposed workers' presumption of a veto power in the hierarchical arrangement of persons, the heart of the mill's "internal organization." Thus in 1935–36, negotiators for the textile companies rejected workers' demands for a different plant doctor or, in the case of Rosellón, their call for one "chosen by the workers."[71] Although a doctor did no supervising, his medical certificate judged a person fit or unfit for hiring, and he treated workers' on-the-job injuries. Whether the doctor treated workers respectfully or appeared fair-minded in his determinations had an important symbolic power, for he shared the upper-class status of the mill's highest employees. To concede that workers might publicly assess his performance, even gain his dismissal, would undermine a wider class hierarchy, along with the simple industrial principle that a company's owners decide who keeps or loses a job.[72]

If labor conflicts in Medellín consistently involved a demand for the dismissal of a higher employee, and strikers demanded "good treatment" as often as they did better wages, then workers did not experience striking as a process of negotiation between "capital" and "labor." In practice, people understood striking by reference to an interpersonal world not indexed by the abstract categories reporters used to describe the events of a strike. Ousting a disliked supervisor, or a self-interested doctor, rallied workers together because it involved an emotional claim. Given the fact of workers' everyday insubordination and infighting, such a demand is not about "respect" or "civility" in a disembodied sense but about workers' control over the tone of workplace interactions involving specific persons. *Lopista* Liberals encouraged workers to strike as a way to negotiate wages and material benefits, but they waged no public argument against supervisors' high-handedness. Nor, of course, did Communist militants make "good treatment" a priority of working-class struggle. Workers experienced strikes in personal terms, in which the negotiation of material benefits was mixed with a nonmaterial sense of pride.

Similarly, neither the Liberal nor the Communist vision allowed space for workers' ambivalence about strikes as a breach of individual loyalty. The moral legitimacy of humbling a disagreeable superior derived, precisely, from the intermingling of pride and personal attachment in workplace relationships. Gaining a sense of the nonmaterial world of workers' feelings about strikes thus allows a historian to learn from the ambivalence that marks retired workers' accounts. The point is not that strikers had mixed feelings but rather that the ambiguity in their stories is itself suggestive evidence of workers' responses to both class-based politics and paternalist ideology. Like Elisa, who opposed strikes in general (and who sometimes crossed picket lines but at other times joined them), loom-fixer Enrique López told a double story about the 1930s. He described his involvement in the 1936 Rosellón strike as "the biggest mistake of my life," yet he presented the mistake in glowing terms, emphasizing the importance of his own contribution and recounting the whole experience as a heroic journey. His self-narration suggests the positive content of this sort of ambiguity; workers' ambivalence about strikes cannot be read simply as a "lack" of class consciousness.

Enrique López's Exemplary Story

Enrique developed his story through a series of conflicting descriptions, with his jokes and listeners' laughter serving to resolve the inherent contradictions. First, his own involvement in the strike was "a mistake" but also a source of pride, a testimony to his and other workers' intelligence and capacity. Second, workers struck because they suffered bad conditions, but the strike wouldn't have happened unless Communist agitators had led them astray. Third, these Communists were both meddling outsiders *and* "experts" who had experience, knew what they were doing, and were therefore legitimate guides. Fundamental tensions, between "bad" disobedience and "good" militancy and between foolishness and justified revindication, shape his remembrance and retelling.

Although I had asked an initial question about the strike, Enrique developed the narrative with few pauses for intervening questions. To my query, "Were you there, in 1936, when there was a strike in the factory?" he responded with an emphatic "Yes, of course!"

Yes. Look, the people here were incredibly badly paid because some people's salaries were completely, well, alarming; people couldn't live on what they got, on what they earned. And so, it happened that, this was in 1935, a man came here, his name was José Antonio Guió, he came from Bogotá; he had just finished directing a strike there . . . and he was a *legitimate* Communist! This guy got, got, what? newsletters, advice . . . all this material for studying and for organizing strikes and unions and all that stuff, he got that stuff in the mail, other men brought it, comrades, they came here and infiltrated the factory to be able to help with this organizing. This man José Antonio Guió came and in a matter of two weeks he organized the union.[73]

Having justified the strike by reference to low wages and having identified outside agitators as simultaneously "good" organizers and "bad" infiltrators, Enrique then described his own role as an enthusiastic new recruit:

But we also did—this was, this was the, the, the biggest mistake of my life. Well, I joined with this man, and I helped him and I did a lot for the movement, because he said to me, he turned to me, he said: "look, Enrique, you are a wise man with a lot of understanding, you know X, Y, and Z person, go, go and take this notebook, this book and you're going to tell them everything we're going to do and you get each of them to sign."

And so I, I was very polite with him and I said: "Gladly! With pleasure!" And I grabbed that folder and, and the pen and I started to talk to the *obreras:* "look, this is going to happen, that is going to happen, this is going to improve, this, that, and the other, and sign here for me and now you will be affiliated with the union, a member of the union, and I'm going to be part of the leadership, see?"; [and they'd say], "well, if it's with you OK, because if it was with some other person we didn't know, no."

Almost all of them signed for me and the union was formed and so . . . he said: "OK, the union is formed, now we're going to have a special meeting . . . we're going to meet at the Guáimaro on this day at this time." Everybody was there, really, this was immense. . . . And that man began to talk, but since he was such an eloquent man and such a good talker and everything, a man of such capability, well, people, people got convinced. . . .

Again, Enrique's telling relies on a double logic: an expert Communist, Guió led him astray, but the organizer couldn't have done it without Enrique's help. Enrique emphasizes his own ability and the *obreras'* respect for him, while maintaining an alibi of youthful naiveté.

His multiple disclaimers, from calling it the "biggest mistake" to his eventual reintegration into the company, free Enrique to tell the story with excitement and enthusiasm:

> This was an experience, an *immense, immense* experience!
> The zero hour arrived, the moment for the strike!
> And we went on strike!
> We went down this street here, one day at noon.
> They sounded the sirens, I put myself in charge of making all the sirens sound and all of that. I gave strategic orders: to one person to sound the whistle on the boiler, to another person to sound the big siren that was for the firemen, to another person to shut off the electricity, to another person to shut off the water. We all got together and we went down the street in a parade to the main plaza.
> We went right down this street! [He motions to the doorway.] Everybody right behind us, because they believed in us. The people were happy, shouting: "Hooray for the strike! Hooray for the workers! Hooray for this, that, and the other!"

With equal gusto, and the same dash of irony, he described their battles with strikebreakers and with the police, who turned fire hoses on the strikers. In response to my questions about women's involvement, for example, he offered a comic anecdote: a story within the story of the leadership role he took on. The women, he said, had been fearless: they got more than men did from the butchers and shopkeepers, and they were more effective at confronting strikebreakers. "Sometimes I run into old *compañeras* [workmates] and we talk about it," he said, prefacing the story he wanted to tell with another quick disclaimer:

> Frankly, the work we undertook back then was something, something else! Avemaría! And so, me? I don't know why they didn't fire me then! I did really bad things, eh, Avemaría! Now I recognize it—think about it: this factory has easy access, entrances everywhere—
> And along this very street . . . the supervisors, the high-up *empleados*, would come up [to the factory] in the mornings, every day! The cashier would come up, the floor boss for weaving, the floor boss for spinning, the lady boss for the finishing room would come up; and so I said to some girls: "OK, whatever we do we need to keep these people out," and they said, "But what can we do? What can we do? We can't beat them up!" And I said, "no, we're not going to beat anyone up, let's go"—There was a big spring that crossed a field over there, and I said, "OK, make a line

here, each one grab a *totuma* [a hollowed-out gourd]. When those people get here you tell them: 'Look, gentlemen, please, don't prejudice our cause, it's for everyone's good and we want to do to all of this the right way,' like that" . . . And then I told them: "OK, if they insist on coming up, I'll make a little sign and you'll understand me and at that moment you grab the *totumas* and you soak these people."

And so then those people were frowning and all of a sudden they were going to continue on up there, and so I said to the girls: "Ready!" They understood me and they grabbed their *totumas* and they soaked all those people right there, all them in their coats and ties and all that, isn't that right? And they had to turn around!

Emphasizing the rustic *totumas*, hollowed-out gourds used in cooking, on the one hand, and the *empleados'* clothing, on the other, Enrique stressed the class-based mockery of female strikers dousing formally dressed men (and a woman). He presented their actions in the same way he presented his own, as youthful high spirits and fodder for a funny story. Undercutting his own insistence that the strike had been a terrible mistake, he took pleasure in the telling. As he developed it, it also became more fully his own story; this was a strike he and his friends had made, not simply a creation of outside agitators. The contradictory way he presented the strike expressed his ambivalence, but it also afforded him a narrative. Instead of being silenced by it, Enrique used anticommunism to tell a story about workers' revindication.

In keeping with its presentation as a youthful folly, however, the error of the strike required personal atonement. Enrique explained that the workers were unable to enforce the strike agreement barring the company from firing activists and that many people had been dismissed. But he was lucky; instead of being fired, he was given a chance to prove himself and, like the prodigal son, to regain entrance to the patriarchal compact. The story of his redemption is a heroic narrative, built around themes of banishment, hard labor, and return. By focusing on his punishment and pardon, it reminds the listener that his strike participation was "bad," a moral transgression.

As Enrique told the story, Rosellón's administrator, Ricardo Correa Jaramillo, put him to work clearing rock from a creek-bed with a pick and a wheelbarrow, explicitly as a punishment for his involvement in the strike. Only by meeting the challenge did he regain his job and his right to speak, as a man, to the manager. This eventual reintegration signaled the beginning of long-term improvements, not only in his own life but also in the life of the company.

This was a huge punishment for me, this was very hard for me! I was not accustomed to that work and I, well, when I got home I couldn't stand the pain in my arms and all that . . . but I reminded myself that I was a man and I faced it, and I stood it! After twenty days I could work as well as any other laborer. And so I made them understand that, because one day the administrator came and he told me: "Hombre! Enrique, you? You have won your laurels here, you should know, I've been informed that you work as hard or harder than many of the others." And so then the field was open for me, to speak to him, and I said to him: "Don Ricardo, I do not believe that you are revengeful with me, it's true that I did many bad things and—"; "Yes, hombre, you shouted all kinds of things against the company and you covered the walls from here to Envigado with slogans and signs and posters and things, and you, well, you turned into a Communist!" And I said: "Don Ricardo, I believe that you will pardon me for this and, that, *someday*, you'll send me back inside."

And for certain, he didn't delay even a whole week in, in sending me back where I was before. I was out there; and he said, "OK, [tell] Enrique to come, that he should go to the weaving room." I arrived in weaving and, well, this was like arriving back home! My friends and my *compañeros* welcomed me back and everything and he said, "OK, you're going to be the mechanic for this section," and then I continued just fine, working hard and with real foundation and punctually and all of that and then came the raises and promotions and changes in wages and all of that and then they started the medical benefits and all of those things and the company began to improve.

Significantly, his redemption continues the ambiguity that throughout marked Enrique's story of the strike. His triumphant return marks an acceptance of the patriarchal order of the factory, but it also signals a final vindication. Not only does he begin an ascent measured by salary increases and promotions but also the company takes a paternalistic turn, toward the provision of "medical benefits and all those things." A bargain is struck: he begins to work harder, to be "punctual," to replace disobedience with loyalty, and the company repays that loyalty with a recognition of his worth as a mechanic and steady, long-term improvement. Enrique's story explains the paternalism of later decades by identifying its origin in the conflicts of the 1930s.

His narrative also points to the importance of gender hierarchy in paternalistic ideology and in the daily organization of millwork. Enrique presents his earlier self's involvement in the strike as a mistake, but one caused by youthful high spirits. That the company also begins to "improve" in general terms is slipped in as part of his own story of learning the rewards of hard work: "the raises and promotions and all that." The prodigal son has learned his lesson, and Don Ricardo appears as the good father. He tests Enrique, punishing him for his hare-brained folly, but also knows when to recognize that the son has grown up and to reaccept him into the family fold.

Don Ricardo's symbolic role as the father who teaches him a lesson is of course paralleled by Enrique's own place in the gender order of adulthood. The story about the strike is one he tells within the larger frame of his and his wife's success at raising a large family, his own role as patriarch and good provider, and his pride in his children's relative success. As he became a responsible family man, Enrique gained a package of family benefits, as part of the new compact between the company and, in his story, its skilled male employees. His narration also captures a key feature of textile companies' provision, through the 1940s and early 1950s, of new benefits and services: it was the anticommunism that emerged in industrialists' response to 1935–36 that fueled the textile companies' shift to a more formal paternalism.

Conclusion

Even five or ten years later, the strikes at Coltejer and Rosellón in 1935–36 would have seemed almost unthinkable—the mills changed that quickly. Thus the first point to be made about Medellín's first big textile strikes is that they happened in workplaces not yet fully controlled by the paternalistic vision for which the textile companies became known. Rather, they were rooted in a fluid shop-floor world marked by workers' easy mobility and by sometimes ribald forms of interaction among female and male workers. Even the citywide textile strikes of the 1930s were the product of a relatively small manufacturing world. Workers and owners still interacted at a face-to-face level and felt that they "knew" one another across the lines of class—for precisely this reason, a worker might experience the act of striking as similar to other, seemingly more personal forms of insubordination. As was true of the Bello strike in 1920, workers demanded the replacement of specific individuals—operatives resented the disrespectfulness of this supervisor, that doctor, these *vigilantas.*

Medellín's textile strikes also grew out of the cross-class world of urban political demonstrations and public expressions of partisan loyalty. Seen not from an electoral perspective but rather from the vantage point of street gatherings, urban political life appears distinctly mixed-sex. Women attended speeches and rowdy meetings in Medellín's central plaza, as had María Elisa, and, during the politicized strikes of 1935–36, they went into the streets alongside male co-workers.

As in 1920, female strikers' behavior in the streets near Coltejer and Rosellón sometimes shocked observers—including their *compañeras.* Reporters' coverage of the Coltejer and Rosellón strikes, however, was markedly different from their coverage of the strike at Bello in 1920. Because the mills were no longer perceived as "female" workplaces, observers wrote about events at Coltejer and Rosellón in the language of political economy, labor legislation, and *Lopista* politics. Discursively, despite the fact of women's involvement, these were "male" strikes. Indeed, the failure to find a language by which to mobilize female workers, or a language that would lessen the distance between "proper" femininity and radical labor activism, may be the key to why leftist labor organizers had so little long-term impact in what were still predominately female workplaces. María Cano might have provided a bridge between the cross-class political identity of a working-class woman like María Elisa, on the one hand, and the radical rhetoric of Communist and left-Liberal union organizers, on the other, but Cano was by this point a national leader, not a local organizer.

Given that the strikes of the 1930s were generally associated with male workers and the "agitation" of largely male Communists and *Lopista* activists, it may seem odd that the textile companies responded by setting up a "family-wage" system. The big firms began to favor male employees and to increase their number, hiring men in previously female jobs: as weavers, spinners, twisting-frame operatives, and packers. The next chapter takes up this question: why and how did anticommunism in Medellín develop hand-in-hand with a normative discourse on gender roles that was inimical to female factory labor? In his notes on "Americanism and Fordism," Antonio Gramsci several decades ago alerted critics of industrialism to this problem: that rules about sexuality and an insistence on "moral virtue" was a key way that twentieth-century capitalists responded to the possibility of workers' mobilization. In Medellín, textile industrialists adopted the moralistic paternalism for which they became locally famous only after workers' ability to organize mass resistance had been demonstrated in the strikes of 1935–36.

FIVE

Gender by the Rules
Anticommunism and *La Moral,*
1936–53

WHETHER OR NOT they supported the strikes, Antioqueños who worked in the textile factories through the 1950s may well have shared Enrique's feeling that the mills had changed for the better. At each of the city's textile mills, owners and managers responded to the possibility of workers' mobilization by turning to a paternalistic system that combined wage increases and generous benefits with patriarchal ideology. The companies began to present themselves both *as families,* with workers cast as children, and as the guarantors of their employees' families. Male workers' benefits enabled them to provide for their children, while female workers were safeguarded against sexual dangers and thus remained potential wives. Workers and owners alike described this paternalistic system of protection and control as *la moral,* translatable as adherence to "morals" or "being proper." By the 1940s, at the mills owned by the Echavarrías, *la moral* involved an explicit exchange: virginity was a precondition of young women's employment. Their policy set a standard, imitated even by Tejicondor and Telsa—two mills that continued to hire married women and single mothers. This chapter traces the way Catholicism, sexual morality, and the ideal of the patriarchal family were joined to anticommunism and work discipline in Medellín's mills. My interest is not only in the shift in disciplinary practice but also in workers' own stake in *la moral.*

Seen as a continuation of the discourse on *la mujer obrera,* as it developed in Medellín in the 1910s and 1920s, the reorganization of the mills after the instability of the 1930s was a fallback decision in favor of the moralistic vision of reformers like Father Gabriel Lizardi and Francisco de Paula Pérez. At the level of shop-floor practice, workers and managers alike knew women to be as often boisterous and insubordinate as delicate or demure. Nevertheless, female workers' purity and their supposed need for moral protection rapidly became the ideological centerpiece of factory discipline in Medellín. Industrialists did not simply manipulate gender and family to secure a paternalistic control. Rather, they enlisted a particular conception of gender in a symbolic reordering of the factory idea, seeking to codify labor discipline through newly strict rules about sexual behavior.[1] Gender itself had to be produced and policed on the shop floor.

As it developed in the late 1930s and through the 1940s, Antioqueño paternalism combined anticommunist repression with material benefits, including medical insurance, access to housing, factory schools, and regular wage increases, as well as cost-of-living bonuses.[2] Some of these were spurred by legislative initiatives directed at large urban employers, ranging from a requirement that companies invest in workers' housing to a decree obliging employers to distribute shoes twice yearly. Yet paternalistic rhetoric required that material benefits appear neither as concessions to the Liberal government nor as compromises with workers whose labor the companies needed but rather as tokens of the mutual respect between a firm and its employees. Catholic gender discourse provided a site and justification for this illusion of mutual respect, not least because it allowed industrialists to represent concessions as gifts. Newly strict definitions of female chastity, elaborate systems for chaperoning working girls, factory beauty contests: these aspects of Antioquia's gender-based paternalism did not merely coincide with the provision of new benefits; they anchored the family symbolism that made workers' concrete gains a sign of loyalty and dependence.

Expansion and the New Paternalism

Strike demands and workers' petitions that had proved difficult or impossible to negotiate in 1935–36 were extended and surpassed in the early 1940s. Workers at Tejidos de Bello, for example, had launched a *pliego de peticiones* in 1936—two weeks after the settlement at Rosellón. The company considered their request for a full-time doctor, resident in Bello, to be "absolutely impossible."[3] Less than a year later, however, the company president reassured stockholders that Bello had successfully weathered the recent wave of extremist "contamination" and that "the firm has greatly expanded its medical services."[4] Workers had also wanted a company-provided bus service, "during bad weather," which management labeled "impracticable." Yet by the late 1930s both Bello and Fabricato ran daily buses.[5] In 1935, workers had demanded a half-hour for breakfast; by the early 1940s, however, all of the large mills provided not only time to eat but also modern cafeterias serving subsidized meals—with landscaped patios adjacent to the eating areas.[6]

Through this period the mills began to occupy the space around them in an entirely different way. They grew laterally, developing a range of off-site extensions, from housing to recreational facilities, subsidized grocery stores, medical offices, and factory chapels. After about 1946, when a new law required large employers to set aside monies for workers' housing, Fabricato extended a previously piecemeal housing policy to plan and fund entire neighborhoods, the first and largest being the Barrio "San José Obrero," built near the main plant in 1947.[7] Coltejer and Rosellón built hundreds of houses in Envigado and Itagüí during the same period.[8] Workers' neighborhoods included schools, with the factories providing the buildings, materials, and teachers' salaries.[9] (Fabricato even kept a record of students' grades, sometimes sending cuts of cloth to those who passed their fifth year.)[10] All of the large textile companies also began to supply practice space and coaches for sports teams: basketball for women and soccer for men.[11] Workers cheered their *compañeros* at games played with other factories' teams, or they read about "their" teams and saw players' photographs in new company magazines, like Coltejer's *Lanzadera* or Fabricato's *Gloria,* both of which began publication in the late 1940s.[12]

Such additions to the mills had changed whole areas of the city; by the early 1950s the factories had become workplaces surrounded by company-sponsored places of nonwork. A worker at Coltejer or Fabricato might now ride a factory bus to work, perhaps after hearing mass at the church in the workers' neighborhood, and she or he might pass newly landscaped company property, a library for afterwork study, and the soccer field on the way. Even workers living not in factory neighborhoods but in older working-class areas were within the companies' orbit; no one in Medellín could miss the billboards and display windows that everywhere promoted fabrics from Fabricato, Rosellón, Coltejer, Telsa, and Tejicondor. In the outlying municipality of Bello, such changes created a company town; Bello did not exist separately from Fabricato. In Medellín the companies created a visual patchwork of modernity; their prominent logos linked downtown offices to company magazines to public installations (including gardens, fountains, and street signs). Clean and stylish, company-maintained city spaces, like the stores that sold their fabrics and the models who smiled out from the textile companies' advertisements, promoted the textile industry as the flowering of the new Medellín.[13]

An economic boom fueled this expanding industrial experiment. As Juan José Echavarría has demonstrated, the world depression helped rather than hindered growth in Antioqueño industry. Lower domestic prices spurred innovation and competition, and companies oriented toward the domestic market gained from the same shock that reduced coffee-producers' export earnings.[14] Textiles were especially key: nationally, the production of cotton goods grew 20 percent annually between 1932 and 1939, at twice the total growth rate for Colombia's manufacturing sector in the same period. Despite a temporary slowdown during World War II, when Colombian firms were forced to postpone machine imports and were often unable to obtain raw materials, including cotton, the country's textile producers benefited from the sustained expansion of the national market for consumer goods.[15] Textiles contributed 56 percent of Colombia's national manufacturing growth in 1927–39 and 67 percent in 1939–45. The larger firms also began export lines that would grow in the immediate postwar years. Coltejer, particularly, profited from the war, as the company won a contract to supply cloth to the U.S. Army. Able to buy machinery in the United States under special license, the company enjoyed a special opportunity to expand. As Coltejer's president, Carlos Echavarría, remembered the frenetic pace of those years: "There were machines running under special tents, while, nearby, buildings were being erected to house them."[16]

In earlier decades, Antioquia's looms and spinning machines had come from English and European suppliers, as well as from New England, but the new looms and spinning machines came primarily from the United States. North American investors were discovering Colombian industry, and foreign capital began to trickle in to the region's manufacturing sector. While local families maintained their control, especially in textiles, higher profits fueled new partnerships. In 1940, after years of negotiations with other firms, including an attempt to buy an existing mill outright, the North American firm of W. R. Grace formalized a partnership with a struggling new firm, Tejicondor.[17] The influx of new capital transformed Tejicondor into a competitor of the Echavarría clan's big mills. By 1944, however, Fabricato had cemented a relationship with Burlington Mills; their joint concern, Textiles Panamericanos, produced synthetic fabrics at a plant in Bello, next door to Fabricato itself. As described in chapter 2, the late 1930s and early 1940s were also years of consolidation, in which Fabricato and Coltejer emerged as the giants of Antioqueño industry, absorbing the Fábrica de Bello and Rosellón, respectively. Taken together, Colombian textile mills more than tripled their stock in machinery between 1930 and 1943.[18] They also phased older machines out of production; Fabricato, Coltejer, and Tejicondor outdistanced their competitors precisely by switching over to automatic looms.[19] Thus, if the managers and major stockholders of the largest mills attempted paternalism on a grand scale, it was because they could suddenly afford it—and because their growing productive capacity required a more stable workforce.

The 1930s and 1940s were also years in which the number of workers at each mill ballooned. In 1928 Coltejer and Rosellón together employed six hundred people, but by 1945 more than six thousand workers kept the two plants running with three shifts of eight hours each.[20] Over the same period the combined workforce of Fabricato and Tejidos de Bello increased from seven hundred to nearly four thousand; by 1946 both mills also had begun a night shift.[21] Tejicondor employed two thousand by 1945, also operating around the clock. More important than this quantitative expansion was the increase in productivity per worker; Alberto Mayor Mora estimates that the annual yardage produced per operative in Colombian mills more than tripled from the late 1920s to the early 1940s.[22] Demand grew even more quickly, however, and mill administrators regularly wrote to the regional representative of the ministry of labor to request permission to work overtime.[23] Managers experimented with new forms of organizing the workday and incentive mechanisms designed to extract more work from each operative, ranging from installing counters on looms and installing clocks to reducing piece-rates.[24] They also began keeping more careful records. Between 1935 and 1940, each of the big textile companies began to maintain a file, or *hoja de vida*, on each worker; where managers had previously jotted brief comments beside workers' names, kept on lists or cards, they now made entries on preprinted forms and filed these alphabetically. Getting a job became more difficult. By the early 1940s, higher wages and the provision of family benefits made workers less likely to quit the textile mills, while personnel managers became more strict about not hiring back those who quit without notice—not least because they now kept better records. Workers were also issued identity cards, without which a person could not enter the mill gate.[25]

A bureaucratic paternalism had replaced the personalistic authority of the industry's early years. By the early 1940s, Medellín's industrial workshops had become large enough that a range of lower-level supervisors separated a worker from the *gerente*. Although the Echavarría brothers and their sons still served as day-to-day administrators at both Coltejer and Fabricato, they now had to cultivate actively a connection with the weavers and spinners. With hundreds (and then thousands) of workers on each shift, that connection could only be established symbolically—even if some of the Echavarrías visited the workshops (or the cafeteria) often enough to maintain the illusion of intimacy.

In the 1910s and early 1920s, by contrast, entrepreneurial capitalists like Tejidos de Bello's Emilio Restrepo or Rosellón's Helidoro Medina had both chaired stockholders' meetings and managed the details of production and discipline. In Fabricato's first few years Jorge Echavarría by himself decided hires, promotions, and pay rates. He often stopped the factory to deliver impromptu moral sermons linked to such decisions, announcing a cost-of-living increase as part of a speech about the virtues of thrift or distributing Christmas bonuses along with exhortations to work hard and behave morally.[26] Don Jorge relied on the direct authority of his presence, as suggested by the following diary entry from 1923:

I announced the contract prices . . . they seemed very low to the poor fools, who only know about non-automatic looms. They began to talk about this in groups and stopped all the looms—When I saw what was happening I stopped the two motors and I said that when the motors started again every loom should be working—Only 4 disobeyed and they were fired immediately—After they were gone I gave the others a stern lecture and told them that what they were wanting was the harsh treatment they had received at Don Emilio's, with his black overseers [negro capataces] and his directives.[27]

Faced with a "tentative rebellion," as he labeled it, Echavarría had raised the stakes: who would face down Don Jorge Echavarría? What began to change in Medellín's factories in the 1930s was precisely this face-to-face relationship with the boss. Echavarría was not a supervisor or an absentee owner but rather a "good *patrón*," different from the also-known Don Emilio. Because he ran the mill directly, Don Jorge could extend informal favors and cultivate a familiarity that softened his authoritarian control. He might condescend to be a godparent or to intervene on behalf of a family member who needed work or specific favor, or he might make an informal loan or help a worker purchase materials to buy a house.

However mythic, anecdotes about Don Jorge are revealing: he gave people rides in his flashy car and drove it to Bello each Christmas, full of presents that he handed out himself. Cultivating a homey informality, the young *gerente* ate packed lunches alongside "his" workers, brought his dog to work with him, and sometimes carried in a Victrola to liven up the workers' day.[28] Don Jorge may have been more consciously benevolent than Don Eduardo (who hired María Elisa Alvarez at Coltejer) or Don Emilio, but all of the early owner-managers were "paternalistic" in that they did favors for their employees and attempted to cultivate a personal loyalty.[29] They were also "patriarchal" in this direct, personalistic way, enforcing moral codes, or not, as they saw fit. In 1930, for example, Emilio Restrepo summarily fired four men and three women who had engaged in unspecified "immoral conduct."[30] Yet this was an informal paternalism, a managerial style that presupposed an intensive knowledge of working people's lives and required a deft feel for how to manage interpersonal relationships of power.[31]

Facing larger workforces and a changed political environment, the next generation of mill administrators (including the younger Echavarrías) sought to remain "good *patrones*" by formalizing their relationship to employees. Although workers continued to request and sometimes receive special favors, they increasingly did so by writing to the company's central office. Leticia Henao, for example, addressed a letter to "Señores Miembros de la Junta Directiva de Fabricato" to request a house in the new Barrio San José.[32] Personal favors became less important than the benefits one enjoyed by working at one of the city's large mills, and these were delineated and administered by white-collar employees not closely connected to the workrooms.[33] The key difference was that, by the late 1940s, textile work involved not a relationship with a *patrón* so much as a connection to a firm—established by bureaucratic and ceremonial practices rather than by cross-class familiarity.

Anticommunism at Fabricato

Thus, the shift to a more complex system of benefits did not represent a break with past practice but rather its application to companies that were richer and newly vulnerable to workers' organization. Formalized and made institutional, an employer's "gifts" could do more than ensure an individual's loyalty. To Medellín's most ambitious factory owners, the extension of new benefits provided a mechanism for social engineering.

Jorge Echavarría himself provides the best example of this change. In 1933, terminally ill, he wrote to shareholders to convince them to fund a recreational center and cafeteria for Fabricato's workers. Calling it his "golden dream," he described plans for a multiroom complex that would serve as a sort of country club for workers: a "Club Fabricato."[34] Like that of the ladies of the Patronato or other advocates of Catholic Social Action, his vision combined heartfelt empathy with crushing condescension. After long hours at the mill, he wrote,

> I would return to my home to enjoy comforts and ... outings, as well as country club gatherings and entertainments. But my thoughts traveled to the cramped and deficient houses of my worktime *compañeros*. . . . They had no entertainment, neither in the afternoons nor on holidays, unless it were to walk through horrible streets or to enter a *cantina* for a few drinks. They had no diversion because there was none to be had, nor could most of them have afforded diversion.
>
> From that time forward I told myself: "Someday, God willing, I will make sure that these poor and deserving people have a good, respectable place for amusement ... where they will have a sense of being at home, a sense of respectability, cleanliness, wholesome fun, and where healthful *sport* [English in original] is encouraged, together with self-respect and respect for one's *compañeros*.

As he imagined it, the Club Fabricato would include an indoor basketball court for women workers, which could double as a theater, and an outdoor soccer field for men, as well as billiard tables and reading rooms. It would also house showers, with towels, "so that workers may take refreshing baths, which they generally fail to do ... in part because they lack the means and in part because they are not accustomed [to bathing]."[35] Echavarría insisted that the building have a cafeteria, with tablecloths and utensils, to avoid the "not very agreeable spectacle" of workers eating in the fields or streets near the mill, using only the "poor containers" in which people carried their lunches. Explicitly, this recreational center would help to create workers in the image of their employers. They too would learn respectable forms of leisure, proper ways of eating and cleaning themselves, and how to regulate their interactions with others.

By providing a Christian atmosphere and healthful recreation, the Club Fabricato would also "counteract the communist ideas that soon may infiltrate and be propagated among our sound and carefully selected personnel."[36] Acutely conscious of the political change wrought by the Liberal Party's ascent and the newfound confidence of Colombian Socialists and Communists, and conscious also of events in the United States and Europe, Don Jorge argued for prevention. He may also have realized that, by 1933, even his "carefully selected" workforce included unionists. As he penned descriptions of his dreamed-of "club," a small group of male workers was organizing to test the provisions of a 1931 law granting the legality of workers' organizations.

Calling themselves the Fabricato Workers' Union, they informed Rudesindo and Ramón Echavarría, Jorge's brothers, of their existence in mid-October of 1933. Immediately, Rudesindo fought back with a petition "from the *empleados*' [meaning white-collar employees] and the *obreros* and *obreras*' of Fabricato." Typed in his office, the header denounced "the subversive activities of elements foreign to the factory" and enumerated the benefits extended by the company.[37] By late May 1934, however, the company's managers faced a surprising level of dissension, as strikers clashed with workers entering Fabricato during a citywide movement in solidarity with Antioquia's railroad workers. Rudesindo dashed off furious messages to Bogotá, demanding that the president guarantee "a commanding authority, implacable against delinquent citizens."[38] Meanwhile, he and Ramón adopted an obvious strategy; given that the 1931 law allowed parallel unions, the company simply organized another and denounced the first as a "black union."[39] As one retired worker explained,

> They [managers] founded what was called a "yellow union" against a "black union," which was against the factory. The ones who started [the "black" union] were men . . . they started going to the women, talking nice and sweet, to see who wanted to join . . . and so [the managers] called me to the office, because I wasn't in the "black" union, to see if I wanted to join the "yellow" union and they signed me right up. . . . When the "black" was finished, they gave us back the dues we'd been paying and the "yellow" finished too.[40]

Distinguishing this first company union from later incarnations, she added that "there weren't any priests, the 'black' [union] was founded by the workers and the other by the factory." Her reference is to 1944, when the factory chaplain, Father Damían Ramírez, preempted another organizing effort. The difference between Rudesindo's high-handedness in 1933 and his careful maneuvering in 1944 demonstrates the consolidation of a new managerial style, one more concerned with legal appearances and more committed to the doctrines of social Catholicism. It also demonstrates how easily the Echavarrías, by the 1940s, combined this new style with an old-fashioned union-busting.

Beginning in 1942, as Alfonso López campaigned for a second presidency, raising unionists' hopes for a return to the "Revolution on the March," Rudesindo became aware of this second organizing effort, an underground movement to organize Fabricato workers into the textile union of the Fedeta. Although weakened by divisions on the left of the Liberal Party and by the Popular Front policies of the Communist Party, the radicalism of the Fedeta terrified Antioqueño industrialists. Supervisors at Fabricato circulated a loyalty oath that seemed to pinpoint the activists: twelve hundred workers signed immediately, but the page for the all-male dyeing room came back blank.[41] Tensions ran high over the following two years, with workers claiming they'd been fired for union activity and Fabricato's lawyer insisting to the labor inspector that they only dismissed the likely perpetrators of specific acts of sabotage: cut cylinders, the disappearance of small tools, urination in the workrooms.[42]

In July of 1944 President López suffered an attempted coup and halfheartedly moved to consolidate his support with pro-labor decrees, including a prohibition on parallel unions (decree 2350 of 1944).[43] Only by moving quickly could the company manage to turn this to its advantage; the company union would have to pre-date anything put together by left-leaning workers. As Fabricato's lawyer put it in a summary he prepared for Medellín's labor inspector,

> Given the issuance of decree 2350 of this year, a group of workers . . . had the idea to organize a factory union, to which workers would belong and which would fight for just goals and by just means, and which would also avoid the organization of a communist union because of the express prohibition against parallel unions.

The lawyer explained that this "group of workers" constituted themselves as a union on 18 October, notified the inspector's office the same day, and received legal recognition (*personería jurídica*) by order of the government ministry on 4 November, an order that was published in the Diario Oficial on 7 November.[44] The dates mattered, of course. The Fedeta-affiliated union had begun the process of seeking legal recognition; electing officers and obtaining a formal letter from the regional labor inspector—dated 6 November. Two days earlier, Fabricato had begun dismissing workers the company claimed not to need, including the newly elected union president. Through mid-November, Fedeta organizers held weekend meetings with Fabricato workers at a public school in Bello. To the activists, 1944 seemed a replay of the clash between "black" and "yellow." "Have we forgotten the experience of 1934?" asked a handbill; "today they don't call us *Sindicato Negro*, but they do call us Communists, by which they seek to do the same as before: to divide and defeat all of us."[45] Other workers, too, drew the same distinction as they had in 1934—between the "union of the street" and the "union of the company."[46] Their phrasing was doubly accurate, given that Fabricato systematically fired union activists and their supporters. As María Cristina Restrepo put it, "the ones who signed up ended up in the street."[47]

All of the workers' handbills cited decree 2350 as their protection. The inspector would impartially determine which was the true union; "Don't be afraid," they insisted, "the government protects and supports us!"[48] Workers were likely unconvinced. That appeal had been more persuasive during López's first presidency (1934–38), when politicized workers at Coltejer and Rosellón could believe that the Liberal Party had more to gain from neutrality than from supporting industrialists. By the middle of his second term, however, López had stopped flirting with populism. Indeed, he was forced to resign in the face of opposition from not only the Conservatives but also the military and power-brokers within his own party. Apart from the unpropitious political situation, even those workers sympathetic to the "street" union probably judged Fedeta activists incapable of mobilizing the workforce. The company had made the choice a clear one: between religion and communism and for or against Fabricato. "The *patrones* started to make lists," one woman explained to the sociologist Luz Gabriela Arango,

> and almost everyone signed up, they told us it was a barrier to communism . . . and that's the way it was. Seems like some workers did get suspended, fired for having participated in the other union. [But] we were all very happy with the [company] union, we stayed together with the company.[49]

A person might sign for both unions, either to disguise the disloyalty or because she or he were naive enough to imagine that managers would not find out who had signed in support of Fedeta. But managers did find out, and supporting the "street" union meant risking a confrontation with a superior. Celina Báez Amado, for example, remembered that she and several friends, all of whom lived at the factory dormitory, had secretly signed for the *sindicato de la calle*, after a co-worker "got our hopes up." "I don't know how our signatures turned up over there [at the office]," she added, remembering the consternation of the nuns who oversaw the dormitory: "The Mother Superior, she was so angry, she wanted to fire us!" Insisting that they had been "tricked" and that they hadn't understood what it was all about, Celina and her friends kept their jobs.[50] Because the purpose of the "company" union was to convince workers that they owed Fabricato a direct and individual kind of loyalty, one's apparent contrition sufficed to prevent immediate dismissal.

In 1934 the "yellow union" had lasted only as long as its challenger, but this second company union would endure through the 1990s—strengthened by a countrywide, church-sponsored organizing drive. More than a company union, Fabricato's Sindicato Textil del Hato became a standard-bearer for anticommunism and for the newly organized Catholic labor central, the Jesuit-led Unión de Trabajadores Colombianos (UTC).[51] The change was ideological. Unlike the puppet union of 1934, which Ramón Echavarría had simply dissolved when it had served its purpose, the reorganized Catholic unions of the UTC spoke on workers' behalf. Through the 1940s and 1950s, the Sindicato Textil del Hato gave workers a safe way to voice complaints: that it was time for a cost-of-living increase, that a new piecework system seemed unfair, or that workers hated the company doctor—who they said barely examined them, didn't bother to change needles, and disrespected female workers.[52] Juan Cadavid, president of the pro-company union, provides a precise illustration of the powers of negotiation (however limited) that workers gained by adherence to anticommunism and by a willingness to inform on their fellows. In 1949 he indicated to Fabricato's general administrator that workers wanted shifts to be rotated, as they were at Fabricato's nearby subsidiary, the Fábrica de Bello. Warning that "many workers" had approached the union about the matter, Cadavid wrote:

> The Union had not wanted, as yet, to make an appeal on behalf of the workers' requests, but given that workers in the different workrooms are signing their names to the petition . . . we wish to move forward and to ask that your office be so good as to study the question with a view to its solution.
>
> It will not escape the Señor Administrator that it is of the utmost importance that the Union handle such labor-related questions. . . . Although it is true that they are respectful, and to our minds have not begun anything serious, the ringleaders who today are preparing petitions and collecting signatures may tomorrow take more serious initiatives.

Even if it were evidently a "yellow union," workers used the Sindicato Textil del Hato to make claims on the new paternalistic compact that its very existence implied. This gave workers only a small space for maneuver, but not even a company union could risk becoming a laughingstock. The union president stated it plainly: "Naturally, the workers want this entity to serve them in some way."[53]

Catholic Moralism

Just as it gave workers some leverage with bosses, anticommunism helped Catholic unionists open a space for dialogue within the UTC. Catholic unions, to work, had to defend workers' interests at least as well as "communist" ones, or so one could argue. In 1948, the president of the pro-Conservative Antioqueño branch of the UTC complained to the archbishop that his organization failed to represent workers, and similar complaints resurfaced through the 1950s, both in Medellín's base unions and at the national level.[54] Catholic unionism derived from the corporatist, quasi-fascist vision of an international church shaken by the specter of communism, but it also contained the seeds of later Catholic progressivism.

At the local level, Catholic unions and the priests who organized them were visibly connected to the employers. Since the first decades of industrialism in Medellín, clergymen appeared in the mills when employers requested their presence. Whether they were there to hang a painting of the Sacred Heart, to inaugurate a new building, or to officiate at a grand festival, they were careful to emphasize workers' obligations and the mill-owners' goodness. In 1932, at Coltejer's all-day celebration of its twenty-fifth anniversary, the invited priest said mass in a specially decorated section of the factory, with not only workers but also owners of various other mills, "matrons and young ladies of society," and a smattering of journalists in attendance. He took as his theme "the good merits that grace Don Alejandro Echavarría," the company's founder, and "the Christian life of workers who follow God's law, bending themselves over the loom, and who distance themselves from odious propaganda and from those who ignore the natural categories that God imposes on a Christian society."[55]

Significantly, such events took place at the workplace itself. Rather than promoting Catholicism as already practiced in Medellín's working-class neighborhoods and the small towns of the surrounding region, industrialists sought to connect religiosity to factory labor. At Fabricato in 1926, for example, Jorge Echavarría fired twenty-two workers who had attended the *fiestas* for the patron saint of Bello—after having warned all employees that work should come first. Yet he worked hard to ensure that all the workers attended a week of religious exercises at the mill, joining the Patronato's campaign to promote regular, factory-sponsored religious retreats.[56] As Alberto Mayor Mora has argued, mill-owners in Medellín attempted to graft a puritan work ethic onto the local stem of Catholicism.[57]

As the companies expanded to include chapels, schools, and the parishes

Llegada del Santísimo
al Club *Fabricato*

Mayo 8 de 1938

From Fabricato's commemorative album. Original caption: "Arrival of the image of our Lord," 8 May 1938. Photographer unknown, reproduction by Fernando Garcés and Foto Garcés. Courtesy of Fabricato.

Father Juan Bautista Bedoya, at Sunday lecture, Fabricato, 1940s. Photographer unknown, reproduction by Fernando Garcés and Foto Garcés. Courtesy of Fabricato.

represented by workers' neighborhoods, their upper-level managers formalized their relationships with priests. In 1940, Fabricato contracted the company's first regular chaplain, charged with combating "the danger, as much Protestant as Communist, that has our workers under siege."[58] The Echavarrías enumerated his duties carefully. Whoever served as chaplain should be "friendly with all the personnel," interesting himself in whatever problems they faced at home. He should celebrate mass at "convenient hours" and be careful to establish hours for Confession "in accordance with the different work shifts." Apart from his regular Sunday duties, he was expected to organize monthly "spiritual retreats" and formal religious exercises each year, as well to deliver moral lectures during the week.[59] The first priest hired failed to impress Fabricato's managers, and they denounced his "laziness," saying that he never left his company-provided house except to engage in activities unconnected to his labors. Although the chaplain in question defended himself angrily, the company had him dismissed and got Father Ramírez in his place.[60] The resident chaplain worked "for" the mill-owners; they paid the regional church for his services and evaluated his conduct. When Father Ramírez was reassigned in 1945, the Echavarrías intervened at the highest level, but to no avail. Fabricato lost the priest that the company afterward eulogized as "the founder of the Union, its soul and guiding spirit."

By the time Ramírez left Fabricato, the Organización Católico-Social Arquidiocesana (OCSA), which he had worked to build, had assumed an institutional role that paralleled the largest firms: it provided medical services for workers affiliated with the Unión de Trabajadores de Antioquia (UTRAN), began financing workers' housing, and operated recreational programs out of community centers maintained by Coltejer and Fabricato, as well as in neighborhoods built by Noel (the country's largest producer of packaged snacks), Pepalfa (knit goods), Indulana (woolens), and others.[61]

As coproducers of propaganda, OCSA and the city's large firms developed a mutually convenient symbiosis. Catholic Social Action's primary organ, *El Obrero Católico*, ran reports on the activities of company unions alongside moralistic exhortations, and the paper's circulation expanded together with company-based forms of paternalism. By the early 1950s, *El Obrero Católico* had a modern look, with comics and articles on health and hobbies, juxtaposed with didactic pieces. When the companies organized an interindustrial league, the weekly paper expanded to include sports pages—focusing especially on company teams.[62] For their part, company-produced magazines included innumerable moral reminders and eulogies to the peace provided by religious observance; Fabricato's *Gloria*, for example, described the company chapel as a place of "gentle silence," in contrast to the "fruitful noise" of the looms, "where the sainted Host is daily elevated and where workers come, in hours of rest, to prostrate themselves on bended knee and give thanks to God for the blessing of work."[63]

Nevertheless, the links between religion and millwork would not have appeared to workers only or even primarily as a strategy of co-optation and repression. Priests represented an irreducible moral authority. For parents whose daughters worked in the mills, the chaplain's presence, joined to the *vigilantas'* watchfulness, could persuade them that the girls' honor would not be jeopardized by long hours in mixed-sex rooms. As María Clara Henao remembered,

> At home, they didn't want us to work, they wanted only the men to work. . . . It was necessity, the situation and everything . . . but Fabricato was beautiful, a beautiful place to work. It had a chaplain whose job it was to check the workrooms. . . . This chaplain, his job was to go by each machine, to give advice, counseling, and if you had to confess, you confessed.[64]

Other retired women described the chaplain's comforting presence without mentioning their parents. Celina Báez remembered that he generally appeared in the evenings, "checking on *la moral*." "He'd show up there . . . just for a moment, and he'd say hello and go on by, no more than that," she said. Concha Bohórquez guessed that the priest had a special permit from the administrator, since no one could enter the mill without one. Or, she said, he may not have needed one, as priests "back then" wore the traditional cassock. In either case, her way of explaining his comings and goings clearly distinguished the chaplain from management as such; his role concerned *la moral*, not production.[65]

The priest heard Confession at the mill, but it remained Confession, a ritual conversation in which workers trusted the priest not to reveal certain kinds of secrets. Similarly, priests circulated in working-class neighborhoods in ways that separated them from the mill-owners. A well-liked priest, like Ramírez, appeared in workers' lives not only as an intercessor vis-à-vis the company but also as a spiritual adviser whose counsel might be sought for a range of problems unconnected with work. Apart from his work with the company union or his role as a moral overseer, the factory chaplain was a man empowered to say mass, give Communion, baptize one's child: practices that transcended the factory.

The image of the Sacred Heart of Jesus, similarly, could never be a uni-dimensional sign of workers' duty to their employer. Since the 1920s, advocates of Catholic Social Action had worked with industrialists to place the image of the Sacred Heart in each of the city's new workrooms. For Alberto Mayor Mora, the icon's appearance marks the emergence of an almost Methodist sense that "God is watching me," a terrifying reminder of the virtue of hard work.[66] But workers may also have seen a symbol of the Lord's protection and of the importance of Christian behavior—in whatever sphere. Workers themselves would have "enthroned" the image in a ceremonial procession, with school girls, flags, and decorated floats; symbolically it was an intervention from outside the factory gate.[67] The Sacred Heart represented a force far beyond that of the mill-owner, which was precisely why an industrialist might want to associate his power and workers' duty to work with that larger power and larger duty. Nevertheless, the force of belief was never wholly "his." Both before and after the public *entronizaciones* of religious images in the 1920s and 1930s, workers carried their own religious imaginations to work.

The real strength of company unions like the Sindicato Textil del Hato, and of Antioqueño paternalism more generally, lay precisely in this ability to build on loyalties beyond the workplace. As Gramsci argued so persuasively, class hierarchy gains legitimacy by its links to a system of values that transcends class. In Colombia, patriotism never assumed the importance it held in Europe, nor did it become so clearly tied to anticommunism as in the United States. Regional pride (*Antioqueñidad*) and invocations of "progress" emerged in anticommunist rhetoric, but they never provided its central anchor. That anchor was *la moral*. Metaphorically, the battle was not between communism and the time-honored hierarchies of class; it was between impiety and faith, lasciviousness and chastity, sinfulness and *la moral*.

By the 1940s, *la moral* defined industrial paternalism in Medellín. Omnipresent, the phrase coursed through the pages of stockholders' reports; through sermons in working-class neighborhoods; and through workers' calculations about the benefits of one employer versus another. In a wide range of discursive contexts, *la moral* appeared where, in the initial decades of the industry, an owner's personal reputation would have been invoked. Now that the mills were too large to be managed by an owner's son or young cousin, someone whose good breeding could provide an aura of respectability, that necessary respectability had to be symbolically produced. Given a quarter-century of debate over the sexual danger faced by *la mujer obrera* and given a population of parents unwilling to compromise their daughters' moral reputations, the new emphasis on morality had a very specific meaning. Religion was linked to the world of work in the same way that Catholic theology was tied to everyday life: the unquestioned "rightness" of female virginity.

Virginity and the Factory "Family"

Just as in an honorable household, women in Coltejer are the focus of the most attention. . . . While a sister is virtuous, her brothers feel pride and her parents are content at having called her to this life. In contrast, there is no home more filled with gloom, more undone, than one in which a woman's virtue is lacking . . .

The only remedy found to date against so great an evil is the grace of God. The woman that loves and fears him carries her virginity in a better custody than if she were under armed guard both day and night . . . but humans have another great remedy, and that is work. The woman who knows sweat and sacrifice and privation because she earns her family's daily bread has to be very good. And the man has to be very evil that would convert her into the object of everyone's scorn, a laughingstock, a disgrace, the shame of all that loved her.

Our workers know how to be gentlemen with their *compañeras* . . . every honorable workman knows he should be a protector toward all of his *compañeras* and a guardian of their dignity, which is the dignity of the factory . . .

Everything belonging to Coltejer is of little worth in comparison to the virtue of our girls. This is superior to the buildings, the machines, the company's shares. If they ever think that one of their workmates is in danger, her *compañeras* should help her, should surround and support her, with the same zeal that men would use in extinguishing a fire.[68]

This 1945 editorial from Coltejer's *Lanzadera* captures perfectly the tone of factory-produced propaganda about female virginity; it also traces the ideological background to the mills' ban on "immoral" women. Mill-workers' families find their extension in the company; working girls find God's grace in their daily labors and in the wages they bring home to their parents. To an extent, the rhetoric matches that of textile capitalists in other parts of the world, who similarly presented their establishments as being "like a family" and as the mainstay of workers' families.[69] Where Coltejer's propaganda surprises is in the vehemence of its association between chastity and capital. Any danger to an *obrera*'s virginity, in this vision, poses a material threat to the mill. Alongside "the buildings, the machines, the company's shares," the "virtue" of female employees is part of the means of production—so much so that *Lanzadera*'s editors compare unchastity to the consuming power of fire.

Coltejer's publicists did not exaggerate. Within the combined logics of anticommunism and Catholic moralism, working girls' virginity *was* a form of capital. It ensured the stability of patriarchal authority—symbolically and materially. The family model could not work well as a mechanism of control if patriarchal relations did not have a disciplinary meaning in workers' own lives. How could industrialists preach obedience to fatherly male authority while at the same time providing young women with the means to support themselves independently of male authority?

Insisting on female employees' total chastity and presenting the factory as their protector solved the logical problem of this disciplinary model. If women worked only while they were virgins, they remained daughters under the authority of a factory-as-father and could be represented as girls awaiting marriage rather than women who might live independently of the family system. This was a family-based, patriarchal logic rather than a set of injunctions applied only to females. Women who became pregnant were dismissed without ceremony, but male workers could also be fired for "immorality." Former workers insisted on this point. Bárbara Alzate de López, who had worked at Rosellón before marrying Enrique, used the same phrasing as dozens of other women and men that I interviewed: "Right away, she was out! And if her boyfriend was from [the mill], he was out too . . . they went looking for the boyfriend and he was out!"[70]

As befitted their representation as "daughters," women who became pregnant or who had "strayed" from *la moral* were questioned by the mill manager. Assuming an avuncular persona, María Cristina Restrepo summarized what he might say: "Look here, what happened to you!? What cliff did you throw yourself off? You'll do me the favor of telling me the story!" She continued in her own voice: "and if she didn't want the person fired, she wouldn't say that it was someone from the factory but instead that it was an individual person [*que era un particular*]—but she was out in the street!" Retired workers either recalled this as a generalized story, or they described what had happened to an acquaintance or, less often, a friend (in one woman's case, her sister). Personnel records tell the same stories in a slightly different way. A woman's file might include a note that "she left because of a pregnancy," or that she had received "the severance pay and bonus that she was entitled to because of her pregnancy and dismissal." Or nothing at all—she may have quit the mill before anyone found out why.[71] Where factory archives provide more detail is on male reactions. Mario Vásquez demanded a special hearing after he was fired for "seducing" a woman working under his direction, claiming that,

> Yes, he had had relations with the worker Margarita Castaño, but he was not the one that had dishonored said operative, it being that the girl in question had given herself easily and for some time now to various men.[72]

Based on this time-honored logic, the regional labor inspector opened an investigation, calling in workers from the same section and questioning Castaño herself, who, according to the inspector, maintained that she "had given in to Vásquez's insinuations once," but that she had lost her virginity some time previously, with another man. Whether she said this sadly or defiantly was irrelevant to the inspector; together with Fabricato's lawyer, who also questioned Castaño, he was concerned only about the history of her virginity. Thus the fact that men were also fired did not mean the absence of a double standard at Fabricato and Coltejer; rather, it helps to pinpoint the meaning of the mills' moralistic practice. Symbolically, female workers were unmarried daughters. Their sexual activity brought dishonor, and required their expulsion—no matter the circumstances. Male workers faced dismissal only if they disrespected a woman respected at the mill, an "obrera señorita," as the manager at Fábrica de Bello put it in the case of another man's complaint to the inspector.[73]

Fabricato's Patronato

By symbolically making their mills "families," especially Catholic families, Antioqueño industrialists made themselves into fathers whose reputations could be damaged by their daughters' and sons' misbehavior—or enhanced by their honorable comportment. Indeed, the best example of patriarchal practice in Medellín's textile workplaces, clearer even than factory-produced propaganda or the expulsion of "immoral" workers, was Fabricato's dormitory for unmarried working girls. By providing daughters with a visible and carefully regulated "home," modeled on the Jesuit-run Patronato of twenty years previous, the company established its reputation for "social labors" and conformity to "evangelical doctrine."[74]

Jorge Echavarría initiated the building of his dreamed-of Club Fabricato in

1933, during the celebration of Fabricato's tenth anniversary. He laid the first stone in a ceremony followed by "beer, milk, games, and dancing . . . until 8:00 P.M."[75] By the time it opened in 1938, however, the Club Patronato had developed in a different direction than the one he had outlined in his letter to the stockholders. Although it housed a cafeteria, game rooms (one for male and another for female workers), and a billiard table that male workers could rent by the hour, Fabricato's showcase building had become less like the workers' country club he imagined and more like a girls' school or convent. Within a few years, more than two hundred girls, or *internas*, lived in its dormitory—each paying a moderate weekly fee for rent and cafeteria meals. Their daily schedule and the rules they lived by were set not by the company but by the Hermanas de la Presentación, nuns from the community that managed the citywide Patronato described in chapter 2. Indeed, Fabricato's managers occasionally despaired at the nuns' strictness. During its first year, for example, the Mother Director disallowed a company-sponsored mixed dance at the Patronato, even though the organizing committee had proposed that this wholesome "distraction" take place there precisely so that the nuns' presence would deter any immorality.[76] Later, in the 1940s, women living at the Patronato were barred from attending even company-sponsored dances at the mill itself.[77] A party like the one Echavarría had thrown to inaugurate the Club Patronato (with beer) would likely have been equally suspect.

Like company boardinghouses in Lowell, Massachusetts, Fabricato's Patronato was meant to allay parents' fears that a daughter's employment in the mill would spell her moral downfall.[78] "Because your parents were such fuss-budgets" (*como eran tan sismáticos los papás de uno*) was how Carolina Arango explained it. She remembered that her mother agreed to let her and a sister start at Fabricato only because a wealthy couple, relatives of the Echavarrías, described the Patronato and assured her the girls would live there, "with the nuns."[79] Another small-town girl, Esperanza Hernández, was sent to live with an aunt in Bello when she got a job at Fabricato; soon, however, the aunt dispatched her to the Patronato, saying that Esperanza was too *avispada*, too outgoing, and that she couldn't take responsibility for her. Acting in loco parentis, Fabricato provided "a new home" for girls who had left their families to work in the city, one that furnished a degree of moral protection often not available within working-class households.[80] Additionally, this "new home" trained *internas* for the day they would marry and manage their own (urban) homes. The Club Patronato offered evening classes in domestic arts, cooking, simple sewing, dressmaking, and needlework, as well as in music, crafts, and even English. Women who left to start their own families were celebrated as part of the company's success story; an anniversary album includes lists of "the young graduates of the Patronato who today form exemplary homes," along with photographs of former *internas* holding well-fed babies.[81] Similarly celebrated were seventeen who had left to take religious vows; their photographs appeared alongside the young wives.[82] Quite apart from the fact that jobs at Fabricato allowed hundreds of women to contemplate a future as wage earners, and that hundreds did, in fact, reach retirement in the mill, the Patronato celebrated a vision of femininity incompatible with prolonged factory labor. As an institution, it was designed to demonstrate (to parents, reformers, and workers themselves) that Fabricato's female employees worked while awaiting marriage, and that while they worked they remained chaste and marriageable. The reassuring stability of the Patronato lay in its evocation of a preindustrial, home-centered gender ideology, in which the only formal alternative to marriage was convent life.

Photographs in the anniversary album show the dormitory organized according to an institutional, orphanage-like aesthetic: rows of identical beds, a separate room with dressers for each worker to store her clothes, and special spaces for washing and ironing.[83] The women followed a set routine, with daily chores and formal religious observance, and were expected to leave the Patronato directly for the factory and to return immediately after their shift. "We'd get up at four in the morning to hear mass . . . we'd hear mass, have breakfast, and go to work," recalled Esperanza Hernández. Shifts rotated, and those who went to work later did chores at the Patronato, cleaning and doing their washing and ironing. The women would have done similar work at home or in rented rooms, but the institution's control over the time and space of leisure made chores at the Patronato rather different. For example, Esperanza remembered the dormitory as "very pretty," explaining that "they wouldn't let anyone come in the dormitory during the day, all the beds [stayed] made right up." Like other women, she praised the orderly neatness but resented not being able to lie down after a long shift. Talking later about the difference it made to move out of the Patronato and rent a house with friends, she emphasized the pleasure of daytime naps: "We would rest, we would lie down . . . it was very different, very different." Living on their own, she said, they also did less housework; keeping a small house to their own satisfaction was a simpler affair than cleaning a huge dormitory to the nuns' standards.[84]

More than other women employed at Fabricato, *internas* faced strict regulation of their behavior and appearance. They were expected to arrive back at the Patronato directly after their shifts and to ask for permission before going anywhere. Acceptable outings included walking up to the town square to shop for small items (in daylight hours) or visiting relatives, but newly arrived *internas* could leave only with a slightly older girl as a chaperone. Even company-sponsored dances might be declared impermissible, especially if they were held at night.[85] No matter where she was going, a woman's

Sewing class at Fabricato's Patronato, 1955. Photograph by Gabriel Carvajal. Courtesy of Fotos Carvajal.

dress required scrutiny; the nuns also checked to be sure nobody wore an inappropriate amount of makeup. As in girls' schools in Medellín in the same period, hemlines were dangerous boundaries.[86] A woman who left the Patronato with a skirt that threatened to show her knees risked having the hem cut out by one of the nuns. "They put my hem down once," recounted Celina Báez, "oh yes, with these little scissors that they carried; [one of the nuns] just opened me up [laughing]. . . . I had to run and change quick, because it was time for my shift."[87] Carolina Arango emphasized the public character of the humiliation, saying, "I was one who used to wear my skirts here [gesturing to her knee]; the Mother Director would come and it was 'you'll do me the favor,' *Pun!* In front of everyone!"[88] Yet to judge from the number of women who told such stories, *internas* commonly shortened their hemlines, testing the limit imposed by the nuns' scissors.

The Patronato combined a parental function with moral policing most clearly in its regulation of *internas'* relationships with boyfriends and potential suitors. On Sundays, the cafeteria was converted into a collective parlor for courtship. Assuming that the young man had asked prior permission of the Mother Director and that the young woman were not being punished for having been out without permission at any time the previous week, a couple could converse under the watchful eyes of the nuns and of their peers. When I asked Carolina if she had a *novio* (boyfriend) while at the Patronato, she replied that she had and that he often visited her there.

Ann: What was that like?

Carolina: No! It was awful! You'd sit there, it was a huge room; all the girls sitting there, with their boyfriends, like this—a little separated-like: this one sat by the door, that one over here. It was all separated, but everyone was there. And the nuns walking up and down . . . no sweetheart, were we chaperoned? Until we had it up to here![89]

In supplying female chaperones—nuns at the Patronato and *vigilantas*, who tended to be older and widowed, in the workrooms—Fabricato pursued a very literal paternalism. The company presented itself as a father figure, by protecting an *obrera*'s virginity and by overseeing suitors' visits. A girl who married from the Patronato was symbolically "given" by Fabricato rather than by her parents, especially if she were orphaned or her parents lived far in the countryside. In a way that went beyond the rhetoric of appreciation in managers' speeches about the "Familia Fabricato" and beyond the propaganda of honor seen in *Lanzadera*'s editorial, the company's role in policing the sexual activity of its "daughters" made it symbolically a patriarchal family.

As in all families, however, the world beyond the household limited parental authority. Women living at the Patronato found ways to see male friends "in the street," a phrase that retired women use to mean both "outside the mill gates" and "outside the Patronato." Lucía Botero explained that "you always managed to scare up a boyfriend":

If you were going out to buy a bar of soap to wash with, and so you saw him. [Or you said] that you were going to see a relative or over to a friend's . . . and really it was because you did your flirting there—so one always had conversations here and there—but woe to you if you got caught talking outside! *Novios* were always supposed to ask permission.[90]

Her own strategy had been to get permission to go to an aunt's house and having her *novio*, who also worked at Fabricato, meet her there. Other women dared more—or at least claimed more in recounting their exploits. When I asked what she'd done during off-hours, Carolina Arango turned first to her memories of the more worldly girls from Medellín, especially those from the working-class neighborhoods of Manrique and Aranjuez. "*Ya sabían el rodaje*" (They knew the ropes), she said, explaining that they went to dance halls: "the bold ones, and the oldest ones, where they'd go was out dancing . . . to party, and many times they drank." They would come back laughing and making fun, telling the more obedient ones what a good time they'd had. Carolina, at least, had listened in awe, and she told the story by contrasting their outings to her own:

They'd get permission, saying they were going such-and-such a place, and afterward they'd come and be laughing and saying: "Oh! The things that happened to us yesterday!" "Ay! At that place, didn't we have a great time dancing though?!" "Ay! What if the nuns—" They'd say: "What if the nuns found out? We'll get fired!" We'd listen to them talk, since we were that much younger, and we were from the country—No! To hear them talk, they were very bold!

The most we could do was to go to up to the plaza for a bit . . . to walk around the park, that was very fine . . . we'd go and see a movie or something. They also showed movies at the Patronato, good ones; they did a lot of things there, get-togethers, everything, and they let us dance on Sundays—but only women by themselves. So boring! Ay! But that was the way things were done.[91]

Carolina's and Lucía's memories, like former *internas'* anecdotes about taking up their hems, serve as reminders of the incompleteness of the story told by formal regulations and industrialists' pronouncements. Fabricato's rigid moral vision cannot be taken as descriptive. Rather, the company's strict insistence on rules is itself evidence of the existence of possibilities and realities not governed by the rules, from the dreamed-of excitement of unchaperoned dancing to the feared consequences of rape. The company demanded chastity, but women nevertheless turned up pregnant—often enough for pregnancies, miscarriages, and cases of successful concealment to be commonly remembered by retired workers, as described in chapter 7.

Beauty Contests and Company Festivals

Given this insistence on female chastity, together with the omnipresence of religious icons in factory workrooms, local observers routinely compared Fabricato to a convent.[92] The analogy is extended to Coltejer, Rosellón, and Tejidos de Bello, since these mills also required that women workers be either virgins or respectable widows. Stories like Lucía's and Carolina's, however, cut against the grain of that representation. The mills remained thoroughly secular environments, where piety, modesty, and an internalized vision of *la moral* coexisted with constant low-level indiscipline and workers' skepticism. At Fabricato, for example, cautious *internas* who rarely left the Patronato worked alongside "fast" girls from Manrique or Aranjuez; country-born girls like Celina shortened their hems to be more fashionable; and the general expectation was that female workers would be courted like other young women.

The analogy between Antioquia's mills and its convents breaks down even at the level of the industrialists' vision. As practiced by the Echavarrías of

Fabricato and Coltejer, Antioqueño paternalism included the ambiguities of a gender ideology that idealized both female modesty and young women's attractiveness. Through the 1940s and early 1950s, all of the large mills had annual beauty contests or *reinados*. The "queen" was supposed to be not only pretty but also a girl with an impeccable moral reputation.[93] Symbolically, the beauty contests paralleled the nuns' chaperoning role; they presented female operatives as marriageable maidens. Still feminine and still virginal, young women worked while awaiting marriage, or so went the message of the *reinados*; female labor thus posed no threat to a family-based gender system. Beauty contests would be unthinkable in a convent; in the world of the mills they acted to mark women's factory labor as a stage, a time before marriage, rather than an exit from women's roles as mothers and wives.

Workers themselves looked forward to the *reinados* and remembered them clearly; most could easily say who had been crowned "queen" and could describe the celebrations that accompanied the crowning of a *reina*. Often, the people I interviewed raised the topic themselves. "Do you know what?" said María Clara Henao, a woman who had worked at Fabricato before her marriage; "Do you know what they did in the factory that was really great? When we had a really good time? A Beauty Pageant. . . . We would choose the prettiest girl in the factory." Brushing aside my overly specific questions about who chose "the prettiest girl in the factory," she insisted that the *reinados* were workers' own celebrations and not something performed by or for management.

> Ann: Whose chose her?
> María Clara: The managers chose her, the administrators, the big people from the factory. They chose the queen and they gave us three days off—to celebrate her, to crown her; we had a really good time . . . we chose the queen.
> Ann: But, so, you also voted for her?
> María Clara: All of us, we were the workers; it wasn't for the white-collar employees.
> Ann: And did the white-collar employees vote?
> María Clara: The white-collar employees were in charge of the pageant, right? But we were the ones that enjoyed the pageant, we the workers.[94]

Reinados were fun. In the weeks beforehand, men and women from different parts of the mill chose someone to represent their section and campaigned for her victory. A 1946 photograph of candidates for the title "Queen of Tejicondor" shows twelve young women standing in front of the mill. Behind them, the side of the building is draped with messages of support: "Queen Isabel," "With Blanca to Victory!" and "Nelly will reign."[95] Gui-

From Fabricato's commemorative album. Original caption: "Queen Margarita," Fabricato, 1940s. Photographer unknown, reproduction by Fernando Garcés and Foto Garcés. Courtesy of Fabricato.

llermo Vélez remembered that, at Coltejer, "they'd pick the prettiest . . . and, obviously, as this or that one's workmate, you wanted what's-her-name to win."[96] The competition may have allowed a sanctioned sort of flirting—a public recognition of the teasing and sexual tension of mixed-sex workplaces. For women, vying for the title of *la más bonita*—or choosing her—likely also involved a desire for homosocial acceptance. However much they derived from the contradictions of patriarchal ideology, at another level the *reinados* were simple popularity contests.

Yet the *reinados* had a specific history of embeddedness within class relations in Medellín. In the late 1910s and early 1920s, socialists had organized celebrations of the first of May that included the acclamation of a young woman as "the flower of work." The title might go to a worker, like Teresa Acosta, who was named "*la flor del trabajo*" in 1924 and who was overcome with nervousness when asked to address the crowd, or to an activist like the Socialist orator María Cano, who was elected the following year.[97] Initially, industrialists had extended funds and letters of support for the first of May

From Fabricato's commemorative album. Procession honoring beauty queens. Photographer unknown, reproduction by Fernando Garcés and Foto Garcés. Courtesy of Fabricato.

celebrations; in 1919 the city's Socialist paper, *El Luchador*, thanked Coltejer's founder, Alejandro Echavarría, and Governor Pedro Nel Ospina, among others, for their backing of the festival—which the paper claimed had drawn six thousand workers. However, Catholic reformers like Father Lizardi and the young ladies of the board of directors of the city's first Patronato de Obreras saw "disadvantages" in the first of May festival. To combat the Socialist celebration, they organized a competing "festival of work" for 4 May. In 1925, with María Cano's notoriety added to the mix, the Patronato's board decided to enlist the help of "respectable industrialists" in a campaign to "contain the already advanced project of the '*Flor del Trabajo*,' which carries with it so many evils."[98]

Whether consciously or not, what the city's "respectable industrialists" did over the long run was to capture some of the appeal of crowning a "flower of work," a working-class sweetheart, through their own carefully orchestrated annual selections of factory "queens." The beauty contests were seamlessly incorporated within other company-sponsored holidays. Fabricato's twenty-year anniversary celebration, for example, included the *reinado* as the centerpiece of a ceremony that included speeches and prizes for loyal workers and was followed by a day of factory-sponsored recreation. The schedule of events planned for "the Fabricato Family" involved all of Bello in the anniversary celebration.

5 A.M.	Reveille. [A band] will go through the streets of Bello announcing the celebration.
6 A.M.	Mass, with Communion, for the souls of our departed companions.
6:30	Breakfast
8 A.M.	Mass (Father Ramírez)
9 A.M.	Coronation of the Queen
	Distribution of prizes awarded . . . to those who have collaborated in the company's success since its founding.
11 A.M.	Foot-ball game [Balón-pie]
12:30	Free Time
1:30	Continuous cinema at the IRIS theater . . . [The movie is titled Spring Bride]
2 P.M.	Basketball contest
3-6 P.M.	Music and Dancing [with prizes for the best couples].[99]

Company anniversaries, masses at Christmas and Easter, October processions for the month of the Virgin, First Communion ceremonies for workers' children: a huge variety of factory celebrations—like the beauty contests—combined anticommunism with festivity, Catholic observance, and gender symbolism. The presence of owners' own families reinforced the central message of such events, that the company was itself a kind of family. High-level employees and their wives attended company-sponsored masses and were seated at special tables during the ceremonial "breakfasts" served to workers after mass. At Fabricato, Rudesindo's wife, Alicia, brought Christmas baskets of gifts and sweets to pass out to workers and their families. She and her husband also presided over the slaughtering of hogs and the distribution of their meat, along with packets of cloth and pay bonuses.[100] Workers from the Rosellón mill, similarly, remember the annual festival of Saint Gertrude, which included raffles and prizes and the obligatory post-mass breakfast. Part of the purpose of such public displays was, in fact, their performative regularity and careful scripting—the fact that they went off flawlessly, with each group playing its part. Addressing himself to "the communist problem," Luis Echavarría evaluated the success of a company-sponsored celebration on 1 May 1944 by noting that it had been "pretty and orderly," especially the awards ceremony, and that "all the details went off perfectly"; he therefore judged the event to have had "a great psychological effect."[101]

Even at mills not owned by the Echavarría clan, public displays of paternalism occupied a central place in evocations of the factory as an extended family. Tejicondor hosted *reinados,* First Communion celebrations, and an annual *fiesta del compañerismo* which involved a prize for the "best *compañero.*" Similarly, at Telsa, whose Jewish owners sponsored considerably less paternalistic display, the annual *fiestas* of First Communion for workers' children were lavish affairs. A consensus on paternalistic practice had emerged to replace the idiosyncrasy and variation among different management styles documented by Inspector Vélez in the 1920s. In part, this increased homogeneity owed to a new corps of mid-level, white-collar employees—especially those hired to manage the details of paternalism: cafeteria managers, coaches for company sports teams, the female social workers who, by the early 1950s, each of the mills hired to visit workers in their homes. Such people knew their counterparts at other mills. By the late 1940s, with thirty thousand people in industrial jobs and ten thousand at Coltejer and Fabricato, Medellín's paternalistic companies constituted a world within themselves and one that set a tone for class and gender relations throughout the city.

Fábricas Alcahuetas

A caveat is necessary here: Tejicondor and Telsa accepted both married women and single women with children. They also offered fewer extra-wage benefits than Coltejer and Fabricato, and Telsa, which was smaller, dependent on wool, and earned less in profit than the big cotton producers, paid significantly lower wages. Seen from the—admittedly illusory—perspective of the statute books, Tejicondor and Telsa were the only large textile mills in Medellín not in outright violation of national labor law. Since 1924, Colombian law had required that factories employing more than fifty women establish day-rooms or *salas-cunas,* so that women could nurse their children during their shifts, a requirement met only (and only briefly) by Tejicondor.[102] An explicit prohibition against dismissing women who became pregnant had been on the books since 1938, as discussed in chapter 1. However, the women and men I interviewed dated legal protections for pregnant women from the late 1950s, whether they supported the change or were suspicious of it. They accurately perceived Tejicondor's and Telsa's more lenient policies— which had their own arbitrarily imposed limits in practice—as a variation in management procedure that bore no relation to formal legislation.[103]

Rather than limiting the illegal discrimination against "immoral" women (and men) at Coltejer and Fabricato, the fact that other mills hired such women helped to consolidate the Echavarrías' moral legitimacy as employers. Moreover, it divided female textile workers into those who worked at mills known for their strict discipline and so were by definition chaste and morally respectable, on the one hand, and those who, at a minimum, had co-workers who "ran around." Gumercinda Báez Amado worked at Telsa but lived with her sister Celina in Fabricato's San José neighborhood. There, she said, they called the bus that picked up Telsa workers "the milk truck," a joke on Telsa's nursing mothers—most of them unmarried—who may have formed only a portion of Telsa's workforce but who would never have been permitted to keep jobs at Fabricato.[104] Cristina Monsalve, a retiree from Rosellón, where strict moral rules were enforced even before the mill was acquired by Coltejer in 1942, expressed the same disdain more caustically: Tejicondor and Telsa, she said, had been "factories of tolerance" (*fábricas alcahuetas*).[105]

Although workers who had reached retirement at Telsa or Tejicondor resented such snobbishness (just as Gumercinda's earlier self had winced at her neighbors' remarks), most subscribed to its basic premise: that employees' sexual lives redounded to a factory's credit or discredit. Both mills had an unwritten rule that an unmarried woman who had more than three children "by then was a whore," as Tejicondor's *gerente* phrased it.[106] Workers shared in this discourse. María Concepción López matter-of-factly described having had a child "by lottery . . . before getting married, understand?" She also complained bitterly that "the Echavarrías are real hypocrites." Yet María Concepción expressed her dislike of specific co-workers, other women at Telsa, by calling them "*concubinas*" (concubines) or "*vagabundas*" (tramps) and insisting that "don't you see, they have no respect for the *factory*?"[107]

As I argue in chapter 7, hearing such seemingly contradictory descriptions in interviews has helped me understand how fluidly women and men move between normative and practical understandings of gender. A hint of this can be gleaned from the way most retired people described the more lenient mills: "As long as she knew how to work," they said, a woman could get a job at Telsa or Tejicondor. María Concepción always phrased things colorfully: "You know, no matter how much of a tramp she was, she could work there, as long as she knew how to work."[108] The description took apart what the Echavarrías and other advocates of Catholic paternalism had tied together: sexual respectability and being a "good worker."

Conclusion

A focus on the disciplinary ideology of *la moral* provides a means of assessing the role of gender in the particular brand of industrial paternalism developed by Medellín's big textile firms. Through the late 1930s and early 1940s, the mills expanded dramatically, employing thousands rather than hundreds of workers and requiring multiple layers of supervisory personnel. Printed work rules and formal systems of hiring took the place of the directives and *regaños* of Don Jorge, Don Eduardo, or Don Emilio. Seeking to maintain a symbolic connection with workers, a new generation of industrialists—particularly the younger Echavarrías of Fabricato and Coltejer—developed an intensely familial discourse, anchored by their claim to act as protective "fathers" for the young women and men they hired. Vis-à-vis men, this claim involved a willingness to extend material benefits to workers' wives and children; vis-à-vis women, it involved the "protection" of workers' reputations through the strict exclusion of unmarried mothers. Gender anchored factory discipline not so much through the separation of women and men, as hierarchically ordered sexes, but more through the policing of a symbolic divide between proper and improper behavior. Men found their actions curtailed, as they were forced to observe factory rules about how to treat female co-workers, but the link between gender ideology and industrial paternalism in Medellín was effected through behavioral controls applied to female workers. Through this period, in which female and male operatives worked alongside one another, textile work was neither "women's work" nor "men's work." Rather, the well-paid jobs offered by Coltejer, Fabricato, the Fábrica de Bello, and Rosellón became jobs defined by their respectability, which meant that they were jobs for family men and for certain categories of women: good daughters, well-behaved *señoritas*, and honorable widows.

In the propaganda produced by Catholic activists, sexual comportment, hard work, and Catholicism were indissolubly joined to one another and to a higher good. This linkage was sometimes crassly manipulative, as in Fabricato's practice of posting slogans on factory walls, such as "To Work is to Pray" or "If you don't care to be honorable for virtue's sake, do it for expediency," but workers' involvement with *la moral* made it more than simply the language of the bosses.[109] Sexual honor and the respectability of public piety were integral aspects of many workers' understanding of themselves as members of a wider community. Alongside or above the direct propaganda of slogans were paintings of Christ, the Virgin, and the Sacred Heart of Jesus, with altars to which workers themselves brought flowers—for reasons that had little to do with factory discipline as such.

Furthermore, the ban on married women and on any heterosexual intercourse outside of marriage was an exclusion that many female wage-earners experienced as an opportunity. In Bello, a whole generation of women purchased their own modest row homes, sharing them with sisters or brothers or friends. If Celina Báez, for example, rejected all suitors to keep her job at Fabricato, she gained more than her employers' favor. She gained independence, her family's respect (since Celina paid most of the bills and educated her nieces and nephews), and a locally accepted "explanation" for her decision to live as an unmarried woman. Like others in her working-class neighborhood, she had her own reasons for dressing respectably, for praying in public settings, for remaining chaste (or for flouting any of those norms).

Taking either gender ideology or industrial paternalism seriously thus requires labor historians to move away from the language of discipline. Asking simply whether workers complied with or resisted workplace strictures will impede a more nuanced understanding of workers' ways of living the exploitative relations of waged labor. Accommodation to class hierarchy at work is necessarily interwoven with ideological structures, such as gender, that extend well beyond any given workplace. The reverse is also true: contestation was never only about the disciplinary hierarchies of the workplace. Workers who ignored or broke mill rules often did so in ways that cannot be called, a priori, forms of resistance. When young women found ways to evade nuns' eyes at Fabricato's Patronato, whether to go dancing in taverns or to meet a boyfriend on a Sunday afternoon, they did not do so as a protest against industrial discipline.

A final example may clarify this point even as it suggests the methodological problems of any attempt to reconstruct workers' subjectivity in alternative ways. As I did in all my interviews, I asked María Cristina Restrepo, a woman who worked twenty-nine years at Fabricato, about the factory *reinados*. She offered descriptions of the fun and festivities that accompanied the selection of a mill's *reina*, descriptions that matched what I had heard from others. In part, these were elicited by my way of framing the question (see below). But María Cristina's larger answer to my question took the form of a revealing story of scandal. What she immediately remembered was a woman who "wasn't fit" to be queen:

Ann: Did they [at Fabricato] also have *reinados,* like other kinds of recreation, like *reinados* or dances?

María Cristina: They had *reinados* almost all the time until one year [. . .] there was a pageant and it turned out that the girl wasn't fit [*no estaba data*], wasn't fit to be a queen, and it all ended right there.

Ann: That is, she wasn't? what?

María Cristina: ¡*No estaba data*!

Ann: Aaaahhh

María Cristina: Because she had lied. And when they found out, that she'd lied about what she was, well then it all went to pot. They fired a lot of people; many mechanics and even supervisors.

Ann: But why?

María Cristina: Because in a *reinado* you see everyone, there's dances, serenades and all that kind of thing . . . because it's not just you, it's this one yes and the other no. And so each one, the one that had ended up being queen, she went out and had a few drinks or whatever. When they found out that the one who'd ended up being queen, she had had a child . . . and a lot of people had known and they had declined to say anything at the factory; and so there's a [gesture],

Ann: A thing, a scandal.

María Cristina: A *tremendous* scandal.[110]

Listening to our voices on tape, I found myself unprepared to hear such a story. I knew that the beauty contests ceased sometime in the late 1950s, when the mills stopped hiring women altogether and industrialists no longer felt a need to resolve publicly the contradictions between the social categories of "woman" and "worker." Yet María Cristina's story posited a different causality; the factory owner ended the *reinados* because a woman was unchaste and because other workers had covered for her. That part of the story seemed to have no empirical base. The following chapter represents what I learned from odd stories like María Cristina's. The myriad, seemingly individual ways that workers complied with, upheld, evaded, or ignored the normative strictures of paternalistic discipline do not act as an obstacle to understanding gender and class in Medellín's mills. Rather, they provide, precisely in their variety, a key to understanding gender and class as on-the-ground relationships, as aspects of everyday practice rather than social abstractions.

SIX

La Moral in Practice,

1936–53

BELLO IS A COMPANY town, and the neighborhoods near Fabricato are full of retired operatives. On one small block I interviewed three women who had known one another as co-workers and neighbors for upwards of fifty years. Gregarious Zoila Rosa Valencia had insisted that I talk also to Ana Rita Arbeláez and Concha Bohórquez, her friends down the street. Concha was stout and healthy, with a terrific sense of humor. Ana Rita I remember vividly: a small, wrinkled woman with snow-white hair. What she most effectively communicated was her gratitude and affection for Fabricato and the Echavarrías. Don Rudesindo had even lent her a photograph of his brother Don Jorge, Ana Rita said, from which a nephew had done a painted portrait. The portrait figured prominently in a set of stories she told about the pride she had taken in being well respected at Fabricato. These included a complicated story about a "calumny" that had been raised against her when she had an abdominal tumor that people had begun to think might be a pregnancy; nothing could have been further than the truth, Ana Rita insisted. After I turned off the tape recorder she grabbed my hand and exclaimed that she was a virgin, "as pure as a rose."[1]

When I returned three years later, with plans for more extensive interviews, Concha and Zoila Rosa told me that Ana Rita had died the previous year; they were sorry she would not see the softbound transcript of our previous conversation. Chuckling, Concha said that Ana Rita had been a fiery little thing, adding, "I'll never forget the day she pulled a knife on me!" A knife? I was flabbergasted. The mental image of any woman at Fabricato pulling a knife on a co-worker was hard to reconcile with what I knew of the

Echavarrías' reputation for strict vigilance, and it certainly jarred with my impression of Ana Rita.

Later, when Concha described a fight she'd had with another workmate, a woman who had bossed her about, she said, and who was "a gossip," I asked her about it:

> Ann: For example, the other day . . . you told me about a fight, well it wasn't a fight, an argument like that one but with Ana Rita . . .
>
> Concha: [A stage whisper.] A knife! . . . yes, it was because I brought her mother into it . . . I said "Your mother!" And so she got really angry and she went to her machine and got a knife . . . with a sharp edge!
>
> Ann: Sharp? . . . weren't you scared?
>
> Concha: No! Bah! And so I thought about complaining [to the manager], but I didn't put in any kind of complaint and I didn't give her any more trouble or anything. And later on . . . I don't know if she invited me to something or what it was she said, but I told her: "No sweetie, ay! You and me, *Nothing doing!*" What do you think? Threatened with a knife for the first time in my life!
>
> Ann: It was the first time?
>
> Concha: Who was going to have threatened me with a knife? [Laughing]. *Virgen Santísima!* And so she said, "Avemaría, it wasn't like I was going to do anything to you." And I said, "No? Well it sure looked like it, by how mad you were."[2]

Concha recounted the memory with nonchalance, almost as a joke. She emphasized its levity by explaining that she had not told any supervisors about the incident, although she did tell other stories in which she complained to supervisors about co-workers. Ana Rita might have pulled a knife, but she had bnot done anything that seemed "beyond the pale" to Concha, who also laughed at herself for having insulted her friend's mother. After hearing many such stories, of the transient interpersonal events that colored retirees' memories of life at work, I began to realize that excluding them would guarantee an artificially sterile reconstruction of workplace relationships. Without ignoring the methodological problems raised by oral history, given that personal narratives are a key source of documentation, this chapter explores the gendered meanings inherent in workers' interaction with one another. What emerges from workers' memories is the other side of *la moral*, the fact that strict behavioral norms easily coexisted with everyday, taken-for-granted lapses from those norms. Workers' knowledge of the rules that applied to being female or male was a practical knowledge, marked by their sense of how, when, and why people will ignore the prescriptive norms of gender. Whether or not a story like Concha's can be empirically verified, the way retirees narrate such memories demonstrates that aggressive or "un-ladylike" behavior was assumed as an ever-present possibility.

Concha and Ana Rita were both women who conformed to Fabricato's strict rules, but the easy way Concha remembered an altercation that breached both workplace regulations and accepted assumptions about feminine comportment suggests that conformity was intermixed with a range of other behaviors. Other workers' memories bear out this claim. Despite, or perhaps because of, a disciplinary system with pretensions to "total" control, the women and men who spent their working lives in Medellín's mills tell stories in which the way women and men "should" behave differs in some degree from the way they do behave. This can be seen most clearly in personal anecdotes about prayers granted, or not granted; about workplace friendships, fights, and romances; and about those things that had been kept "very much in secret," like abortion, illegitimacy, and concealed love relationships.[3] Women's and men's lives were shaped by the straitjackets of gender, certainly, but also by the "little tradition" that accompanies a society's rules about gender.

Pierre Bourdieu has made this point with a metaphor drawn from organized religion. A society's formal rules, what women and men are exhorted to do, constitute an "orthodoxy," he argues. This orthodoxy will be most accessible and carefully articulated where those holding cultural power face the possibility of "heterodoxy," a public expression of nonconformity by some group of people. Bourdieu separates the formal discourses of orthodoxy and heterodoxy from the informal, uncodified world of everything "that goes without saying," which he abbreviates as "doxa." This is the sum of un-spoken knowledge, of familiarity with the behaviors others expect from one's body-in-the-world. It maps the everyday, interpersonal terrain he calls the "habitus." Bourdieu insists, however, on the permeability of the boundary between doxa and orthodoxy: the prescriptions handed down by cultural authorities will overlap with what, for their intended audience, "goes without saying" as good and right. Similarly, heterodoxic claims will have added power when they can make political an unspoken knowledge that already exists at the level of doxa.

Bourdieu's schema is generally understood in static terms, but the evidence available for Medellín points to a more dynamic understanding of the concepts he has developed. The appearance of factories in Medellín introduced the city to "modern" heterodoxies, from the notion that "modern" women might ignore the strictures of an earlier generation to the socialist argument that collective bargaining, rather than mediation by religious authorities, should be the mechanism for ensuring that wealthy elites maintained their access to labor. In the late 1930s and through the 1940s, industrialists effectively imposed *la moral* as an "orthodoxy." That is, *la moral* existed as an overt, publicly known set of norms—not as the sum total of experience. It did not "go without saying" that workers would piously obey their superiors or that women would be chaste. Chastity, Catholicism, and the importance of gender roles had to be ceaselessly promoted to be of any disciplinary use to factory managers. If, as Bourdieu argues, the processes of the doxa can only be described in retrospect, then stories of everyday interactions are precisely where one should look to apprehend workers' understandings, in practice, of the disciplinary formalities of *la moral*.[4]

Oral History as Evidence of an Alternative Religiosity

Retired people's memories of their religious experiences demonstrate the usefulness of an approach premised on the mutual permeability of official norms and unofficial practices rather than on the existence of a spectrum running from "resistance" to "accommodation." Workers' practice of Catholicism included beliefs and customs not emphasized by the priests that industrialists employed to deliver sermons, hear confessions, and oversee public ceremonies. It was not that everyday religious forms contradicted the public piety of the mills, but neither did the prayers and rituals workers most remembered have much to do with working hard or being respectful.

Most people had thoroughly enjoyed the masses, First Communions, and yearly spiritual exercises sponsored by the companies. One week each year, work stopped early to allow time for prayer, and, on that Sunday, everyone dressed in their best clothes for an outdoor mass at the mill. Whether they found the sermon boring or profound, workers welcomed the opportunity to make Confession and engage in spiritual reflection. The chance to see and be seen was no less appealing. As Celina Báez Amado remembered,

> On Sunday, they'd give us Holy Mass, with Communion. You'd go in new clothes, as elegantly as you could; as pretty as you could. . . . And [it was] with a procession up to the Plaza, to the Virgin of the Rosary. There were fireworks! And music! But it was a party! . . .
> Even if it was only a pair of stockings, you tried your best, to buy something new to wear, a little something, or the best you had.[5]

Simply by planning their outfits and admiring one another's clothing, by participating as themselves, workers partially recast the meaning of the company-sponsored event. While spiritual exercises did not cease to be a showcase for sermons about how one should behave oneself, the event became more like the customary practices of a small-town religious holiday. Like other forms of sociability, dressing up before their co-workers was something people did for reasons independent of mill-owners' paternalistic designs. In no sense did shopping for new stockings or a pretty hat "resist" the enforced religiosity of textile workplaces. (Jorge Echavarría, for example, had explicitly told workers to "get out your Sunday best" for the archbishop's 1923 visit of blessing to Fabricato.) Seen from the perspective of workers' wider "habitus," however, the chance to be seen at one's best, and to engage with others in religious celebration, transformed the companies' disciplinary Catholicism into something convivial and multidimensional. A festival in which the workers "made a beautiful float for the Virgin . . . and each work-room came out with a wreath of flowers, singing praises to Her," owed more to the region's long traditions of popular religiosity than to the paternalistic designs of any given firm.[6]

Retired people described their own engagement with Catholicism in var-ied ways. Concha Bohórquez chuckled that "I've been a real pew-licker (*lam-beladrillos*) . . . always in the church praying," and Cristina Monsalve re-membered the fervor with which she had wanted to become a nun. Ofelia Gómez, however, laughed out loud at my asking if she had been very Cath-olic, saying simply, "I've always been lazy when it comes to religion." In general, people's memories of prayer involved desire: they told stories of asking for a saint or a specific incarnation of the Virgin Mary to help them get a job, a house, or a particular piece of good luck. These were often self-deprecating. Concha made fun of herself by saying that she had gone every day to Bello's replica of the Calvary, before she was hired, to pray for a place at Fabricato: "I prayed to Christ Crucified, Oh completely! With what faith! And after I got the job I never went back [laughs] . . . he'd given me my little miracle." A woman from Rosellón, Susana Gómez, told a story of remem-bered hilarity—about a miracle *not* experienced. She and a cousin had made a special donation to the church of the Virgen del Perpetuo Socorro, in prepara-tion for a day of job-hunting. One gatekeeper shouted at them to move on, that they were getting in the way of workers' coming on shift. Another, according to Susana, threatened to call the dog catcher. Stopping at a corner, she remembered telling her cousin: "Hey, look how fast the Virgen del Per-petuo Socorro worked our miracle!" As she told the story, they looked at one another, there in the street, and began laughing so hysterically that passersby also began laughing, at seeing them with tears of mirth rolling down their faces.[7]

María Elisa Alvarez was less light-hearted. One of the days I interviewed her, she had turned two cherished statuettes of saints against the wall; "they're being punished," she said, explaining that they had not yet helped her nephew find a job. She prayed the Rosary every night and had prayed it at her loom on Tejicondor's night shift, yet she was self-disparaging: "I don't pray . . . I don't know how to pray, I only know how to ask for things."

Her memories bespeak the importance, in her life, of miracles made by worshipful prayer. Although María Elisa despaired that the Virgin "has not wanted to make any more miracles for me . . . perhaps because I have become more wicked," she described three miraculous interventions in careful detail. One had been wrought by the Christ of an outlying neighborhood church and two by María Auxiliadora, the Virgin she most often turned to in need. Of these, María Elisa said, the last one "was a much larger miracle . . . because it was as if your face were exchanged for a dark-skinned face." She explained that, in the 1930s, one of her two brothers became sick with a terrible fever. Just then, after months of unemployment, the municipal warden sent for him, to offer him a job at the jail. Ill as he was, there was no chance that he would pass the required medical exam. Although the two brothers looked nothing alike, "one was white . . . blonde-haired, the other was dark, with wavy hair," as she explained, the healthy one decided to present himself in his brother's stead. Getting caught in such an act of fraud would have meant a fine or an arrest, according to María Elisa, who stressed the family's anxiety.

> I said to my other brother, Nano, "Avemaría, my God . . . What are we going to do? He's going to lose the job that's there for him, and with us being so poor!"
>
> [Speaking in Nano's voice] "What are we going to do? I'm taking the risk! I'll get him the health certificate." It was a Saturday. No *señorita*, look, at home, at breakfast, we didn't talk about anything else, we were so desperate. . . . On Sunday I left and I went to [the church of] María Auxiliadora at 8:00 A.M. . . . I went there and I knelt down, I just spoke to her of this huge necessity I had: [As if praying] "My God! María Auxiliadora! What is it? His face is so different, I know it's very different, I know it. Ay! don't tell me again that it's different, I know it's different María Auxiliadora, but change it for me. I need for you to change [Nano's face] for José's face!"[8]

When she arrived from work the next day, Nano showed her the certificate he had gotten in José's name. No one had questioned him; the woman who drew his blood only remarked that he had lost weight since leaving military service. With his new certificate, José got the job, "and we could relax." Fifty years later, María Elisa told the story with emotional intensity and conviction: "Tell me that wasn't a miracle, a huge one, *señorita*. If you only knew . . ." For María Elisa, it went without saying that the Virgin would not judge her or her brother by the illegality of the petty fraud they were attempting. In her story, it is normal for poor people to bend or break the rules to help a family member get a job; what was extraordinary, and miraculous, was how well it worked that day.

Workers' ways of praying for material goods and earthly interventions did not frontally conflict with the view of Catholicism that mill-owners had harnessed to paternalistic discipline, one that emphasized hard work, sexual self-control, and proper behavior. The nuns at Fabricato's Patronato, for example, had encouraged workers in the traditional practice of painting a picture of the house they desired and placing it on a home altar (together with a bowl of beans and other foodstuffs as an offering) on 3 May, the day of the Holy Cross.[9] Nevertheless, retirees' stories of prayers trace the varied ways that workers' own religious practices extended beyond, and thus reframed, the enforced religiosity of textile workplaces.

Compañerismo and Talk

In precisely the same way, workers' memories of mixed-sex interaction in the mills added layers of subjective experience to the official rules of factory work. If Christian piety constituted the foundation of *la moral*, the walls of this paternalistic edifice were built of injunctions that concerned workingwomen's interaction with males of any class, including their co-workers. Factory supervisors around the world have attempted to limit sociability whenever operatives' talking, bickering, and fooling around interfered with production, but the *vigilanta* system made Medellín's mills unusually strict.[10] Especially during the 1940s, when the textile workforce was thoroughly mixed-sex, mill rules made a whole range of everyday behaviors (conversation, having any sort of argument, flirting with a person of the other sex, etc.) into infractions likely to result in a reprimand, docked pay-packets, or formal suspensions. Like alternative religious practices, however, workers' conviviality reframed mill discipline more than it resisted the behavioral restrictions plant managers sought to enforce.

As with other aspects of *la moral*, the limits factory administrators placed on workers' social interaction developed as much from reformers' concerns as from industrialists' interest in maintaining output. Through the 1920s, Medellín's factory inspector had worked to convince the city's industrialists that they should require silence during work hours. Inspector Vélez praised mills that maintained "a strict vigilance," as at Tejidos Hernández, where, he said, "conversations among workers are not permitted, that is to say, between men and women workers. Morality thus proceeds very well."[11] Where he heard talk or casual banter, Vélez tried to penalize the *vigilanta* on duty; he warned one manager to intervene with a *vigilanta* who, according to the inspector, "through her pusillanimity, authorized chatting between men and women workers."[12] For Catholic reformers like Vélez, silence marked a factory as clean and respectable, a "temple of work."[13]

As discussed in chapter 5, this was precisely the image that a new generation of industrialists, led by the Echavarrías, hoped to project. In 1935, when managers at Fabricato and the Fábrica de Bello drew up their first formal lists

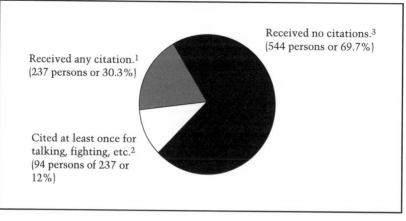

Received no citations.[3]
(544 persons or 69.7%)

Received any citation.[1]
(237 persons or 30.3%)

Cited at least once for talking, fighting, etc.[2]
(94 persons of 237 or 12%)

Figure 8   Percentage of workers entering Medellín's mills between 1918 and 1960 who were cited or suspended during their employment. On sampling method, see Introduction, note 10.

[1]Includes persons written up for poor work, absenteeism, insubordination, tardiness, and other infractions.

[2]Includes persons written up for talking, fighting, arguments, and gossip. See fig. 9.

[3]Includes 181 persons who stayed at their jobs for less than one year, a group that generally left or were dismissed without formal citations.

of regulations, they banned all conversation "unrelated to work." Through the 1940s and 1950s, both women and men risked a verbal reprimand or a suspension without pay if they were caught chatting, "distracting co-workers," or playing "hand-games" (*juegos de manos*). Particularly at Fabricato and Tejicondor, where industrialists took a special pride in presenting themselves as innovators and their mills as ultramodern, workers commonly received formal disciplinary citations for engaging one another in talk of some kind. Taking all the mills together, of those persons who received any type of citation (approximately one third), 24 percent were cited for talking (figures 8 and 9). More women were written up for "arguments" (*disgustos*) than for fights (*peleas*), while the reverse was true of men, patterns that likely reflect supervisors' attitudes as much as any difference in behavior. If fighting and arguing are considered together, women and men got into trouble over altercations with workmates at about the same rate (16 percent of women who received any citation and 15 percent of men who received any citation).

The retired people I interviewed, most of whom had entered the mills in the early 1940s, described interaction with co-workers as a normal part of the factory day. To the question, "Could one talk during work hours?" Lucía Jiménez gave a typical response: "No, not during work hours, but we had

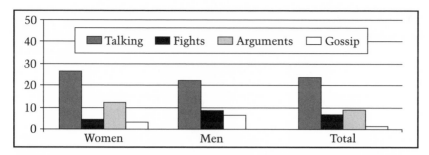

Figure 9   Persons written up for behavior involving co-workers, as a percentage of those cited or suspended. On sampling method, see Introduction, note 10.

compañeras . . . it's like, 'We can't talk during work hours?' we were all there together—but yes, we could."[14] Asking for advice, covering for a person who felt ill, or airing hurt feelings were constants of workers' communication. Depending on the supervisor or *vigilanta*, these might seem to involve conversation "unrelated to work," and many people, decades later, described suspensions that had seemed to them unfair, when they had been reprimanded or suspended for "talking" but the conversation in question had been about their labors.[15]

For their part, upper-level administrators recognized and encouraged certain aspects of workers' sociability while attempting to outlaw others. They not only sponsored company sports teams and dances but also formal rituals, like Tejicondor's "Celebration of *Compañerismo*," in which workers elected each year's "best *compañero*."[16] To the extent supervisors at all levels of the mill hierarchy relied on workers' understandings of *compañerismo* to aid them with training and motivating operatives, sociability was essential to a factory's success. Recalling the day that she arrived in Fabricato's spinning section in 1944, for example, María Cristina Restrepo emphasized her own fear and her co-workers' helpfulness:

> María Cristina: I was scared to death to see those machines . . . I said: "I'll die of fright." . . . Horrible, dreadful, that terrible heat, all that cotton . . . and then, after a week I felt all right, the girls, the *compañeras*, perfect.
> Ann: Really good friends?
> María Cristina: Really good friends, really good *compañeras*, the first three days one doesn't know where to put one's clothes [laughs]. I didn't know where the bathroom was, nothing. . . . You don't know where you came in or where you have to go to get out; you pay [attention], it's like, the door was here, by the picture of the Virgin and the Sacred Heart—but I'd keep losing track. Just huge! [But] one girl, really nice, very polite, she really stuck by me.[17]

As a key component of *compañerismo*, talking with co-workers was part of the work process, rather than an evasion of work, despite the fact that it formally transgressed the rules. Yet workers' understandings of what made a good *compañero* or *compañera* included a wide variety of behaviors, only some of which were valuable to supervisors' and administrators' attempts to keep up production. If managers attempted to limit everyday forms of sociability, it was precisely because of this variety. The problem, for attempts at a total kind of discipline, was the fluidity of the line between shop-floor exchanges that helped workers get through the day, on the one hand, and those that distracted women and men from their tasks, on the other.

Flirting

Unsurprisingly, retirees remembered flirtation and courtship as quotidian aspects of workers' social interaction—despite the company's explicit rule against mixed-sex conversation. When I asked if one saw *noviazgos* (courtships) at the mill, Concha joked: "*Avemaría!* The Father used to say that if a thousand people started at Fabricato in December, two thousand got married the next December."[18] The *vigilantas* had been strict, she said, but conversations between *novios* happened "on the run, on the wing." A couple that had done their courting at Fabricato remembered clearly how they managed to see each other while working in different sections of the mill:

> Ann: How did you meet each other?
> Eugenio Márquez: Well right there in the same factory, she would pass by and look and I would pass by and look—
> Ester Gómez de Márquez: In the shifts . . . I had to pass by his section, [it was] a walkway.
> Ann: Yes, and so it was like you kept an eye out for each other?
> Eugenio: An electric eye![19]

Often, courtships started at the mill and were pursued in the evening and on Sundays; young men either stood under their *novia*'s window or visited in the family parlor. At Rosellón, Cristina Monsalve's *novio* (and future husband) could not easily leave his place at the sizing machine, but he sent sweets to her loom with friends and, later, began spending evenings with her and her parents.[20] As María Cristina Restrepo remembered of her youth as a spinner in Fabricato's main plant, "it was very simple . . . you would meet in the factory, and over there's the house and there's the street."[21]

Certainly, mixed-sex interaction at work facilitated an informality not available within conventional structures for visiting or spending time with a person of the opposite sex. Many women enjoyed an easy, teasing *compañerismo* with male workers without involving themselves in the negotia-

One of several family portraits included in a commemorative album compiled by Fabricato in the late 1940s. Nicolás Gómez, a worker at the mill, and his wife Ana María Ramírez de Gómez, who had also worked at Fabricato, with their child. Photographer unknown, reproduction by Fernando Garcés and Foto Garcés. Courtesy of Fabricato.

tions of courtship and marriage. María Cristina, who remained single and reached retirement at Fabricato, described a moment of playfulness between her, three male co-workers, and the shift supervisor:

Working one Sunday, some guys, workers, came over to talk to me; and then the supervisor saw us and so I said: "*The* Supervisor, *The* Supervisor; but don't you move." And so he came over and [said], "Come," all four, it was four guys, *compañeros* from right there, the same workroom, "Come here, I am going to ask you a question." All of us shaking; yes [laughter.] . . . And so he said: "Tell me, what [perfume] does Cristina wear that everybody hangs around her machines all the time?"

And so one of them was more bold, and he said to him . . . "Look, it's simple. I went to ask her if since we were working on Sunday and we didn't go to mass, if it was a sin . . . do you think it is?" And so he said, "You guys always win, that's what," the supervisor said. And so I said, "*Avemaría*, it's not like it's won," I said.

But we did say, "they're going to suspend us." Fine. And so he said "fine, you all like to talk to Cristina, on Sunday we're going to work, but I'm going to put her to work whitewashing, who wants to hold the ladder for her?"; so they all jumped up, "I'll hold the ladder!" [laughter.] That was a whole conversation there too.[22]

Other workers recounted similar anecdotes, in which playfulness or a well-chosen rejoinder ensured that a supervisor responded with good humor. At Tejicondor, María Elisa Alvarez remembered that her co-workers would sometimes pair up and dance when the electricity went out, with others clapping and singing for accompaniment. Once, she said, a top administrator caught her friend Mira Gaviria dancing:

> A really nice boss, he came and found a couple dancing, the guy had his pants rolled up to here and the girl had hers rolled halfway up her leg . . . because, they said, they were going to be a pair of *campesinos* dancing . . .
>
> We had swept the workroom, me and Mira, who was like a best friend. We had already cleaned the place and we'd cleaned our machines. . . . And Mira said, "we're going to sing." She sang . . . she sang really beautifully; she sang "Los Aviadores."
>
> "But we can't dance to this tune," said a guy, Ricardo . . . "and they're saying they're going to dance, you hear?"
>
> . . . And those two were dancing. When Don Zeledón came in . . . some of them turned around to look at him, but not us, we were dying of laughter, naturally! . . . When he comes and says, "But how well they dance! I'll invite you to the party we're going to have in December!"
>
> Mira answered him, "We'll be there, dancing, Don Zeledón!" [She said,] "Don Zeledón, there's nothing to do. If we have to be doing something, here's a cigarette, go and smoke it!"[23]

By the 1950s and 1960s, however, most mills could generate their own electricity and thus experienced less "down-time." Workers' relationships with shift supervisors and higher-level managers also changed dramatically, making the degree of informality María Elisa describes progressively less likely, as described in chapter 7. Yet what most clearly marks María Elisa's story as a memory from the 1940s is the mixed-sex nature of the workplace and of worktime. Tejicondor's spinning room is, in her memory, a place inhabited by young men and women both. This fact colors the moments of leisure that happen in the interstices of a workday: here, down-time becomes dance time.

Jealousy and Harassment

Whether it involved romance or simple fun, mixed-sex sociability also shaped women's work relationships with other women (and men's relationships with one another). Many retired women remembered being made fun of for not having boyfriends. Among the women who stayed on until Tejicondor was almost all male, said María Elisa, was one whom she refused to speak to for well over ten years. I asked why, and Elisa was direct: "Because she had said something stupid about me and Mira Gaviria . . . she said, 'well aren't they a pair of queers [*un par de maricas*].'" Similarly, Gumercinda Báez Amado employed the third person to repeat "what others said" about her and her sister:

> "The Báez sisters sure are serious aren't they?" . . . and they'd criticize like always in life, there's a lot of criticism: "That old maid over there, dressing up saints because she couldn't undress drunks."[24]

Petty jealousies also flourished. Speaking in a light-hearted way, Bárbara Alzate de López emphasized Enrique's inconstancy during their courtship, which took place largely at Rosellón. Bárbara also detailed the recriminations she suffered at the hands of what she called his "*media-novias*" (semi-girlfriends).

> Bárbara: I really kept an eye on them [his girlfriends], because they did me plenty of mischief. . . .
> Ann: And, like what sort of things?
> Bárbara: Those machines where you go up like this [gestures], and they have, these big windings of thread . . . well they'd take—to leave me stranded—they'd take all the thread . . . they'd steal my thread. . . . There was a man that loaded the thread and he said: "Ay! Look, they stole your thread, look how they left you dry!" And me, "Ay!" and so he'd run and fill me up. [Laughter.][25]

As a "mechanic" or loom-fixer, she explained, Enrique had been especially able to strike up conversations with women; mentioning this allowed her to return to what were clearly stories her daughters (present at the interview) had heard before, about how popular their father had been with women.

> Ann: And was that something you saw a lot at the factory, boyfriends and girlfriends?
> Bárbara: Yes, you saw it a lot, but you couldn't talk at the factory, and woe to him who had his conversations there, "Out!" Yes, they would fire him!
> Ann: . . . And so Enrique didn't come to talk to you?
> Bárbara: No, we'd go out in shifts . . . he'd come out of weaving and I'd meet him here and he'd meet me over here, and so we'd go on talking while we ate lunch, he'd go to lunch and I'd be coming back, and they'd sound the siren and all that and we would talk. But he sure got me vexed, because he was a ladies' man . . . he had *girlfriends*. . . .
> I'd find out that he'd gone out with someone, that they saw him in such-and-such a place with so-and-so: I'd find out on Monday. And me,

no, I didn't pay any mind to that, but he did have a girlfriend in weaving, which made me a little bit mad.

Ann: How was that?

Bárbara: Because she; he left me to go out with her . . . she worked in weaving with him, so when I would be going out and waiting for him, he had already left with her, and so, tell me who would put up with that? And so she made fun of me, his girlfriend, we'd run into each other at the cinema and she'd say . . . like, "Blessed *Saint* Bárbara!" [laughter].[26]

Enrique himself explained that the loom-fixers had more mobility and more opportunities for conversation than most workers. "They talked a lot, chatted with the *obreras* . . . to talk with an *obrera* while you were fixing her loom? This was very common." He added, however, that many *vigilantas* had been quick to suspend an *obrera* for talking to a mechanic, even if she were only responding to his questions.[27] Daily relations between loom-fixers and female operatives were thus colored by inequalities of status: tradesmen escaped the petty authority of *vigilantas* or room supervisors. They were considered highly skilled workers and were well paid; they also derived advantage from masculine privilege, as only men could be loom-fixers.

What a man might term "chatting with an *obrera*" ranged from welcome flirtation to unwelcome insistence, and women sometimes reported male behavior that they found "disrespectful." At Fabricato in 1935, three women signed statements that the supervisor of the packing and finishing section directed unwanted compliments to them and attempted to fondle them at their work. Clara Saldarriaga and Socorro Pérez complained that José Delgado "constantly" commented on their clothing and that he touched them while they worked. Margarita Arroyave said that he would send her to work in narrow parts of the warehouse and then walk back and forth, "with the aim of rubbing his body against mine"; he had also offered to give her money every week if she would let him kiss her, she said. Clara, Socorro, and Margarita may have initiated the complaint themselves, or they may have been encouraged to come forward by a *vigilanta* or upper-level administrator. José Delgado was summarily fired, and "disrespect toward an *obrera*" and "immoral acts in the workroom" appear as reasons for men's firings from Coltejer in the same period.[28] If the Echavarrías' patriarchal vision limited women's behavior, it also constrained men's.

In interviews, women emphasized the moral protections that the Echavarrías' policies guaranteed them, but they also articulated their ability to defend themselves directly—using a wide range of strategies. María Cristina Restrepo convinced a male co-worker to leave her alone by persuading her brother to pose as a boyfriend. Ofelia Gómez, who worked at Coltejer in the 1940s, remembered having to do more: "I carried a pocket-knife," she explained;

A *compañero* told me, "look out when the electricity goes out, they're going to grab you," I took out the pocket-knife and I had it open and the lights were about to come back on when this guy grabbed me and I cut him—right then and there they took him to the emergency room. And that one got fired, that one got fired.[29]

Some women felt vulnerable in ways that extended beyond the shop floor. Cristina Monsalve structured her narrative around the fact of widowhood, saying that a young widow struggles with "the world, the devil, and the flesh." "A widow," she insisted, "is more delicate than a single girl . . . you can converse with anyone and with whoever comes along, but the widow: [people will say,] 'look at that widow, so shameless!' " Male workers, she said, viewed her differently, and she recalled a confrontation with a loom-fixer:

Cristina: One day a mechanic thought that I looked like very good—
Her daughter: Or he thought you looked easy, he thought you looked easy,
Cristina: Ay! [He said to me,] "How good you look, you haven't got a single bad piece [of breast meat], you're like a chicken!" [*No tiene presa mala, ¡está como la gallina!*]
Ann: Ay!
Cristina: "I'd throw away four-hundred pesos on you tonight," and I said: "and why don't you throw them away on your mother, you *scoundrel*! What have I done to you for you to say such things to me? Look, I'm not going to the office to tell what you said to me because they'll fire you and you have children, but I know how to defend myself from you." And look, and he's still alive . . . and I won't speak to him—he's old, old but I won't speak to him.[30]

Reported Speech and Unladylike Behavior

This was an anecdote Cristina had recounted many times over; her daughter knew it, and Cristina described the event to me, using exactly the same language, on two separate occasions. However briefly, retired people's ability to switch from answering questions to narrating stories allowed them to shift our conversations in the present away from the question/answer format of "an interview" and toward more culturally familiar ways of describing interpersonal exchanges in the past.[31] Key to this shift was the inclusion of heterogeneous perspectives within recounted anecdotes. By reproducing others' words, retired people expanded their own voices. Figuratively, they called witnesses who corroborated their self-presentations, whether as upstanding paragons of "good reputation," as silly youngsters who later learned better, or as women who, whatever else, had stood up for themselves.

Women were especially careful to bring managers or shift supervisors into accounts of their conflicts with co-workers. Their own belligerence or sharpness of tongue was thus set off by the fact of having been a good worker. Cristina, for example, had nursed a grievance against a woman who had spread a rumor that she had gotten pregnant (a grievance similar to Ana Rita's). The *vigilanta* of the women's toilets, whose job it was to make sure that no one used the bathroom as a place to talk or smoke, had begun telling others that Cristina seemed "to be in a compromised state." Given the extreme sanction attached to an illegitimate pregnancy, these were fighting words. A co-worker informed Cristina:

> She told me, "Girl, look what she's saying . . . that you're pregnant." And I said: "Yeah? And they're going to be twins, one for her and the other for you," I answered her like that. When I told myself, "keep quiet? No. Wait and see," and I went to the office . . .
>
> I told Don Antonio . . . "Do me the favor of calling the *vigilanta* for the bathrooms, because she's telling my *compañeras* that I'm in a compromised state." And I took off my apron—you had to wear an apron there, right?—And I told him: "You are a married man, go right ahead, check me, because it's easily known . . ."

As Cristina told the story, she then spoke up to defend the woman, asking Don Antonio not to take it to the general manager's office: "I told him . . . she is the mother of five children, as am I, and perhaps they'd fire her and that would pain me a lot, not for her but for the children." Her conversation with Don Antonio provides a foil for the story's conclusion, as Cristina described her own willingness to confront the woman:

> I said to her, look, aahh, when I'd get sick? [menstruate] I'd leave the toilet full and I said to her, "Look, there they are for you to baptize." I tormented her with that until they fired her: "Look, there it is so that you can baptize it, and watch how you talk!" Because that was a calumny . . . and look, I left with my retirement and she left fired.[32]

What might appear as vulgarity in another person's telling is firmly defined as standing up for oneself, not by a direct claim so much as by the juxtaposition of three dialogues: with the friend who tells her about the rumor being circulated, with Don Antonio, and with the *vigilanta*.

Cristina took special pains to defend her position as a respectable widow, but the same narrative strategy appeared in dozens of similar stories. Even

María Concepción López, who had retired from Tejidos Leticia (where the Rabinoviches had tolerated behavior that would have gotten a person fired at Coltejer, Fabricato, or Tejicondor) and who actively disassociated herself from what she termed the "hypocrisy" of the Echavarrías' moral discipline, included managers' voices in her stories of everyday quarrels. Her voice quickened with enthusiasm as she remembered her ability to fight well, and her description of the enmity between herself and a woman nicknamed "the butterfly" was animated.[33]

> Ann: Did you sometimes have like fights with the *obreras*, with *compañeras*? And what were they like?
>
> María Concepción: *Of course!* Over there in the Leticia factory I fought [laughter]. One time I had this *compañera*—because there were two shifts—and there was this one, from here, also from Bello; she kept after me! [*me tenía dedicada*]. They called her "the butterfly."
>
> Ann: And why?
>
> María Concepción: I don't know, because she looked like it [laughter]. OK, and what do you think? every day she'd be coming out and I'd be going in and she'd say: "Hey you, look, you left the selvages on the floor," and I'd tell her: "Not hardly, I picked them all up, it's you that leaves them for me." And we fought, hear? We grabbed each other there in the bus, I was shoving her between the wheels of the bus—because I was sure strong then . . . I was just hanging on to her hair.[34]

Immediately, she added that she'd gone to see Samuel Rabinovich, or "Don Samuel," to tell him that she had again tangled with "the butterfly." As she chose to remember the conversation, María Concepción had simply announced: "You decide if you're going to give me the pink slip," to which he had replied, "I won't fire you, María, you're useful to me here."[35] She also emphasized her skill as a weaver; explaining that their fight was about a fine chiffon they were weaving. "That's the hardest stuff to work on," she said; "you had to use an iron rod to stretch it out, so I'd let the selvages grow, because [otherwise] it gets so *twisted*." Recounting another fight, this time with a man she described as a homosexual, and whom she said she had hit in the face, María Concepción admitted that Bernardo Rabinovich had suspended her for a week. But, she said, she had stayed away until he sent a man to say he needed her to return to the mill. Certainly, calling the Rabinovich brothers as witnesses made it easier for María Concepción to tell stories of her toughness and fractious behavior. Given that Tejidos Leticia imposed fewer rules of behavior than Medellín's other mills, however, her memories suggest her awareness of larger social proscriptions and norms of femininity more than they indicate that she pushed against mill rules. To put it another way, women's descriptions of the fights they had at work point to the intermixture between factory strictures (whatever their specific form) and the cultural "doxa" that shaped Antioqueños' evaluations of one another's public comportment. Women were expected not to fight and not to insult one another in vulgar terms; stories about having done such things are thus more easily told when they are offset by the disclaimer of having been a good worker.

For workingwomen, as for their employers, how one behaved toward co-workers was an integral part of the code of *la moral*. With sexual restraint, "good workers" were expected to practice politeness and to be good *compañeros*; women, in particular, were expected to comport themselves like ladies. In the all-encompassing vision of Catholic paternalism, this went together with not shortening one's hemlines, not drinking, and not sneaking out to go dancing. (And, as Cristina's story suggests, not being a gossip was also part of *la moral*. Indeed,) by 1950, any worker entering Coltejer signed a statement that, "I have been notified that all gossip or ridicule of any worker, on or off company property, will be grounds for immediate dismissal." Apart from agreeing to abide by the factory regulations as printed, this was the only special directive a person was required to sign.[36]

When a person was found out "spreading rumors or telling secrets" or "listening to and passing on *gossip* in the workroom," the supervisor had it written or typed into their file.[37] This marked a change; Eduardo Echavarría, in the 1920s, had often observed that this or another worker was "chatty" (*charlatana, charlatán*) or "a fighter" (*peleadora, peleador*), but he had written it down only when a person left the mill. As the mills became more formally paternalistic and more bureaucratic, however, managers monitored workers' interaction more closely. To take two examples: A sixteen-year-old boy who entered as machine-cleaner and oiler in 1944 was suspended seven times in the fifteen months he stayed at Fabricato. He received two two-day suspensions for "arguing with a co-worker" (*por disgustar con un compañero*) and for "playing" in the workrooms, two eight-day suspensions for outright fights, and three others, of varying lengths, for poor work and disobedience. A seventeen-year-old girl at Tejicondor, a weaver named Haydeé Angel, received thirteen one-day suspensions in six years: six times for imperfect cloth, three times for stopping work (including once when she was caught putting on makeup before the quitting siren had sounded, a common cause for suspension), twice for chatting with companions, and once for "picking a fight." Haydée finally quit when slapped with a two-week suspension, which her supervisor explained to his superiors in writing. After their shift, as the weavers were getting ready to leave, another woman remarked that he, the supervisor, was very strict, which was a good thing too, since "there were some people that used to spend a lot of time in the washrooms combing their hair and fixing themselves up." Haydée shot back that she would comb her hair "whenever she darn well pleased [*cuando le diera la verraca gana*], and thank goodness she had hair to comb, not like some people, who don't have anything to comb." According to whoever told the supervisor what happened, the first woman said nothing, but turned her back, "and then Haydée threw a bottle and hit her in the head."[38]

Haydée would likely tell the story differently, especially if her telling were in an interview conducted fifty years later. The retrospection involved in oral histories, along with the way people generally reshape the stories they tell to include multiple voices and witty rejoinders, as in the narratives discussed above, are often used to dismiss oral historical work. Yet notes made at the time, as in personnel files, contain their own distortions. Recordkeepers were more likely to describe altercations between women, like the incident recorded by Haydée's supervisor, as *disgustos* or arguments, whereas men got written up for "fights," as noted above. The categories used by supervisory personnel also varied by mill. At Coltejer, for example, almost no one was written up for talking. At Tejicondor, by contrast, talking accounted for more than 25 percent of the citations received by women and 20 percent of those received by men. A quantitative examination of the reasons for workers' suspensions offers information about what supervisors wrote down, about whom, in specific workplaces, but no way of guessing how often the cited behavior went on without being recorded or how workers thought about their interactions with one another. Nor can it be used to chart the verbal reminders that generally preceded a person's being written up. Interviews, similarly, are excellent sources for understanding some things but poor sources for understanding others. They blur the line between fact and fantasy, revealing more about how workers entered one another's imaginations than about their on-the-ground interaction.

El Delito Más Grande: Pregnancy

When María Cristina Restrepo told me her odd story, of a beauty queen at Fabricato who lost her crown when the factory discovered that she had secretly had a child, I excitedly asked if other women, too, had concealed pregnancies:

> Ann: Because many people have told me—were there really some women who had their children in secret?
> María Cristina: But, I don't know except of one case, or two cases, of women who had children and in the factory no one knew. Because there is this one, from the Bello mill ... when she had [her child] it was a three-day holiday and after the three days she went back to work.
> Ann: And nobody noticed?

María Cristina: But it was because we used these pajama-like things [an over-smock], crossed-over like this and with pockets here and here. And so; she was fat and on a fat person you'd only notice it a little bit. But first of all, the person who was working in the factory and who got pregnant, was going to be fired, practically speaking . . . because by working there you made an agreement: that there would be discipline in the factory, that wouldn't be anything offensive, because you could not discredit the company.[39]

María Cristina then described another woman, whose secret went undiscovered for many years, but "one day they found out, they found out . . . they found out that she had lied to the company and so they fired her." As if to soften the implied judgment, she immediately added a third example in which the company had relented:

Another girl, also from weaving, they called her when her son had a bicycle accident, and so they said *oops!* After that she could not deny it, but since she was close to retirement, she only had about four or six years to go, they let her finish.

She implies that the woman was "allowed" to stay as a concession to her seniority in the mill; María Cristina suggests a moral revindication; the woman's temporal distance from her "immorality" lessens the stain on her character. As in her first description, of the wayward *reina,* it is clear that María Cristina does not want the mill discredited. She may have underscored the "agreement" a woman entered into by working at Fabricato precisely because my questions seemed inappropriate. Earlier in our interview she had described *la moral* in distinctly positive terms. Like other retirees, she pointed to the key symbols of Catholic paternalism: female chastity, the presence of priests in the workrooms, careful oversight, and sexual protection for working women.

Ann: In this earlier period, was it women? Were they all single, or were there married women too?

María Cristina: They did not allow married women there, no. And not *fracasadas* (fallen women) either, not in any way. There, it was a good thing I think . . . it was very orderly, a lot of morality. What one wore, no one dressed badly . . .

You'd be on the night shift, and when you were least thinking of it the priest would be right there. There, no one could put out his hand out like this; a man couldn't touch you.[40]

I would not now ask the sort of "leading question" I put to María Cristina, but given that retirees responded even to this type of question in a wide variety of ways, their memories cannot be simply attributed to my presence.

Some produced anecdotes like María Cristina's, of women *que se fajaban*, referring to those that girdled themselves with strips of cloth to conceal their bellies.[41] Others simply disallowed the question. For Eugenio Márquez, concealing a pregnancy was "materially impossible," and Celina Báez said flatly that "they always found out and fired them," even those who tried to bind their bellies down.[42] Concha, too, doubted anyone had managed to hide a pregnancy, whatever I had heard. Girls in that position might try it for a while, she said, but they knew it was hopeless, so "they'd leave all quiet-like, before they got fired."[43] Even where people described stories of successful concealment as fabrications, however, they acknowledged that women had gotten pregnant, of course. The fact of secret liaisons, "seductions," and aborted or concealed pregnancies went without saying. Anecdotes about such things circulated as part of the collective memory of *la moral.*

I asked about concealment because retired people had mentioned it as a possibility in interviews recorded by other researchers. Four years before I met María Concepción López, she had told labor historian Ana María Jaramillo that "you couldn't work if you were married . . . but why would you say anything?"[44] Additionally, I had seen a few suggestive notes in factory personnel records, such as an entry in a woman's file that "she didn't work out—has 1 child of 3 years and hadn't said anything," or a comment that another woman had returned after a year's absence, with the observation that she had "adopted" a child. At Fabricato, I also came across documentary evidence of abortion, something that I had not expected to find. A folded newspaper clipping was stapled to the *hoja de vida* of Virgelina Rodríguez, who had worked at the mill for one year, in 1947–48, when she was nineteen. More than two decades later, Bello police arrested Rodríguez, by then a well-known midwife, for poisoning a woman who had sought an abortion.[45] The dead woman had apparently contracted Rodríguez for help in inducing a miscarriage. After other methods had failed, Rodríguez gave her a liquid poison, Folidol, and the woman died within an hour. Significantly, the police arrested Rodríguez because she killed someone, not because she customarily performed abortions. Although she was only nineteen when employed at Fabricato and probably not yet a midwife, she may have been a person (even then) who knew something about where to go to terminate a pregnancy.

Stories of concealment fit easily within a melodramatic logic of moral redemption; they could be told without overtly passing judgment on either the woman or the company. The passage of years, a mother's love for her child, and the fact that the companies had been forced to change their policies of exclusion: all of these made space for stories that had been scandalous but were now legitimate memories of "life back then." None of this applied to abortion, however, which most retired women classed as sinful or "a crime." Yet descriptions of women's ways of ending a pregnancy may have circulated much as did stories of concealment, creating a community story that some people could tell more easily than others. In the course of an informal group interview, in which no one gave their real names, I asked if women had ever induced miscarriages. A man standing nearby jumped in with a breezy, generalized account of *teguas*, or traditional herb-doctors:

> Man's voice: The girl, the girl would notice that her menstruation had not come . . . and that she had had relations with a man, and so, by means of one of these *teguas* she would say, "look, this is happening," and so he'd give her a brew and there you go.
> Ann: And this, this really worked?
> Susana Osorio [the woman to whom I had directed the question]: AVEMARÍA! Girl, did it work?[46]

My tendency not to ask men about abortion practices may thus have been a mistake; knowledge of abortion practices did nothing to imperil a man's respectability. The same may have applied to women who placed themselves outside the limits drawn by *la moral*. María Concepción López, for example, recounted helping a friend abort without any indication of embarrassment, and without my having asked about it. In describing her enmity with "la Mariposa," whom she offhandedly called a *vagabunda* (tramp), María Concepción remembered helping a friend who had gotten pregnant for the fourth time.

> María Concepción: [Speaking of "la Mariposa."] A *vagabunda* . . . she found her way around there in the factory . . . another one, C——, did too. Women like that. But there was another one that already had like three children, right there in the factory, and finally she said to me: "María, tell me, Ay! If I have another child Don Samuel said he'd kick me out,"
> Ann: Yes? Would he really fire——?
> María Concepción: Oh yes, he was going to fire her, because that would already be four. . . . And so I told her: "Ay! Let me talk to this Indian." . . . And I talked to the Indian and he gave me some leaves and said: "cook them and give them to her and give them to her by spoonfuls, count it out by spoonfuls." And she didn't have any more, she's retired now and she didn't have any more. . . . But the Indian died, the one that knew; what do you know?[47]

Only when I asked how she had known to go to this *indio* did she stop short, telling me about an earlier difficulty he had helped her resolve only after I turned off the tape recorder. Because her account concerns Tejidos Leticia, the city's most lenient mill, María Concepción's descriptions are only partially about mill rules; they point outward, toward more widely familiar practices. No less than she did, workers at Coltejer or Fabricato moved within a regional culture marked by a range of attitudes more than by moralists' hard and fast distinctions. The difference was that María Concepción refused the moral hierarchy that shaped most *Antioqueños'* ways of describing this range.

For the majority of retirees, especially those from Coltejer, Rosellón, and Fabricato, the mills' rigid sexual code was a direct product of the industrialists' uprightness. They remembered their employers and the factories as exceptional places, positioned at one end of the cultural range that constituted the society they had known. A person might pity an unmarried mother, or speak approvingly of new laws preventing the companies from firing pregnant women, but feel intense nostalgia for the earlier, more draconian rules and all that they symbolized. According to Susana Osorio, a girl who got pregnant "was repudiated by everyone . . . what a horrible thing!" To explain, however, she added that, "it was because, here, the people that invented this, the ones that made Medellín an industrial place, were good people . . . very strict and very clean and very kind."[48]

People told their stories from well within the boundaries of *la moral.* If the memories they chose to relate transgressed those boundaries, they did not therefore critique the mills' rigidity or, much less, condemn the employers' paternalism. Few wished to place themselves "beyond the pale" as completely as María Concepción did. Rather, memories of transgressive behavior in the past were communicated by reference to a moral yardstick only partially offset from the one employers had used to measure workingwomen's behavior. María Cristina, for example, used both the nation's new legal rules and the claim that the women she described had raised their children in a socially proper way to downplay the fact that their acts of concealment had transgressed against the Echavarrías' rules. Retirees' ability to substitute one moral standard for another and thus speak about unsanctioned behavior in the past derived in part from the enormous cultural shift that separated Medellín in the 1990s from the same city fifty years before. Nevertheless, their ways of telling stories about what people "got away with" in the past suggest that the mills' strict rules, even then, had provided workers with only one of a set of possible standards for judging behavior.

Nena's Story

I interviewed Ana Palacios de Montoya, who called herself Nena, after her husband, Jairo, had proudly told me, in the course of an interview about his years as a chauffeur at Coltejer, that he and his wife had married secretly. I has asked Jairo if he had met her at Coltejer, and he explained that he himself had gotten her a job at the plant, after they became lovers. He had worked directly for the personnel manager and had simply asked for a favor, saying he wanted to help the daughter of a poor family he knew. "I slipped her in secretly," he said. His revelations added yet another layer of complicity and betrayal to the constant ethical dilemmas of interviewing. He invited me to their home, and when I arrived Nena had less access to the range of strategies a person can use to put off or distract a question-asking outsider. What she did have, however, was a storytelling power that she used to shift the interchange away from my questions and toward her ways of narrating.[49] This enabled her to move fluidly between descriptions of the gratitude she owed Coltejer and an accounting of the suffering the company's rigid policy had caused her.

Setting the tone for a narrative rich in symbolic allusion, Nena described her first day at the mill as a bodily subterfuge:

> They started to examine us, and some doctor told me he had noticed something in my heart. So I told him that I was embarrassed because you had to take off all your clothes, from here [gestures toward her waist]. I told him I was embarrassed and also I was scared and so I passed. When really I had suffered attacks to my heart [*ataques al corazon*] when I was young.[50]

She had successfully hidden her heart's secret, and this opening anecdote gained significance as Nena proceeded with her story of long concealment and the attainment of a seemingly impossible dream: happiness in marriage *and* a retirement pension from Coltejer. When she met Jairo, in 1943, Nena said, she had worked as a servant, which she hated: "the *señoras* put you down a lot and, no, that wasn't for me." She had loved millwork, and insisted that "I still sometimes dream that I'm at work . . . I wasn't bored with it even for a single day." Like María Concepción, Nena claimed the moral legitimacy of having been a good worker and highly skilled: "I'm very lucky with the looms," she explained; "they sent me like four letters about my work, because it was exemplary."

In loving detail, Nena recounted how she bought a lot and built a house through *cesantías* (yearly bonuses of unused severance pay) and loans from the company, with help from Our Lady of Perpetual Help and an old neighbor. Her house stood as a testament to the company's good faith: when she needed cement or paint or money to pay tradesmen, she had gotten loans from Coltejer. After saving and scrimping to finish the first floor, said Nena, she had dreamed of adding a second story:

> I told myself, "no, I've got to save enough to finish the upstairs, so that when my old man is old and me too, won't it be great, me sitting there with him on the balcony . . ." It's just like I dreamed it would be, just like I thought it would happen, it happened for me.

In developing her narrative, Nena transformed the second-story balcony into a symbol both of her long efforts to earn a company pension and of her and Jairo's enduring affection for one another. Her life's trajectory, as she presented it, was a unidirectional movement toward a retirement shared with her *viejo* in the house she built with years of labor in the factory. As she recounted it,

> We've known each other since '43 and we've loved each other since '43 and you should know that today is like '43; we've known each other all this time and our repertory for conversation hasn't run out, we're the same people. We're the same people, us two—if he's here and I'm in the kitchen, he's like "Are you coming? You're coming? Coming? Are you finished?" [She laughs.] So that I'll go over where he is. Together on the balcony, together in bed lazing around [*haciendo perro*], together sitting here. . . .
>
> All those difficulties, all the suffering, because you do suffer, seeing that you have to go to work and leave the children. . . . That is really horrible. You really suffer; and I'd say, "Ay! to get my retirement!" What I wanted most of all was to see myself with my old man, when we'd be old, sitting together on this balcony, talking.

The moral counterweight to her respect for Coltejer was love. She and Jairo loved each other still, and the house, with its balcony, symbolized that love. Describing it and their shared life as pensioners reinforced Nena's critique of Coltejer's ban on married women, pregnancy, and sexual pleasure even as it allowed her to express loyalty to the company.

"I'll be frank," she said: "we loved each other since '43 but we didn't get married until '61." When she became pregnant, she remembered, Jairo had suggested an abortion:

> Nena: We were afraid to get married, because of my job. And so I had my daughter without being married, you understand, right?
>
> Ann: Yes . . . a person couldn't get married, she'd be fired, right?
>
> Nena: Of course, yes. And so . . . he said, "Aren't you going to take something for it?" [*No se va a tomar algún mejoral?*] And I told him, well, then all three of us will have to go somewhere else, you, me, and my mamá. . . . Fine, [speaking in a low voice] I had her, before we were married, right? . . . I had her baptized and I gave her the name María de Jesús Palacios, which is my name.
>
> But when I came out he said . . . "What name did you give her?" And I told him that I put down María de Jesús Palacios. And so he said, "No, she is a Montoya." I just said, "well, that's up to you." And so later on, when we got married, then she could be legitimized, and he went and

changed it. . . . But with us, it was more than anything this fear that they'd find out at the factory because it was just the biggest crime,

Ann: Yes.

Nena: You got married and you had to leave. You could get married, but you left.

She insisted on the thoroughness of Coltejer's prohibition, emphasizing that her own story was entirely exceptional:

Nena: Look, that was *the biggest crime,* that or any other crime. There was a girl there who had a baby, and you should have seen the wrangling that went on with that girl, until they fired her. That was the biggest crime, because they were so selfish [*egoistas*].

Ann: And were there a lot of women who got married or who had—

Nena: No, no, no one. No one got married, no one.

Ann: Not even secretly?

Nena: No. Not secretly and not in any other way. And if they went out with men or whatever they did it very much in secret because it was a crime, married or single.

I asked how she had managed to conceal her pregnancy, and Nena responded that, in part, it was a matter of bodily luck:

Nena: It's because the weight doesn't show on me. Now because I'm old and fat and I've got a big belly, but back then it didn't show *at all.* I went to the, when she was born they had to take her out with forceps and everything, and in the hospital they said, "no, go over there because there's a lot, a lot of women ahead of you; you must be having a miscarriage." They thought that. And I was dying, I was just dying because it was already time. Anyway, until I finally had her.

Ann: And how much time? Did you go back to work?

Nena: No, I was so lucky that this was, we went out on vacation on December sixteenth and she was born on January second, and so I stayed home that month of vacation and from there I could go back to work.

Ann: And nobody knew?

Nena: *Nobody* knew, nobody . . . I didn't move even one button on one skirt, nothing, nothing.

"Imagine it," she remembered; "the only thing that grew was my bust, but drastically! I became very busty." She pumped out the milk as best she could, Nena said, and kept folded towels in her bra, which she would change in the factory bathroom. Repeatedly, I asked her to explain what she had thought or felt, or to clarify seeming impossibilities. Nena responded with tales of her body and its particularities, including descriptions of later ailments and trips to doctors and *teguas*. She even explained that one of the company doctors had been a trusted friend, and that he had examined her only a few months after the birth but had not said anything at the mill. Like the house, her body provided an alternative standpoint from which to tell an unsanctioned story about the past. Rather than reject *la moral* or the complex edifice of Coltejer's paternalistic rhetoric, she fit her own story of subterfuge into a discursive frame which, by itself, left no room for her memories.

Conclusion

Workers' stories of the social world of millwork do not offer direct evidence of past behavior but rather are a source for understanding how women and men experienced *la moral* in their own lives. Rooted in gender norms, the paternalistic structure of mill discipline partially overlapped with notions of how women and men should behave that most Antioqueños simply took for granted. Yet cultural assumptions about what one is expected to do need not be confused with everything else that "goes without saying" in a given context. Prescriptions are not descriptions. In Medellín's mills, where industrial discipline was linked to the constant reiteration of rules about sexuality, workers assumed a slippage between gender ideology and gender practice. Rules against mixed-sex talk and against flirting, for example, were understood to have been made to be broken.

Understanding *la moral* as it functioned in practice, rather than simply in terms of the disciplinary ideologies it represented, allows a fuller reconstruction of the subjective work lives of women and men in Medellín's mills. No line separated the institutional religiosity of the mills from the world of private prayers and saintly intercessions. Similarly, the spiritual exercises sponsored by the textile companies inherited the feel of small-town religious festivals. The injunction to be modest, chaste, and ladylike had meaning for female mill-workers, and workers' self-descriptions reflect key aspects of *la moral*. Stories that cut against the grain of a community memory of the totality of mill regulations are therefore told in ways that mark them as anomalous. Verbal altercations appear as exceptions to the rule of *compañerismo*, and women's descriptions of their quick-wittedness in arguments or their ability to fight are often set off by references to having been good women and good workers.

Yet the permeability between the "orthodoxy" of *la moral* and the more flexible world of "doxa," to use Bourdieu's terminology, was only one aspect of workers' relationship to the patriarchal ideology of the mills. The boundary between "doxa" and the radical "heterodoxy" of the fact that people broke mill rules was no less porous. The rigid separation of chaste and unchaste behavior, for female employees, which the Echavarrías represented as equivalent to the division between women who kept their jobs in the mills and women who "failed" to, could be blurred in practice. Workers heard stories about female operatives who had children that they never mentioned at work, about *mujeres que se fajaban,* women who bound down their bellies during pregnancy, and about men who maintained secret relationships with mill girls. Such stories, no less than the rules themselves, were part of the normative field of gender in Medellín. A changing working-class "habitus" overlapped with *la moral* without being reducible to it.

SEVEN

Masculinization and *El Control,*

1953–60

THE SYSTEM OF industrial discipline that I have abbreviated as *la moral* fell victim to its own success, and to the general success of Antioqueño industry. Through the 1940s and early 1950s, the textile firms made record profits, and Medellinense industrialists wielded more political power than ever before. In massive publicity campaigns, the national manufacturer's association, the ANDI, dominated by Antioquia's textile firms, identified industrial development with "progress" and "modernity." At a national level, the association insisted that its members were concerned not only with "private interests" but also with "national progress and the strengthening of the Colombian economy."[1] At the level of the firm, this rhetoric of progress and modernity was no less powerful. By the early 1950s, each of Colombia's big textile companies had undertaken expensive restructuring programs. Self-consciously, textile managers attempted to remake Medellín's flagship industry. They followed international debates about industrial engineering, hired North American advisers, and created wholly new systems for training employees. This chapter traces the undoing of *la moral* as Antioqueño industrialists embraced a new disciplinary model, one modeled on the reworking of Frederick W. Taylor's ideas, and on "Methods Time Management" (MTM) in the parlance of the time. Seen from the top down, the change is simple to assess. As one of Fabricato's top executives summed it up: "If in the past control has been exercised over conduct, it is now exercised over results."[2] My purpose, however, is to describe changes in disciplinary practice from the bottom up. How did workers experience the reorganization of the shop floor in the period 1953–60?

Workers in Medellín's big textile firms used the terms *el incentivo, el estandar,* and *el control* to describe the disciplinary system imposed on them with the adoption of MTM in the early 1950s. *El incentivo* and *el estandar* referred to two new labor management techniques: incentive pay and the development of the "standard hour" as a means for evaluating workers' performance. *El control* was an ironic modification of *control de la calidad,* or quality control. All three terms referred concretely to the institution of time and motion studies; *el control,* for example, was used as a verb: "Oh yes, I was controlled" (*a mi me controlaron*), said Ana Rita Arbeláez. "I was controlled by one that had a little machine [a stopwatch] . . . the *controlista,* the one that comes to do the control."[3]

In Medellín's mills, the adoption of neo-Taylorist forms of discipline marked a definitive shift to an all-male labor force, and *el control,* in women's memories, describes an experience of displacement. While both women and men remembered *el control* with bitterness, women's stories are particularly marked by anger at the engineers' lack of respect for their skill. They narrate remembered conversations, with co-workers and with the *controlistas,* in ways that emphasize their own sense of pride, a pride that was explicitly gendered. For long-time female employees on the verge of retirement, aware that the mixed-sex workplaces they had known were becoming all male, *el control* marked not only a loss of workers' control over the labor process but also the end of women's access to well-paid industrial jobs.

Industrialists' New Political Role

What workers called *el control* or *el estandar* and managers termed "industrial engineering" was an expensive new import for Medellinense industrialists. As a technology of labor management, it required not merely an occasional foreign technician (as had been present in Medellín's mills since the 1910s, when Miguel Solvés and Francisco Charpiot worked for Don Emilio) but rather on a battery of experts from the prominent U.S. firm Barnes Textile Associates.[4] Their ability to hire foreign advisers and to commit resources to the changes recommended by those advisers, such as the creation of new departments of industrial engineering within each firm and the implementation of plantwide time and motion studies, reflected the factory owners' new wealth and their new sense of the stability of Colombia's industrial policy. By 1950, Antioqueño manufacturers, led by the Echavarría clan, wielded enormous political power at the national level. The decision to pursue a more capital-intensive form of production was taken in a moment of confidence. Despite rising levels of violence in the countryside, intense partisan conflict, and, in 1953–58, Colombia's first experience with military rule, the early 1950s were an economic golden era for Medellín's big factory owners.

Industrialists' relationship to the Colombian state had changed significantly since the 1930s. López's declaration of a "Revolution on the March" had been poorly received by the Medellinense elite not only because he had seemed dangerously populist and too willing to cooperate with Colombia's tiny Communist Party but also because he never fully endorsed protectionism. López mocked the notion that a small number of factories producing light consumer goods would make Colombia the "Belgium or Switzerland of the tropics." While he sometimes supported industrialists' interests and was willing to take credit for the sector's expansion under his presidency, López favored agriculture and the export of primary products over manufacturing. He viewed tariff barriers as "a tax on the many to benefit the few," as Richard Stoller summarizes it, and he pursued an excess-profits tax to redress the balance. Such ideas lost ground through the 1940s, as the "Revolution on the March" faded, first during the Liberal administrations of Eduardo Santos (1938–42) and of López himself (in his turbulent second term, 1942–45) and then during the Conservative presidencies of Mariano Ospina (1946–50) and Laureano Gómez (1950–53).[5]

What did provide a constant counterweight to Medellín's textile capitalists' demands for increased import tariffs was the country's powerful coffee lobby. Indeed, Colombia's midcentury political history can be read through the conflicts among coffee interests, manufacturers, and big importers.[6] These conflicts, and their resolution in the creation of a heterogeneous capitalist elite, internally divided along regional lines and by economic sectors but nevertheless willing to negotiate a developmentalist model based on state subsidies, is too complex to detail here. More important for this discussion is an understanding of the chief mechanism by which such conflicts and negotiations entered the public arena. Given the effectiveness with which the Federation of Coffee Growers pursued the interests of its most powerful members, importers and big distributors created their own organization, as did manufacturers, with the founding of the ANDI in 1944. Controlled by Medellín's largest industrialists, although nominally a national body, the ANDI became one of the country's most powerful political lobbies. The clearest sign of industrialists' strengthened position, and of the success of the ANDI's attempts to win over public opinion, was Colombia's refusal, under Ospina, to sign the GATT agreement.[7]

Ospina openly defended the manufacturing interests of his home state of Antioquia, championing a policy of "integral protection" that ranged from subsidies for importers of industrial machinery to state support for the production of domestic cotton to a simple increase in the tariff (1950). *Lopista* Liberals attacked Ospina's policies and those of Gómez, a far more virulent Conservative, but the key to understanding industrialists' changing role is to notice that protectionism became less and less a partisan issue over the

Table 8. Coltejer, 1940–50

Total Workforce	1940	1,320	
	1942	3,392	
	1944	5,031	
	1946	6,093	
	1948	7,186	
	1950	7,384	
Net Profits (in pesos).	1940	833,908.00	
Not adjusted for inflation (15%).	1942	3,061,444.00	
	1944	6,474,658.00	
	1946	10,768,923.61	
	1948	14,612,646.68	
		Total Shareholders	Shares held
Stockholders and Shares	1940	951	250,597
	1942	2,600	1,627,484
	1944	5,029	2,993,075
	1946	7,115	4,065,287
	1948	12,157	5,869,701
	1950	15,610	7,988,977

Source: Alfonso Mejía Robledo, Vidas y empresas de Antioquia: Diccionario biográfico, bibliografico, y económico (Medellín: Imprenta Departamental de Antioquia, 1951), pp. 219–20.

course of the 1950s. The ANDI built bipartisan support by financing Liberal as well as Conservative candidates and by emphasizing economic nationalism; by the mid-1950s the Liberal Party leaders Carlos and Alberto Lleras (future presidents both) supported the political vision of a national industrial future.[8] Indeed, the ANDI may have prefigured the elite bipartisan negotiations of the National Front in the 1960s. Certainly, an incapacity to grasp the new political role of industrialists contributed to the failure of Rojas Pinilla's attempt at military dictatorship. In 1953, General Rojas Pinilla had taken power amid general applause, supported by Ospinista Conservatives, Liberals, and the country's economic power brokers. Military rule was welcomed by a nation torn apart by rural violence, which the sectarianism of Gómez would only continue to fuel. Soon, however, Rojas Pinilla began to dabble in populism—and to experiment with fiscal policy. In Medellín and around the country, large employers simply sent their workers home, with pay. Their "strike," or rather their lockout, spelled the end for the general. A bipartisan coalition, backed by business interests across competing sectors of the economy, then moved toward a power-sharing arrangement, the National Front, that lasted for more than a decade.

National industry had come of age economically as well as politically—the two being tightly interwoven in midcentury Colombia. Medellinenses controlled the ANDI because that city now enjoyed an undisputed hegemony in the size, longevity, and technical sophistication of its industrial ventures. Antioqueño industry was also fantastically profitable through the 1940s and 1950s, allowing for sustained capital reinvestment. Fabricato almost tripled its capital stock during this period. Worth one hundred million pesos in 1955, the company rivaled Antioquia's two largest firms, Coltejer and the cigarette producer Coltabaco—with these top three companies accounting for the vast majority of capital investment in Antioqueño manufacturing.[9] Coltejer's financial progress can be traced in table 8. Although the same level of data is not available for the 1950s, qualitative evidence suggests that the company's marked growth continued through the early 1960s. For both Fabricato and Coltejer, growth in this period also depended on stock issues. More than eight thousand Colombians owned stock in Fabricato by the late 1960s.[10] By then, as indicated in chapter 1, and visible in table 8, Coltejer was one of the most widely held companies in Latin America. Thus, the Medellinense firms that embarked on the restructuring programs outlined in this chapter were markedly different from their predecessors, which had pioneered the gender-specific controls of *la moral*. By the 1950s, through their control of the ANDI, Antioquia's big textile firms had positioned themselves as the nation's most forward-looking and sophisticated enterprises. The decision to leave aside a form of labor discipline modeled on traditional sexual mores in favor of one centering on productivity and industrial efficiency was entirely in keeping with this new national role.

El Control

MTM resulted from several decades of experimentation, and studious self-promotion, by a wide range of engineers, "experts," and consultants. Centered in the United States and overseen by trade associations like the American Institute of Industrial Engineers, this far-reaching movement cannot accurately be described simply as "Taylorism," although that remains the umbrella term most often applied. By the 1950s, Taylor's ideas—many of which he had synthesized from others' work—had been tinkered with and redirected toward the kind of detailed motion study pioneered by Taylor's contemporaries Frank and Lillian Gilbreth.[11] Even in Britain and the United States, textile mills seem not to have adopted what the Gilbreths called "micromotion study" with stopwatches and careful records of workers' movements, until the late 1940s.[12] Through the 1950s, in reviews written for the industry, terms like "incentive plan," "mechanical time studies," "work simplification," and "standards departments" are identified with "modern" management and are described as new, if increasingly widespread, supervisory methods.[13] Thus Antioquia's industrial workplaces did not come late to "Taylorism," which graduates of Medellín's National School of Mines had brought to Coltejer and other local firms in the 1930s.[14] Rather, the region's textile companies adopted MTM and "payment by results," to use the rhetoric associated with neo-Taylorism, only a few years behind their counterparts in Europe, Australia, and the United States. Time and motion studies, imported together with new machinery and other labor-saving technologies, were being undertaken in textile mills in Brazil, Egypt, Mexico, and India in the early 1950s, at the same time as in Colombia, and, indeed, the Colombian experience became a model for other textile firms in other Latin American countries, as Peter Winn suggests in his discussion of the Yarur mill in Chile.[15]

As applied in Medellín, "payment by results" depended on the notion of a "standard hour," a measure of what an operative on a particular machine should accomplish in sixty minutes. Because their function was to define this measurement for each job in the mill, the new departments of industrial engineering created at Coltejer, Fabricato, and Tejicondor were generally referred to as departments of "standards," using the English word—from which workers derived their own term *el estandar.* Consultants' methods mirrored those applied in North American textile mills. At Coltejer, Fabricato, and Tejicondor, the imported advisers initiated factory-wide tours of observation, in which analysts with stopwatches and clipboards recorded workers' movements. They scrutinized machine processes and work patterns throughout the mill, suggesting ways to improve cotton quality and examining workers' authorized and unauthorized breaks as carefully as they monitored what operatives did at their machines. The goal, from the engineers' perspective, was not to fine-tune discrete processes but rather to assess the potential for change at the level of the entire plant. Their suggestions ranged from eliminating specific hand motions to rearranging the physical layout of the workrooms. At Coltejer, for example, employees kept their bicycles near their machines so that they would not be stolen, but this meant that people worked on their bicycles during their shifts. The consultants therefore had a bicycle shed built at the plant gate.[16] Workers were intensely aware of the unceasing nature of this scrutiny. At Fabricato, according to Concha Bohórquez, time and motion observers told workers that they should behave normally and that they should feel free to take breaks, eat, or talk to co-workers. But, she said, "you knew that would count against you—you'd have to be very dumb."[17]

The results of the engineers' time and motion studies were used to define a "best way" to perform any given operation and to set hourly production quotas for different jobs. Unlike straight piece-rates (common in Antioquia's mills since the 1910s), workers' earnings on *el estandar* were determined by a time-based rate, measured by the number of units per hour they had achieved in a given day. A person who produced sixty "units" per hour had reached *el estandar*, and was paid at a daily rate that included a bonus for having met the standard. A person who produced more than sixty received a significant increase in their daily earnings, as one's pay-rate increased proportionately with output.[18] Engineers at Coltejer attempted to convince workers of the system's fairness by insisting that the "standard hour" included an allowance for the breaks a person required for "personal needs" and "physical fatigue."[19] Tejicondor's in-house magazine asserted that the new quotas were carefully calibrated to demand no more physical energy than "walking 4.83 kilometers per hour on level ground." "As this system is based in mathematics," *Revista Tejicondor* opined, "its exactitude is immediately apparent."[20] Skilled operatives could also be motivated by pride and competitiveness, and the companies celebrated those who achieved rates of 80, 100, or even 120 standard units per hour (in the latter case, a person had worked at twice the rate the engineers had determined to be optimal for a given job).[21]

The establishment of a parallel layer of management, in the new departments of industrial engineering, caused resentment among workroom supervisors. The new system changed their relationship with those they supervised and limited their authority—as the new engineers and visiting consultants reported directly to top management. Don Luis Henao, a former supervisor from Coltejer, and one who had come up through the ranks, expressed his disagreement with incentive pay by way of a story of pride and reversal typical of textile employees' memories of their conversations with workplace superiors. His immediate boss, he said, "was always getting mad at me, because I was the supervisor there and I was in disagreement with this, with Standards."

> Don Luis: And so I told him, I didn't tell him anything; until one day, seeing that it was a problem, they called me in for a meeting with him, and also with the other man on my shift and with the head of personnel. They invited me in there and the first question they asked me was "Why are you in disagreement with Standards?" And I told him: "Simply because it doesn't make for quality. What are we doing? We're pulling the threads out . . . and making cylinders [of warp], for the looms, where a hundred or two hundred are damaged" . . .
>
> Eh! And so the administrator comes and tells me, "Unfortunately, yes, it's true. Luis H., you have hit the nail on the head. You are *right*. They just sent back I don't know how much merchandise from Germany, because it was defective." . . . and, since then, I was the most highly regarded man there.
>
> Ann: And did they get rid of Standards?
> Don Luis: No, it continued, but with a lot more moderation . . . be-

cause there were people that earned a lot of money but didn't produce quality. . . . Now they've modified it a lot; now at Coltejer quality is everything.[22]

To win over mid-level supervisors, like Don Luis, as well as ordinary workers, the companies recruited *controlistas* from among the ranks of skilled operatives and those with seniority at the mill. As in the United States, engineers "sold" the new system by recycling propaganda produced by Frederick Taylor almost fifty years previously, and Taylor himself (along with Adam Smith and Charles Babbage) was eulogized in printed material produced for Coltejer's and Fabricato's in-house training courses, run by the companies' newly created industrial engineering departments.[23] When I asked retiree Eugenio Márquez, for example, about *el estandar*, he remarked that "I read a little bit about the history of industrial engineering." Without mentioning Taylor by name, he recounted, in abbreviated form, one of the most famous of the many (probably apocryphal) vignettes employed by the "father of scientific management" to justify and promote his ideas. For Eugenio, however, the story of Taylor's experiments with workmen in the pig-iron section of Bethlehem Steel served as a condemnation of Fabricato's "arbitrary" incentive system.

In itself, Eugenio's abbreviated reference to Taylor's story, which he embedded within an explanation of *el estandar*, points to the enormous complexity with which texts of all kinds circulate in the twentieth century. Taylor's *Principles of Scientific Management*, published in 1911, restated the ideas he had presented in his 1903 book, *Shop Management*; what was new was the inclusion of numerous autobiographical anecdotes.[24] Of these, the story of the pig-iron handlers seems to stand out in the minds of Taylor's readers, perhaps because he wrote it in dialogue and partially in dialect: it is a classic example of the persuasive power of reported speech. From Ralph Barnes to Daniel Bell to Harry Braverman, readers of *Principles of Scientific Management* return to Taylor's discussion of a Pennsylvania Dutchman he called Schmidt.[25] Taylor claimed to have trained Schmidt (as he believed one might train an "intelligent gorilla") to handle almost six times more pig-iron per day than his workmates regularly handled, and paid him 60 percent more than the others received.[26] Whether or not Schmidt ever existed, he could be used, by the late 1950s, to promote incentive pay among workers at a Colombian textile firm. In shortened form, the pig-iron handler could then be invoked, almost four decades later, by a worker faced with the problem of explaining the "standard hour system" to a young interviewer who had never worked in a textile mill. "Industrial engineering," said Eugenio,

began with a person who had two workers, at an iron company, laboring. And this man was a mechanical engineer. He began watching—so the story goes, I wasn't there. He saw that there was a man who produced more than the others . . . but who was paid the same. And so this mechanic, or, better, this engineer . . . said: "The person that works at sixty units per hour, I'll pay him more. And the person that produces more than sixty, I'll pay him according to his output." . . . To me, this man seems to have been very fair, because he wanted to stimulate the one that worked hardest. But here, they do the opposite. . . . What happens is that if someone goes over, they come and increase the number of units—like as if to say, "This one's really good, let's squeeze some more juice out of him."[27]

While both Taylor and his detractors used the pig-iron anecdote as a stand-in for scientific management as a whole, Eugenio recounted it as part of a critique of *el estandar* that was specific to Fabricato. "Speaking concretely, I'm referring only to this company," he emphasized, saying that he could not claim to know how well or how badly the system had worked in other places. Like many retirees, he acknowledged that a good worker had in fact earned more on incentive pay, at least at first, and he insisted that the system was not bad in itself; rather, it had been "badly applied."[28]

Pride in Work

Eugenio's central criticism of *el estandar* at Fabricato was that it measured workers without regard for human variation. Some people pick things up quickly and some do not, he said, putting himself in the second group: "Right? It's like saying you have to think the same as me right at this moment, or me think the same as you. No man! Maybe we do think the same about something, but the normal thing is for you to be thinking something different."[29] Other retirees expressed their resentment of the standard hour system in similar terms, describing it as a system that pretended to measure one worker against "another person who doesn't have the same ability or the same way of doing something, or maybe who's sick."[30] For María Elisa Alvarez, the question was one of each person's "pace." "There was a worker there who I couldn't stand," she said, describing a bobbin-cart pusher who worked more quickly than the others. Using a floor manager's voice, she presented his story as a moral commentary:

After that . . . he started not being able to manage the work. . . . He got operated on for an ulcer and when he came back to work, he couldn't really do anything. To where one of the floor supervisors, one of the bosses, one of the important ones, told him: "Frankly, R——, you're useless to me now. You got a lot of people fired, and that's what really bothers me, all the *compañeros* I had to lay off, not because I wanted to but because of the *estandar* system. I knew their pace; but the pace you were using, it wasn't your real pace."[31]

A worker who has a faster pace than other people, concluded María Elisa, should "sneak over" to help a co-worker; in spinning, for example, she said that the right thing to do was to doff somebody else's machine (replace full bobbins with empty ones) whenever a person had extra time. "If that can't be done, because the standards man is standing there right next to you, well that's that," she said, but a fast worker should keep up a normal pace and not "make war" on his or her *compañeros*.

Yet María Elisa's own fast pace, and her knowledge of a job she had taken pride in, by 1953, for almost twenty-five years, was what she most emphasized in recounting her experiences with *el estandar*. Like several of the retired women I interviewed, she used time and motion study to tell a seemingly contradictory story, about her own speed and skill, on the one hand, and about the widely hated company speed-up, on the other. When a man from the standards department arrived in her section, *urdidoras*, said María Elisa, she had warned him, indirectly, that he would not be able to keep up with her: "I told him, 'look, I can't work at your pace because I have my own . . . you won't believe me but your pace is not the same as mine, even if you're a man and I'm a woman.'" The problem, she said, was that he had to stop to make notes on his clipboard; he could not follow her hand movements as she fixed breaks in the yarn and rethreaded the machine. Recounting their conversation as she remembered it, María Elisa switched back and forth between his voice and her own.

> Then the machine shut off. . . . [He asked me,] "Why did it shut off?" and I told him, "because of a sliver" . . . a long bit of yarn that didn't go through the twisting-frame right. Fine. I gave him the sliver. Fine. [Using his voice,] "And what do I do with it?" . . . "It has to be taken to the supervisor of the main spinning, so that they can correct the problem, it's a problem with the machine." "How do you know the problem's with the machine?" "Look . . . if you don't understand why it broke, you have to go find out in the main spinning room, because that's where the problem is."
>
> He went . . . and they found a serious problem. Fine. He came back to my machine and he said "let's continue." We tried, but no, that guy couldn't work with me at all.[32]

Tejicondor's standards department tried again, she said, sending her a woman whom they had trained for time and motion study but who had previously worked alongside María Elisa. "Look J——," María Elisa remembered having told her,

"Ask me anything, but I'm not going to answer any of your questions."
Fine. And that's what I did, I said, "Me, I'm not going to follow behind
any of my *compañeros*, harrying and persecuting them." She said, "Well
here I come, ready to harry you and persecute you!" And me, "well,
alright then, at least I'll have someone to talk to!" So we went and took
all the notes, since she also knew spinning . . . we got along just fine. She
was there maybe a day, when the supervisor said, "This is stupid, it's
stupid to put standards on the girls in *urdimbre*, these girls keep up a
pace! More than that?" Well, they left us alone then, and I kept working
and seeing my *compañeros* all worn out, with those standards.[33]

Her description of *el estandar* was a story of individual triumph embedded
within a larger narrative of loss. "Standards were one of the worst things that
ever happened in the mill," for María Elisa. Indeed, the shift to neo-Taylorist
discipline was the only aspect of her working life at Tejicondor that she
remembered with a sense of having been wronged.

María Elisa's narrative strategy was typical. Retired workers used anecdotes about the new system to tell stories of strength and skill rather than of
weakness. Their stories recall the North American legend of John Henry.
Even as they conceded that the increased presence of industrial engineers
changed the work process irremediably, former operatives emphasized the
public recognition of their own knowledge, experience, and ability. Whether
they existed only in memory or had taken place, in some form, at the time,
the conversations that retirees remembered having with those who had
come to clock their movements demonstrate that the pride which machine-
tenders took in their jobs derived from the social experience of work and not
simply from their loyalty to a given employer.

While men also remembered confrontations with engineers and lower-
level observers from the mills' new standards departments, women's stories
about the standard hour system were especially vivid. More than male retirees, they communicated exasperation and resentment in long, carefully
recounted dialogues. Susana Gómez, for example, who had retired from
Rosellón, explained that instead of *el incentivo* she had called it *el sin-
sentido* (literally, "nonsense"). She remembered arguing with the engineers
and comparing their methods to those of a dictator.

They would say, "Hey now, don't get mad, you don't have to get mad!"
And I'd tell them "*Ay mijo!* You better go and thank God that I'm not a
swearing woman, because I'd have used the big one on you by now,
because all of you, you're like Fidel Castro; all you need is for them to
give you a revolver and you'd be Fidel Castro. Because the thing is, you
are really corrupt and really shameful, and you're just here watching us,
you're just sitting there, in your suits and ties, and we're here with our

hands full. *No mijo!* You don't know what it's like to sit yourself down to work eight hours!"[34]

As had María Elisa, Susana maintained that the man the standards department had sent to observe her had given up in frustration: "Finally they got tired of it and they left me alone." María Cristina Restrepo, similarly, remembered having won an individual victory over the man Fabricato had assigned to observe her. She used her own memory of his words to describe the man's defeat, rather than a back-and-forth dialogue, but her way of remembering the incident mirrors Susana's and María Elisa's stories. "After three days," she said,

> He went and called over another one of the men from *el control*, and he told him, "look, I can't believe this work. This cotton is awful, it's impossible. She never stops working, it's constantly [*es constantamente*]; I'm the one getting dizzy, not her."[35]

In women's accounts, the standard hour system appears as a direct affront to the pride and skill with which long-time female operatives approached their jobs. Mediated by the rhetoric associated with *la moral*, the public image of Medellín's textile companies had for years centered on their female workers. As industrial efficiency took the place of *la moral*, women who had spent their lives in the mills found themselves symbolically and materially displaced.

Women's Exclusion from Textile Jobs

Male participation in the textile workforce had increased over a long period, as outlined in the introduction to this book. By the 1930s men made up more than a third of Antioquia's textile workers, and by midcentury half the region's mill-workers were male (see table 1, above). Nevertheless, the application of *el estandar* in the early 1950s marked a definitive shift. Following a trend associated with the introduction of the standard hour system and MTM in cotton mills in other countries at the same time, female participation in the workforce declined in direct proportion to the growing role of technical engineers.[36]

Previously, male participation had expanded as the textile companies themselves expanded. In the boom years of the 1930s and 1940s, men entered the mills in increasing numbers, but women continued to be hired. With the reorganization of the mills after the massive time and motion studies of the early 1950s, however, the companies reduced their hiring across the board. By monitoring cotton quality more carefully, on the one hand, and demanding higher levels of output from fewer workers, on the other, Fabricato, Tejicondor, and Coltejer were able to increase production while cutting the labor force.[37] The ratio of outgoing to incoming males stayed near 1:1, while the corresponding figure for women rose dramatically, to 3:1.[38] Thus the mills made the transition from a largely female to a nearly all-male workforce without mass layoffs; men replaced women who retired or left in the course of normal labor turnover—if they were replaced at all. Through the early 1970s, this meant that long-time female employees reached retirement as one or two of a handful of women still working at weaving or spinning machines.

Certain jobs, however, were abruptly reclassified as "men's jobs," especially in spinning, which had remained more heavily female, through the 1940s, than other sections of the mills. At Tejicondor, for example, the engineers from American Associated recommended that "only male doffers be retained after the application of incentives," given the increase in workload.[39] At Fabricato, Zoila Rosa Valencia remembered a similar switch in the *mecheras*, or fly-frames, section. "These guys showed up," she said, "to reduce personnel, or whatever, . . . and what do you know, they took all the women off the machines." She and her co-workers were each assigned a male trainee, Zoila scoffed, "and when they learned how, or whatever, they gave our machines to those men." Turning the story around, she used it to underscore the women's unappreciated skill:

> I put up a real fight about that . . . we told them, "There's just one question. Ever since they took these machines away from us the machines in the main workroom have been shutting down, but when we were working we always kept ahead of them and they always had yarn. . . ." I used to tell them, "If the men are so macho how come the machines are all shut down?"[40]

Concha Bohórquez described the change as one that outsiders, "*misteres*," had brought to the mills. (In Colombia, *mister* is a non-pejorative term for North American men.) While she was more light-hearted in narrating her experiences with *el estandar*, she too made it a story of individual vindication: she had refused to be intimidated. In her memory, the newly impersonal work relations introduced in the mid-1950s do not displace the earlier, paternalistic Fabricato of the Echavarrías; rather, the two coexist in nostalgic tension. Rudesindo Echavarría, Concha said, had intervened to stop the dismissal of women workers.

> Concha: People said that two *misteres* came, to organize the factory, with this *standar*. And they said that all the women had to leave the factory . . . that women were only good for sleeping with. That's what they [the *misteres*] said.

Ann: That's what they said?

Concha: And so people said that we were going to get fired. . . . The ones that were going to be fired . . . they got sent to the basement. . . . And one day I got sent to the basement . . . it was because there was no cotton or something like that; and so we were supposed to go pick over some cotton—the cotton was in these huge bags, these sacks. It was so hot! And there were a lot of us, so I laid myself down on one of these sacks and I just went to sleep.

Ann: [Laughs.]

Concha: Ay! When all of a sudden they wake me up and tell me: "Hey, five of the 'big whites' [slang for bosses] came by here and they saw you sleeping!" . . . And I said, "Bah, what are they going to do to me? They're not going to do anything to me." So a minute later I got called to the office, and they asked me how was it that I dared to be sleeping? And I just said, "Avemaría! If you had the chance to sit down there you'd see, you'd fall asleep straight off, because it's just perfect!" [Laughing.] They didn't say anything else to me . . . but the other girls, they got it.

Ann: Did a lot of women get fired?

Concha: Lots! A lot of women, until what's his name, Don Rudesindo Echavarría, he came. Don Rudesindo Echavarría, and he stopped the firing of women . . . and so they didn't fire some of them, and the ones in the basement? They had to give them their jobs back.[41]

Rudesindo Echavarría may well have made a public announcement of concern or, in fact, stopped the personnel department for dismissing long-term female employees. Certainly, the opposition between the Echavarrías and later managers was less sharply drawn at Fabricato than at other mills. Jorge Posada, who oversaw the company's massive program of time and motion studies in 1953–57 and who later became Fabricato's president, promoted the standard hour system without distancing himself from paternalistic forms. Posada visited the workrooms, as the Echavarrías had always done, and he used religious language in the articles he wrote for *Fabricato al Día*.[42] Nevertheless, Concha's story is more evocative as a *story* than as evidence of what Don Rudesindo may or may not have said publicly. Her narrative fits a community narrative in which *el estandar* marks the end of the "good old days," when the Echavarría family ran the mills directly. The introduction of time and motion studies appears in workers' memories as a watershed dividing an earlier period, when "the human person counted," as a retired man from Rosellón put it, from the impersonal world introduced by the new engineers. The action attributed to Don Rudesindo, of protecting women from being fired, enacts that division within Concha's memory.

Concha's anecdote brings together diverse strands of the shift from *la moral* to *el control*. What changed with the shift to neo-Taylorist management techniques were precisely the kind of workplace relationships Concha narrates. With fewer operatives managing more machines, workers were now not often together, "a lot of us," in one part of the plant, with relatively lax supervision; in this context, Concha's day in the basement stands out as unusual. The new speed of work meant precisely that one had fewer opportunities for such unauthorized breaks: a nap on a soft sack of cotton is symbolically the antithesis of MTM. Finally, the story's resolution, a personal encounter leavened by humor, harks back to an earlier style of interaction, as seen in workers' stories about the 1930s and 1940s. With great economy, Concha's story captures key aspects of workers' experience of the changes associated with time and motion study—from the *misteres'* recommendation that women be replaced to the insecurity of seeing one's workmates laid off. Yet hers is a light-hearted narration, transformed by nostalgia into a symbolic, farcical story rather than a tragic one.

Modern Managers, Modern Unionists

Embracing a new vision of capital-intensive processes and efficient workrooms, Medellín's textile employers abandoned *la moral* in favor of workplace agreements, which set out employees' rights and responsibilities in more specific terms. This involved a conscious rhetorical shift, separating a new, more North American style of management from previous patterns. *Revista Tejicondor,* for example, exhorted workers to use new terms: "Don't say overseer [*Vigilante*]—say SUPERVISOR. Don't say Administration—say EXECUTIVE OFFICE," proclaimed the company magazine. Similar messages likely appeared in posters on factory walls.[43] Managers themselves made the distinction, as long-time workers did, between "then" and "now," as is evident in the statement by a manager at Fabricato, quoted above: "If in the past control has been exercised over conduct, it is now exercised over results. If in the past awards were given for good attendance, they will now be given for efficiency."[44]

A contemporary description of the change in Medellinense managers' sense of themselves is provided by the work of a gifted ethnographer trained at the Harvard Business School in the late 1950s. In 1960, Charles Savage traveled to Medellín and, with the support of the leadership of the ANDI, including Rodrigo Uribe, Carlos Echavarría's nephew and then CEO of Coltejer, undertook to study the transition from a "patronal culture" of workplace organization to "Taylorist-oriented systems of work measurement." Savage decided against conducting his study in the textile mills, feeling that they were too large; he may also have found them too noisy for conversation to happen easily.[45] He chose two chinaware plants and a large menswear firm, which Savage called "El Dandy." In the latter, MTM seems to have been applied in a way identical to the textile mills. A standards department was created at El Dandy, and engineers conducted extensive time and motion studies to establish an incentive pay system, which workers bitterly resented, and which led to a drawn-out strike. Savage had sympathy for the neo-Taylorist engineers, and their innovative spirit was, in part, what he set out to describe. Nevertheless, he became increasingly critical of their methods. He termed them the *doctores,* using the title of address that distinguished the young engineers from traditional *patrones,* addressed with the honorific *don.* He reports that one of the *doctores,* Ramón García, admonishing a worker: "I am not *don* Ramon. I am *Doctor* García."[46] Indeed, Savage became convinced that the intensity of the *doctores'* desire to overturn the paternalistic structures of the 1930s and 1940s made "Taylorism more than a method for organizing factory work; it became the emotional center of their world, the mortar that held it together." A perceptive observer, Savage is persuasive in claiming that the young engineers' identity as professional men and modernizers was at stake in the day-to-day interactions he observed. The lunchtime rituals of the *doctores* at one of the chinaware firms he studied speak volumes:

> The *doctores* devised a clever social mechanism to enforce their norms. Its primary setting was the luncheon table in the company house where they gathered at noon. Only the managers who enjoyed the doctoral designation lunched together. . . . The doctores punished infractions of their norms with jokes that centered around a biblical name-calling game devised by one of them. They called the plant manager the Father, the assistant manager the Son, and the production manager the Holy Spirit. They poked fun at Don Paco [a "patronal" manager who organized social activities] by labeling him Saint Vincent, Apostle of Charity. They underscored the standards manager's leading role in factory reform by designating him Martin Luther. Names like Pontius Pilate, Herod, and Judas were assigned temporarily to anyone whose behavior became suspect. The terms were used in the jovial, intimate spirit of fraternity that the doctores maintained when they were by themselves.[47]

In the textile mills, where *el estandar* was accompanied by a shift in the sexual makeup of the workforce, the *doctores* tilted not only against the windmills of patron-client relations but also against the specific "invented tradition" of *la moral.* The shift to an almost all-male workforce made the sexual controls of the 1940s wholly obsolete. By the mid-1960s, both companies accepted married women and unmarried mothers—even if few new women were being hired. Ana Palacios de Montoya, for example, had married Jairo Montoya in 1961, before her retirement from Coltejer, knowing that she could now do so without endangering her job—although she still hesitated to tell her workmates. At Fabricato, the convent-like Patronato began to be seen as an anachronism. Treading carefully, so as not to antagonize the order of the Hermanas de la Presentación, the company closed the dormitory in several stages over the decade 1963–74.[48] Now that the operatives were male, workers' comportment (at and away from work) ceased to be a focus of discipline. Drinking on the weekend, being seen in a "bad" part of town, going out dancing, finding oneself the subject of malicious gossip: things that might have meant a woman's firing were unimportant to a man's employment.[49] Similarly, the beauty contests and elaborate religious festivals of earlier years disappeared, although sporting events and other recreational activities continued to expand at all of the city's factories.

While the workrooms were mixed-sex, and thus dangerous, the family-centered rhetoric of Antioquia's large textile firms had leaned toward images of protection. The largest mills were symbolically fathers, able to protect hundreds of sexually vulnerable females while preparing them as future wives. As outlined in chapter 5, this imagery had included male workers. Their wages and increasing extra-wage benefits allowed them to sustain their own families; the companies' generosity passed through them to their wives and children. With women's gradual exclusion, the textile factories expanded the "family wage" system they had begun to envision in the 1940s. Through the 1950s and 1960s, the mills subsidized unprecedented numbers of mortgages for workers with families, whether by building low-cost homes or by setting up separate lending entities.[50] With housing came a renewed attention to domesticity. Social workers, or *visitadores sociales,* evaluated the home life of those who applied for jobs, visited current workers' homes, and arranged classes and recreational activities directed toward workers' wives and families.[51] By 1965, for example, more than five hundred wives and daughters of Fabricato workers were taking classes in embroidery, cooking, dressmaking, folk dancing, and the like. Antioquia's textile employers also increased their role as the educators of workers' children: Coltejer, for example, employed twenty teachers for nine hundred children by 1955.[52] The difference was that the imagery of the 1950s excluded female employees. Factory managers now defined their ideal worker, quite explicitly, as a male head-of-household. As Jorge Posada explained it, Fabricato would benefit in direct proportion to "the character of a worker's family atmosphere, which allows him to render more efficient work-shifts through conditions of good health, diet, housing, and entertainment."[53]

High-level managers like Posada were attempting to fashion a new style of discipline, one not dependent on the control of workers' sexuality. They embraced a new phrase, "industrial relations," and the big firms soon established formal departments with that name. But workers' attitudes were also changing. In the charged political atmosphere of the late 1950s and early 1960s, company unions at Fabricato and Tejicondor, as well as at each of Coltejer's legally separate subsidiaries (Coltefábrica, Planta de Acabados, Doña María, Rosellón, and Sedeco), were taken over from within.[54] A new generation of working-class militants drew inspiration from radical worker movements across Latin America, as well as from the radical student activism of the period. For their part, older unionists had gained experience and self-confidence through their participation in anticommunist federations at a national and international level. The combination meant that the mill-workers' unions no longer depended on having either the blessing or the organizational help of the company owners. Increasingly, too, young church-men supported workers' demands rather than attempting to moderate them. By 1968, for example, company priests at both Coltejer and Fabricato were firmly aligned with the Catholic left.[55]

For the first time since 1936, Antioquia's textile conglomerates faced unions willing to strike over wage demands and working conditions, and the standard hour system became a lightning rod for worker dissatisfaction, as had happened at El Dandy. Workers at Tejicondor struck for four months in 1959, unsuccessfully demanding that the company suspend the standard hour system.[56] Representatives of workers' organizations at other mills distanced themselves from Tejicondor's union, widely denounced as communist, but they followed its lead.[57] Citing "the terrible results obtained by Standards Engineering," Coltejer's two unions launched a sustained campaign against the new system. In 1958 and again in 1960, company president Carlos Echavarría roundly refused to consider any modifications to the new system, countering that modern techniques of industrial engineering were necessary for the country's progress and that workers earned more with incentive pay than would otherwise be possible.[58] By 1962, however, Coltejer workers' demands for better wages, and for a negotiated solution to the question of el estandar, led to the company's first strike in nearly three decades. A longer strike in 1967, together with ongoing conflicts at other textile mills definitively laid to rest the notion that Antioquia's history of paternalistic work relations would protect its central industry from labor conflict.[59]

Although the textile unions failed to reverse the speed-up associated with incentive pay, all of the large firms were forced to train union representatives in time and motion study and in the computation of incentive pay scales. Remembering the experience thirty years later, a retired union leader from Tejicondor summed up his view of el estandar. "It's a bad analogy," said Pedro González Cano, "but I'm going to make an analogy for you."

> You take a dog and tie a stick to it here, here on its neck; and you tie this
> stick so that the end sticks out over the dog's head. And you're going to

tie a sausage on the stick there, so the dog will run to eat that sausage. And the more he runs the more he gets tired. And he's never going to catch that sausage, right? That is the system of *el estandar.* No one can catch up; no one catches up because that's the system it has.[60]

Conclusion

As a veteran of the polarized strike at Tejicondor, and a unionist trained in MTM, Don Pedro expressed himself with unusual bluntness. Most workers' criticisms of *el control* were more indirect. As had Luis Henao and Eugenio Márquez, retirees tended to attack the way standards had been applied in the workrooms they knew rather than arguing that time and motion study or incentive pay systems were evil in themselves. Indeed, retirees praised the introduction of new, more modern machines and the improvement in cotton quality that allowed each operative to work more efficiently. By the 1960s, with newly imported systems for monitoring humidity, more efficient spinning machines, improved sizing techniques (for preparation of the warp) and fully automated looms, workers were tending numbers of machines that would have seemed incredible to their younger selves.[61] Most felt pride. Ana Palacios de Montoya, for example, had entered Coltejer in the 1940s, when most weavers operated ten or twelve looms each; by the time she retired, she said with satisfaction, "I was tending sixty-four."[62]

In reference to the machines themselves, workers tended to speak with amazement and a technical kind of appreciation. Remembering that she had once worked on machines that required an operative to pull out damaged cloth *"by hand!"* Susana Osorio laughed that "the world wasn't so advanced back then!" A friend of hers added, "Sure! It had to be like that! You had to help the machines with *your hand;* now it's all electronic!"[63] Proud of their former employers' "modernity" and "progress," retirees often asked if I'd gone on factory tours or if I'd seen the newest computerized machines (I had). They were well aware that technological improvements had meant fewer jobs, and they described the layoffs and reshufflings that accompanied the installation of new machinery.[64] Yet the generation that had worked through the 1940s and 1950s tended not to blame the new technology for the changes that made the factories "not what they used to be." Rather, as had Savage, they blamed the arrogance of the new engineers. What most stood out in their memories was the way *el control* had changed the social experience of work.

Women's memories of time and motion study reflect their knowledge that the new engineers favored men. Concha's mordant description, of two *misteres* who had informed the Echavarrías that women were "good only for sleeping with," points to the contradictory relationship between class and gender in the shift toward a new disciplinary system. The minority of women that remained at the mills to retirement age, as Concha had done, had been symbolically excepted from the equation of femininity, sex, and marriage. The local orthodoxy that female operatives should be virgins had imposed on them a rigid discipline, but it had also made it possible for women who followed the rule of *la moral* to command a level of respect at work. In the new order represented by the units of the standard hour system, however, the mills had no place for women workers—whether chaste or unchaste.

Yet masculinization had not begun with *el estandar*. Since the late 1930s, mill-owners had been steadily replacing female operatives with males—even as they organized an elaborate set of rationales and special rules to smooth over the contradictions of employing women of marriageable age. The advice dispensed by North American textile engineers merely capped a process that had begun with the identification of *la mujer obrera* as a being separate from *la clase obrera*.

CONCLUSION

GENDER WAS KEY TO the consolidation of industrial discipline in Medellín—before, during, and after the intense paternalism of 1936–53. In the initial decades of the industry, mill-owners faced pressure to behave in ways that recognized a special moral responsibility toward young female employees. Not only local churchmen but also many of the women entering the mills (and the women's families) expected that female operatives should be treated with the respect reserved for *señoritas*. Women working outside their families' homes, in places where they intermingled with men, would maintain that status only if they were clearly identified as virgins. After divisive strikes in 1935–36, the sons of Medellín's first industrial entrepreneurs began to move away from the ad hoc disciplinary forms of their fathers and toward a more hegemonic model, a local version of the Fordist ideal, which I have abbreviated with the term *la moral*. As factory managers consolidated this disciplinary model, the publicly acclaimed virginity of female employees became the symbolic center of work relations in the textile industry.

La moral did more than ensure the sexual chastity of the majority of Medellín's women workers. As manufacturing began to be seen as the life's blood of a new, modern Antioquia, it provided the region's industrialists with a means of legitimizing their expanding power. In 1936–53, the Echavarrías turned their mills into showplaces for an industrial model that joined fervent Catholicism to capitalist factory production. That their paternalistic practice depended upon the high returns generated by protectionist tariffs did not weaken the appeal of such a model. Medellín's wealthiest industrialists offered a vision of industrial "progress" that would not disrupt the familiar hierarchies of social rank and patriarchal family organization. Explicitly anticommunist, *la moral* incorporated piety, sexual self-control, and proper behavior in public with the injunction to work hard and be loyal to one's employer. Because this form of industrial discipline linked one's behavior at work to a complex set of social values that extended well beyond the workplace, I have analyzed it by applying Gramsci's concept of hegemony. Millowners solidified their class position, which enabled them to generate profit from the waged labor of thousands of employees, by selectively drawing on the behavioral norms by which Antioqueños, in general, judged women and men.

This book has explored the subjective and interpersonal dimension of factory labor by reference to a reconstructed chronology of workplace discipline in Medellín. The distinct periods I outline for the city's textile workplaces, 1905–35, 1936–53, and 1953–60, reflect changes that are measurable at a very local level but that are also linked to specific moments in the transnational circulation of ideas about industrial production. Nor can local changes in gender and work relations be understood without reference to regional and national structures—Medellín's urban growth, the fantastic expansion of Antioqueño industry in the 1940s and early 1950s, and the partisan conflicts that have shaped the Colombian state. In calling this chronology "reconstructed," I mean simply that it is a product of research and argumentation rather than a given. Defining and debating how to periodize the past is the bread-and-butter of what historians do, yet it is often so wholly taken for granted that it is presumed to have no theoretical dimension. Especially on the relatively small scale of case studies in social history, periodization can seem a routine procedure—necessary, but not something that alters the analysis being presented. Throughout the preceding chapters, however, developing a localized chronology, one rooted in mill-workers' experiences, has been an explicit goal.

The chronological structure outlined here reflects not only the emergence of new disciplinary models but also the changing way that workers experienced and acted on the hierarchical arrangements of the factory. From the first appearance of textile jobs, with the inauguration of the Fábrica de Bello in 1905, through about 1935, millwork was relatively easy to come by. Although Medellín's first factories were small enough to operate with only a few hundred machine-tenders, workers tended to come and go as they pleased, and factory managers often found themselves short-handed. It was not unusual for wealthy men like Don Jorge Echavarría or Don Emilio Restrepo to send for young women by name, advising them they were in need of hands. Indeed, workers' instability provided industrialists with their chief justification for not following the directives of Medellín's factory inspector, charged with "policing" the new workshops. Factory owners resented legislation that set their establishments apart. From the perspective of local history, their objections had some merit. Throughout the period 1905–35, the quotidian forms of interaction between owners and workers made the central class relationship of millwork similar to that of other local forms of employment, such as might exist between a man of wealth and the domestic servants working in his home, or between a shopkeeper and his errand boy.

Similarly, relations among workers in the new factories echoed the fluid sociability of the city's streets. Only later, in the late 1930s and through the 1940s, did *la moral* create workplaces marked by rules of silence and the constant monitoring of mixed-sex interaction. The first generation of factory workers in Medellín, the vast majority of them women, faced no such rigid forms of policing. Rather, the evidence is that they "talked back" to millowners with impunity, walked off the job when displeased, and got into public fights. They exasperated the young society ladies of the Patronato de Obreras, who found that "the woman worker" conformed but little to the image charity-minded reformers had formed of her. Female factory workers were also capable of taking action to enforce reforms of their own, as did strikers in Bello in 1920, who mobilized to force the dismissal of supervisors they accused of "seduction" and rape.

By 1935–36, as national politics began to reflect an international discourse about the redistributive possibilities of revolutionary change, Medellín's increasingly wealthy manufacturers found themselves forced to contemplate the possibility that the modern, industrial city they dreamed of might confront modern, industrial forms of class conflict. Textile workers, male and female, began to participate in left-liberal and communist models of worker activism, one that included combative unions, *pliegos de peticiones*, mass rallies, and the possibility of solidarity campaigns that could bring the city to a halt, as in the 1935 Coltejer strike. In that strike, as at Rosellón the following year, and in bitter unionization campaigns at Fabricato, cotton mill-workers in Medellín seemed poised to join an emerging movement of urban workers and to be a local source of support for President López's "Revolution on the March."

In ensuing years, however, unionism made little headway in the mills. Radical labor organizing was a poor fit with a local political tradition of cross-class partisan identification. Additionally, the textile factories were still largely female spaces, and Colombian languages of unionism (as was true of their counterparts around the world) did little to speak to working-women—in contrast to the national languages of Liberalism and Conservatism. The differences and similarities between the Bello strike, in 1920, and the strikes at Coltejer and Rosellón in 1935–36 are instructive. In 1920, in the absence of an organized Antioqueño labor movement, reporters and self-appointed gentlemen negotiators viewed the Bello strikers' actions through the lens of "outraged maidenhood." They largely ignored the fact that the strikers sought not only the supervisors' dismissal but also higher pay and changes in onerous work rules. In 1935–36, reporters and politicians flown in from Bogotá viewed the textile strikes through the lens of class conflict, making the strikes seem to be as much about *Lopista* labor policy (centered on male workers) as about workers' on-the-ground complaints. Nevertheless, a focus on workers' own actions demonstrates important continuities between these "female" and "male" strikes. At Coltejer and Rosellón, as at Bello, the demands workers most insisted on were for the dismissal of specific individuals. For both female and male workers in this period, just as ordinary work relations turned on face-to-face interactions and personalistic structures of authority, so too did the extraordinary—strikes.

Medellín's first generation of textile entrepreneurs, Alejandro Echavarría (1859–1928) of Coltejer, Emilio Restrepo (1852–1932) of the Fábrica de Bello, and Jorge Echavarría (1889–1934) of Fabricato, would have found it difficult to predict the direction the industry would take in the late 1930s and through the 1940s. The mills began to expand rapidly, investors from the United States became interested (as evinced by the participation of W. R. Grace in Tejicondor), while the political situation continued to be volatile. In this context, mill-owners chose to pursue a more formally paternalistic strategy of discipline, one which combined anticommunism and the injunction to work hard with Catholic piety and normative gender ideology. Industrialists themselves, rather than the reform-minded legislators and churchmen of previous decades, undertook to "protect" *la mujer obrera* from any possible corruption. Her male co-worker, too, was enjoined to be respectful of women. In Coltejer's company magazine, for example, male workers were exhorted to "be gentlemen" in their behavior toward female co-workers, in keeping with the company's claim that "everything belonging to Coltejer is of little worth in comparison to the virtue of our girls," and at Fabricato, workers were straightforwardly told that "to work is to pray." Industrialists thus linked the obedience they demanded of employees to the larger obligations of the Catholic faithful. Through 1936–53, the definition of a "good worker" explicitly included piety and, for females, chastity.

As retirees' memories demonstrate, however, a worker might simultaneously embrace the identities of a "good worker" or a "good woman," and ignore, at least occasionally, the rigid definitions that industrialists sought to attach to both. Whether it is traced at the level of factory rules or of workers' own investment in *la moral*, formal ideology reflects women's and men's lives at work only inadequately. For millhands, it "went without saying," to use Bourdieu's concept of "doxa," that women and men often acted in ways that contravened the disciplinary ideology of *la moral*. The *vigilantas* might be charged with enforcing the ban on mixed-sex conversation, but people nevertheless pursued courtships during work hours, with some male workers "being gentlemen" and others failing to. Public fights might mark a woman as disorderly or *alborotada*, not at all an ideal worker, but female operatives nevertheless fought. Illegitimate pregnancies might be seen as "the greatest crime," and never spoken of openly, but retirees had heard numerous stories about secret abortions and concealed births—what Ann Twinam, in reference to colonial Latin America, refers to as "private pregnancies."[1] The fact that *la moral* functioned effectively as a form of hegemonic discipline in no way undermines the evidence that mill-workers contested that discipline in myriad and constant ways.

I have argued that industrialists invested in *la moral* as a means of resolving the problems inherent in their reliance on a mixed-sex workforce. Influential local reformers had pursued a decades-long campaign against the presumed moral danger of female factory labor. In this discursive context, textile capitalists attempting to present themselves as the guardians of Colombia's industrial future could ill afford not to position themselves as protective "fathers" vis-à-vis their employees. So long as they employed women, that fatherhood required the policing of female workers' sexuality. Unsurprisingly, then, the final shift toward an all-male workforce, on the advice of North American advisers charged with implementing the standard hour system at Fabricato, Coltejer, and Tejicondor, augured the collapse of *la moral*. The elaborate rituals of a gender-based disciplinary system, such as the beauty contests and religious processions that retirees fondly remembered, now appeared anachronistic. To factory managers who thought of themselves as modern engineers, the *doctores* of Charles Savage's ethnographic descriptions, these were relics of a "patronal" past. The mills remained paternalistic, but family wage ideology replaced female virginity as the central symbol of the employer-employee relationship.

The change would have been clear to an observer of the Club Patronato built by Jorge Echavarría and his brothers in the 1930s. Although Don Jorge had envisioned it as a cafeteria and recreational center for male as well as female employees, through the early 1960s it functioned primarily as a convent-like dormitory for young women. With women's exclusion from textile jobs, the Patronato then became a center for classes in homemaking and crafts for workers' wives. Perhaps even more symbolically, by 1998 Don Jorge's Patronato had become a space of thoroughly mixed-sex interaction. No longer owned by Fabricato, it now functioned as a health clinic for Bello residents, including a high percentage of the company's elderly retirees, male and female.

Although the story of women's exclusion from production jobs frames this study, its analytic focus has been to understand the conditions for women's *inclusion*. In Medellín, at least by the 1930s, textile jobs were good jobs. For decades, women worked alongside men, doing work that was well paid, respected, and ensured them unparalleled benefits. Culturally, what made this possible was the intensity of the sexual controls placed on female employees at the "best" textile firms. Their chastity placed them temporarily outside the sexual economy of the family, yet did so in a way that guaranteed their respectability. The textile companies celebrated the marriageability of "our girls," and thus publicly emphasized the idea that women worked in the mills only for a short portion of their lives. In practice, however, female turnover rates did not diverge significantly from male turnover rates. Many women left millwork rapidly, as did many men. A smaller, mixed-sex group, however, stayed at their jobs for a lifetime.

Understanding what factory work meant in women's lives, given the conditions of their inclusion in Medellín's labor aristocracy, requires a model of gender that does not rest solely on the cultural differentiation of male and female. I have treated gender as a normative field in which femininity and masculinity gain meaning not only by contrast to one another but also by reference to a complex hierarchy of what are "proper" and "improper" behaviors for gendered selves. Such a conception is truer to the way womanhood and manhood function ideologically than is a model of gender that is focused on the opposition of female to male. As a discourse that made mixed-sex workplaces socially acceptable in Medellín, *la moral* was effective not because it narrowed the distance between "being a woman" and "being a man" but because it drew on the long-established, deeply meaningful distinction between virginal and nonvirginal females to reinforce a notion that some women could move freely in mixed-sex spaces without compromising their respectability. During the period of the most intense paternalistic discipline, female operatives at Medellín's largest mills derived social status from the rules imposed by their employers. A job at Coltejer, Rosellón, Fabricato, Pantex, or the Fábrica de Bello (known as "Fabridos" after 1939) ensured a woman's reputation for "proper" feminine behavior. The status of women employed at Tejicondor or Telsa was less stable, a fact that retirees from these mills remembered in a variety of ways. María Elisa Alvarez, who had worked at Tejicondor, told stories that emphasized her conformity to the norms of respectable femininity, while María Concepción López, who reached retirement at Telsa, plainly manifested that she resented the "hypocrisy" of those who would judge her for being an unmarried mother. Like women who had reached retirement in the Echavarrías' mills, however, María Elisa and María Concepción lived the distinctions of *la moral* as a familiar outgrowth of a gender system that extended well beyond the mills. In this sense, the case study offered here allows a theoretical argument that is not confined to the (admittedly unusual) constellation of class and gender relations that pertained in Medellín's textile industry.

As regards gender history and feminist theory, the argument has two parts.

First, the distinction of male and female will be meaningful in ways that vary according to the existence of cultural codes identifying varieties of possible males and females. Distinctions between "good girls" and "bad girls," for example, may shape a woman's life experience as powerfully as does the fact that she is not male. Such distinctions will often structure a society's labor markets, guide people's decisions about reproduction, function as signposts for the status of social groups (as scholarship on the intersection of sexuality and racial ideology has demonstrated), and influence the meaning of selfhood in a given cultural context. Second, conceiving of gender as a normative field rather than as a binary allows for the flexibility and changeability that marks human societies. Bourdieu's concepts of "doxa," "orthodoxy," and "hetero-doxy" are particularly useful for understanding practice as permeated by but still distinct from the ideological structures of gender. The rules of *la moral* were, literally, "made to be broken," even if most people conformed to them most of the time.

From the perspective of theoretical debates about gender and class, the Antioqueño case would appear to provide evidence for the argument that the two reinforce one another in a direct relationship. Factory owners manipulated the value attached to virginity to buttress their own authority, and female operatives, who earned less, on average, than males, were subject to more stringent rules of behavior. Femaleness would thus seem to compound the subordinate status ascribed to workers. Yet I have argued that paternalistic discipline, as it developed in Medellín, is instead evidence of the tensions and contradictions between gender and class. Chastity, modesty, obedience: what constituted female propriety for an *obrera* overlapped with a more general ideal of feminine behavior. This was true despite the material difference between a female mill-worker's life and the life of either an upper-class society lady or a married working-class woman who performed labor primarily in the context of her own household. The effectiveness of *la moral* derived from its apparent universality, its cross-class structure. Being female in twentieth-century Medellín meant that one's life could be evaluated by reference to a normative field that centered on an idealized image of a woman who depended on the benevolent protection of a male provider. Whether or not a woman herself articulated an alternative vision, as did Celina and Gumercinda Báez Amado, who exclaimed "marriage was not for us, thank God!" the gender ideology of the dominant society existed as an index by which she might be judged and found wanting. Being a mill-worker meant that one supported oneself, and often one's family of origin, with daily wage labor—taking on a social role theoretically reserved for men (although never, in practice, entirely a male role). Thus *obreras* in Medellín did not live their social roles as women and as workers as a "seamless entity" but rather as a set of injunctions and experiences that were often contradictory.

By sharing their memories, retired mill-workers provided me with a map to a complex social world, one made up not of stereotyped *obreros* and *obreras* but of a wide variety of female and male selves. Taking subjectivity seriously has for me meant accepting the inaccuracies and exaggerations of people's own descriptions of their lives. A memory that cannot be verified, or one that can be proven to be empirically false, may help outline the interpersonal, emotional world in which any historical actor exists. Historians working on the decision-making processes of people whose political position makes them appear larger than life include such "subjective" evidence as a matter of course. Accounts of the lives of artists or scientists are less rather than more convincing when they exclude references to how a person understood the events of her or his own life, such as the way a particular memory was recounted to friends until it became myth, for example. The best oral histories of working-class communities therefore draw on the older genres of biography and autobiography, as well as on the anthropological and literary approaches that historians still tend to treat as "new."[2]

For research about the past, the lesson of oral history is not that the self-perceptions of persons with wildly different relationships to the mechanisms of political and economic power have an equivalent historical role. Rather, it is that "subjectivity" cannot be set in opposition to "objectivity" when what is being investigated involves human agents in changing (and unequal) relationships with one another. With other labor historians who accept the challenge of constructing a model of working-class identity that definitively breaks with that strand of the Marxist heritage that derived "social conscious-ness" from "social being," I have assumed that workers' self-perceptions and their perceptions of community cannot be derived from their status as "work-ers." Categories such as "workers," "managers," "women," or "men" have meaning in people's own lives only in the "how" of practical behavior and practical relationships. To understand effectively the dynamics of any given workplace, or other social space, a researcher must ask questions about both the objective structures of production *and* the subjective "structures of feel-ing" by which labor, or other social interaction, is realized in that time and place. Such a double strategy makes visible what Bourdieu terms the "dialec-tical relation" between the subjective and the objective.[3]

In listening to workers' memories, I have looked for evidence not of what it was that made up a "worker's consciousness" or "identity," understood in abstraction, but rather for evidence of how workers perceived their own behavior in relationships with others: bosses, supervisors, co-workers, fam-ily members. Necessarily, such evidence is available to the oral historian only as retrospection. Where memories speak to questions about workers' self-perceptions and their perceptions of others (that is, to questions about their subjective relationship to the social world of work), they do so in ways colored by the present. I have taken this retrospection to mean that workers' stories must be approached *as stories*—with the assumption that an active mind is continually shaping, editing, and embellishing that part of memory that is brought forth in conversation. In the broadest sense, my aim has been to attend both to discourse, understood by reference to regimes of representation that shape what a person thinks, feels, and says about self and society, and to practice, understood as the realm of everyday social exchange, of doing and acting, in which meanings are never fixed. However suggestively, my analysis of stories like María Elisa's recounting of conversations with Don Eduardo, Enrique's chronicle of his role in the 1936 strike, or Nena's striking memory of hiding a pregnancy made "criminal" by Coltejer's inflexibility, has aimed to address what appear to me as the two central difficulties of poststructuralist approaches to subjectivity: First, that an emphasis on representation can obscure agency and, in particular, obscure the dynamism made possible by agents' relationships to other agents. Second, that subjectivity exists in time, and thus any theory of the subject must be part of a larger explanation of how change happens in human societies.

Not only theoretically but also substantively, this study has emphasized change over time. By describing qualitative, subjective shifts in the way mill-workers, mill-owners, supervisors, and other Antioqueños understood gender and work relations in Medellín's textile mills, I have sought to challenge some of the preconceptions that obscure the history of ordinary people in Latin America. Chief among these is the vague but persistent notion that technological changes from outside the region are the only motor of change. Whether the reference is to modern workplaces or "modern girls," the implication is often that everything new comes from without. As Colombians are fond of reminding North Americans, however, where there are exporters there are also importers. Without neglecting the role of a world market in technology and in ideas about how to organize industrial production, and without ignoring the transnational nature of debates about factory work for women, I have examined the way Antioqueños themselves shaped the social interaction at the heart of the factory model. Gender relations changed in Medellín as a result not only of foreign ideas and the adoption of foreign practices but also because local people argued about, pushed against, and attempted to control the way their society defined women's and men's work.

APPENDIX
Persons Interviewed

Pseudonyms have been used where requested. With the exception of the interview with Barbara Rabinovich, all were conducted in Spanish. Translations used in the text are mine.

1. María Elisa Alvarez, Medellín, 8, 11, 22 July 1994
2. Blanca Luz Angel, Bello, 11 Oct. 1990
3. Carolina Arango, Bello, 7 Oct. 1990 and 8 Aug. 1994
4. Ana Rita Arbeláez, Bello, 8 Oct. 1990
5. Bárbara Alzate de López (pseud.), Envigado, 2 Aug. 1991
6. Gonzalo Alzate, Bello, 16 Oct. 1990
7. Celina Báez Amado, Bello, 2 Oct. 1990 and 9 Aug. 1994
8. Gumercinda Báez Amado, Bello, 22 Feb. 1991
9. Concha Bohórquez, Bello, 23 Oct. 1990 and 12 July 1994
10. Feliciano Cano, Medellín, 19 Oct. 1990
11. Ramón Cano, Medellín, 29 Oct. 1990
12. Victor Cardona, Medellín, 21 Feb. 1991
13. Rubén Chaverra, Medellín, 29 Oct. 1990
14. María de los Angeles Estrada (pseud.), Itagüí, 16 July 1991
15. Fabio Garcés, Medellín, 30 Oct. 1990
16. Ofelia Gómez (pseud.), Medellín, 18 July 1991
17. Laura Gómez Arango, Bello, 3 Oct. 1990
18. Ester Gómez de Márquez (pseud.), Bello, 16 Oct. 1990
19. Pedro Nel Gómez Jiménez, Medellín, 8 Oct. 1990
20. Pedro González Cano (pseud.), Medellín, 2 Nov. 1990
21. Luis H. Henao, Medellín, 22 Nov. 1990
22. María Clara Henao (pseud.), Bello, 17 Oct. 1990
23. Lucía Jiménez, Envigado, 21 May 1991
24. Juan Esteban Loiza, Medellín, 29 Oct. 1990
25. Enrique López (pseud.), Envigado, 30 July 1991
26. María Concepción López, Bello, 22 May 1991
27. Eugenio Márquez (pseud.), Bello, 16 Oct. 1990
28. Cristina Monsalve (pseud.), Envigado, 30 July 1991
29. Gerardo Monsalve, Medellín, 8 Oct. 1990

30. Jairo Montoya (pseud.), Medellín, 9 Oct. 1990

31. Margarita Montoya (pseud.), Envigado, 24 July 1991

32. Ivan Muñoz (pseud.), Bello, 1 Nov. 1990

33. Ana Palacios de Montoya (pseud.), Medellín, 8 Nov. 1990

34. Carolina Posada de Sánchez, Bello, 23 Oct. 1990

35. Barbara Rabinovich, Philadelphia, 18 June 1995

36. María Cristina Restrepo (pseud.), Bello, 23 Oct. 1990

37. Ofelia Restrepo (pseud.), Bello, 10 Oct. 1990

38. Angel Sánchez, Bello, 23 Oct. 1990

39. Enrique Tamayo, Medellín, 29 Oct. 1990

40. María Luisa Tamayo Casas, Envigado, 21 May 1991

41. Ofelia Uribe (pseud.), Medellín, 29 July 1994

42. Zoila Rosa Valencia, Bello, 8 Oct. 1990

43. Prudencia Vallejo, Bello, 18 Oct. 1990

44. Camila Vélez, Bello, 18 Oct. 1990

45. Guillermo Vélez, Medellín, 2 Nov. 1990

46. Ramón Antonio Vélez, Medellín, 15 May 1991

Note: The following persons were interviewed informally and as a group—Juan Alzate, Jaime Ruiz, Alvaro Muñoz, María Zapata, Luis Castrillón, Susana Gómez, Susana Osorio, and Gonzalo Ardila, Envigado, 24 July 1991 (all are pseudonyms). This was an impromptu recording session, consisting of taped conversations with retired Rosellón workers who were waiting for their pension checks in a line that stretched down the block.

NOTES

Introduction

1 For general overviews of the move away from import substitution in Latin America see: Victor Bulmer-Thomas, *The Economic History of Latin America Since Independence*, Cambridge Latin American Studies, vol. 77 (New York: Cambridge University Press, 1994), pp. 278–88, 377–87, 419; Eliana Cardoso and Ann Helwege, *Latin America's Economy: Diversity, Trends, and Conflicts* (Cambridge: MIT Press, 1995), pp. 98–107; and James Dietz, "A Brief Economic History," and Oswaldo Sunkel, "From Inward-Looking Development to Development from Within," both in *Latin America's Economic Development: Confronting Crisis*, 2d ed., ed. James Dietz (Boulder: Lynne Rienner, 1995), pp. 3–19 and 355–81.

2 During the first two years of the Gaviria administration, the policies associated with *apertura* were transformed from the relatively cautious gradual plan announced in February 1990 (by Gaviria's predecessor) to a much more radical liberalization program. See José Antonio Ocampo, "La internacionalización de la economía colombiana," in *Colombia ante la economía mundial*, ed. Miguel Urrutia M. (Bogotá: Tercer Mundo and Fedesarrollo, 1993), pp. 17–66. An indication of the effect on manufacturers oriented toward the domestic market is provided by Ocampo's figures (p. 50) on nominal and effective rates of protection for consumer nondurables, which dropped from 63 percent to 17.5 percent and from 137 to 41 percent, respectively. For the general context of *apertura* debates in Colombia, see José Antonio Ocampo, "La apertura externa en perspectiva," in *Apertura económica y sistema financiero: Compilación de los documentos presentados en el XII simposio sobre mercado de capitales*, ed. Florángela Gómez Ordóñez (Bogotá: Asociación Bancaria de Colombia, 1990), pp. 40–97, as well as Gabriel Misas Arango, "De la industrialización sustitutiva a la apertura: El caso colombiano," in *Gestión económica estatal de los ochentas: Del ajuste al cambio institucional*, vol. 2, ed. Luis Bernardo Florez E. and Ricardo Bonilla González (Bogotá: Centro de Investigaciones Para el Desarrollo CID, 1995), pp. 5–61.

3 Subsectors within the textile industry varied enormously with regard to efficiency. Juan José Echavarría, "Industria y reestructuración," in Florángela Gómez Ordóñez, ed., *Apertura económica y sistema financiero*, p. 137; on the growth of firm-level debt in Colombian manufacturing see p. 139. For additional discussion of the problem of productivity in Colombian manufacturing, see Juan Gonzalo Zapata, "¿Es necesaria una reestructuración en la industria nacional?" in his *Reflexiones sobre la industria colombiana* (Bogotá: Fescol, 1990), pp. 19–47. A suggestion of the trepidation with which the big textile firms faced the *apertura* can be seen in a qualitative survey done by Juan José Echavarría and Pilar Esguerra; see their essays and commentaries in the Zapata volume, as well as Echavarría's comments in Luis Jorge Garay, ed., *Estrategia industrial e inserción internacional* (Bogotá: Fescol, 1992), p. 371 n. 2.

4 Interview with María Elisa Alvarez, Medellín, 8 July 1994.

5 Interview with Gonzalo Ardila, as part of an informal group interview, recorded with pensioners during a four-hour period as they waited in line to receive retirement checks, Envigado, 24 July 1991.

6 Interview with Susana Osorio, as part of group interview, Envigado, 24 July 1991.

7 See Rafael Samuel, *Theatres of Memory* (New York: Verso, 1994) and Christopher Shaw and Malcolm Chase, eds., *The Imagined Past: History and Nostalgia* (Manchester: Manchester University Press, 1989).

8 For discussions of the complexity of nostalgia in working-class memory, see Daniel James, *Doña María's Story: Life-History, Memory, and Political Identity* (Durham: Duke University Press, forthcoming); Verena Stolcke, *Coffee Planters, Workers, and Wives: Class Conflict and Gender Relations on São Paulo Plantations, 1850–1980* (New York: St. Martin's Press, 1988), chap. 6; Tamara Hareven, *Family Time and Industrial Time* (New York: Cambridge University Press, 1982), pp. 79–81 and 371–82; and Douglas R. Holmes, *Cultural Disenchantments: Worker Peasantries in Northeast Italy* (Princeton: Princeton University Press, 1989), chap. 1.

9 For current discussions about proletarianization, see essays by Berlanstein, Reid, and Sewell in Leonard Berlanstein, ed., *Rethinking Labor History: Essays on Discourse and Class Analysis* (Urbana: University of Illinois Press, 1993), as well as William Reddy, *Money and Liberty in Modern Europe: A Critique of Historical Understanding* (New York: Cambridge University Press, 1987). For summaries of the debate over a longer period, which includes an articulation of the role of gender in the historiography of European industrialization, see essays by Peter Stearns and Louise Tilly in Michael Adas, *Islamic and European Expansion* (Philadelphia: Temple University Press, 1993).

10 My sampling methods were straightforward. After an initial survey, based primarily on conversations with company archivists, I estimated that the factory archives in which I had been granted permission to do research housed a total of 65,000 records for persons hired before 1960. This total reflected the records available for seven mills: Tejicondor, Fatelares, Fabricato, including the formerly separate Fábrica de Bello, and Coltejer, including that company's downtown plant, as well as its subsidiaries, Rosellón and Sedeco. Aiming for a sample of 1,000, I entered the data from every sixty-fifth record, after a random start. Because the total number of records was lower than my estimate, approximately 50,000, in the end my sample contained 781 cases. Although strategies of personnel management and recordkeeping changed over the years, most records con-

tained information on the employee's sex, age, birthplace, civil status, and level of education or literacy, as well as the dates of employment. Employee files also contained observations as to a person's conduct and reprimands received, including a note as to whether that person left voluntarily or was dismissed.

11 Interview with María Elisa Alvarez, Medellín, 22 July 1994.

12 My own observations support this, as do those of Dawn Keremitsis, based on a 1974 interview she conducted with Dr. Hernando Villa, vice president of Coltejer. Keremitsis, "Latin American Women Workers in Transition: Sexual Division of the Labor Force in Mexico and Colombia in the Textile Industry," *The Americas* 40 (1984): 496 and 503.

13 See laws 53 and 197 of 1938 and their accompanying decrees: 1632 and 2350 of 1938, as well as 953 and 1766 of 1939. Ibid., pp. 374–79, and Ernesto Herrnstadt, *Tratado del derecho social colombiano*, 2d ed. (Bogotá: Editorial ABC, 1947), pp. 156–61. These laws were ignored by the regional labor inspectors, as well as by Antioqueño industrialists. Antioquia's labor inspectors limited themselves to requiring the mills to pay a severance penalty to women fired for pregnancy; Rosa Obdula Gallego, for example, was paid $122.50 pesos "for the dismissal she received for the reason of being pregnant." Gustavo Ruiz, Inspector Seccional del Trabajo to Sr. Gerente de la Fábrica de Tejidos de Bello, and Gerente to Carlos Restrepo, Inspector del Trabajo, 28 August 1939; for other cases, see Gustavo Ruiz to Eugenio Sanín, 6 August 1941 and Administrador Fabricato to Rudesindo Echavarría, 16 March 1946. All citations from vols. 881 and 911, Archivo Fabricato (hereafter AF; translations of all archival documents are mine). See also Luz Gabriela Arango, *Mujer, religión e industria: Fabricato 1923–1982* (Medellín: Universidad de Antioquia, 1991), p. 272.

14 Male workers received bonuses on the birth of a child, according to retirees. Their wives also had access to special medical benefits. Fabricato, for example, began offering free prenatal service to male workers' wives in May of 1950. Eduardo Arias Robledo to Junta Directiva del Sindicato Textil del Hato, 18 April 1950, vol. 908, AF. On the provision of other extra-wage benefits in the 1940s and 1950s, see chapter 5.

15 Interviews with Luis Castrillón, as part of group interview, Envigado, 24 July 1991, and Zoila Rosa Valencia, Bello, 8 October 1990. See also Keremitsis, p. 495, and Arango, *Mujer, religión e industria*, p. 72.

16 Keremitsis, p. 496. Alberto Mayor Mora makes a similar assumption in *Etica, trabajo, y productividad en Antioquia* (Bogotá: Tercer Mundo, 1984), p. 296. Arango's argument, in *Mujer, religión e industria*, is somewhat distinct, as explained below.

17 Arango, *Mujer, religión e industria*, pp. 273–79. Arango's statistical work is incomplete, as she had access only to a fraction of the personnel records dating from the period 1923–50. Her book therefore includes a number of faulty conclusions, such as that the majority of Fabricato's workers remained at the firm until retirement; these do not, however, invalidate her work as a whole.

18 For an exhaustive discussion of "economy" and "culture" as concepts in the history of work, see Richard Biernacki, *The Fabrication of Labor: Germany and Britain, 1640–1914*, Studies on the History of Society and Culture, vol. 23 (Berkeley: University of California Press, 1995). My approach differs from that of Biernacki, who is more concerned with attaching a separate causality to culture. See pp. 16–37 and 472–82.

19　Enrique Echavarría, *Historia de los textiles en Antioquia* (Medellín: Tip. Bedout, 1943), p. 16. The workforce in British cotton mills was about 60 percent female in the 1900s and 1910s; Brian R. Mitchell, *British Historical Statistics* (New York: Cambridge University Press, 1988), pp. 377 and 379. Pedro Nel Ospina also met with agents for textile machinery firms in New York in 1902. He was particularly impressed with the Dobson and Barlow Company, which, as he wrote to Emilio Restrepo, had exported machines to the United States, Russia, Japan, India, Peru, and Mexico, among other countries. Pedro Nel Ospina to Sr. Emilio Restrepo, 15 May 1902, AGPNO/6/12, Fundación Antioqueña de Estudios Sociales (hereafter FAES).

20　Medellinense capitalists began importing textile machinery after ring frames and the "self-acting" mule had replaced older mule-frame machines. This technological shift had allowed mill managers in Britain (in Scotland more than in Lancashire), the United States, and Japan to replace adult male spinners with female and child "piecers," as the new machines required less physical strength and a shorter period of apprenticeship. Mary Blewett, "Manhood and the Market: the Politics of Gender and Class among the Textile Workers of Fall River, Massachusetts, 1870–1880," in *Work Engendered: Toward a New History of American Labor*, ed. Ava Baron (Ithaca: Cornell University Press, 1991), pp. 92–113. See especially pp. 93 n. 2, 96–97, and 111; Hareven, *Family Time and Industrial Time*, pp. 397–98; E. Patricia Tsurumi, *Factory Girls: Women in the Thread Mills of Meiji Japan* (Princeton: Princeton University Press, 1990), p. 106. See also Mary Freifeld, "Technological Change and the 'Self-Acting' Mule: A Study of Skill and the Sexual Division of Labor," *Social History* 11 (Oct. 1986): 319–43, and William Lazonick, "Industrial Relations and Technical Change: The Case of the Self-Acting Mule," *Cambridge Journal of Economics* 3 (1979): 231–62.

21　Engineers' report by Howard A. Finley, 18 July 1955, Consultores extranjeros, Correspondencia, Archivo Tejicondor (hereafter AT).

22　See María Patricia Fernández-Kelly, *For We Are Sold, I and My People: Women and Industry in Mexico's Frontier*, Aihwa Ong, *Spirits of Resistance and Capitalist Discipline: Factory Women in Malaysia*, and Fernández-Kelly and June Nash, eds., *Women, Men, and the International Division of Labor*, in the SUNY Series in the Anthropology of Work (Albany: State University of New York Press, 1983 and 1987). Also Susan Tiano, *Patriarchy on the Line: Labor, Gender, and Ideology in the Mexican Maquila Industry* (Philadelphia: Temple University Press, 1994); Kevin Yelvington, *Producing Power: Ethnicity, Gender, and Class in a Caribbean Workplace* (Philadelphia: Temple University Press, 1995); Devon Gerardo Peña, *The Terror of the Machine: Technology, Work, Gender, and Ecology on the U.S.-Mexico Border* (Austin: Center for Mexican American Studies, University of Texas at Austin, 1997); and Norma Iglesias Prieto, *Beautiful Flowers of the Maquiladora: Life Histories of Women Workers in Tijuana*, Translations from Latin America Series (Austin: University of Texas Press, Institute of Latin American Studies, 1997).

23　"Fordism" is used here in a general sense, to describe employers' interest in combining paternalism with the progressive adoption of capital-intensive technologies, as well their self-positioning as social engineers. For a classic description, from the perspective of long-term change in North American industry, see Richard Edwards, *Contested Terrain: The Transformation of the Workplace in the Twentieth Century* (New York: Basic Books, 1979). See also Antonio Gramsci's compelling treatment, "Americanism and Fordism," in *Selections from the Prison Notebooks* (New York: International Publishers, 1971).

24 Mary Nolan, *Visions of Modernity: American Business and the Modernization of Germany* (Oxford: Oxford University Press, 1994).

25 For provocative discussions of Fordist approaches in Brazil, see Barbara Weinstein, *For Social Peace in Brazil: Industrialists and the Remaking of the Working Class in São Paulo, 1920–1964* (Chapel Hill: University of North Carolina Press, 1996), and José Sergio Leite Lopes, *A tecelagem dos conflictos de classe na "cidade das chaminés"* (São Paulo: Editora Marco Zero, 1988). See also Peter Winn, *Weavers of Revolution: The Yarur Workers and Chile's Road to Socialism* (New York: Oxford University Press, 1986). For an overview of the era of Import Substitution Industrialization (ISI), see Bulmer-Thomas, pp. 278–88. Examples of welfare capitalism also can be found outside of the ISI sector through this period, particularly in export enclaves characterized by permanent installations—such as the Braden Copper Company, described by Thomas Klubock, *Contested Communities: Class, Gender, and Politics in Chile's El Teniente Copper Mine, 1904–1951* (Durham: Duke University Press, 1998). I thank Michael Jiménez for directing my attention to this point.

26 See Berlanstein, ed., *Rethinking Labor History*, as well as Reddy, *Money and Liberty*. For summaries of the debate over a longer period, which include an articulation of the role of gender in the historiography of European industrialization see the essays by Stearns and Tilly in Adas, *Islamic and European Expansion*.

27 *Semana*, 6 September 1947, as cited in Eduardo Sáenz Rovner, *La ofensiva empresarial: Industriales, políticos, y violencia en los años 40 en Colombia* (Bogotá: Tercer Mundo, 1992), p. 85 (emphasis in original; translation mine). According to Sáenz Rovner, the cartoon appeared first in *Michín* and was then reproduced in other publications.

28 The classic discussion is Eric Hobsbawm, "The Labour Aristocracy in Nineteenth-Century Britain," in *Labouring Men: Studies in the History of Labour*, ed. Hobsbawm (London: Weidenfeld and Nicolson, 1964), pp. 272–315.

29 Juan José Echavarría, "External Shocks and Industrialization: Colombia, 1920–1950" (Ph.D. diss., Oxford University, 1989), p. 145 n. 15.

30 Medellín, *Anuarios Estadísticos* for 1916–48 (Medellín: Imprenta Municipal).

31 International Labour Office (ILO), *Textile Wages: An International Study* (Geneva: ILO, 1952), p. 20. The other two countries with comparable rates were France and South Africa. In the latter this wage differential cannot be interpreted in terms of gender only, as the female textile workforce in the 1940s was largely white, whereas the ILO's figures for male earnings seem to reflect an average of African, "colored," and white males. See Iris Berger, *Threads of Solidarity: Women in South African Industry, 1900–1980* (Bloomington: Indiana University Press, 1992).

32 Interviews with Lucía Jiménez, Envigado, 21 May 1991; Susana Gómez, as part of group interview, Envigado, 24 July 1991; Ofelia Restrepo, Bello, 10 Oct. 1990; and others.

33 Interview with Celina Báez Amado, Bello, 2 Oct. 1990.

34 Interview with Gumercinda Báez Amado, Bello, 22 Feb. 1991.

35 Interview with Ana Palacios de Montoya, Medellín, 8 Nov. 1990.

36 Interview with Celina Báez Amado, Bello, 1 Oct. 1990.

37 Interview with Ana Palacios de Montoya, Medellín, 8 Nov. 1990.

38 See Ava Baron's critique of what she terms "categorical theories," in her introduction to *Work Engendered*, p. 21. A discussion of this point from the perspective of Latin American labor history can be found in John French and Daniel James, eds., *The Gendered Worlds of Latin American Women Workers: From Household to Factory to the Union Hall and Ballot Box* (Durham: Duke University Press, 1997), pp. 4–5, 17, 21.

39 See Margaret Somers, "Narrativity, Narrative Identity, and Social Action: Rethinking English Working-Class Formation," *Social Science History* 16, no. 1 (1992): 591–630, esp. pp. 606–10, as well as her "The Narrative Construction of Identity: A Relational and Network Approach," *Theory and Society* 23, no. 5 (1994): 605–49.

40 For two recent attempts to ground Marx's theoretical work by reference to the immediate cultural contexts of England and Germany, see Somers, "Narrativity," and Biernacki, *Fabrication of Labor.*

41 "Insofar as millions of families live under economic conditions of existence that separate their mode of life, their interests and their culture from those of the other classes, and put them in a hostile opposition to the latter, they form a class. Insofar as there is merely a local interconnection among these small-holding peasants, and the identity of their interests begets no community, no national bond and no political organization, they do not form a class"; *The Eighteenth Brumaire of Louis Bonaparte*, as cited by Raymond Williams, *Keywords: A Vocabulary of Culture and Society* (New York: Oxford University Press, 1983), p. 68.

42 From *The German Ideology*, as cited in ibid., pp. 67–68.

43 Ira Katznelson, "Introduction," in Katznelson and Aristide Zolberg, eds., *Working-Class Formation: Nineteenth-Century Patterns in Western Europe and the United States* (Princeton: Princeton University Press, 1986). I am drawing also on Margaret Somers's discussion in "Class Formation and Capitalism: A Second Look at a Classic," *European Journal of Sociology* 37, no. 1 (1996): 180–203.

44 See discussion in Kathleen Canning, "Gender and the Politics of Class Formation: Rethinking German Labor History," *AHR* 97 (June 1992): 736–68.

45 Edward P. Thompson, *The Making of the English Working Class* (London: Victor Gollancz, 1963), p. 9.

46 For a summary of debates about the crisis of the class concept, see Reddy, *Money and Liberty.*

47 William H. Sewell, "Toward a Post-Materialist Rhetoric for Labor History," in Berlanstein, ed., *Rethinking Labor History*, pp. 27–32.

48 Joan Scott applies the more expansive definition, Kathleen Canning the more specific. Scott, *Gender and the Politics of History* (New York: Columbia University Press, 1988), pp. 4–5, 66–67; Canning, *Languages of Labor and Gender: Female Factory Work in Germany, 1850–1914* (Ithaca: Cornell University Press, 1996), pp. 10–11.

49 The phrase is Alf Lüdkte's, as cited in Canning, *Languages of Labor and Gender*, p. 13.

50 In this paragraph I am drawing on Joan Scott, "The Evidence of Experience," *Critical Inquiry* 17 (summer 1991): 793–97; Judith Butler, *Gender Trouble: Feminism and the Subversion of Identity* (New York: Routledge, 1990); and Laura Frader and Sonya Rose, *Gender and Class in Modern Europe* (Ithaca: Cornell University Press, 1996), in addition to work by Sewell, Somers, and Canning, cited above. I am also working within the conceptual framework demarcated by

Pierre Bourdieu in *Outline of a Theory of Practice* (New York: Cambridge University Press, 1977) and *The Logic of Practice* (Stanford: Stanford University Press, 1990), as well as that evident in Raymond Williams's essay "Structures of Feeling," in his *Marxism and Literature* (New York: Oxford University Press, 1977), pp. 128–35.

51 The anthropological literature on honor and shame recognizes this explicitly, as does new research on homophobia and prostitution. For summaries of both, with an exploration of the usefulness of this emerging work for Latin American gender studies, see Norma Fuller, "En torno a la polaridad mariansimo-machismo"; Marta Lamas, "Cuerpo e identidad"; and Nora Segura, "Prostitución, género, y violencia." All three appear in *Género e identidad: Ensayos sobre lo femenino y lo masculino*, ed. Luz Gabriela Arango, Magdalena León, and Mara Viveros (Bogotá: Tercer Mundo Editores, 1995), pp. 241–64, 61–82, and 193–212, respectively. For aspects of the rich discussion of this issue in Anglo-American feminist theory, see Gloria Anzaldúa, *Borderlands/La Frontera: The New Mestiza* (San Francisco: Aunt Lute, 1987); bell hooks, *Ain't I a Woman: Black Women and Feminism* (Boston: South End Press, 1981) and *Yearning: Race, Gender, and Cultural Politics* (Boston: South End Press, 1990); María Lugones and Elizabeth Spelman, "Have We Got a Theory for You! Feminist Theory, Cultural Imperialism, and the Demand for 'The Woman's Voice,'" *Women's Studies International Forum* 6, no. 6 (1983): 573–81; Chandra Mohanty, Lourdes Torres, and Ann Russo, *Third World Women and the Politics of Feminism* (Bloomington: Indiana University Press, 1991); and Gayatri Spivak, *In Other Worlds* (New York: Routledge, 1988). Within feminist social history, Joan Scott and Sonya Rose provide working definitions of gender that, like the one presented here, include a recognition of the ways gender produces divisions among persons of the same sex while at the same time reifying the male-female dichotomy. See Scott, *Gender and the Politics*, p. 43, and Sonya Rose, *Limited Livelihoods: Gender and Class in Nineteenth-Century England* (Berkeley: University of California Press, 1992), p. 15. The difference between my conceptualization and each of theirs is primarily one of emphasis. The reference to Gayle Rubin is to "The Traffic in Women: Notes on the 'Political Economy' of Sex," in *Toward an Anthropology of Women*, ed. Rayna Rapp Reiter (New York: Monthly Review, 1975), pp. 157–210; reprinted in *Feminism and History*, ed. Joan Scott (New York: Oxford University Press, 1996), pp. 105–51.

52 As noted above, the anthropological literature on honor/shame is key to this discussion, although it is too large to be summarized here. In addition to the starting point provided by the brief discussion of Julian Pitt-Rivers and Roberto da Matta, in Fuller, "En torno a la polaridad," pp. 241–43 and 250–53, see the essays in J. G. Péristiany, ed., *Honour and Shame: The Values of Mediterranean Society* (Chicago: University of Chicago Press, 1966), and Carmelo Lison-Tolosana, *Belmonte de los Caballeros: A Sociological Study of a Spanish Town* (Oxford: Clarendon Press, 1966). For work on the related divisions between "house" and "street," as conceptualized for Brazil, see Gilberto Freyre, *Sobrados e mucambos: Decadência do patriarcado rural e desenvolvimento do urbano* (Rio de Janeiro: J. Olympio, 1951); Roberto da Matta, *A casa & a rua: Espaco, cidadania, mulher e morte no Brasil* (Rio de Janeiro: Editora Guanabara, 1987); and Sandra Lauderdale Graham, *House and Street: The Domestic World of Servants and Masters in Nineteenth-Century Rio de Janeiro* (Austin: University of Texas Press, 1992). See also the sophisticated discussion provided by Verena Stolcke (formerly Martinez-

Alier), *Marriage, Class, and Colour in Nineteenth-Century Cuba: A Study of Racial Attitudes and Sexual Values in a Slave Society*, 2d ed. (Ann Arbor: University of Michigan Press, 1989).

53 Ann Laura Stoler, "Carnal Knowledge and Imperial Power: Gender, Race, and Morality in Colonial Asia," as reprinted in Scott, ed., *Feminism and History*, pp. 209–66.

54 Martinez-Alier, *Marriage, Class, and Colour*, p. 24.

55 Evelyn Brooks Higginbotham, "African-American Women's History and the Metalanguage of Race," *Signs* 17, no. 2 (1992): 251–74. Reprinted in Scott, ed., *Feminism and History*, pp. 193–94.

56 A provocative example is Marilyn Maness Mehaffy's work on visual representations in the late nineteenth century, "Advertising Race/Raceing Advertising: The Feminine Consumer(-Nation), 1876–1900," *Signs* 23, no. 1 (1997): 131–73. Other feminist work influencing my approach to gender-based differentiation includes Jane Fishburne Collier, "Rank and Marriage: Or, Why High-Ranking Wives Cost More," in *Gender and Kinship: Essays Toward a Unified Analysis*, ed. Jane Fishburne Collier and Sylvia Junko Yanagiasko (Stanford: Stanford University Press, 1987), pp. 197–220; Donna Haraway, "Gender for a Marxist Dictionary: the Sexual Politics of a Word," in her book *Simians, Cyborgs, and Women* (New York: Routledge, 1991), pp. 128–48; Carol A. Smith, "Race-Class-Gender Ideology in Guatemala: Modern and Anti-Modern Forms," *Comparative Studies in Society and History* vol. 37 (1995): 723–49; and Gayatri Spivak, "French Feminism in an International Frame," in her *In Other Worlds*, pp. 134–54.

57 For a discussion of the meaning of domestic service in the region for Latin American feminism, see Elsa Chaney and Mary García Castro, *Muchachas No More: Household Workers in Latin America and the Caribbean* (Philadelphia: Temple University Press, 1989), pp. 197–267.

58 Any listing of so large and influential a literature will overlook some key contributions, but see Domitila Barrios de Chungara, with Moema Viezzer, *Let Me Speak! Testimony of Domitila, a Woman of the Bolivian Mines*, trans. Victoria Ortíz (New York: Monthly Review, 1978); Angela Davis, *Women, Race, and Class* (New York: Random House, 1981); Cherríe Moraga and Gloria Anzaldúa, *This Bridge Called My Back: Writings by Radical Women of Color* (Watertown, Mass.: Persephone Press, 1981), as well as the above cited work by hooks, Lugones and Spelman, and Mohanty, Torres, and Russo.

59 Elizabeth Jelín, "The Bahiana in the Labor Force in Salvador, Brazil," in June Nash and Helen Safa, eds., *Sex and Class in Latin America* (Boston: Bergin and Garvey, 1980), pp. 129–46 (paper initially presented at a conference on "Feminine Perspectives in the Social Sciences in Latin America" held in Buenos Aires in 1974).

60 Rubin, "The Traffic in Women."

61 Heidi Hartmann, "The Unhappy Marriage of Marxism and Feminism: Toward a More Progressive Union," *Capital and Class* 8 (1979), as reprinted in *Women and Revolution*, ed. Lydia Sargent (Boston: South End Press, 1981), p. 10.

62 Anne Phillips and Barbara Taylor, "Sex and Skill: Notes Toward a Feminist Economics," in *Feminism and History*, pp. 317–30. Veronica Beechey also makes this point in *Unequal Work* (London: Verso, 1987); see p. 11. Heleieth Saffiotti makes a similar argument, although about race more than gender, in her discussion of the particularities of the Brazilian economy and the implications of slavery for class and gender relations: *Women in Class Society* (New York: Monthly Review,

1978). See also the comprehensive essay by Laura Frader and Sonya Rose in their edited volume, cited above.

63   Laura Lee Downs, *Manufacturing Inequality: Gender Division in the French and British Metalworking Industries, 1914–1939* (Ithaca: Cornell University Press, 1995), p. 4. Sonya Rose, in her *Limited Livelihoods,* agrees with the first part of Downs's argument, but she is more attentive than Downs to the gaps and contradictions within gender ideologies, as discussed below. For Downs, gender is "stable"; for Rose, "unstable" (pp. 4 and 13, respectively).

64   Rubin, "The Traffic in Women," pp. 112–13, and Gerda Lerner, *The Creation of Patriarchy* (New York: Oxford University Press, 1986), p. 239.

65   Ruth Milkman, *Gender at Work: The Dynamics of Job Segregation by Sex During World War II* (Urbana: University of Illinois Press, 1987), p. 7.

66   Ibid. and see: Freifeld, "Technological Change and the 'Self-Acting' Mule"; Jane Mark-Lawson and Anne Witz, "From 'Family Labor' to 'Family Wage'? The Case of Women's Labor in Nineteenth-Century Coalmining," *Social History* 13, no. 2 (1988): 151–73; Martha May, "Bread before Roses: American Workingmen, Labor Unions, and the Family Wage," in *Women, Work, and Protest,* ed. Ruth Milkman (London: Routledge and Kegan Paul, 1985), pp. 1–21.

67   See James and French, eds., *Gendered Worlds,* p. 16, and essays by Heidi Tinsman and Thomas Klubock in the same volume. Other salient examples include Ana María Alonso, *Thread of Blood: Colonialism, Revolution, and Gender on Mexico's Northern Frontier* (Tucson: University of Arizona Press, 1995); Susan Besse, *Restructuring Patriarchy: The Modernization of Gender Inequality in Brazil* (Chapel Hill: University of North Carolina Press, 1996); Matthew Gutmann, *The Meanings of Macho: Being a Man in Mexico City* (Berkeley: University of California Press, 1996); John Humphrey, *Gender and Work in the Third World: Sexual Divisions in Brazilian Industry* (London: Routledge, 1989); Deborah Levenson-Estrada, *Trade Unionists against Terror: Guatemala City, 1954–1985* (Chapel Hill: University of North Carolina Press, 1994); Helen Safa, *The Myth of the Male Breadwinner: Women and Industrialization in the Caribbean* (Boulder, Colo.: Westview Press, 1995); and work by Stolcke cited above.

68   Heidi Hartmann, "Capitalism, Patriarchy, and Job Segregation by Sex," in *Capitalist Patriarchy and the Case for Socialist Feminism,* ed. Zillah Eisenstein (New York: Monthly Review, 1979), p. 208. See also Silvia Walby, *Patriarchy at Work* (Cambridge: Polity Press, 1986), p. 45. For a recent examination of "the fatal flaws of misogyny and patriarchy" in working-class radicalism in Britain, see Anna Clark, *The Struggle for the Breeches: Gender and the Making of the British Working Class* (Berkeley: University of California Press, 1995). Clark's work traces connections between sexism and class domination but without the determinism of "dual systems" approaches.

69   Scott, *Gender and the Politics,* p. 35. Ava Baron extends this point by focusing on the way gender is created "not simply outside production but also within it," *Work Engendered,* p. 37.

70   Scott, *Gender and the Politics,* p. 60.

71   Scott, "The Evidence of Experience," p. 797.

72   This point is made by Frader and Rose, p. 20.

73   Scott, *Gender and the Politics,* pp. 44–49.

74   Ibid., p. 49.

75   There are numerous examples of recent scholarship that avoid both pitfalls. An

excellent, nuanced example is Ava Baron's study of masculinity in the printing trades, "An 'Other' Side of Gender Antagonism at Work: Men, Boys, and the Remasculinization of Printers' Work, 1830–1920," in *Work Engendered*, pp. 47–69.

One. Medellín, 1900–1960

1 *Life*, 29 Sept. 1947, pp. 109–16.

2 Ibid., p. 114.

3 From the country's central artery, the Magdalena River, the looms likely were loaded onto rail cars. In 1905, however, the railroad was finished only as far as Caracolí; between that small town and Bello, mule train remained the only means of transporting cargo.

4 Enrique Echavarría, *Historia de los textiles*, p. 19.

5 Constanza Toro, "Medellín: Desarollo urbano, 1880–1950," in *Historia de Antioquia*, ed. Jorge Orlando Melo (Medellín: Suramericana de Seguros, 1988), p. 302; Catalina Reyes, "¿Fueron los viejos tiempos tan maravillosos? Aspectos de la vida social y cotidiana de Medellín, 1890–1930" (master's thesis, Universidad Nacional, sede Medellín, 1993), pp. 26–45.

6 Echavarría, *Historia de los textiles*, p. 17.

7 Emilio Restrepo C. to Señor Alcalde Municipal de Bello, also to Señor Ministro de Industrias, 26 April 1928, Copiador 11, p. 6, Archivo Fabricato (hereafter AF).

8 Echavarría, *Historia de los textiles*, p. 29.

9 In addition to work by Botero Herrera, cited below, see the essays in two compilations edited by Jorge Orlando Melo: *Historia de Antioquia*, cited above, and *Historia de Medellín* (Medellín: Suramericana de Seguros, 1996).

10 The material in this paragraph depends on Botero Herrera, "Historia de la ciudad de Medellín," unpublished manuscript, pp. 19–25, which also suggests that easier access to southern Cauca trade routes gave Medellín an advantage; James Parsons, *Antioqueño Colonization in Western Colombia*, rev. ed. (Berkeley: University of California Press, 1968), p. 24; and Ann Twinam, *Miners, Merchants, and Farmers in Colonial Colombia*, Latin American Monographs, vol. 57 (Austin: University of Texas Press, 1982), pp. 50–55, 76–80, 95–96.

11 An important exception is Mary Roldán, "Genesis and Evolution of *La Violencia* in Antioquia, Colombia (1900–1953)" (Ph.D. diss., Harvard University, 1992).

12 For a discussion of the positive dimensions of the myth of *Antioqueñidad*, including the notion that this was a region characterized by democratic social structures, upward mobility, stable families, and a wholesome Catholicism, see Roldán, "Genesis and Evolution," pp. 120–24.

13 *Life*, 29 Sept. 1947, p. 110.

14 Ann Twinam, "From Jew to Basque: Ethnic Myths and Antioqueño Entrepreneurship," *Journal of Interamerican Studies and World Affairs* 22 (Feb. 1980): 81–107.

15 Parsons, *Antioqueño Colonization*, pp. 3–4, and Twinam, *Miners, Merchants*, pp. 8–12. Representative of Antioqueño writing on *la raza* are Gabriel Arango Mejía, "Las familias antioqueñas," Gustavo González Ochoa, "La raza antioqueña," and Julio César Arroyave, "Psicología del hombre antioqueño," all in *El pueblo antioqueño*, ed. La revista Universidad de Antioquia (Medellín: Universidad de Antioquia, 1942). See also F. Gómez Martínez and Arturo Puerta, *Biografía económica de las industrias de Antioquia* (Medellín: Editorial Bedout, 1945), pp. 9–10.

16 For example, Arroyave, "Psicología," p. 141, and Parsons, following local writers, *Antioqueño Colonization*, pp. 102–8. Everett E. Hagen took the argument rather further, using the popularity of beauty contests and the region's supposed high rates of prostitution to suggest a connection between Antioqueños' sexual vigor (or their "need-aggression") and a supposed entrepreneurial spirit: *On the Theory of Social Change: How Economic Growth Begins* (Homewood, Ill.: Dorsey Press, 1962), pp. 371, 377, 380.

17 Ibid. Hagen's argument was psychological, that insecurity about their status in the eyes of other Colombians prompted entrepreneurial initiative among Antioqueños, but he also maintained that Basque immigration might have played a role in shaping *Antioqueñidad*. Thus ethnicity, psychology, and culture continued to be interwoven in explanations that were logically identical to that positing a Jewish heritage. For another example, see Luis Fajardo, *The Protestant Ethic of the Antioqueños: Social Structure and Personality* (Cali: Universidad del Valle, n.d.). Twinam provides a useful discussion of such cultural arguments, "From Jew to Basque." See also William Paul McGreevey, *An Economic History of Colombia, 1845–1930* (Cambridge: Cambridge University Press, 1971), pp. 185–88.

18 In 1991, for example, I met a North American reporter in Bogotá who trotted out all the old arguments without skepticism: that *Antioqueños* have large families and worship their mothers, that the department's name is taken from Antioch in Syria and that this proves it was settled by Jews, and that the Antioqueños' knack for making money cannot be denied.

19 Ann Twinam provides an overview of this debate in her *Miners, Merchants;* see also Roger Brew, *El desarrollo económico de Antioquia desde la independencia hasta 1920* (Bogotá: Banco de la República, 1977); Alvaro López Toro, *Migración y cambio social durante el siglo diez y nueve* (Bogotá: Ediciones Universidad de los Andes, 1970); and Frank Safford, "Significación de los Antioqueños en el desarrollo económico colombiano, un examen crítico de las tésis de Everett Hagen," *Anuario colombiano de historia social y de la cultura*, 3 (1965): 49–69. Luis Ospina Vásquez, *Industria y protección en Colombia, 1810–1930*, 4th ed. (Medellín: FAES, 1987), first published in 1955, also implies an argument along these lines.

20 Mariano Arango, *Café e industria, 1850–1930* (Bogotá: Carlos Valencia Editores, 1977); Santiago Montenegro, "La industria textil en Colombia, 1900–1945," *Desarrollo y sociedad* 8 (1982): 117–73; José Antonio Ocampo and Santiago Montenegro, *Crisis mundial, protección e industrialización* (Bogotá: Fondo Editorial Cerec, 1984); Bernardo Tovar Zambrano, "La economía colombiana (1886–1922)," in *Nueva Historia de Colombia*, vol. 5 (9 vols.; Bogotá: Planeta, 1989), hereafter abbreviated as *NHC*. But see Marco Palacios, who argues that coffee was relatively unimportant in Antioqueño development: "El café en la vida de Antioquia," in *Los estudios regionales en Colombia: El caso de Antioquia*, ed. Fundación Antioqueña de Estudios Sociales (Medellín: FAES, 1982), pp. 85–98. Palacios's recent synthesis of twentieth-century Colombian history, on the other hand, allows a role for coffee but places the rise of Medellín in the more general context of the decline of the Santanders and the expansion of Antioquia; he suggests that the very size of the Antioqueño area, coupled with the fact that no other city rivaled Medellín for dominance within the region, is what explains the concentration of wealth in Medellinense financial enterprises. Marco Palacios, *Entre la legitimidad y la violencia: Colombia, 1875–1994* (Bogotá: Norma, 1995), p. 83.

21 Fernando Botero Herrera, *La industrialización de Antioquia: Génesis y consolidación, 1900–1930* (Medellín: CIE, 1985), and Juan José Echavarría, "External Shocks and Industrialization" (Ph.D. diss., Oxford University, 1989). See also commentaries by Jaime Jaramillo Uribe, José Antonio Ocampo, Marco Palacios, and others in Fundación Antioqueña de Estudios Sociales, *Los estudios regionales*, pp. 1–19, 97–114, 217–30.

22 For a later period, the violent years of the 1940s, Eduardo Sáenz Rovner, in *La ofensiva empresarial*, has partially taken up Ospina Vásquez's political approach, although his arguments tend in a somewhat different direction than Ospina's.

23 But see Juan José Echavarría, "External Shocks and Industrialization," for a revisionist argument that protectionism was less important to Colombian industrialization than has been thought.

24 Ospina Vásquez, p. 491, cited by Palacios, "El café," p. 87.

25 On his sympathy with Hagen, see the prologue to the second edition, Ospina Vásquez, pp. 9–12, and McGreevey, p. 189.

26 Ospina Vásquez, p. 543.

27 José Olinto Rueda, "Historia de la población de Colombia: 1880–2000," in *NHC*, vol. 5, pp. 357–96.

28 Anthony James Beninati, "Commerce, Manufacturing, and Population Redistribution in Medellín, Antioquia, 1880–1980: A Case Study of Colombian Urbanization" (Ph.D. diss., State University of New York at Stony Brook, 1982), pp. 139, 159, 165.

29 The material in this and the following paragraph is drawn from Botero Herrera, "Historia de la ciudad de Medellín," pp. 174–78, 96–198.

30 In 1912, the Junta Directiva declared that "from this point on, visitors will not be permitted in the factory . . . except when expressly invited." Complimentary tours were also arranged for visiting luminaries, especially politicians with a voice in debates about protectionism. In 1919, for example, Bello's municipal government petitioned the mill's manager to close the factory and give workers a holiday to commemorate the visit of Marco Fidel Suárez; Restrepo refused precisely because he wished Suárez to tour the factory while in operation. Actas 3, 10, and 20, in "Libro de Actas de la Junta Directiva" (Fábrica de Bello) in the Sala Histórica, AF, also Emilio R. to Sr. Presidente del Concejo Municipal de Bello, 2/3/1919 Copiador 15 (1918/1919), p. 186. Operatives' wages are taken from Emilio Restrepo to Ministro de Hacienda, 8 March 1916, Copiador 12, p. 3, AF. Kids under twelve earned between $0.10 and 0.25, women were paid 0.16–0.40, while men (including mechanics and construction workers) received 0.35–1.30. Well into the 1950s, factory tours continued to be a local pastime for wealthy tourists and for the city's elite. A Philadelphian who married into Medellín's most established Jewish family (owners of Tejidos Leticia) described factory visits as a standard part of showing Medellín to visitors in the 1950s and 1960s. Interview with Barbara Rabinovich, Philadelphia, 18 June 1995.

31 Botero Herrera, "Historia de la ciudad de Medellín," pp. 32–64, 96–104, 110, 176–77, 180, 283. See also Fernando Botero Herrera, "Regulación urbana e intereses privados," in Melo, ed., *Historia de Medellín*, pp. 326–43.

32 Jorge Echavarría (a younger relative, not to be confused with Don Jorge), described his arrival at Burlington, in Cramerton, North Carolina, with enthusiasm: "They will give me the same training that the [Americans] that join the company get. . . . I have to work fifty-five hours a week and I'll get $60.00 U.S. per week." Jorge

Echavarría to Luis Echavarría, 3 June 1950, Correspondence vol. 912, AF. See also Roldán, "Genesis and Evolution," p. 219.

33 Botero Herrera, *La industrialización*, pp. 60–65; Echavarría, *Historia de los textiles*, pp. 22–28; Ospina Vásquez, p. 425; Parsons, *Antioqueño Colonization*, p. 180.

34 Echavarría, *Historia de los textiles*, pp. 35–45, and Anita Gómez de Cárdenas, *Medellín: Los años locos* (Medellín: Fabricato, 1985), pp. 57–71. Fabricato was incorporated in 1920, immediately prior to a severe financial crisis in Medellín. The company did not begin operation until 1923.

35 *Fabricato al Día* 112 (July–August 1973), p. 25; Echavarría, *Historia de los textiles*, p. 39; and Ospina Vásquez, p. 426.

36 Gómez de Cárdenas, p. 68.

37 Ibid., pp. 30–31, 45, 68; *Fabricato al Día* 112 (July–August 1973), p. 29.

38 Echavarría, "External Shocks and Industrialization," pp. 384–85. See also Echavarría, *Historia de los textiles*, pp. 46–47; Santiago Montenegro, "Breve historia de las principales empresas textileras," *Revista de extensión cultural* 12 (July 1982): 50–66; see p. 65.

39 Sáenz Rovner, pp. 38–39.

40 In 1966, the company initiated a second partnership with Burlington Mills to found Tejidos la Esmeralda, and, in 1970, in association with Nicaraguan capitalists, Fabricato launched Fabritex, in Managua.

41 See Alberto Mayor Mora, "Historia de la industria colombiana, 1930–1968," *NHC*, vol. 5, pp. 333–56; see also "Datos históricos: 80 años de Coltejer," *El Colombiano*, 22 October 1987, and Coltejer, "Coltejer: Una publicación del departamento de relaciones públicas de Coltejer," printed pamphlet, April 1970, Archivo Coltejer (hereafter AC).

42 Roldán, "Genesis and Evolution," p. 113.

43 On the Violence, see: Charles Bergquist, Ricardo Peñaranda, and Gonzalo Sánchez, eds., *Violence in Colombia: The Contemporary Crisis in Historical Perspective* (Wilmington, Del.: SR Books, 1992); Germán Guzmán, Orlando Fals Borda, and Eduardo Umaña, *La violencia en Colombia*, 2 vols. (Bogotá: Círculo de Lectores, 1988; first published 1963); Paul Oquist, *Violence, Conflict, and Politics in Colombia* (New York: Academic Press, 1980); and Gonzalo Sánchez and Donny Meertens, *Bandoleros, gamonales, y campesinos: El caso de la violencia en Colombia* (Bogotá: El Áncora, 1983). An excellent discussion of the literature on the Violence is provided by Gonzalo Sánchez, "*La Violencia* in Colombia: New Research, New Questions," *Hispanic American Historical Review* 65, no. 4 (1985): 789–807.

44 Largely, not exclusively: on urban violence in these years, especially the events of 9 April, see Arturo Alape, *El Bogotazo: Memorias del olvido* (Bogotá: Editorial Pluma, 1983); Herbert Braun, *The Assassination of Gaitán: Public Life and Urban Violence in Colombia* (Madison: University of Wisconsin Press, 1985); and Medófilo Medina, *La protesta urbana en Colombia en el siglo veinte* (Bogotá: Ediciones Aurora, 1984).

45 The material in this paragraph draws on chaps. 6 and 7 of Roldán, "Genesis and Evolution."

46 Ibid., p. 516. Roldán's argument goes further, as she sees the industrialists as having modeled the internal discipline of their firms on their idealized vision of social relations in the central, traditionally "Antioqueño" towns near Medellín

and in the relatively homogeneous coffee towns in the southwest (pp. 192–98, 201, 211–12). Because I see this vaunted paternalistic industrial system developing in response to workers' behavior and in response to intra-elite debates within Medellín, my argument has a different emphasis. In my view, industrial discipline was neither so complete nor so backward looking.

47 Sáenz Rovner, p. 218. Many of the retired workers I interviewed remembered being sent home "when they [los patrones] overthrew Rojas Pinilla," and several were outspoken about their support for the populist general, whom they said had protected workers' interests. Interestingly, a number of retired workers moved the factory closings backward in time to 1948, saying that they had been sent home when Gaitán was killed but not remembering the employer-led protest against Rojas. The shift made sense in terms of a larger national story about 9 April 1948, although relatively little disruption occurred in Medellín and the mills had remained open. For a similar case of the way memory can be reshaped by national and regional narratives, see Alessandro Portelli, The Death of Luigi Trastulli and Other Stories: Form and Meaning in Oral History (Albany: State University of New York Press, 1991), pp. 1–28.

48 See Mary Roldán, "La política de 1946 a 1958," in Historia de Antioquia, ed. Melo, pp. 161–75.

49 Ibid., pp. 164–65; also her "Genesis and Evolution," p. 373.

50 An erudite discussion of the Colombian church in this period is provided by Fernán González, "La iglesia católica y el estado colombiano, 1930–1985," in NHC vol. 2, pp. 371–96. For radically divergent views of Builes, see Darío Acevedo Carmona, La mentalidad de las élites sobre la violencia en Colombia, 1936–1949 (Bogotá: El Áncora Editores, 1995), and Jaime Sanín Echeverri, Obispo Builes (Bogotá: Editora Geminis, 1988). On the tight link between Medellinense industrialists and the social Catholics, see Alberto Mayor Mora, Etica, trabajo, y productividad.

51 Interview with Antonio Pineda, conducted by Jorge Bernal, Bello, 10 June 1987.

52 Interview with Estanislao Bedoya, Medellín, 15 October 1990, and with Susana Osorio, as part of group interview, Envigado, 24 July 1991.

53 Interview with María Cristina Restrepo, Bello, 23 Oct. 1990.

54 Interview with Concha Bohórquez, Bello, 12 July 1994.

55 Ibid.

56 Ibid.

57 The cédula system was developed piecemeal, beginning in the early nineteenth century, and was expanded in the 1920s and 1930s. By 1935, adult males required a cédula to vote, and government-issued identity cards were issued to women and minors as their counterpart to the cédula. Among the identifying information contained in the cédula or identity card is a classification of the person's skin color. See República de Colombia, Registraduría nacional del estado civil (Bogotá: Registraduría, 1988), pp. 76–79. I thank Marco Palacios for forwarding to me his own notes on the cédula system.

58 Interview with María Clara Henao, Bello, 17 Oct. 1990.

59 Humberto Ramírez Gómez, "Relación de Basket Ball en el presente año," 15 December 1939. Correspondence, vol. 878, AF. Interestingly, basketball was considered a women's sport and was not played by men, for whom the factories promoted football (soccer).

60 Interview with María Elisa Alvarez, Medellín, 8 July 1994.

61 Botero Herrera, *La industrialización*, p. 169.

62 Interview with María Elisa Alvarez, Medellín, 8 July 1994.

63 Ibid.

64 Interview with Eugenio Márquez, Bello, 16 Oct. 1990.

65 Juan Alzate, as part of group interview, Envigado, 24 July 1991, and interviews with Laura Gómez Arango, Bello, 3 October 1990; Gumercinda Báez, Bello, 22 Feb. 1991; Estanislao Bedoya, Medellín, 15 Oct. 1990; and Eugenio Márquez, Bello, 16 Oct. 1990.

66 Interview with María Elisa Alvarez, Medellín, 8 July 1994.

67 Interview with Concha Bohórquez, Bello, 12 July 1994.

68 Interview with Ofelia Uribe, Medellín, 29 July 1994.

Two. The Making of *La Mujer Obrera*, 1910–20

1 Interview with María Elisa Alvarez, Medellín, 8 July 1994.

2 For comparison, see Robert Gray, "The Languages of Factory Reform in Britain, c. 1830–1860," in *The Historical Meanings of Work*, ed. Patrick Joyce (New York: Cambridge University Press, 1987), p. 143.

3 Ibid., and see Patricia Hilden, "The Rhetoric and Iconography of Reform: Women Coal Miners in Belgium, 1840–1914," *Historical Journal* 34, no. 2 (1991): 411–36, as well as Joan Scott, " 'L'ouvrière! Mot impie, sordide' . . ." in her *Gender and the Politics of History*, pp. 139–63.

4 See, for example, the weekly *Colombia*, 25 Feb.–10 March 1920.

5 For an excellent summary of Rerum Novarum and the approach to the problem of female labor that it implied, see Sandra McGee Deutsch, "The Catholic Church, Work, and Womanhood in Argentina, 1890–1930," *Gender and History* 3, no. 3 (1991): 304–22; esp. p. 308.

6 *El Social*, 22 July 1917.

7 Scott, " 'L'ouvrière!' " and Hilden, "Rhetoric and Iconography."

8 The material in this paragraph is drawn from *El Luchador*, 24 Jan. 1920 and 28 Nov. 1919. A 1922 poem in the same newspaper evoked similar themes, comparing *la obrerita, hija del la montaña*, to a rose, a "hard-working bee," a "butterfly" flying between the "dark spiderwebs" of the city.

9 *El Luchador*, 8 Nov. 1918. Jorge Issacs, *María* (Madrid: Espasa-Calpe, 1983). See Doris Sommers's analysis of the importance of this nineteenth-century novel in *Foundational Fictions: The National Romances of Latin America* (Berkeley: University of California Press, 1991).

10 Jaime Sanín Echeverri, *Una mujer de cuatro en conducta*, 5th ed. (Medellín: Editorial Bedout, 1980). I would like to thank the author for discussing the novel with me and for sharing so generously his memories of Medellín with me, his foreign-born niece.

11 Acta of July 1912, Libro de Actas de la Junta Directiva del Patronato de Obreras, hereafter abbreviated as "Libro de Actas," held by the religious order of the Hermanas de la Presentación, Medellín. I thank Antonio Lopera for taking an interest in this research and facilitating my work with the uncataloged papers of the former Patronato. Further references to these papers are indicated by the abbreviation PO.

12 Actas of March 1914 and of May 1916, Libro de Actas, PO.

13 Entries for 1, 15, and 22 Oct. 1916, and for 5 Nov. 1916; also 14 Jan. 1917 and 11 March 1917 in the manuscript volume titled "Historial de la Casa," PO.

14 Entries for 10 and 24 Dec. 1916 and 3 June 1917, "Historial de la Casa," PO.

15 Medellín, *Anuario Estadístico* of 1916–17, p. 41. This was the first year in which city statisticians undertook what became a yearly survey of women workers; men were not surveyed, as mentioned above. For 1916 they found 2,056 *obreras*, 716 of whom worked in the *trilladoras*, and in 1917 the figure was 2,143, with 718 in *trilladoras*. City figures did not include women working in Bello, Itagüí, or Envigado.

16 Entry for 11 Feb. 1917, "Historial de la Casa." Also the Acta of March 1916, Libro de Actas, PO.

17 Actas of Nov. 1914, Aug. 1917, and April 1921, also the entries for 8 April 1917 and 29 June 1918, "Historial de la Casa," PO. See also *El Social*, 19 Aug. 1917, which printed a thank-you to the Ferrocarril de Antioquia for having given 250 tickets for a Patronato-sponsored outing; the tickets were given to those who had attended more than seven Sunday lectures.

18 The organization of the dormitory/restaurant attempted a convent-like separation from men; even the messenger, gardener, and doorkeeper were female, as indicated by notes taken by the city's factory inspector: "Hay una Directora General, una sirvienta, una portera, una manadera, y una jardinera." Acta 693, 29 May 1920, Libro de Actas del Inspector de Fábricas, Signatura 8929, Archivo Histórico de Antioquia (hereafter AHA). Further references to the records of the inspector are given with the number of the Acta, the date, and the archive location (Signatura), abbreviated as S.

19 Acta of Oct. 1915, Libro de Actas, PO.

20 Acta of Dec. 1915, Libro de Actas, PO.

21 Acta of Oct. 1916, Libro de Actas, PO.

22 See, for example, a didactic piece in the Catholic paper *El Obrero*, 3 Feb. 1912.

23 Acta of Oct. 1915, Libro de Actas, PO.

24 Actas of Nov. 1916, April 1916, and April 1913, Libro de Actas, PO.

25 *Negra* is an extremely unstable term in Colombian Spanish; it can mean "black woman" or "mulata," or "dear," or "sweetie," depending on the context, and it can be applied to women of almost any combination of hair and skin color. For "*mujer-hombre*" see *El Obrero Católico*, 25 June 1927.

26 In February of 1922, for example, "the Señoritas . . . proposed to the Reverend Father Director to do spiritual exercises in various factories, saying that they would arrange with each owner and manager." Acta of Feb. 1922, Libro de Actas, PO.

27 Actas of Jan. 1915, April 1918, and Jan. 1923, Libro de Actas, as well as entries for 1 Oct. 1916 and 1 Sept. 1918, "Historial de la Casa," PO. The ladies also directed choral groups at several factories; Actas of March 1916 and Aug. 1920, Libro de Actas, PO.

28 Elvira Escobar, Presidenta de la Junta del Patronato de Obreras to los Directores de las siguientes Fábricas, 13 Dec. 1918, in the manuscript volume titled "Libro de Anotaciones Secretaría," PO.

29 Actas of Feb. and June 1919, Libro de Actas, PO. The board also arranged special meetings between themselves and female supervisors at the mills: Acta of April 1914.

30 Acta of Oct. 1915, Libro de Actas, PO.

31 Such arguments relied on the examples of the Russian and Mexican revolutions, the activities of the International Workers of the World in the United States, and the strike movement in Britain. Secretario de Gobierno, *Memoria a la Asemblea de 1917* (Medellín: Imprenta Oficial, 1917), pp. 7–13. Further citations are to *Memoria*, with the year indicated.

32 See, for example, Father Lizardi's piece in *El Social*, 18 March 1917, which was placed in the official record as part of *Memoria*, 1917, p. 291.

33 *El Social*, 29 April 1917.

34 "Que la mirada policiva penetra a las fábricas"; *Memoria*, 1917, p. 9.

35 "*Entregarse*," the word Pérez used, is also commonly used to refer to a woman's surrender of her virginity.

36 *El Social*, 8 July 1917; see also 18 March and 30 Sept. 1917.

37 *El Social*, 22 July 1917.

38 *El Social*, 12 Oct. 1917.

39 *El Social*, 18 March 1917.

40 *Memoria*, 1917, p. 18.

41 Joaquín Emilio Jaramillo to Administrador de la Fábrica de Tejidos Hernández, 19 July 1919, S. 8562, p. 28, AHA.

42 Vélez replaced Joaquín Jaramillo in mid-February of 1920, during the Bello strike; it seems likely that the public embarrassment of the women's action prompted Jaramillo's dismissal. Incidentally, it is only after Vélez's appointment that the inspector's Actas de Visita exist in the departmental archive.

43 Daniel Vélez to Secretario de Gobierno, 5 July 1920, in which Vélez informs him that the *matrona* at the shoe factory "Rey Sol" is required to work like the others and is thus a *vigilanta* in name only, S. 8562. See also the inspector's Actas de Visita for Rosellón and the Fábrica de Bello, Acta 121, 12 June 1920, S. 8930; Acta 428, 26 April 1922, S. 8932; and Acta 1513, 19 Feb. 1927, S. 8944, AHA.

44 *Memoria*, 1924, p. 272. See also the inspector's report for 1922, in which year twelve administrators were fired for moral violations, and 1923, when eight *vigilantas* and thirteen administrators were thus "punished." The act of quantifying such actions was, of course, itself part of the discourse of progress and modernity manipulated by the inspector.

45 Acta 1476, 7 July 1922, S. 8934; also Acta 628, 24 April 1920, S. 8929, AHA.

46 Antioquia, Secretario de Gobierno, *Informe* (Medellín: Imprenta Oficial, 1922), p. 47. See also later *Informes*, cited by year.

47 Actas 1476, 7 July 1922, S. 8934, and 764, 28 July 1920, S. 8928, AHA.

48 Inspector de Fábricas, "Fábrica de Tejidos Rosellón," 21 July 1920, S. 8930, p. 56, AHA.

49 Acta 705, 19 June 1920, S. 8929, p. 220, AHA.

50 Antioquia, *Mensajes que los gobernadores de Antioquia han dirigido a la Asamblea del Departamento, 1911–1929* (Medellín: Imprenta Municipal, 1929), p. 713 and again on p. 718.

51 Acta 458, 3 July 1922, S. 8932, AHA. In 1923, an administrator at the Fábrica de Bello was accused "of having wanted to corrupt two *obreras*," but the inspector concluded that he was innocent and had observed "exemplary" conduct. Acta 597, 19 April 1923, S. 8932, AHA. See also a letter by Vélez's predecessor to a *trilladora* owner, insisting that the plant administrator had "tried to seduce"

various *obreras* there. Joaquín Emilio Jaramillo to Alcalde Municipal, 19 Aug. 1919, S. 8562, p. 31, AHA.

52 A loose note, on 8½-by-4-inch paper, appearing in S. 8935. Later Actas suggest that Angel remained at the mill for years afterward: Acta 1875, 3 April 1923, S. 8935, AHA. See also the inspector's denunciation of an unnamed mill (almost certainly Bello) in Antioquia, *Mensajes*, p. 715.

53 The owner of Tejidos Unión argued with the inspector in the mill, and then dragged Vélez off to the government secretary's office, there winning a month's reprieve.

54 Antioquia, *Memoria*, 1926, p. 254, and *Memoria*, 1933, p. 231. See also *Mensajes*, p. 715.

55 Sherry Ortner, "Resistance and the Problem of Ethnographic Refusal," in Terrence McDonald, ed., *The Historic Turn in the Human Sciences* (Ann Arbor: University of Michigan Press, 1996), pp. 281–304, as cited by Canning, *Languages of Labor and Gender*, p. 14.

56 Actas of Nov. 1915, April 1917, and Sept. 1927, Libro de Actas, PO.

57 Only *jóvenes* lived in the dormitory. Actas of June 1915 and March 1924, Libro de Actas, and see the entry for 26 March 1917, "Historial de la Casa," PO.

58 Acta of May 1915, Libro de Actas, PO.

59 Acta of May 1915, Libro de Actas, PO.

60 Acta of March 1916, Libro de Actas, PO.

61 Acta of March 1917, Libro de Actas, PO.

62 Actas of June 1918 and Aug. 1920, Libro de Actas, and the entry for 17 Dec. 1916, "Historial de la Casa," PO.

63 They also resolved to buy some cheap items, that would cost *obreras* only a few *vales*, along with expensive goods requiring many. Actas of 7 Oct. 1915 and 3 Dec. 1923, Libro de Actas, PO.

64 Ana Escobar Uribe, y otras, to Honorables Diputados de la Asamblea Departamental de Antioquia, 8 March 1917. In "Comprobantes de Ordenanzas Sancionadas," 1917, S. 6333, AHA.

65 Acta of Sept. 1923, Libro de Actas, PO.

66 Acta of March 1924, Libro de Actas, PO.

67 Entries for 17 Dec. 1916 and 29 June 1918, "Historial de la Casa." Also Acta of May 1925, Libro de Actas, PO.

68 *El Correo Liberal*, 13 Feb. 1920. I thank Alberto Mayor for generously sharing this and other articles on the Bello strike.

69 The Liberal papers *El Sol, El Correo Liberal*, and *El Espectador* strongly supported the strikers, as did the Socialist papers *El Luchador* in Medellín and *El Socialista* in Bogotá. Among politicians of national standing, not only the Conservative Pedro Nel Ospina but also the Liberal Alejandro López involved themselves in negotiations behind the scenes, as did the archbishop of Medellín (allied with the Conservatives). Pedro Nel Ospina to Ricardo Restrepo C. AGPNO/C/26, folio 395, FAES; Emilio Restrepo to Illmo. Sr. Arzobispo de Medellín y Reverendo P. Gabriel Lizardi, S.J., 5 March 1920, Copiador 16, p. 352, AF; and Alejandro López to Alfonso Mejía, 12 March 1920. See also *El Espectador*, 14 Feb. 1920. I thank Professor Alberto Mayor for sharing a copy of both this article and López's letter with me. See also Secretario de Gobierno to Don Emilio Restrepo, 18 Feb. 1920, S. 8570, p. 28, AHA.

70 See Michel-Rolph Trouillot, *Silencing the Past: Power and the Production of History* (Boston: Beacon Press, 1995), p. 23.

71 In Medellín in January and early February, tailors struck for ten days, shoemakers for nine, glass workers for seven, and railroad workers at the Cisneros station for two. Mauricio Archila Neira, *Cultura e identidad: Colombia, 1910–45* (Bogotá: Cinep, 1991), pp. 222 and 435–36.

72 *El Correo Liberal*, 13 Feb. 1920.

73 He also used "Señor Impertinente," *El Espectador*, 14 Feb. 1920.

74 Ibid.

75 Ibid.

76 Ibid. See also *El Espectador*, 1 March 1920, which published a long ballad dedicated to "*vuese finosura/Besthabé.*"

77 *El Luchador*, 17 Feb. 1920.

78 Ibid.

79 Ibid. *El Luchador* reported that González and Tamayo had been "ready to fight and capable of detaining the *obreras* and *obreros* who didn't care to accept the strike," but that Espinal had argued for "the freedom of the *obreras* that have stayed at work; [and that] the rest of the *obreras* applauded her" (14 Feb. 1920). The Socialist paper thus tried to present her as a fair, morally upright defender of the *obreras* rather than as a "striker."

80 This description was offered by a "group of gentlemen" who met in the offices of *El Correo Liberal* and published a manifesto in solidarity with the strikers; see *El Espectador*, 2 March 1920.

81 *El Espectador*, 14 Feb. 1920.

82 Ibid.

83 See *El Correo Liberal*, 13 Feb. 1920; *El Espectador*, 14 and 23 Feb. and 5 March 1920; *El Luchador*, 14, 17, 20, and 27 Feb. 1920.

84 *El Luchador*, 27 Feb. 1920.

85 *El Espectador*, 5 March 1920. Writers at *El Sol*, a more centrist Liberal paper, similarly insisted that only the intervention of "honorable gentlemen" (*caballeros honorables*) would ensure a resolution in Bello. *El Sol*, 16 Feb. 1920.

86 *El Luchador*, 25 Feb. 1920.

87 Marco Palacios has suggested this in a personal communication, based on his own research.

88 "Sultán" appears in *El Socialista*, 17 Feb. 1920 and *El Espectador*; "Nabab" in *El Correo Liberal*, 13 Feb. 1920; and "harem" in *El Luchador*, 25 Feb. 1920.

89 *El Espectador*, 14 Feb. 1920, and *El Luchador*, 17 Feb. 1920. See also *El Correo Liberal*, 13 Feb. 1920. In the latter report Teódulo is described as being so surprised and frightened by the women's rebellion that he appeared "so pale he was almost white" (*hasta blanco de puro pálido*).

90 *El Espectador*, 26 Feb. and 10 March 1920.

91 *El Luchador*, 17 Feb. 1920.

92 *El Luchador*, 14 Feb. 1920.

93 Ibid.

94 See P. A. Pedraza, *Excursiones presidenciales* (Norwood, Mass., 1909), p. 165, cited by Constantine Alexander Payne, "Growth and Social Change in Medellín, Colombia," Senior Honors Essay in History, Stanford University, 1984, p. 32.

95 Interview with Antonio Pineda, conducted by Jorge Bernal, Bello, 10 June 1987, as well as my own interview with María Concepción López, Bello, 22 May 1991.

96 "Condiciones que propone la asamblea general de accionistas de la Compañía de Tejidos de Medellín a las obreras de su fábrica de Bello, para poner fin a la huelga," Copiador 16, pp. 347–48, AF. Reproduced in *El Espectador*, 14 Feb. 1920. The wage increase actually granted appears to have been closer to 25 percent, but this was still a significant increase. "Lista del jornal diario que ganan los obreros," Copiador 16, p. 365.

97 Emilio Restrepo to Illmo. Sr. Arzobispo de Medellín y Reverendo P. Gabriel Lizardi, S.J., 5 March 1920, Copiador 16, p. 352, AF.

98 Emilio Restrepo to Sres. Echeverri Hermanos, 11 March 1920, Copiador 16, p. 363, AF.

99 "Libertad de calzarse o no," in "Condiciones que propone la asamblea general de accionistas" (see note 97 above).

100 *El Correo Liberal*, 13 Feb. 1920 contains a brief reference to *female* strike-breakers: "*las remisas a la huelga.*"

101 *El Luchador*, 17 Feb. 1920.

102 *El Espectador*, 14 Feb. 1920; emphasis added.

103 Charpiot he saw as having "promoted" the strike. Emilio Restrepo to Leopold Cassella & Company, 16 Feb. 1920, Copiador 16, AF. See also *El Espectador*, 14 Feb. 1920. Antonio Pineda remembered Espinal being fired, as well as one Alfredo Holguín, whom he said had been a strike leader. Interview with Antonio Pineda, conducted by Jorge Bernal, Bello, 10 June 1987.

104 *El Luchador*, 14 Feb. 1920 and *El Espectador*, 5 March 1920.

105 *El Correo Liberal*, 13 Feb. 1920.

106 Of a similar incident in Tampa, for example, Nancy Hewitt asks, "was offering their skirts to men a derogation of femaleness?" See " 'The Voice of Virile Labor': Labor Militancy, Community Solidarity, and Gender Identity among Tampa's Latin Workers, 1880–1921," in Baron, ed. *Work Engendered*, p. 159.

107 Interview with María Concepción López, Bello, 22 May 1991.

Three. New Workers, New Workplaces, 1905–35

1 Echavarría, *Historia de los textiles*, p. 21.

2 Interview with María Elisa Alvarez, Medellín, 8 July 1991.

3 Later in the interview, she related that when she asked for another raise years later, during another stint at Coltejer, he responded the same way again: "It's always the same, to buy coconut candy . . . it's disgusting, buying from that lady! A lot of uncleanliness! Anti-hygienic!" Ibid.

4 Ibid.

5 Ibid. Such memories provide a way of reinterpreting what scholars of the region often describe as a "social egalitarianism" deriving from the structure of the mining economy and the fact that slavery was less important here than in some Colombian regions. See Mayor Mora, *Etica, trabajo, y productividad*, p. 271, as well as the discussion in Roldán, "Genesis and Evolution," pp. 123–24.

6 See Acta 169, 28 Sept. 1920; Acta 189, 4 Nov. 1920; and Acta 291, 23 May 1921, S. 8930; Acta 484, 22 Aug. 1922, S. 8932, AHA.

7 Actas 121, 12 June 1920, and 353, 13 Oct. 1921, S. 8930, AHA. See also Acta 189, 4 Nov. 1920, cited above, where Vélez prefaces his complaint that the mill employs minors with the comment, "Although in this establishment little attention, not to say none, is paid to the observations of the undersigned . . ."

8   Ibid.

9   "Que el Señor Gerente le había dicho que por ahora se abstenga de cumplir tal
    ley." Acta 1602, 1 Oct. 1922, S. 8934, AHA.

10 Acta 807, 7 Sept. 1920, S. 8928, and Acta 1040, 16 June 1921, S. 8933; as well as
    Acta 173, 5 Oct. 1920, S. 8930, AHA.

11 Acta 715, 22 June 1920, S. 8929, AHA.

12 Acta 169, 28 Sept. 1920, S. 8930. See also Actas 144, 169, 189, 230, and 255, AHA.

13 His emphasis. Acta 203, 20 Dec. 1920, S. 8930, AHA.

14 Acta 663, 21 May 1920, S. 8929, and Acta 765, 28 July 1920, S. 8928, AHA.

15 Acta 800, 2 Sept. 1920, S. 8928, AHA. See also Acta 767.

16 Cited by Mayor Mora, *Etica, trabajo, y productividad*, p. 257.

17 Emilio Restrepo to Jesus María Marulanda, 29 Nov. 1912, Copiador 8, p. 113, AF.

18 Ibid.

19 Don Emilio had ordered Fiddies, in writing, to continue speaking to Solvés, and
    they nearly came to blows on at least one occasion. Emilio Restrepo to W. H.
    Fiddies, 7 July 1912 and Eusebio Restrepo to Emilio Restrepo, 14 Aug. 1912.
    Copiador 7, pp. 417 and 459–72, AF.

20 Eusebio Restrepo to Emilio Restrepo, 14 Aug. 1912. Copiador 7, pp. 459–72, AF.

21 For a nuanced discussion of the performances required of elite actors and the
    significance of seemingly petty challenges to power, see James Scott, *Domination
    and the Arts of Resistance* (New Haven: Yale University Press, 1990), esp. pp. 10–
    11 and 45–69.

22 For the years 1938–42, an accounting of accidents suffered by mill-workers is
    available in vol. 881, AF. In this four-year period, at least twenty workers at
    Fabricato suffered serious accidents to their fingers, with many having one or
    more finger joints amputated.

23 Entry for Margarita Hoyos, Libro de Personal, 1918–34; this handwritten logbook
    is held at the public *hemeroteca* of Coltejer, in Itagüí; I thank Gabriel Alzate and
    Orlando Ramírez for their assistance in locating it. Future references to this
    source include the employee's name and the abbreviation LP, AC. See also entries
    for Tulia Muñoz, and Luis Vasco, who was dismissed for being "*grosero y al-
    tanero*" (rude, or foul-mouthed, and uppity), with the note that he was "a rude
    sambo, who took advantage of our necessity for workers—he threatened the su-
    pervisor that they would have to work things out in the street."

24 Entry for Teresa Montoya; see also the entry for Nicolasa Henao, among others.
    LP, AC.

25 From *hojas de vida* held in the Sala Histórica, AF. See also entries in the Coltejer
    log, such as that for Celia Bedoya, who was fired for concealing faults in the fabric
    she wove and for being "a bad worker" but was then rehired—later quitting be-
    cause she hated weaving drill. LP, AC.

26 Entries for Evangelina Mesa, Ana Montoya, María Saldarriaga, Berta Suárez, and
    Ramón Tejada. LP, AC.

27 At Fabricato, too, there seems to have been some inconsistency in the mill's early
    years, when Don Jorge sometimes hired married women; Arango, *Mujer, religión
    e industria*, p. 48.

28 See entries for: Marco Holguin Ortíz, Carlos Jaramillo, and Ana Molina. Of
    Josefina Ocampo, for example, the manager wrote, "She said she was leaving to
    work in a carpentry shop, later we found out that she was at the Medinas'. She
    behaved loutishly, since we paid her apprenticeship for her to go work for others."

Many entries, however, are simple statements, as is that for Inés López, who "left without giving notice, going over to the C.C. [Compañía Colombiana] de Tabaco," or Margarita Hincapié, who "left without giving notice to go over to Posada Tobón [a bottling plant]." LP, AC.

29 In interviews, retirees stressed how easily they'd entered the mills: the owner or manager had seen them in the street and called them over; they'd gone to ask for work and started the same day; or a supervisor had sent for them after hearing from a friend or relative that they were available to work. Interviews with Ana Rita Arbeláez, Bello, 8 Oct. 1990; Estanislao Bedoya, Medellín, 15 Oct. 1990; Fabio Garcés, Medellín, 30 Oct. 1990; and with Luis Castrillón, as part of group interview, 24 July 1991. By the early 1990s, of course, getting hired in the mills had become far more difficult, meaning that retirees' memories of how easily they had gotten work were shaped by what they knew of young relatives' unsuccessful attempts. For a discussion of workers' mobility in the early period, see also Mayor Mora, *Etica, trabajo, y productividad*, pp. 256–57.

30 Entries for Rubén Berrio and Carmen Morales Alzate. See also the notes made about Rosario Gil Cardona, Ana González, Santiago Grisales, Hernando Hernandez, Alejandro and Alicia Londoño Uribe, and Julia Mora Alvarez. LP, AC.

31 Sometimes, the administrator suspected falsehood. When one woman's mother said she was home sick, for example, he investigated and found out she'd gone to work at Tejidos Hernández. Entry for Rosario Franco. LP, AC.

32 Entries for Eloisa Echeverri, Ana Gómez Osorio, and Margarita Hoyos Posada. See also entries for Juan de Dios Idárragon, who "left because he wouldn't work Whitaker"; Antonia Acosta, who "left without giving notice, someone was sent to ask him and he said he had to take some medicine, we believe it was because he wouldn't work Kaiser Drill"; and Dolores Acosta Díaz, who quit rather than cut overalls. Mercedes Acevedo left rather than work a damaged cylinder, muttering upon going that "she wouldn't be back to work in this god-damned factory," a blasphemy which was duly reported and noted down beside her name. LP, AC.

33 Entry for Ana Marín García. LP, AC.

34 Entries for Rosa Betancur and José Gaviria. See also the entry for Ramón Bermudez, who was ordered to carry bobbins, "for lack of boys," and who "said he wouldn't . . . and if they obligated him to he'd quit." LP, AC.

35 See entries for Margarita Espinosa Escobar, Manuel Estrada Muñoz, Julia Mora Alvarez, Ana López Naranjo, Felisa Uribe Arcila, and Emilia Valencia González. LP, AC.

36 Entry for María de la Paz Flórez Villa; and see also that for María Villa. Other references to "dirty-mouthed" and "vulgar words" include Ernestina Ríos, and Rosalina Ruíz. LP, AC.

37 Entry for Otilia Quiros Montoya; and dozens of similar entries. LP, AC.

38 Entry for Ana Molina. LP, AC.

39 Entry for Margarita López. LP, AC.

40 An entry for one Camilo Torres, for example, reads: "*Sambo altanero*. Rude and vulgar, he left after mistreating the foreman"; see also the entry for Martina Oporto. "*Sambo*" appears more often than "*Negro*," although the latter was also used, as in the description of Alfonso Mesa: "A shameless, unwilling, troublesome Negro." LP, AC.

41 Entries for Angela Franco and Florentina Gómez, as well as for Carolina Gaviria, Dolores Jaramillo, Ana Mejía, and Evangelina Múnera. LP, AC.

42 Personnel file in author's quantitative sample.

43 Entry for Alejandrina Mejía. LP, AC.

44 Entry for Angela Ríos. See also the notes made about Isabel Ospina, Sofía Tabares, and Luis Vasco. LP, AC.

45 Personnel file in author's quantitative sample. The same woman was rehired twice after this incident.

46 Entry for Eduardo Arango Gutiérrez. LP, AC.

47 Entries for Otilia Posada Gutiérrez and Lucila García Tamayo. LP, AC.

48 Entry for María Fernández. See also entries for Dolores Jaramillo, Margarita Hincapié, Concha Estrada, Gabriel Montoya, and Miguel Hernández Múnera. LP, AC.

49 Entry for Dolores Vélez. Other examples include Jesús Flórez, Leonor Hincapié, Carmen Sierra, and Lastenia Vélez, who was, according to the manager, "bad, unsupportable, and chatty with the men." LP, AC.

50 Entries for Carmen Ramírez, and María Palacio. See also entry for Mariela Ortíz, who was "fired for mistreating her co-worker, using bad words." LP, AC.

51 Entry for Ana Escobar Gallego and for Gabriela and Ligia Posada. See also the note for María Jaramillo. LP, AC.

52 Entries for María Rendón, Amalia Toro, Lucila Mejía, and Cruz Uribe. LP, AC.

53 From personnel files in author's quantitative sample. Judging also from interviews, petty altercations also seem to have been common in the lines to leave the factory after finishing a shift.

54 Entries for Leogilda Morales and Ana de J. Puerta. LP, AC.

55 Alf Lüdtke, "Cash, Coffee-Breaks, Horseplay: *Eigensinn* among Factory Workers in Germany circa 1900," in *Confrontation, Class Consciousness, and the Labor Process*, Contributions in Labor Studies, no. 18, ed. Michael Hanagan and Charles Stephenson (New York: Greenwood Press, 1986), and Lüdtke, "Organizational Order or *Eigensinn?* Workers' Privacy and Workers' Politics in Germany," in *Rites of Power: Symbolism, Ritual and Politics Since the Middle Ages,* ed. Sean Wilentz (Philadelphia: University of Pennsylvania Press, 1985). For discussions of the impact of the concept in German historiography, see Geoff Eley, "Labor History, Social History, *Alltagsgeschichte:* Experience, Culture, and the Politics of the Everyday—A New Direction for German Social History?" *Journal of Modern History* 61 (June 1989): 297–343, and David F. Crew, "*Alltagsgeschichte:* A New Social History 'From Below'?" *Central European History* 22 (fall 1989): 394–407.

56 Lüdtke does argue that *Eigensinn* constitutes a form of resistance to factory discipline; he sees conviviality and rough play as fostering a "reciprocal appreciation" and as a cultural practice that happens in time "stolen" from an employer. I am thus using the notion in a somewhat different sense than he does.

Four. Strikes, 1935–36

1 The only person I interviewed who did remember the 1920 strike was María Concepción López, who remembered Betsabé Espinal as a "revolutionary," but who insisted that the strike had nothing to do with sexual harassment. Interview with María Concepción López, Bello, 22 May 1991.

2 Interview with Ana Palacios de Montoya, Medellín, 8 Nov. 1990.

3 As Mauricio Archila Neira emphasizes for the 1934 strike of the Ferrocarril de Antioquia: "a general strike in Medellín, of all places." *Cultura e identidad*

obrera, p. 284. Daniel Pécaut describes it similarly; *Orden y violencia: Colombia 1930–1954*, vol. 1, trans. Jesús Alberto Valencia (Bogotá: Siglo XXI, 1987), p. 213.

4   In describing this "defect," she inserted a commonly heard Colombian maxim, roughly translatable as "the world is not broken, and if one day it breaks, I'll put it over my head like a *ruana* and at least I'll be covered up," to stress her own unwillingness to let fear of being without work stop her from leaving a job. Interview with María Elisa Alvarez, Medellín, 8 July 1994.

5   Interview with María Elisa Alvarez, Medellín, 11 July 1994. María Elisa did not work at Coltejer in 1935. She had quit a short time before the strike and then returned a few years afterward, only to quit again when Don Eduardo again refused to give her a raise.

6   Ibid.

7   Interview with Cristina Monsalve, Envigado, 30 July 1991.

8   Ignacio Torres Giraldo, *María Cano, mujer rebelde* (Bogotá: Publicaciones de la Rosca, 1972), pp. 5–10.

9   Interview with María Elisa Alvarez, Medellín, 11 July 1994.

10 Elisa described herself and her sisters as having always understood the "five stars" of womanliness: to be a good daughter, a good wife, a good mother, a good Christian, and a good citizen. Ibid.

11 For example, she recounted getting in trouble for telling "off-color" stories [*cuentos verdes*], to a patient when she cleaned at a hospital, saying, "I told him the story about the baby Jesus and he didn't laugh, so I said 'what you want is a dirty story, I'm going to tell you a *dirty* one" [*un cuento verde; un cuento cochino*].

12 On María Cano see: Mauricio Archila Neira, "La clase obrera colombiana, 1886–1930," *NHC*, vol. 3 (1989): 219–55, as well as Torres Giraldo, *María Cano*. For a sensitive reading of the latter, see Ana María Jaramillo, "María Cano sigue floreciendo," *Re-Lecturas* 2, no. 5 (1989): 34–35. See also Gilberto Mejía, *Memorias: El comunismo en Antioquia (María Cano)* (Medellín: Ediciones Pepe, 1986).

13 See Susan Besse, "Pagú: Patrícia Galvão—Rebel," in *The Human Tradition in Latin America: The Twentieth Century*, ed. Judith Ewell and William Beezeley (Wilmington, Del.: Scholarly Resources, 1987); Patrícia Galvão, *Industrial Park: A Proletarian Novel*, trans. Elizabeth and K. David Jackson (Lincoln: University of Nebraska Press, 1993); and Elena Poniatowska, *Tinísima*, trans. Katherine Silver (New York: Farrar, Straus, Giroux, 1996).

14 Interview with María Elisa Alvarez, Medellín, 11 July 1994.

15 See the discussion by Carolyn Steedman, *Landscape for a Good Woman: A Story of Two Lives* (New Brunswick, N.J.: Rutgers University Press, 1987). The reference is to Richard Sennett and Jonathan Cobb, *The Hidden Injuries of Class* (New York: Vintage Books, 1973).

16 Interview with María Elisa Alvarez, Medellín, 11 July 1994.

17 Ibid., for this quotation and for the discussion in the next paragraph.

18 Germán Colmenares, "Ospina y Abadía: La política en el decenio de los veinte," in *NHC*, vol. 1, pp. 243–68.

19 For a concise discussion of this period, one that contextualizes the role of the church, see Palacios, *Entre la legitimidad*, pp. 96–124.

20 Coffee exports are measured in 60 kg bags. A condensed history of the coffee industry in this period is José Antonio Ocampo's "Los orígenes de la industria cafetera, 1830–1929," *NHC*, vol. 5, pp. 213–32. See also Jesús A. Bejarano, "La

economía colombiana entre 1922 y 1929," pp. 51–76 in the same volume, as well as Marco Palacios, *Coffee in Colombia, 1850–1970: An economic, social, and political history* (Cambridge: Cambridge University Press, 1980).

21 Bejarano, p. 53.

22 Ibid., p. 64.

23 Palacios, *Entre la legitimidad,* p. 125.

24 Archila, *Cultura e identidad,* pp. 223–27.

25 Archila, "La clase obrera colombiana," provides a summary of their role.

26 For overviews of popular radicalism in this period see Palacios, *Entre la legitimidad,* pp. 117–22 and Charles Bergquist, *Labor in Latin America* (Stanford: Stanford University Press, 1986), pp. 274–375.

27 On Conservative Carlos E. Restrepo's creation of a dissident "Republican" faction, see Jorge Orlando Melo's essay in *NHC,* vol. I, pp. 215–40. David Bushnell, however, minimizes the extent of Restrepo's split and insists that he "was in reality a Conservative." *The Making of Modern Colombia* (Berkeley: University of California Press, 1993), p. 162. A discussion of Olaya is provided by Palacios, *Entre la legitimidad,* p. 129.

28 Richard Stoller, "Alfonso López Pumarejo and Liberal Radicalism in 1930s Colombia," *Journal of Latin American Studies* 27, no. 2 (1995): 367–97.

29 Alvaro Tirado Mejía, "López Pumarejo: la revolución en marcha," in *NHC,* vol. I, p. 320. See also his *Aspectos políticos del primer gobierno de Alfonso López Pumarejo, 1934–1938* (Bogotá: Procultura, 1981). For a nuanced discussion of conflicting traditions within the Liberal Party, see Michael Jiménez, "The Limits of Export Capitalism: Economic Structure, Class, and Politics in a Colombian Coffee Municipality, 1900–1930," Ph.D. diss., Harvard University, 1986, pp. 471–72.

30 See Stoller, "Alfonso López Pumarejo," for an extended discussion of the meaning of López's radical rhetoric.

31 Tirado Mejía, "López Pumarejo," pp. 343–45. See also Bushnell, pp. 189–90, and Pécaut, p. 107, both of whom point out that the extension of the suffrage only increased (about equally) the strength of the two traditional parties. For an overview of López's administration, see Palacios, *Entre la legitimidad,* pp. 146–48, 155–56.

32 Bushnell, p. 188.

33 Stoller, p. 374.

34 Archila, *Cultura e identidad,* pp. 223 and 277. Pécaut delineates three reasons for the strike wave in 1934–38: the continuing economic crisis, a Communist Party decision to "test" López, and workers' own belief that he would ensure fair arbitration. Pécaut, p. 213.

35 Archila, *Cultura e identidad,* p. 299, as well as his "La clase obrera colombiana," p. 245.

36 In Spanish, the Unión Nacional Izquierdista Revolucionaria.

37 The Acción Patriótica Económica Nacional, or APEN, is outlined in Tirado Mejía, "López Pumarejo," pp. 308–9.

38 This marked a change for the Colombian Communist Party; before 1935–36 they had been wholly intransigent, attacking López and left-leaning Liberals almost as bitterly as they attacked Gaitán, in whom they saw a *caudillo* and a fascist. Pécaut, pp. 202–4, Archila in *NHC,* vol. 3, p. 251. See also Medófilo Medina, *La*

protesta urbana, pp. 45–52. Palacios points to the farcical nature of the Colombian Communists' notion of a "popular front" with *Lopismo*, *Entre la legitimidad*, p. 158.

39　*El Colombiano*, 22 June 1935; no scholarly history of Colombian labor legislation exists, but a brief outline of the legal history of *cesantías* (severance pay) is available in Ernesto Herrnstadt, *Tratado del derecho*, p. 277. Paid vacations had been formally required as part of a package of labor legislation passed under Olaya; see Archila, *Cultura e identidad*, p. 273.

40　On the demand for breakfast time see *El Diario*, 20 June 1935.

41　*El Diario*, 31 May 1935. Some observers referred to this union as the Sindicato de Textiles de la Fábrica de Coltejer; it's not clear whether its members understood this to be company-oriented or a union linking workers from multiple cloth mills.

42　*El Diario*, 12 and 13 June 1935.

43　*El Diario*, 17 and 18 June 1935; *El Tiempo*, 19 June 1935; and *La Defensa*, 17 and 18 June 1935.

44　See Mejía, *El comunismo*, p. 293. Very little research has been done on the Fedeta and its affiliated unions. See Ivan Darío Osorio, *Historia del sindicalismo Antioqueño, 1900–1986* (Medellín: Instituto Popular de Capacitación, n.d.), pp. 49–61.

45　*El Diario*, 20 June 1935. The Ministry of Industry later became the Ministry of Labor.

46　Ibid.

47　See, for example, the president's letter to Antioquia's railroad workers' union, published in Ibid.

48　*La Defensa*, 17 June 1935.

49　*El Diario*, 18 June 1935.

50　See, for example, Mayor, *Etica, trabajo, y productividad*, p. 288.

51　Compare, for example, *El Colombiano* (Conservative) with *El Correo Liberal* and *El Espectador* (both Liberal) for 1920, and *La Defensa* (Conservative) with *El Diario* (Liberal) for 1935.

52　*El Diario*, 20 June 1935. For a brief discussion of *El Diario*'s place in the internecine squabbles of Antioqueño Liberals, see Jorge Orlando Melo, "La política de 1904 a 1946," in *Historia de Antioquia*, ed. Melo, p. 159.

53　*El Diario* and *El Colombiano*, 22 June 1935; the newspapers printed the text of the settlement, but most of its articles state only that a specific point of the *pliego* has been "accepted" or not. Whether or not the workers' demand for breakfast time was allowed, for example, is difficult to determine.

54　See Osorio, *Historia*, p. 38, and Secretario de Gobierno, *Memoria*, 1936, p. 165, AHA.

55　*El Diario*, 18 and 21 Jan. 1936; *El Colombiano*, 17 Jan. 1935, as cited by Mayor, *Etica, trabajo, y productividad*, p. 288. See also Mejía, *El comunismo*, p. 294. In my interview with Enrique López, he also described the women's fundraising activities and claimed that they had been more effective than men in getting donations of food.

56　*El Diario*, 7 Jan. and 17 Feb. 1936.

57　"Era muy *sapa*, por todo sapiaba a uno"; interview with Cristina Monsalve, Envigado, 30 July 1991. Cristina also described the women's contempt for Cleofe and their insults, saying that they had called her "that damned old tattle-tale!"

58　Interview with Margarita Montoya, Envigado, 24 July 1991.

59　Mejía's transcription of this *pliego*, *El comunismo*, p. 294, refers to "los obreros," in the masculine form, while the version published by *El Diario* on 14 Jan. uses "obreras" when the reference is to spinning or weaving.

60 *El Diario*, 14 Jan. 1936, and Mejía, *El comunismo*, p. 295.

61 Mejía, *El comunismo*, pp. 268 and 291–301.

62 Ibid., p. 293.

63 Secretario de Gobierno, *Memoria*, 1936, p. 9, AHA.

64 *El Heraldo de Antioquia*, as cited by Mejía, *El comunismo*, p. 300. Envigado was a hotly contested municipality, where votes divided evenly between Liberals and Conservatives in 1931 and 1946. See Melo, "La política de 1904 a 1946," p. 152.

65 "Informe que presente el gerente de la Compañía de Tejidos de Rosellón a la asamblea general de accionistas," 26 Feb. 1936, File location 31-2-01, AC.

66 Secretario de Gobierno, *Memoria*, 1936, pp. 10–12, AHA.

67 Ibid.

68 "Lista de Empleados," 12 April 1933, Copiador 82, p. 103, AF. Teódulo was also still doing errands for Don Emilio in August of 1920, six months after the strike. See Emilio Restrepo to Sr. Tesorero de Bello, 3 Aug. 1920, Copiador 17, p. 132, AF.

69 Male dyers led this one-day strike, to judge from whom the company fired. See *El Luchador*, 3 Feb. 1920, and the factory inspector's record of Rosellón's charges against the technician Agustín Busquet, 21 July 1920, Libro de Actas del Inspector de Fábricas, p. 56, S. 8930, AHA.

70 *La Defensa*, 21 June 1929.

71 *El Diario*, 14 Jan. 1936.

72 Workers' complaints about the plant doctor at Fabricato in the 1940s moved even that mill's company union to action; the union president notified the *gerente* that workers "are constantly presenting us with complaints" about the carelessness with which he seemed to examine them. They complained also that he vaccinated people without changing needles and that the clinic was disorganized. Carlos Jaramillo to Rudesindo Echavarría, 8 March 1945, and Juan Cadavid to Jorge Duque, 8 Feb. 1949, Bound vol. 908, AF.

73 Interview with Enrique López, Envigado, 30 July 1991. The excerpts in the rest of this chapter are also from this session.

Five. Gender by the Rules:
Anticommunism and *La Moral*, 1936–53

1 See Pierre Bourdieu, *In Other Words: Essays toward a Reflexive Sociology* (Stanford: Stanford University Press, 1990), p. 80, for a discussion of "codification."

2 Beginning in the mid-1940s, Fabricato incorporated a floating cost-of-living benefit, *la prima móvil*, into workers' pay packets. Tejicondor adopted *la prima móvil* in 1943, Coltejer in 1950. Adolfo Restrepo al Inspector Seccional de Trabajo, 6 Sept. 1943, Libro de correspondencia general, 1943, AT; Coltejer, *Balance e informes*, 1 March 1951, AC.

3 Wary of more strikes, the governor named the same arbitrator who had helped settle the Rosellón conflict. For the *pliego de peticiones*, management's reaction, and the Bello settlement, see *El Diario*, 17–18 Feb. and 3 March 1936, as well as "Diario del periodo de conciliación entre la Fábrica de Bello y sus obreros," 26 Feb. 1936, bound vol. 881, AF.

4 "Informe del gerente a la asamblea general" (Fábrica de Bello), 15 Feb. 1937, bound vol. 843, AF.

5 Fabricato purchased the Bello mill in 1939 (although they continued to be administered separately), and it's not clear whether the latter's bus service began before or after that date; in 1941 management began charging a nominal fee. Carlos Mejía Uribe to Directores de Fabricato and Fábrica de Bello, 20 May 1941, AF. Coltejer also began a bus service during these years. See "Reseña Histórica de Coltejer" in *Lanzadera* 2, no. 18 (1957), pp. 36–46.

6 A photograph of Coltejer's cafeteria appears in *Life*, 29 Sept. 1947. Tejicondor built its own cafeteria in 1941, deciding that workers should no longer simply eat where they wished on the grounds. Interestingly, Tejicondor's managers expressly indicated that "we judge it best for the firm," referring to seating in the planned cafeteria, "not to establish any separation between men and women." Memorandum de la gerencia general a administración, 24 Sept. 1942, AT. Fabricato's cafeteria was part of its Patronato, discussed below.

7 Fabricato's new neighborhood began with a hundred houses, built according to different plans: some were larger than others and some included a separate "servant's room." See "Correspondence and Contracts," bound vol. 739, AF. Fabricato again increased its spending on housing construction in 1962, with 139 new houses in San José Obrero and 57 in Bello's Barrio Santa Ana: Arango, *Mujer, religión e industria*, p. 178. See also *Fabricato al Día* 112 (July–Aug. 1973), p. 26.

8 Rosellón had built a number of houses in "Barrio Rosellón" in the 1910s, but the firm began a more complete housing policy in 1941, a year in which the firm built forty-four houses. *Boletín Comercial* 19–20 (May–June 1914), pp. 464–65, cited by Botero, *La industrialización*, p. 144, and "Informe del gerente a la asamblea general de accionistas," Rosellón, 1942, file location 17–1–05, AC. See the photographs in Coltejer's "Album de Coltejer," at the company's public *hemeroteca* in Itagüí, as well as the summary in *Balances e informes*, Coltejer, first semester, 1954, pp. 3–4, file location 17–1–06, AC.

9 A teacher appears on Fabricato's payroll as early as 1924, when very few workers were married, but the company seems to have begun its first schools in 1942, when a religious brotherhood was contracted to provide six teachers for 110 boys. The company paid tuition for girls at the school Inés del Sagrado Corazon and maintained a primary school for 120 younger children. Bound vol. 795, AF. By the 1970s, Fabricato funded more than four thousand scholarships—at a variety of age-levels—for workers' children and for workers themselves. *Fabricato al Día* 112 (July–Aug. 1973), p. 20. See also Arango, *Mujer, religión e industria*, p. 164. Within a few years, Coltejer and Rosellón together provided space for nine hundred students a year. *Balances e informes*, Coltejer, second semester, 1955, pp. 20–21, AC.

10 See letters to schools in bound vol. 795, AF.

11 By 1941 Tejicondor had a (female) basketball team and a (male) soccer team. But it was Fabricato that led the employers' sports effort: the Echavarrías built "*a complete soccer field*" in Bello in 1948. *Gloria* 15–16 (Nov.–Dec. 1948), p. 55 (emphasis in original).

12 *Lanzadera* was preceded by *Ecos de Coltejer*, a newsletter aimed at workers; by 1949 it had been reorganized as *Lanzadera* and began publishing more sophisticated prose, although it was still directed at Coltejer's employees. *Gloria* was directed toward the wider national audience of consumers of Fabricato's products, although it also seems to have been circulated to workers at the plant and it certainly included photographs and didactic essays directed to workers. In invest-

ing in such in-house publications, Medellín's textile firms followed standard international practice; articles on the usefulness of "employee publications" appeared in *Textile Industries* with some regularity. See *Textile Industries* 111, no. 12 (Dec. 1947): 73–77 and 114, no. 4 (April 1950): 183–90.

13 The visual archive maintained by FAES documents the textile companies' visual impact on Medellín.

14 Echavarría, "External Shocks and Industrialization."

15 Jesús Bejarano Ávila, "La economia colombiana entre 1930 y 1945," in *NHC*, vol. 5, pp. 115–49. The industry depended, at least in part, on imports of raw cotton and cotton yarn until 1960, when the domestic supply of cotton began to catch up with the textile mills' demands.

16 Cited in Manuel Restrepo Yusti, "Historia de la industria, 1880–1950," in Melo, ed., *Historia de Antioquia*, p. 278. See also Mayor Mora, "Historia de la industria colombiana," and Santiago Montenegro, "El surgimiento de la industria textil en Colombia, 1900–1945," in *Crisis mundial, protección e industrialización*, ed. José Antonio Ocampo and Santiago Montenegro (Bogotá: Fondo Editorial Cerec, Fescol, 1984).

17 Explaining the company's intense interest in Antioquia's textile industry to local consular officials, "the Grace representative . . . stated that one textile mill in Medellín made a profit of $400,000 pesos in 1936 on a capital investment of $800,000." Grace also expressed the firm's irritation at the Antioqueños' clannishness and their funding of publicity campaigns directed against foreign capital. William Dawson to secretary of state, RG59, 821.6551/2, box 5663, 1937, also Gerald Keith, chargé de affaires ad-interim, despatch no. 750, RG59, 821.655/4, NARA.

18 Mayor, "Historia de la industria," pp. 335–36.

19 Stockholders of Tejidos de Bello were informed in 1935 that the company could not survive the competition if it did not move to automatic looms, as all of the other mills were making the transition. Martín del Corral, "Informe a la asemblea general de accionistas," 12 Aug. 1935, bound vol. 843, AF. Rosellón also modernized its stock of looms: "Informe del gerente a la asembleal general de accionistas, Rosellón," 14 Aug. 1936, file location 17-1-05, AC. The large firms nevertheless attempted to limit this competition by signing a pact to restrict loom imports between 1933 and 1935. Acta 68, Libro de Actas, pp. 264–71, Sala Histórica, AF.

20 Coltejer switched to three shifts in 1943. "Historia," company pamphlet, April 1970, AC.

21 Figures for Coltejer and Fabricato in 1945 include their newly added subsidiaries: Rosellón and Tejidos de Bello. Reference is made to three shifts in the Fabricato's 1946 report to the minister of labor. Gerencia de Fabricato to Sr. Inspector de Trabajo, 20 Feb. 1947, bound vol. 881, AF.

22 Mayor, "Historia de la industria," p. 336. Managers reported continual increases in productivity in this period. See for example, Martín del Corral, "Informe a la asemblea general de accionistas," 15 Feb. 1937, bound vol. 843, AF.

23 Factory correspondence files include many such requests; one example is Carlos Restrepo R. to Ministerio de Trabajo, Higiene, y Prevención Social, 14 March 1944, AF.

24 In 1934 Fabricato bought counters for its new automatic looms, and attempted to buy more for the existing mechanical looms. Acta 90, 23 Jan. 1934, Libro de Actas, p. 379, AF. Tejidos de Bello purchased three hundred dollars worth of "watch-

clocks" in 1934. Ricardo Restrepo Wills to Detex Watch-Clock Corp., 5 March 1934, Copiador de Cartas 85, p. 92; Tejidos de Bello also reduced piece-rates during the first wave of the crisis: internal memorandum, "Precios a como estaban y como deben rebajarse los obreros y obreras de la Fábrica de Bello," 19 March 1931, Copiador 79, p. 234, AF. Tejicondor experimented with multiple shifts, moving between two nine-hour and three eight-hour shifts in the early 1940s and keeping careful records of each shift's levels of productivity. Gerente general de Tejicondor to Juan Fernández Botero, Inspector del Trabajo, 2 Oct. 1943, AT.

25 An identity card from Fabricato, issued to an apprentice on the sizing machines (engomadoras), is printed with motivational slogans: "Only your own efforts can move you forward" and "Your conscience is worth a thousand witnesses." AF.

26 Mayor, Etica, trabajo, y productividad, pp. 268 and 343, nn. 59–60.

27 From Jorge Echavarría's diary for 1923–26. Cited by Gómez de Cárdenas, Medellín, p. 67.

28 Fabricato al Día 112 (July–Aug. 1973), pp. 28–29, 34. See also Mayor, Etica, trabajo, y productividad, p. 343, n. 58.

29 Emilio Restrepo built houses for workers and seems to have made personal loans to some families. Actas 13 and 35, Libro de Actas, p. 91, Sala Histórica, AF. Pablo Jaramillo to Sr. Administrador de la Fábrica de Bello, 19 Feb. 1928, bound vol. 880, AF. Helidoro Medina claimed to maintain a fund for workers' family emergencies. Civismo, 10 May 1919, p. 62. Additionally, the Echavarrías of Coltejer distributed aguinaldos or Christmas bonuses, as did administrators at other mills, according to the Patronato de Obreras. Entry for 24 Dec. 1916, "Historial de la Casa," PO.

30 Emilio Restrepo to Señor Alcalde Municipal de Bello, 10 July 1930, Copiador 78 (1929–30), p. 413, AF.

31 See Mayor, Etica, trabajo, y productividad, pp. 271, 279–80, for a discussion of the roots of an Antioqueño work ethic based on close relationships between workers and bosses. Mayor emphasizes the example of patrones with experience doing manual work.

32 Leticia Henao to Señores Miembros de la Junta Directiva de Fabricato, filed with her personnel file for 1947–55. Marta Roldán, similarly, sent a letter to Fabricato's central office, not addressed to any one person, requesting the company's financial help in arranging for her to begin a novitiate at a convent. Letter of 3 July 1946, bound vol. 911, AF. This volume includes numerous other letters requesting loans. Similar letters appear among Coltejer's personnel files.

33 Between 1940 and 1945, Coltejer's ratio of white-collar employees to workers increased from 1:27 to 1:11. From Coltejer, Balances e informes, 1945, AC.

34 Photographs of the Club Patronato in the 1940s include reading rooms and show groups of women and men playing cards; there were also billiard tables and gardens. Album del Patronato, Sala Histórica, AF.

35 Jorge Echavarría to Accionistas de Fabricato, 15 March 1933. Cited in Arango, Mujer, religión e industria, p. 142, and reproduced in E. Livardo Ospina, Los Hilos Perfectos: Crónica de Fabricato en sus 70 años (Medellín, Fabricato, 1990), pp. 27–29.

36 Ibid.

37 Petition dated 24 Oct. 1933, bound vol. 908, AF.

38 Fabricato to Excmo. Señor Presidente de la República, 5 June 1934. Also Fabricato to Ministros Gobierno, telegram, 5 June 1935, bound vol. 908, AF.

39 The junta first consulted a lawyer and debated when would be "the opportune

moment for the company to promote the unionization of its workers." Acta 85, 1 Dec. 1933, Libro de Actas, pp. 348–49, Sala Histórica, AF. Fabricato's managers seem to have first organized a white-collar union, the "Sindicato Asociación Profesional de Fabricato," and then the "Sindicato Textil del Hato." Florentino Morales D. to Señor Administrador, 1 May 1934, and Oscar Agudelo and Gabriel Valderrama to Rudesindo Echavarría, 20 May 1934, bound vol. 908, AF.

40 Quoted by Arango, *Mujer, religión e industria*, p. 155.

41 Petition, with signatures, 2 March 1942, bound vol. 908, AF.

42 Eugenio Sanín to Sr. Inspector de Trabajo, 21 Aug. 1944, bound vol. 908, AF.

43 Pécaut, pp. 346–47; Archila, *Cultura e identidad*, p. 354.

44 Internally prepared summary of events, dated 25 Nov. 1944. With this is a letter informing the company of the union's formation, dated 19 Oct., bound vol. 908, AF.

45 Printed handbill, 10 by 16 in., bound into vol. 908 with other papers from Nov. 1944, AF.

46 Interviews with Celina Báez Amado, Bello, 2 Oct. 1990; María Cristina Restrepo, Bello, 23 Oct. 1990; and María Clara Henao, Bello, 17 Oct. 1990.

47 Interview with María Cristina Restrepo, Bello, 23 Oct. 1990.

48 Printed handbills, bound into vol. 908, AF. Workers perceived the fact that the school was lent to the union as a sign of government support. Interview with Ivan Muñoz, Bello, 1 Nov. 1990. A departmental undersecretary and the town mayor supported the union and spoke at the meetings at the *escuela modelo*; at one meeting the regional labor inspector was slated to speak, but he withdrew his support at the governor's urging, according to Fabricato's lawyer.

49 Arango, *Mujer, religión e industria*, p. 155.

50 Interview with Celina Báez Amado, Bello, 1 Oct. 1990. Retired workers almost always stressed their own loyalty to the company, even those who said they had signed for the Fedeta. Celina used the word *engañada*; others simply said that they'd quit when they understood that "this was bad because it went against the other one [the company union]," as one man explained in an interview, saying, "I've never liked to go against the factory." Interview with Antonio Pineda, conducted by Jorge Bernal, 10 July 1987.

51 Formally constituted in 1946, the UTC had its strength in Antioquia where it extended the activities of the Unión de Trabajadores de Antioquia (UTRAN), an association of Catholic unions opposed to the Fedeta. For analyses of the expansion of Catholic unionism, see Archila, *Cultura e identidad*, p. 361; Osorio, *Historia del Sindicalismo*, pp. 127–34; Pécaut, pp. 429–39.

52 Carlos Jaramillo to Rudesindo Echavarría, 19 Oct. 1944, 8 March 1945, 28 July 1945, bound vol. 908, AF. Additionally, workers used the union to complain that the company didn't pay transportation costs when a family had to travel to Medellín for the lung examination required to live in a company house; to request that leather shoes rather than *tenis* (sneakers) be distributed; to circulate a petition that shifts be rotated.

53 Juan Cadavid to Jorge Duque, 21 Jan. 1949, bound vol. 908, AF.

54 Pécaut, pp. 433, 436; see also Archila, *Cultura e identidad*, p. 314, who points to the splits between the Juventud Católica and Catholic Social Action. At Coltejer in 1950, the company union faced an internal split when a group of members publicly accused the UTRAN-affiliated union of being "patronal"; to function as a barrier to "communism," a company union had to pretend not to be wholly yellow— turning a seeming statement of fact into a political offensive. Luis Eduardo Bernal

(president of the UTRAN) to Director de La Defensa, 15 March 1950, and Unsigned [Fabricato] to Juan B. Bedoya, 21 March 1950, AF.

55 *El Colombiano*, 24 Oct. 1932, reproduced in *Lanzadera* 2, no. 18 (Sept.–Oct. 1957).

56 Jorge Echavarría, diary entry for 2 Oct. 1926, as cited by Mayor, "Historia de la industria," p. 256; see also pp. 268 and 343, n. 61. On the Patronato's self-conscious campaign, see Actas of Feb. 1922 and Jan. 1923, Libro de Actas, PO. As part of their effort, the ladies of the board encouraged factory owners to give workers a cash bonus to attend the exercises. Elvira Escobar to "los directores de las siguientes fábricas," 13 Dec. 1917, "Anotaciones Secretaría," PO.

57 Mayor, *Etica, trabajo, y productividad*, p. 19.

58 Ramón Echavarría to Rvdo. Padre Lubín Gómez, 30 April 1940, bound vol. 155, AF.

59 Ibid.

60 Correspondence between Pbro. Roberto Jaramillo, Arzobispo Joaquin García B., and *gerente*, Fabricato, Jan. 1943, AF.

61 Humberto Bronx and Javier Piedrahíta, *Historia de la arquidiócesis de Medellín*, cited by Arango, *Mujer, religión e industria*, p. 168.

62 Arango, *Mujer, religión e industria*, p. 168. For a discussion of circulation and the early trajectory of *El Obrero Católico*, see Mayor, *Etica, trabajo y productividad*, pp. 305–9.

63 *Gloria* 36 (May–June 1952). Additionally, many OCSA-sponsored programs occupied company space itself: Catholic youth groups and "Centros de Acción Sindical" were located within the mills but run by Catholic priests, serving as sites for recruitment for both Catholic Social Action and the pro-company unions.

64 Interview with María Clara Henao, Bello, 17 Oct. 1990.

65 Interviews with Celina Báez Amado, Bello, 9 Aug. 1994, and with Concha Bohórquez, Bello, 12 July 1994.

66 Acta of April 1918, Libro de Actas, PO. Also Mayor, *Etica, trabajo, y productividad*, pp. 262, 309–12.

67 For a description of an *entronización* at Rosellón, one organized, according to *El Obrero Católico*, by workers at the mill, see Mayor, *Etica, trabajo, y productividad*, p. 312.

68 *Lanzadera* 8 (3 Feb. 1945). Reproduced as an appendix in Mayor, *Etica, trabajo, y productividad*, pp. 525–26.

69 See, for example, Jacquelyn Dowd Hall, et al., *Like a Family: The Making of a Southern Cotton Mill World* (Chapel Hill: University of North Carolina Press, 1987); as well as Patrick Joyce, *Work, Society, and Politics: The Culture of the Factory in Later Victorian England* (Brighton: Harvester Press, 1980), and Judy Lown, *Women and Industrialization: Gender at Work in Nineteenth-Century England* (Minneapolis: University of Minnesota Press, 1990).

70 Interview with Bárbara Alzate de López, Envigado, 2 Aug. 1991.

71 Interview with María Cristina Restrepo, Bello, 23 Oct. 1990; also personnel files in author's quantitative sample.

72 Written statement of Gustavo Ruiz S., Inspector del Trabajo, 17 Oct. 1941, bound vol. 881, AF.

73 According to the manager, Miguel Betancur was fired "for seducing and making pregnant the *obrera señorita* Rosa Gallego, having committed the same fault in

earlier years with the *obreras señoritas* Laura López and Isabel Ríos." Fábrica de Bello to Carlos Restrepo, Inspector de Trabajo, 30 Sept. 1939, bound vol. 881, AF.

74　*Gloria* 11 (Jan.–Feb. 1948) and 36 (May–June 1952).

75　Arango, *Mujer, religión e industria*, p. 146.

76　Carlos Jaramillo, Teresa Cadavid, Julieta Cardona, and Adelaida Restrepo to Director de Fabricato, 5 March 1938, bound vol. 833, AF. Carlos Jaramillo was an upper-level employee and later president of the company union.

77　Interview with Celina Báez Amado, Bello, 9 Aug. 1994. The nuns also refused the company union's request to show movies at the Patronato, although the union had assured them that they would only screen moral productions and their reason for purchasing the film projector was that "while we fail to instill a sufficient level of culture in our workers we will have advanced but little in the anticommunist campaign we seek." Juan Cadavid to Luis Echavarría, 25 May 1949, bound vol. 908, AF.

78　Thomas Dublin, *Women at Work: The Transformation of Work and Community in Lowell, Massachusetts, 1826–1860* (New York: Columbia University Press, 1979), pp. 77–78. Fabricato's experiment nevertheless differed significantly from the Lowell dormitories, which were modeled on boardinghouses rather than on schools or convents. While almost all of Lowell's workforce lived in the dormitories, only a fraction of the women employed at Fabricato lived at the Patronato. Additionally, the Lowell women had evening visitors and only a ten P.M. curfew, while Fabricato's *internas* had to return immediately after work and received visitors only on Sundays.

79　Interview with Carolina Arango, Bello, 8 Aug. 1994.

80　Interview with Esperanza Hernández, conducted by Ana María Jaramillo, Bello, 1987. A pictorial history of the institution entitled "El Patronato de Fabricato," held in the company's Sala Histórica, AF, explains that "it was founded to the beautiful end that the young *obreras* of Fabricato, who have had to abandon their homes . . . would find in it a new home."

81　"El Patronato de Fabricato," Sala Histórica, AF.

82　See also *Gloria* 11 (Jan.–Feb. 1948), for an article on the beauty pageants that similarly paired "*obreras* who have chosen the religious life" with those "who have married workers within the company."

83　In the album "El Patronato de Fabricato," AF.

84　Interview with Esperanza Hernández, conducted by Ana María Jaramillo, Bello, 1987.

85　Interview with Celina Báez Amado, Bello, 9 Aug. 1994.

86　My grandmother compared the stories I told her about the Patronato's insistence on skirts below the knee to her own school experiences, laughing about how she and other girls would hike up the skirts of their uniforms as they walked past boys' schools.

87　Interview with Celina Báez Amado, Bello, 1 Oct. 1990.

88　Interview with Carolina Arango, Bello, 7 Oct. 1990. Lucía Botero, similarly, exempted herself but insisted that many did try to get out with a shortened skirt: "I never fought about that, but many did that, they'd be going out the door—with the nun right behind them. She'd cut out their hem right there and they'd have to come back and change into a longer one [skirt] and then later taken the hem down on that one." Interview with Lucía Botero, conducted by Ana María Jaramillo, Bello, 1987.

89   Interview with Carolina Arango, Bello, 8 Aug. 1994.

90   Interview with Lucía Botero, conducted by Ana María Jaramillo, Bello, 1987.

91   Interview with Carolina Arango, Bello, 8 Aug. 1994.

92   See Arango, *Mujer, religión e industria*, p. 20.

93   Fabricato's magazine tied the *reinados* to the Patronato and to "the preeminent place given to morality." *Gloria* 11 (Jan.–Feb. 1948).

94   Interview with María Clara Henao, Bello, 17 Oct. 1990.

95   The names of the would-be *reinas* are written on the back of the photograph: "Nelly Florez, spinning, Blanca Ramírez, finishing, Isabel [no last name given], weaving," AT.

96   Interview with Guillermo Vélez, Medellín, 2 Nov. 1990.

97   *El Luchador*, 1 May 1924. On María Cano as the "flower of work," see Torres Giraldo, *María Cano*, and Jaramillo, "María Cano."

98   Acta of July 1925, Libro de Actas, PO.

99   Programa acordado por la familia Fabricato, 4 Aug. 1943, bound vol. 842, AF.

100 Interview with Lucía Botero, conducted by Ana María Jaramillo, Bello, 1987. See also Archila, *Cultura e identidad*, p. 129.

101 Luis Echavarría to Rudesindo Echavarría and Guillermo Villa, 12 May 1944, AF.

102 Article 2 of Law 48 of 1924. Colombia, Ministerio de Industrias, *Compilación de leyes obreras, 1905–1927* (Bogotá: Oficina General del Trabajo, 1929), p. 66. See also presidential decrees insisting on the *salas-cunas:* Decree 1722 of 1937 and 972 of 1943. Available in Campo E. Barón Serrano, *Legislación del trabajo* (Bogotá: Librería Voluntad, 1948), pp. 386–87.

103 At Tejicondor, for example, the *salas-cunas* were controversial among mill managers and upper employees. In November 1943, only a few months after the company had inaugurated its *salas-cunas*, the plant doctor attempted to convince the board of directors that accepting "those who have been turned away as a social ill in Bello or in Envigado" would only "swell the ranks of those who to fulfill their maternal duties have to be bad workers or vice-versa . . . bad mothers." Gerente a Administración, 12 Nov. 1943, Libro Memorandum, 1943. See also Acta of 28 Oct. 1943, Libro de Actas, AT.

104 Interview with Gumercinda Báez Amado, Bello, 22 Feb. 1991.

105 Interview with Cristina Monsalve, Envigado, 30 July 1991.

106 Acquaintances of long-time Tejicondor *gerente* Adolfo Restrepo quote him thus. One or two mistakes he would overlook, but with the third or fourth pregnancy, a woman "by then was a whore."

107 Interview with María Concepción López, Bello, 22 May 1991.

108 Ibid.

109 Arango, *Mujer, religión e industria*, p. 64, here, as elsewhere, the translation is my own.

110 Interview with María Cristina Restrepo, Bello, 23 Oct. 1990.

Six. *La Moral* in Practice, 1936–53

1   Interview with Ana Rita Arbeláez, Bello, 8 Oct. 1990.

2   Interview with Concha Bohórquez, Bello, 12 July 1994.

3   Susana Osorio, speaking of illegitimacy, said: "Very much in secret, it had to be, because it wasn't just the factory that condemned you. You were condemned at home, by the neighbor, the priest, the mayor, everything, everything that was

law condemned it. And even the girl herself wouldn't accept that people would be able to say that she had a love child [*hijo natural*], that's what a child like that would be called." Interview with Susana Osorio, as part of group interview, Envigado, 24 July 1991.

4   See Pierre Bourdieu, *Outline of a Theory of Practice*, p. 168, as well as his other works, including *The Logic of Practice* and *Language and Symbolic Power*, trans. John B. Thompson (Cambridge: Harvard University Press, 1991).

5   Interview with Celina Báez Amado, Bello, 9 Aug. 1994.

6   Arango, *Mujer, religión e industria*, p. 166, for Don Jorge's instructions to workers before the archbishop's visit, see Ospina, *Los Hilos perfectos*, p. 23.

7   Interviews with Concha Bohórquez, Bello, 12 July 1994; Cristina Monsalve, Envigado, 30 July 1991; Ofelia Gómez, Medellín, 18 July 1991; and Susana Gómez, as part of group interview, Envigado, 24 July 1991.

8   Interview with María Elisa Alvarez, Medellín, 8 July 1994.

9   Interview with Celina Báez Amado, Bello, 1 Oct. 1990.

10 Tejidos Leticia was an exception, as explained in chap. 5.

11 Acta 427, 18 Aug. 1927, S. 8949, AHA. See also Acta 1476, 7 July 1922, S. 8934, AHA. Mary Roldán has commented on Antioqueño elites' equation of silence and moral uprightness in "Purifying the Factory, Demonizing the 'Public Service Sector': The Role of Ethnic and Cultural Difference in Determining Perceptions of Working Class Militancy in Colombia, 1940–1955." Paper presented at the Eighth Latin American Labor History Conference, Princeton University, April 1991.

12 Acta 1533, 9 Aug. 1922, S. 8934; Acta 1513, 19 Feb. 1927, S. 8944; Acta 121, 12 June 1920, S. 8930; and Acta 428, 26 April 1922, S. 8932, AHA. See also Daniel Vélez to Secretario de Gobierno, 5 July 1920, S. 8562, which informs him that the *matrona* at the shoe factory "Rey Sol" is so only in name.

13 Acta 884, 24 April 1920, S. 8928, AHA.

14 Interview with Lucía Jiménez, Envigado, 21 May 1991.

15 Interviews with María Clara Henao, Bello, 17 Oct. 1990, and María Cristina Restrepo, Bello, 23 Oct. 1990.

16 "Publicación del Departamento de Capacitación," 29 Nov. 1958, bound with *Revista Tejicondor*, AT.

17 Interview with María Cristina Restrepo, Bello, 23 Oct. 1990.

18 "And the December after that three thousand would come back to get separated again, they were sick of being married," laughed Concha, quoting the company priest but adding that "he was just kidding." Interview with Concha Bohórquez, Bello, 12 July 1994.

19 Interview with Eugenio Márquez and Ester Gómez de Márquez, Bello, 16 Oct. 1990.

20 Interview with Cristina Monsalve, Envigado, 30 July 1991.

21 Interview with María Cristina Restrepo, Bello, 23 Oct. 1990.

22 Ibid.

23 Interview with María Elisa Alvarez, Medellín, 22 July 1994.

24 Ibid., and interview with Gumercinda Báez Amado, Bello, 22 Feb. 1991.

25 Interview with Bárbara Alzate de López, Envigado, 2 Aug. 1991.

26 Ibid.

27 Interview with Enrique López, Envigado, 30 July 1991.

28 From personnel files in author's quantitative sample.

29 Unrecorded interview with Ofelia Gómez, Medellín, 18 July 1991; from author's notes.

30 Interview with Cristina Monsalve, Envigado, 30 July 1991.

31 See Charles Briggs, "Learning How to Ask: Native Metacommunicative Competence and the Incompetence of Fieldworkers," *Language and Society* 13, no. 1 (1984): 1–28.

32 Interview with Cristina Monsalve, Envigado, 30 July 1991.

33 Many retired workers commented on the way co-workers applied nicknames to one another. Interviews with María Elisa Alvarez, Medellín, 22 July 1994; Ofelia Uribe, Medellín, 29 July 1994; and Juan Alzate, as part of group interview, Envigado, 24 July 1991.

34 Interview with María Concepción López, Bello, 22 May 1991.

35 Ibid.

36 Personnel records for Rosellón and Sedeco (subsidiaries of Coltejer), AC.

37 Emphasis in original; these and similar entries are found in personnel records from personnel files in author's quantitative sample, whether from Coltejer, Fabricato, or Rosellón.

38 A pseudonym is used here. Personnel file, AT.

39 Interview with María Cristina Restrepo, Bello, 23 Oct. 1990.

40 Ibid.

41 Interview with Ofelia Restrepo, Bello, 10 Oct. 1990.

42 Interviews with Eugenio Márquez, Bello, 16 Oct. 1990; Celina Báez Amado, 9 Aug. 1994; and Gonzalo Alzate, Bello, 16 Oct. 1990.

43 Interview with Concha Bohórquez, Bello, 12 July 1994.

44 María Concepción López, interview by Ana María Jaramillo and Jorge Bernal, Bello, 1987. See also Arango, *Mujer, religión e industria*, p. 76.

45 Unidentified newspaper clipping stapled to the *hoja de vida* of María Virgelina Rodríguez Carmona, AF.

46 Interview with Susana Osorio, as part of group interview, Envigado, 24 July 1991.

47 Interview with María Concepción López, Bello, 22 May 1991.

48 Interview with Susana Osorio, as part of group interview, Envigado, 24 July 1991.

49 I do not mean to imply that the interchange was thereby less charged with inequality, only that I had less control than researchers sometimes assume. Useful discussions of the unethical dimensions of oral research include Barbara Myerhoff, *Number Our Days* (New York: Simon and Schuster, 1978) and her *Remembered Lives: The Work of Ritual, Storytelling, and Growing Older*, ed. Marc Kaminsky (Ann Arbor: University of Michigan Press, 1992); Sherna Berger Gluck and Daphne Patai, eds., *Women's Words: The Feminist Practice of Oral History* (New York: Routledge, 1991); Ann Oakley, "Interviewing Women: A Contradiction in Terms," in *Doing Feminist Research*, ed. Helen Roberts (London: Routledge and Kegan Paul, 1981), pp. 30–61.

50 Interview with Ana Palacios de Montoya, Medellín, 8 Nov. 1990; excerpts throughout the rest of this chapter are from this same interview.

Seven. Masculinization and *El Control*, 1953–60

1 Alfonso Mejía Robledo, *Vidas y empresas de Antioquia: Diccionario biográfico, bibliográfico, y económico* (Medellín: Imprenta Departamental de Antioquia, 1951), p. 215.

2　Jaime Mejía Duque in *Fabricato al día* 112 (July–Aug. 1973), quoted by Arango, *Mujer, religión e industria*, p. 94.

3　Interview with Ana Rita Arbeláez, 8 Oct. 1990.

4　Robert B. Mitchell, for Barnes Textile Associates, Inc., "Report of Production Engineering Department Installation," Nov. 1953, Hemeroteca, AC, and Folder consultores extranjeros, Correspondencia, AT. See also Mayor Mora, "Historia de la industria," p. 349.

5　The material in this paragraph is drawn from Stoller, "Alfonso López," p. 373. See also Palacios, *Entre la legitimidad*, p. 180.

6　See Palacios, *Entre de legitimidad*, pp. 174–79, and Sáenz Rovner, *La ofensiva empresarial*.

7　Palacios, *Entre la legitimidad*, p. 175.

8　Ibid., pp. 179–80.

9　Yusti, "Historia de la industria, 1880–1950," p. 278, and E. Livardo Ospina, *Los hilos perfectos: Crónica de Fabricato en sus 70 años* (Medellín: Fabricato, 1990), p. 262.

10　Ospina, *Los hilos perfectos*, p. 262.

11　Proponents of "Motion and Time Study" as Ralph Barnes (cited below) argued it should be called, the better to extend credit to the Gilbreths as well as to Taylor, generally included long sections on the Gilbreths in the potted histories that were a standard feature of texts on industrial engineering. Generally, such histories begin with Taylor himself, although some evoke a pseudo-anthropological view of prehistory in their drive to legitimize incentive-pay systems. See R. Marriott, *Incentive Payment Systems* (London: Staples Press, 1961), and John Hutchinson, *Managing a Fair Day's Work* (Ann Arbor: Bureau of Industrial Relations, University of Michigan, 1963). See also Ralph Barnes, *Motion and Time Study*, 2d ed. (New York: Wiley and Sons, 1940); Marvin Mundel, *Motion and Time Study: Principles and Practice*, 3d ed. (Englewood Cliffs, N.J.: Prentice Hall, 1960); and Benjamin Niebel, *Motion and Time Study: An Introduction to Methods, Time Study, and Wage Payment*, 3d ed. (Homewood, Ill.: Richard Irwin, 1962). On Taylor and Taylorism, see Judith A. Merkle, *Management and Ideology: The Legacy of the International Scientific Movement* (Berkeley: University of California Press, 1980); Daniel Nelson, *Frederick W. Taylor and the Rise of Scientific Management* (Madison: University of Wisconsin Press, 1980); and Chris Wright, "Taylorism Reconsidered: The Impact of Scientific Management within the Australian Workplace," *Labour History* 64 (May 1993): 35–53.

12　The War Department's endorsement of standards during World War II spurred industrialists' interest in the United States, where time and motion consultancy boomed in 1945–48 and labor unions became more willing to accept the methods of industrial engineering. Ralph M. Barnes, "The Changing Concept of Industrial Engineering," in Barnes, ed., *Motion and Time Study Applications*, 4th ed. (New York: John Wiley and Sons, 1961), p. 1; Niebel, *Motion and Time Study*, p. 12; and Marriott, *Incentive Payment*, p. 23.

13　For example, Norbert Lloyd Enrick, ed., *Time Study Manual for the Textile Industry* (New York: Textile Book Publishers, 1960), which refers to standards departments as having become "recently" popular among textile manufacturers. His bibliography lists articles on time study and incentive pay that appeared in the trade press from the 1940s and 1950s. See also ILO, *Payment by Results*, Studies and Reports, New Series, no. 27 (Geneva: ILO, 1951), and ILO, Textiles Committee, *The Effects of Structural and Technological Changes on Labour Problems in the Textile Industry* (Geneva: ILO, 1968), p. 32.

14 Mayor Mora, "Historia de la industria," p. 345, n. 98, and Yusti, "Historia de la industria, 1880–1950," p. 273.

15 On "Taylorism" in Colombian and Antioqueño industry, see Charles H. Savage and George Lombard, *Sons of the Machine: Case Studies of Social Change in the Workplace* (Cambridge: MIT Press, 1986). For a sense of the international dimensions of "Methods Time Management" and the like, see Wright, "Taylorism," and ILO, *Payment by Results.* Also ILO, Textiles Committee, *Problems of Productivity in the Textile Industry* (Geneva: ILO, 1955), pp. 47–54, 87–104, and *Effects of Technological Developments on Wages and on Conditions and Level of Employment in the Textile Industry* (Geneva: ILO, 1958), pp. 35–36, 88, 93. For a description of "modernization" in the Mexican context in the 1950s, which seems to have involved new looms more than time and motion studies, see Jorge Durán, *Los obreros del Río Grande* (Guadalajara: Colegio de Michoacán, 1986), pp. 185–95. See also Peter Winn, "A Worker's Nightmare: Taylorism and the 1962 Yarur Strike in Chile," *Radical History Review* 58 (1994): 3–34.

16 English in original. H. M. Trammell to Luis Uribe A., 16 June 1953, in Vicepresidencia, Contraloria, AC.

17 Interview with Concha Bohórquez, Bello, 23 Oct. 1990.

18 For a contemporary ethnographic description, at a plant near Medellín, see Savage and Lombard, p. 164.

19 "Curso de ingeniería industrial, parte 4: La medición del trabajo por cronometraje," Publicaciones del Departamento de Ingeniería Industrial, Hemeroteca, AC.

20 *Revista Tejicondor*, Jan. 1960, p. 7.

21 Mayor Mora, "Historia de la industria," p. 349, and interview with Ana Palacios de Montoya, Medellín, 8 Nov. 1990.

22 Interview with Luis Henao, Medellín, 22 Nov. 1990.

23 Some of this material is conserved in the company's *hemeroteca* in Itagüí. See "Curso de ingeniería," cited in note 19.

24 Frederick W. Taylor, *Shop Management* (New York: American Society of Mechanical Engineers, 1903), and *Principles of Scientific Management* (New York: Harper and Brothers, 1911). See also Castonguay, "Engineering and Its Discontents," pp. 298–99 and Merkle, *Management and Ideology*, p. 29.

25 Barnes, *Motion and Time Study*, p. 140, and Harry Braverman, *Labor and Monopoly Capital* (New York: Monthly Review Press, 1974), pp. 102–6, who also cites Bell at some length.

26 Taylor, *Principles of Scientific Management*, pp. 41–48.

27 Interview with Eugenio Márquez, Bello, 16 Oct. 1990.

28 Interviews with Estanislao Bedoya, Medellín, 15 Oct. 1990, Feliciano Cano, Medellín, 19 Oct. 1990; Ramón Cano, Medellín, 29 Oct. 1990; Luis Castrillón, as part of group interview, Envigado, 24 July 1991; Pedro Nel Gómez Jiménez, Medellín, 8 Oct. 1990; and Eugenio Márquez, Bello, 16 Oct. 1990. See also interview material quoted in Arango, "Las obreras en la industria textil, 1950–1970," in Melo, ed., *Historia de Medellín*, p. 488.

29 Interview with Eugenio Márquez, Bello, 16 Oct. 1990.

30 Interview with Estanislao Bedoya, Medellín, 15 Oct. 1990. Estanislao echoed Eugenio's phrasing, describing *el estandar* as a system that treated workers as

though they were machines and asking the rhetorical question: "How can you compare a big strong guy to a girl over there maybe who's sick?"

31 Interview with María Elisa Alvarez, Medellín, 22 July 1994.

32 Ibid.

33 Ibid.

34 Interview with Susana Gómez, as part of group interview, Envigado, 24 July 1991.

35 Interview with María Cristina Restrepo, Bello, 23 Oct. 1990.

36 For suggestive material on the link between MTM, the introduction of new machinery, and "payment by results," on the one hand, and women's exclusion from textile jobs, on the other, see the following publications by the Textiles Committee of the ILO: *Problems of Women's Employment in the Textile Industry* (Geneva: ILO, 1953), pp. 2–5, 22; *Effects of Technological Developments*, p. 112, and *The Effects of Structural and Technological Changes*, p. 45.

37 Mayor Mora, "Historia de la industria," p. 349.

38 Figures based on author's sample of personnel records, as described above in my introduction, note 10.

39 Engineers' report by Howard A. Finley, 18 July 1955, Folder consultores extranjeros, Correspondencia, AT.

40 Interview with Zoila Rosa Valencia, Bello, 8 Oct. 1990.

41 Interview with Concha Bohórquez, Bello, 23 Oct. 1990. For a similar oral history account, in which the town's priest intercedes with the Echavarrías, see Arango, *Mujer, religión e industria*, p. 82.

42 Posada also solicited operatives' input, introducing suggestion boxes and awarding prizes to workers who submitted ideas that saved the company money. Arango, *Mujer, religión e industria*, pp. 91 and 94.

43 Emphasis in original. "No diga Vigilante—diga SUPERVISOR. No diga Administración—diga GERENCIA FABRICA," *Revista Tejicondor*, Dec. 1959, p. 14. Similarly, in 1954, Coltejer's "gerencia" was renamed "presidencia."

44 Jaime Mejía Duque in *Fabricato al Día* 112 (July–Aug. 1973). Quoted by Arango, *Mujer, religión e industria*, p. 94.

45 Savage and Lombard, p. 12.

46 Ibid., p. 109.

47 Ibid., p. 110.

48 Arango, *Mujer, religión e industria*, p. 185. The nuns continued to run the cafeteria that operated on the first floor of the Patronato building. For its part, Tejicondor defended its policy of accepting *madres solteras*, although it was also reducing female hiring dramatically. See "Madres que trabajan," *Revista Tejicondor*, Feb. 1960, p. 2.

49 The female *vigilanta* disappeared as well; there was no longer any need to pay a person to monitor mixed-sex conversation.

50 Between 1950 and 1965, for example, Fabricato distributed more than one thousand houses to workers; after 1965, the company established a community mortgage fund—although Arango points out that buying a home on a worker's salary became progressively more difficult through the 1960s and 1970s. *Mujer, religión e industria*, p. 178. Coltejer, too, dramatically increased its housing stock in the postwar years, building both rental units and houses for sale to loyal workers in various "*barrios obreros*," including a company neighborhood named "Alejandro Echavarría" after Coltejer's founder. See photographs of workers' housing and

accompanying text in Coltejer, *Balances e informes*, first semester, 1954, pp. 3–4, and first semester, 1955, p. 5; also second semester, 1955, AC. Tejicondor, similarly, established a credit fund to help workers buy homes. "Novena Publicación del Departamento de Capacitación," Oct. 1959, bound with *Revista Tejicondor*, AT.

51 At Tejicondor, the *visitadora social* was charged with determining "the environmental conditions of the applicant." "Septima Publicación del Departamento de Capacitación," May 1959, bound with *Revista Tejicondor*, AT.

52 Coltejer, *Balances e informes*, second semester, 1955, AC.

53 Quoted in Arango, *Mujer, religión e industria*, p. 176. In this spirit, Medellín's textile manufacturers spearheaded the creation of Colombia's first regional organization for family subsidies, the *Caja de Compensación Familiar de Antioquia* or COMFAMA (developed in 1953–57). Family-wage ideology in Antioquia reached its fullest expression in COMFAMA, which has grown to include grocery stores, subsidized pharmacies, training programs, resort-like vacation spots, and urban recreational centers reminiscent (to North American eyes) of the YMCA and YWCA. The history of this important institution has yet to be examined from the perspectives of social history. For informative *apologias* of COMFAMA's founding see the institution's self-published history, *Comfama* (Medellín: Comfama, 1990), and Jaime Sanín Echeverri, *Crónicas de Medellín* (Bogotá: Banco Central Hipotecario, n.d. [1987]), pp. 139–46.

54 Interviews with Luis Henao, Medellín, 22 Nov. 1990, and with Pedro González Cano, Medellín, 2 Nov. 1990. Coltejer's legal subdivision was itself an anti-union strategy, as it required that workers at each plant be organized in separate unions. For a chronicle of infighting within the UTRAN, which was affiliated with the anticommunist UTC, see Osorio, *Historia del Sindicalismo*, pp. 127–65.

55 Arango, *Mujer, religión, e industria*, p. 188. Significantly, the first public split between the UTRAN and the ANDI, with the regional hierarchy taking the side of the ANDI, occurred in 1951, as a direct result of mass dismissals at Coltejer. Osorio, *Historia del Sindicalismo*, pp. 134–35.

56 Osorio, *Historia del Sindicalismo*, p. 92. The previous year the union had unsuccessfully demanded the reversal of standards as part of a collective bargaining agreement.

57 Interview with Pedro González Cano, Medellín, 2 Nov. 1990; and see Osorio, *Historia del Sindicalismo*, p. 151.

58 See Mayor Mora, "Historia de la industria," p. 350, and Osorio, pp. 144–45.

59 By 1961, neither Tejicondor's union nor either of Coltejer's two negotiating units remained affiliated with the Catholic-led UTC, despite the federation's increasingly independent political line. A decade later, Fabricato's union also voted to leave the federation. Arango, *Mujer, religión, e industria*, pp. 190–94.

60 Interview with Pedro González Cano, Medellín, 2 Nov. 1990.

61 For a summary of technological developments in the 1940s and 1950s, many of which were applied in Medellín, see ILO, Textiles Committee, Sixth Session, *Effects of Technological Developments*, pp. 14–29.

62 Interview with Ana Palacios de Montoya, Medellín, 8 Nov. 1990.

63 Interview with Susana Osorio, as part of group interview, Envigado, 24 July 1991.

64 Interviews with Gumercinda Báez Amado, Bello, 22 Feb. 1991, and Gonzalo Alzate, Bello, 16 Oct. 1990.

Conclusion

1   Ann Twinam, "Honor, Sexuality, and Illegitimacy in Colonial Spanish America," in Asunción Lavrin, ed., *Sexuality and Marriage in Colonial Latin America* (Lincoln: University of Nebraska Press, 1989), pp. 118–55.

2   See, for example, Luisa Passerini, *Fascism in Popular Memory: The Cultural Experience of the Turin Working Class*, trans. Robert Lumley and Jude Bloomfield, Cambridge Studies in Modern Capitalism (New York: Cambridge University Press, 1987); Alessandro Portelli, *The Death of Luigi Trastulli*; and Daniel Bertaux and Paul Thompson, eds., *Between Generations: Family Models, Myths, and Memories* (New York: Oxford University Press, 1993), as well as other work by both Bertaux and Thompson, especially the pioneering essay by Bertaux and Isabelle Bertaux-Wiame, "Life Stories in the Baker's Trade," in *Biography and Society: The Life History Approach in the Social Sciences*, ed. Daniel Bertaux, Sage Studies in International Sociology (Beverly Hills: Sage Publications, 1981).

3   Pierre Bourdieu, *In Other Words*, p. 126.

BIBLIOGRAPHY

Archives and Manuscript Collections

Archivo Histórico de Antioquia, Medellín (AHA)

Fundación Antioqueña de Estudios Sociales, Medellín (FAES)

United States National Archives and Records Administration, College Park, Maryland (NARA)

Corporate archive and personnel files, 1907–60, Compañía Colombiana de Tejidos (Coltejer), Itagüí (AC)

Corporate archive and personnel files, 1923–60, Fábrica de Hilados y Tejidos del Hato (Fabricato), Bello (AF)

Corporate archive and personnel files, 1935–60, Tejidos el Cóndor (Tejicondor), Medellín (AT)

Newspaper collection, library of the Universidad de Antioquia, Medellín

Personnel files, 1939–60, Fábrica Textil de los Andes (Fatelares), Medellín

Uncatalogued papers of the former Patronato de Obreras, held by the religious order of Hermanas de la Presentación, Medellín (PO)

Newspapers and Magazines

Civismo
Colombia
El Colombiano
El Correo Liberal
La Defensa
El Diario
Ecos de Coltejer
El Espectador
Fabricato al Día
Gloria
Lanzadera

El Luchador
El Obrero Católico
El Social
El Socialista
El Sol
El Tiempo

Government Publications

Antioquia. 1929. *Mensajes que los gobernadores de Antioquia han dirigido a la Asamblea del Departamento, 1911–1929.* Medellín: Imprenta Municipal.

——, Secretario de Gobierno. 1916–26. *Informes.*

——. 1917–40. *Memorias.*

Colombia. 1917. *Informe de Hacienda, 1916.* Bogotá: Ministro de Hacienda.

——, Ministerio de Industrias. 1929. *Compilación de leyes obreras, 1905–1927.* Bogotá: Oficina General del Trabajo.

——. 1932–33. *Boletín de Comercio e Industria.* Bogotá: Ministro de Industrias y Trabajo.

——. 1933–45. *Memoria al Congreso Nacional.* Bogotá.

——. 1947. *Primer Censo Industrial.* Bogotá: Contraloria General de la República.

——. 1953. *Leyes, decretos: El trabajo de la mujer.* Bogotá: Imprenta Nacional. Medellín. 1916–49. *Anuarios Estadísticos.* Medellín: Imprenta Municipal.

Books and Essays

Acevedo Carmona, Daró. 1995. *La mentalidad de las élites sobre la violencia en Colombia, 1936–1949.* Bogotá: El Áncora Editores.

Adas, Michael. 1993. *European and Islamic Expansion.* Philadelphia: Temple University Press.

Alape, Arturo. 1983. *El Bogotazo: Memorias del olvido.* Bogotá: Editorial Pluma.

Alonso, Ana María. 1992. "Work and Gusto: Gender and Recreation in a North Mexican Pueblo." In *Worker's Expressions: Beyond Accommodation and Resistance,* ed. Doris Francis, Daniel Nugent, and John Caligione. Albany: State University of New York Press.

——. 1995. *Thread of Blood: Colonialism, Revolution, and Gender on Mexico's Northern Frontier.* Tucson: University of Arizona Press.

Anzaldúa, Gloria. 1987. *Borderlands/La Frontera: The New Mestiza.* San Francisco: Aunt Lute Press.

Arango, Luz Gabriela. 1991. *Mujer, religión e industria: Fabricato 1923–1982.* Medellín: Universidad de Antioquia.

——. 1996. "Las obreras en la industria textil, 1950–1970." In *Historia de Medellín.* Vol. 2, ed. Jorge Orlando Melo. Medellín: Suramericana de Seguros.

Arango, Mariano. 1977. *Café e industria, 1850–1930.* Bogotá: Carlos Valencia Editores.

Arango Mejía, Gabriel. 1942. "Las familias antioqueñas." In *El pueblo antioqueño,* ed. La revista Universidad de Antioquia. Medellín: Universidad de Antioquia.

——. 1942. *Genealogías de Antioquia y caldas.* Medellín: Imprenta Departamental.

Archila Neira, Mauricio. 1989. "La clase obrera colombiana, 1886–1930." In *Nueva historia de Colombia.* 9 vols. Ed. Jaime Jaramillo Uribe. Bogotá: Planeta. 3: 219–55.

———. 1991. *Cultura e identidad: Colombia, 1910–1945.* Bogotá: Cinep.

Arroyave, Julio César. 1942. "Psicología del hombre antioqueño." In *El pueblo antioqueño*, ed. La revista Universidad de Antioquia. Medellín: Universidad de Antioquia.

Barnes, Ralph. 1940. *Motion and Time Study.* 2d ed. New York: Wiley and Sons.

Barnes, Ralph, ed. 1961. *Motion and Time Study Applications*, 4 ed. New York: Wiley and Sons.

Baron, Ava, ed. 1991. *Work Engendered: Toward a New History of American Labor.* Ithaca: Cornell University Press.

Barón Serrano, Campo E. 1948. *Legislación del trabajo.* Bogotá: Librería Voluntad.

Barrios de Cungara, Domitila, with Moema Viezzer. 1978. *Let Me Speak! Testimony of Domitila, a Woman of the Bolivian Mines.* Trans. Victoria Ortiz. New York: Monthly Review.

Beechey, Veronica. 1987. *Unequal Work.* London: Verso.

Behar, Ruth. 1990. "Rage and Redemption: Reading the Life Story of a Mexican Marketing Woman." *Feminist Studies* 16, no. 2: 223–58.

Bejarano Ávila, Jesús A. 1989. "La economía colombiana entre 1922 y 1929." In *Nueva historia de Colombia.* 9 vols. Ed. Jaime Jaramillo Uribe. Bogotá: Planeta. 5: 51–76.

Beninati, Anthony James. 1982. "Commerce, Manufacturing, and Population Redistribution in Medellín, Antioquia, 1880–1980: A Case Study of Colombian Urbanization." Ph.D. diss., State University of New York at Stony Brook.

Berger, Iris. 1992. *Threads of Solidarity: Women in South African Industry, 1900–1980.* Bloomington: Indiana University Press.

Bergquist, Charles. 1986. *Labor in Latin America: Comparative Essays on Chile, Argentina, Venezuela, and Colombia.* Stanford: Stanford University Press.

Bergquist, Charles, Ricardo Peñaranda, and Gonzalo Sánchez, eds. 1992. *Violence in Colombia: The Contemporary Crisis in Historical Perspective.* Wilmington, Del.: SR Books.

Lenard Berlanstein, ed., 1993. *Rethinking Labor History: Essays on Discourse and Class Analysis.* Urbana: University of Illinois Press.

Bertaux, Daniel, and Isabelle Bertaux-Wiame. 1981. "Life Stories in the Baker's Trade." In *Biography and Society: The Life History Approach in the Social Sciences*, ed. Daniel Bertaux. Sage Studies in International Sociology. Beverly Hills: Sage Publications.

Bertaux, Daniel, and Paul Thompson, eds. 1993. *Between Generations: Family Models, Myths, and Memories.* New York: Oxford University Press.

Besse, Susan. 1987. "Pagú: Patrícia Galvão—Rebel." In *The Human Tradition in Latin America: The Twentieth Century*, ed. Judith Ewell and William Beezeley. Wilmington, Del.: Scholarly Resources.

———. 1996. *Restructuring Patriarchy: The Modernization of Gender Inequality in Brazil.* Chapel Hill: University of North Carolina Press.

Biernacki, Richard. 1995. *The Fabrication of Labor: Germany and Britain, 1640–1914.* Studies on the History of Society and Culture, vol. 23. Berkeley: University of California Press.

Blewett, Mary. 1991. "Manhood and the Market: The Politics of Gender and Class among the Textile Workers of Fall River, Massachusetts, 1870–1880." In *Work Engendered: Toward a New History of American Labor*, ed. Ava Baron. Ithaca: Cornell University Press.

Botero Herrera, Fernando. 1985. *La industrialización de Antioquia: Génesis y consolidación, 1900–1930.* Medellín: CIE.

———. 1996. "Regulación urbana e intereses privados." In *Historia de Medellín,* Vol. 1., ed. Jorge Orlando Melo, Medellín: Suramericana de Seguros.

Bourdieu, Pierre. 1977. *Outline of a Theory of Practice.* Trans. Richard Nice. New York: Cambridge University Press.

———. 1992. *The Logic of Practice.* Stanford: Stanford University Press.

———. 1991. *Language and Symbolic Power.* Trans. John B. Thompson. Cambridge: Harvard University Press.

———. 1990. *In Other Words.* Stanford: Stanford University Press.

Braun, Herbert. 1985. *The Assassination of Gaitán: Public Life and Urban Violence in Colombia.* Madison: University of Wisconsin Press.

Braverman, Harry. 1974. *Labor and Monopoly Capital.* New York: Monthly Review.

Brew, Roger. 1977. *El desarollo económico de Antioquia desde la independencia hasta 1920.* Bogotá: Banco de la República.

Briggs, Charles. 1984. "Learning How to Ask: Native Metacommunicative Competence and the Incompetence of Fieldworkers." *Language and Society* 13, no. 1: 1–28.

Bulmer-Thomas, Victor. 1994. *The Economic History of Latin America since Independence.* Cambridge Latin American Studies, vol. 77. New York: Cambridge University Press.

Butler, Judith. 1990. *Gender Trouble: Feminism and the Subversion of Identity.* New York: Routledge.

Campos Rivera, Diego. 1988. *Derecho laboral colombiano.* 5th ed. Bogotá: Temis.

Canning, Kathleen. 1992. "Gender and the Politics of Class Formation: Rethinking German Labor History." *AHR* 97 (June): 736–68.

———. 1996. *Languages of Labor and Gender: Female Factory Work in Germany, 1850–1914.* Ithaca: Cornell University Press.

Cardoso, Eliana, and Ann Helwege. 1995. *Latin America's Economy: Diversity, Trends, and Conflicts.* Cambridge: MIT Press.

Chaney, Elsa, and Mary García Castro. 1989. *Muchachas No More: Household Workers in Latin America and the Caribbean.* Philadelphia: Temple University Press.

Clark, Anna. 1995. *The Struggle for the Breeches: Gender and the Making of the British Working Class.* Berkeley: University of California Press.

Colmenares, Germán. 1989. "Ospina y Abadía: La política en el decenio de los veinte." In *Nueva historia de Colombia.* 9 vols. Ed. Alvaro Tirado Mejía. Bogotá: Planeta. 1: 243–69.

Crew, David F. 1989. "*Alltagsgeschichte:* A New Social History 'From Below'?" *Central European History* 22 (fall): 394–407.

da Matta, Roberto. 1987. *Casa y a rua: Espaco, cidadania, mulher e morte no Brasil.* Rio de Janeiro: Ediroa Guanabara.

Davis, Angela. 1981. *Women, Race, and Class.* New York: Random House.

Deutsch, Sandra McGee. 1991. "The Catholic Church, Work, and Womanhood in Argentina, 1890–1930." *Gender and History* 3, no. 3: 304–22.

Dietz, James. 1995. "A Brief Economic History." In *Latin America's Economic Development: Confronting Crisis.* 2d ed., ed. James Dietz. Boulder: Lynne Rienner.

Downs, Laura Lee. 1995. *Manufacturing Inequality: Gender Division in the French and British Metalworking Industries, 1914–1939.* Ithaca: Cornell University Press.

Dublin, Thomas. 1979. *Women at Work: The Transformation of Work and Community in Lowell, Massachusetts, 1826–1860.* New York: Columbia University Press.

Durán, Jorge. 1986. *Los obreros del Río Grande.* Guadalajara: Colegio de Michoacán.

Echavarría, Enrique. 1943. *Historia de los textiles en Antioquia.* Medellín: Tip. Bedout.

Echavarría, Juan José. 1989. "External Shocks and Industrialization: Colombia, 1920–1950." Ph.D. diss., Oxford University.

Echavarría, Juan José. 1990. "Industria y Reestructuración." In *Apertura económica y sistema financiero: compilación de los documentos presentados en el XII simposio sobre mercado de capitales,* ed. Florángela Gómez Ordoñez. Santa Fé de Bogotá: Asociación Bancaria de Colombia.

Edwards, Richard. 1979. *Contested Terrain: The Transformation of the Workplace in the Twentieth Century.* New York: Basic Books.

Eley, Geoff. 1989. "Labor History, Social History, *Alltagsgeschichte:* Experience, Culture, and the Politics of the Everyday—A New Direction for German Social History?" *Journal of Modern History* 61 (June): 297–343.

Enrick, Norbert Lloyd, ed. 1960. *Time Study Manual for the Textile Industry.* New York: Textile Book Publishers.

Fajardo, Luis. n.d. *The Protestant Ethic of the Antioqueños: Social Structure and Personality.* Cali: Universidad de Valle.

Faue, Elizabeth. 1991. *Community of Suffering and Struggle: Women, Men, and the Labor Movement in Minneapolis, 1915–1945.* Chapel Hill: University of North Carolina Press.

Fernández-Kelly, María Patricia. 1983. *For We are Sold, I and My People: Women And Industry in Mexico's Frontier.* SUNY Series in the Anthropology of Work. Albany: State University of New York Press.

Fernández-Kelly, María Patricia, and June Nash, eds. 1987. *Women, Men, and the International Division of Labor.* SUNY Series in the Anthropology of Work. Albany: State University of New York Press.

Fishburne Collier, Jane. 1987. "Rank and Marriage: Or, Why High-Ranking Wives Cost More." In *Gender and Kinship: Essays Toward a Unified Analysis,* ed. Jane Fishburne Collier and Sylvia Junko Yanagiasko. Stanford: Stanford University Press.

Foucault, Michel. 1980. *Power/Knowledge.* Ed. Colin Gordon. New York: Pantheon Books.

Frader, Laura, and Sonya Rose. 1996. *Gender and Class in Modern Europe.* Ithaca: Cornell University Press.

Freifeld, Mary. 1986. "Technological Change and the 'Self-Acting' Mule: A Study of Skill and the Sexual Division of Labor." *Social History* 11 (Oct.): 319–43.

French, John D., and Daniel James, eds. 1997. *The Gendered Worlds of Latin American Women Workers: From Household and Factory to the Union and Ballot Box.* Durham: Duke University Press.

Freyre, Gilberto. 1951. *Sobrados e mucambos: Decadência do patriarcado rural e desenvolvimento du urbano.* Rio de Janeiro: J. Olympio.

Fuller, Norma. 1995. "En torno a la polaridad mariansimo-machismo." In *Género e identidad: Ensayos sobre lo femenino y lo masculino,* ed. Luz Gabriela Arango, Magdalena León, and Marta Viveros. Bogotá: Tercer Mundo Editores.

Fundación Antioqueña de Estudios Sociales. 1979. *Los estudios regionales en Colombia: El caso de Antioquia.* Medellín: FAES.

Galvão, Patrícia. 1993. *Industrial Park: A Proletarian Novel.* Trans. Elizabeth and K. David Jackson. Lincoln: University of Nebraska Press.

Garay, Luis Jorge, ed., 1992. *Estrategia industrial e inserción internacional.* Bogotá: Fescol.

Glickman, Rose. 1984. *Russian Factory Women: Workplace and Society, 1880–1914.* Berkeley: University of California Press.

Gluck, Sherna, and Daphne Patai, eds. 1991. *Women's Words: The Feminist Practice of Oral History.* New York: Routledge.

Gómez de Cárdenas, Anita. 1985. *Medellín: Los años locos.* Medellín: Fabricato.

Gómez Martínez, F., and Arturo Puerta. 1945. *Biografía económica de las industrias de Antioquia.* Medellín: Editorial Bedout.

Gómez Ordóñez, Florángela, ed., 1990. *Apertura económica y sistema financiero: Compilación de los Documentos Presentados en el XII Simposio Sobre Mercado de Capitales.* Bogotá: Asociación Bancaria de Colombia.

González, Fernán. 1989. "La iglesia católica y el estado colombiano, 1930–1985." *Nueva historia de Colombia* 2: 371–96.

González Ochoa, Gustavo. 1942. "La raza antioqueña." In *El pueblo antioqueño,* ed. La revista Universidad de Antioquia. Medellín: Universidad de Antioquia.

Gramsci, Antonio. 1971. *Selections from the Prison Notebooks.* New York: International Publishers.

Gray, Robert. 1987. "The Languages of Factory Reform in Britain, c. 1830–1860." In *The Historical Meanings of Work,* ed. Patrick Joyce. New York: Cambridge University Press.

Gutiérrez de Pineda, Virginia. 1968. *Cultura y familia en Colombia.* Bogotá: Tercer Mundo y Departamento de Sociología, Universidad Nacional.

Gutmann, Matthew. 1996. *The Meanings of Macho: Being a Man in Mexico City.* Berkeley: University of California Press.

Guzmán, Germán, Orlando Fals Borda, and Eduardo Umaña. 1988 (1963). *La violencia en Colombia.* 2 vols. Bogotá: Círculo de Lectores.

Hagen, Everett E. 1962. *On the Theory of Social Change: How Economic Growth Begins.* Homewood, Ill.: Dorsey Press.

Hall, Jacquelyn Dowd. 1986. "Disorderly Women: Gender and Labor Militancy in Appalachian South." *Journal of American History* 73: 354–82.

Hall, Jacquelyn Dowd, et al. 1987. *Like a Family: The Making of a Southern Cotton Mill World.* Chapel Hill: University of North Carolina Press.

Haraway, Donna. 1991. *Simians, Cyborgs, and Women.* New York: Routledge, 1991.

Hareven, Tamara. 1982. *Family Time and Industrial Time.* New York: Cambridge University Press.

Hartmann, Heidi. 1979. "Capitalism, Patriarchy, and Job Segregation by Sex." In *Capitalist Patriarchy and the Case for Socialist Feminism,* ed. Zillah Eisenstein. New York: Monthly Review.

——. 1981. "The Unhappy Marriage of Marxism and Feminism: Toward a More Progressive Union," *Capital and Class* 8 (1979). Reprinted (1981) in *Women and Revolution,* ed. Lydia Linda Sargent. Boston: South End Press.

Herrnstadt, Ernesto. 1947. *Tratado del derecho social colombiano.* 2d ed. Bogotá: Editorial ABC.

Herrero, Daniel, and Bernard Kapp, eds. 1974. *Ville et Commerce: Deux essais d'histoire hispano-américaine.* Paris: Editions Klincksieck.

Hewitt, Nancy A. 1991. "'The Voice of Virile Labor': Labor Militancy, Community

Solidarity, and Gender Identity among Tampa's Latin American Workers, 1880–1921." In *Work Engendered: Toward a New History of American Labor*, ed. Ava Baron. Ithaca: Cornell University Press.

Higginbotham, Evelyn Brooks. 1996. "African-American Women's History and the Metalanguage of Race," *Signs* 17:2 (winter 1992): 251–74. Reprinted (1996) in *Feminism and History*, ed. Joan Scott. New York: Oxford University Press.

Hilden, Patricia. 1991. "The Rhetoric and Iconography of Reform: Women Coal Miners in Belgium, 1840–1914." *Historical Journal* 34, no. 2: 411–36.

Hobsbawm, Eric. 1964. "The Labour Aristocracy in Nineteenth Century Britain." In *Labouring Men: Studies in the History of Labour*, ed. Hobsbawm. London: Weidenfeld and Nicolson.

Holmes, Douglas R. 1989. *Cultural Disenchantments: Worker Peasantries in Northeast Italy*. Princeton: Princeton University Press.

Honig, Emily. 1986. *Sisters and Strangers: Women in the Shanghai Cotton Mills, 1919–1949*. Stanford: Stanford University Press.

hooks, bell. 1981. *Ain't I a Woman: Black Women and Feminism*. Boston: South End Press.

———. 1990. *Yearning: Race, Gender, and Cultural Politics*. Boston: South End Press.

Humphrey, John. 1989. *Gender and Work in the Third World: Sexual Divisions in Brazilian Industry*. London: Routledge.

Hutchinson, John. 1963. *Managing a Fair Day's Work*. Ann Arbor: Bureau of Industrial Relations, University of Michigan.

Iglesias Prieto, Norma. 1997. *Beautiful Flowers of the Maquiladora: Life Histories of Women Workers in Tijuana*. Austin: University of Texas Press, Institute of Latin American Studies.

International Labour Office (ILO). 1951. *Payment by Results*. Studies and Reports, New Series, no. 27. Geneva: ILO.

———. 1952. *Textile Wages: An International Study*. Geneva: ILO.

———, Textiles Committee. 1953. *Problems of Women's Employment in the Textile Industry*. Geneva: ILO.

———. 1955. *Problems of Productivity in the Textile Industry*. Geneva: ILO.

———. 1968. *The Effects of Structural and Technological Changes on Labour Problems in the Textile Industry*. Geneva: ILO.

Issacs, Jorge. 1983. *María*. Madrid: Espasa-Calpe.

James, Daniel, and French, John, eds. Forthcoming. *Doña Maria's Story: Life-History, Memory, and Political Identity*. Durham: Duke University Press.

Jaramillo, Ana María. 1989. "María Cano sigue floreciendo," *Re-Lecturas* 2, no. 5: 34–35.

Jelín, Elizabeth. 1980. "The Bahiana in the Labor Force in Salvador, Brazil." In *Sex and Class in Latin America*. Boston: Bergin and Garvey.

Jiménez, Michael. 1986. "The Limits of Export Capitalism: Economic Structure, Class, and Politics in a Colombian Coffee Municipality, 1900–1930." Ph.D. dissertation, Harvard University.

———. 1989. "Class, Gender, and Peasant Resistance in Central Colombia, 1900–1930." In *Everyday Forms of Peasant Resistance*, ed. Forrest Colburn. Armonk, N.Y.: M. E. Sharpe.

———. 1990. "'Mujeres incautas y sus hijos bastardos': Clase, género y resistencia campesina en la región cafetera de cundinamarca (primera parte)." *Historia Crítica* 3: 69–82.

Joyce, Patrick. 1980. *Work, Society, and Politics: The Culture of the Factory in Later Victorian England*. Brighton: Harvester Press.

Joyce, Patrick, ed. 1987. *The Historical Meanings of Work*. New York: Cambridge University Press.

Kaplan, Temma. 1982. "Female Consciousness and Collective Action: The Case of Barcelona, 1910." *Signs* 7 (spring): 547–66.

———. 1987. "Women and Communal Strikes in the Crisis of 1917–1922." In *Becoming Visible: Women in European History*, ed. Renate Bridenthal and Claudia Koonz. Boston: Houghton Mifflin.

———. 1992. "Making Spectacles of Themselves: Women's Rituals and Patterns of Resistance in Africa, Argentina, and the United States." El Trabajo de las Mujeres: Pasado y Presente. Universidad de Málaga, 1–4 December.

Katznelson, Ira, and Aristide Zolberg, eds. 1986. *Working-Class Formation: Nineteenth Century Patterns in Western Europe and the United States*. Princeton: Princeton University Press.

Keremitsis, Dawn. 1984. "Latin American Women Workers in Transition: Sexual Division of the Labor Force in Mexico and Colombia in the Textile Industry." *The Americas* 40: 491–504.

Kessler-Harris, Alice. 1975. "Where Are the Organized Women Workers?" *Feminist Studies* 3 (fall): 92–109.

Klubock, Thomas. 1998. *Contested Communities: Class, Gender, and Politics in Chile's El Teniente Copper Mine, 1904–1951*. Durham: Duke University Press.

Lamas, Mara. 1995. "Cuerpo e identidad." In *Género e identidad: Ensayos sobre lo femenino y lo masculino*, ed. Luz Gabriela Arango, Magdalena León, and Mara Viveros. Bogotá: Tercer Mundo Editores.

Lambertz, Jan. 1985. "Sexual Harassment in the Nineteenth Century English Cotton Industry." *History Workshop Journal* 18 (spring): 29–61.

Lamphere, Louise. 1985. "Bringing the Family to Work: Women's Culture on the Shopfloor." *Feminist Studies* 11 (fall): 519–40.

Lauderdale Graham, Sandra. 1992. *House and Street: The Domestic World of Servants and Masters in Nineteenth-Century Rio de Janeiro*. Austin: University of Texas Press.

Lazonick, William. 1979. "Industrial Relations and Technical Change: The Case of the Self-Acting Mule." *Cambridge Journal of Economics* 3: 231–62.

Leite Lopes, José Sergio. 1988. *A tecelagem dos conflictos de classe na "cidade das chaminés."* São Paulo: Editora Marco Zero.

Lerner, Gerda. 1986. *The Creation of Patriarchy*. New York: Oxford University Press.

Levenson-Estrada, Deborah. 1994. *Trade Unionists against Terror: Guatemala City, 1954–1985*. Chapel Hill: University of North Carolina Press.

Lison-Tolosana, Carmelo. 1966. *Belmonte de los Caballeros: A Sociological Study of a Spanish Town*. Oxford: Clarendon Press.

Lown, Judy. 1990. *Women and Industrialization: Gender at Work in Nineteenth-Century England*. Minneapolis: University of Minnesota Press.

López Toro, Alvaro. 1977. *Migración y cambio social durante el siglo diez y nueve*. Bogotá: Ediciones Universidad de los Andes.

Lüdtke, Alf. 1985. "Organizational Order or *Eigensinn?* Worker's Privacy and Worker's Politics in Germany." In *Rites of Power: Symbolism, Ritual and Politics Since the Middle Ages*, ed. Sean Wilentz. Philadelphia: University of Pennsylvania Press.

———. 1986. "Cash, Coffee-Breaks, Horseplay: *Eigensinn* among Factory Workers in

Germany circa 1900." In *Confrontation, Class Consciousness, and the Labor Process. Contributions in Labor Studies, no. 18*, ed. Michael Hanagan and Charles Stephenson. New York: Greenwood Press.

Lugones, María, and Elizabeth Spelman. 1983. "Have We Got a Theory for You! Feminist Theory, Cultural Imperialism, and the Demand for 'The Woman's Voice.'" *Women's Studies International Forum* 6, no. 6: 573–81.

Mark-Lawson, Jane, and Anne Witz. 1988. "From 'Family Labor' to 'Family Wage'? The Case of Women's Labor in Nineteenth-Century Coalmining." *Social History* 13, no. 2: 151–73.

Marriott, R. 1961. *Incentive Payment Systems*. London: Staples Press.

Martínez-Alier, Verena. 1989. *Marriage, Class, and Colour in Nineteenth-Century Cuba: A Study of Racial Attitudes and Sexual Values in a Slave Society*. 2d ed. Ann Arbor: University of Michigan Press.

May, Martha. 1985. "Bread before Roses: American Workingmen, Labor Unions, and the Family Wage." In *Women, Work, and Protest*, ed. Ruth Milkman. London: Routledge and Kegan Paul.

Mayor Mora, Alberto. 1984. *Etica, trabajo, y productividad en Antioquia*. Bogotá: Tercer Mundo.

——. 1989. "Historia de la industria colombiana, 1930–1968." In *Nueva historia de Colombia*. 9 vols. Ed. Alvaro Tirado Mejía. Bogotá: Planeta. 5: 333–56.

——. 1990. "Institucionalización y perspectivas del taylorismo en Colombia: Conflictos y sub-culturas del trabajo entre ingenieros, supervisores y obreros en torno a la productividad, 1950–1990." IV Coloquio Colombiano de Sociología, Universidad de Valle, November.

McGreevey, William Paul. 1971. *An Economic History of Colombia, 1845–1930*. Cambridge: Cambridge University Press.

Medina, Medófilo. 1984. *La protesta urbana en Colombia en el siglo veinte*. Bogotá: Ediciones Aurora.

Mehaffy, Marilyn Maness. 1997. "Advertising Race/Raceing Advertising: The Feminine Consumer(-Nation), 1867–1900." *Signs* 23, no. 1: 131–73.

Mejía, Gilberto. 1986. *Memorias: El comunismo en Antioquia (María Cano)*. Medellín: Ediciones Pepe.

Mejía Robledo, Alfonso. 1951. *Vidas y empresas de Antioquia: Diccionario biográfico, bibliografico, y económico*. Medellín: Imprenta Departamental de Antioquia.

Melo, Jorge Orlando, ed. 1988. *Historia de Antioquia*. Medellín: Suramericana de Seguros.

——. 1996. *Historia de Medellín*. Medellín: Suramericana de Seguros.

Merkle, Judith A. 1980. *Management and Ideology: The Legacy of the International Scientific Movement*. Berkeley: University of California Press.

Milkman, Ruth. 1987. *Gender at Work: The Dynamics of Job Segregation by Sex during World War II*. Urbana: University of Illinois Press.

Milkman, Ruth, ed. 1985. *Women, Work, and Protest*. London: Routledge and Kegan Paul.

Misas Arango, Gabriel. 1995. "De la industrialización sustitutiva a la apertura: El caso colombiano." In *Gestión económica estatal de los ochentas: Del ajuste al cambio institucional*. Vol. 2, ed. Luis Bernardo Florez E. and Ricardo Bonilla González. Bogotá: Centro de Investigaciones Para el Desarrollo (CID).

Mitchell, Brian R. 1988. *British Historical Statistics*. New York: Cambridge University Press.

Mohanty, Chandra, Lourdes Torres, and Ann Russo. 1991. *Third World Women and the Politics of Feminism*. Bloomington: Indiana University Press.

Montenegro, Santiago. 1982. "Breve historia de las principales empresas textileras." *Revista de extensión cultural (de la Universidad Nacional de Colombia, Seccional de Medellín)* 12 (July): 50–66.

———. 1982. "La industria textil en Colombia, 1900–1945." *Desarrollo y sociedad* 8: 117–73.

———. 1984. "El surgimiento de la industria textil en Colombia, 1900–1945." In *Crisis mundial, protección e industrialización*, ed. José Antonio Ocampo and Santiago Montenegro. Bogotá: Fondo Editorial Cerec, Fescol.

Moraga, Cherríe, and Gloria Anzaldúa. 1981. *This Bridge Called My Back: Writings by Radical Women of Color*. Watertown, Mass.: Persephone Press.

Mundel, Marvin. 1960. *Motion and Time Study: Principles and Practice*. 3d ed. Englewood Cliffs, N.J.: Prentice Hall.

Murray, Kevin. 1989. "The Construction of Identity in Narratives of Romance and Comedy." In *Texts of Identity*, ed. John Shorter and Kenneth Gergen. London: Sage.

Myerhoff, Barbara. 1978. *Number Our Days*. New York: Simon and Schuster.

———. 1992. *Remembered Lives: The Work of Ritual, Storytelling, and Growing Older*, ed. Marc Kaminsky. Ann Arbor: University of Michigan Press.

Nelson, Daniel. 1980. *Frederick W. Taylor and the Rise of Scientific Management*. Madison: University of Wisconsin Press.

Niebel, Benjamin. 1962. *Motion and Time Study: An Introduction to Methods, Time Study, and Wage Payment*. 3d ed. Homewood, Ill.: Richard Irwin.

Nolan, Mary. 1994. *Visions of Modernity: American Business and the Modernization of Germany*. Oxford: Oxford University Press.

Oakley, Ann. 1981. "Interviewing Women: A Contradiction in Terms." In *Doing Feminist Research*, ed. Helen Roberts. London: Routledge and Kegan Paul.

Ocampo, José Antonio. 1989. "Los orígenes de la industria cafetera, 1830–1929." In *Nueva historia de Colombia*. 9 vols. Ed. Jaime Jaramillo Uribe. Bogotá: Planeta. 5: 213–32.

———. 1990. "La apertura externa en perspectiva." In *Apertura económica y sistema financiero: Compilación de los documentos presentados en el XII simposio sobre mercado de capitales*, ed. Florángela Gómez Ordoñez. Santa Fé de Bogotá: Asociación Bancaria de Colombia.

———. 1993. "La internacionalización de la economía colombiana." In *Colombia ante la economía mundial*, ed. Miguel Urrutia M. Bogotá: Tercer Mundo and Fedesarrollo.

Ocampo, José Antonio, and Santiago Montenegro, eds. 1984. *Crisis mundial, protección e industrialización*. Bogotá: Cerec, Fescol.

Ong, Aihwa. 1987. *Spirits of Resistance and Capitalist Discipline: Factory Women in Malaysia*. SUNY Series in the Anthropology of Work. Albany: State University of New York Press.

Oquist, Paul. 1980. *Violence, Conflict, and Politics in Colombia*. New York: Academic Press.

Osorio, Ivan Darío. 1986. *Historia del sindicalismo Antioqueño, 1900–1986*. Medellín: Instituto Popular de Capacitación.

———. 1988. "Historia del sindicalismo." In *Historia de Antioquia*, ed. Jorge Orlando Melo. Medellín: Suramericana de Seguros.

Ospina, Livardo E. 1990. *Los hilos perfectos: Crónica de Fabricato en sus 70 Años.* Medellín: Fabricato.

Ospina Vásquez, Luis. 1987. *Industria y protección en Colombia, 1810–1930.* 4th ed. Medellín: FAES.

Palacios, Marco. 1980. *Coffee in Colombia, 1850–1970: An Economic, Social, and Political History.* Cambridge: Cambridge University Press.

——. 1982. "El café en la vida de Antioquia." In *Los estudios regionales en Colombia: El caso de Antioquia*, ed. Fundación Antioqueña de Estudios Sociales. Medellín: FAES.

——. 1995. *Entre la legitimidad y la violencia: Colombia, 1875–1994.* Santa Fé de Bogotá: Norma.

Parsons, James. 1968. *Antioqueño Colonization in Colombia.* Rev. ed. Berkeley: University of California Press.

Passerini, Luisa. 1987. *Fascism in Popular Memory: The Cultural Experience in the Turin Working Class.* Trans. Robert Lumley and Jude Bloomfield. Cambridge Studies in Modern Capitalism. New York: Cambridge University Press.

Payne, Constantine Alexander. 1984. "Growth and Social Change in Medellín, Colombia." Senior Honors Essay in History, Stanford University.

Pécaut, Daniel. 1987. *Orden y violencia: Colombia 1930–1954.* 2 vols., trans. Jesús Alberto Valencia. Bogotá: Siglo XXI.

Peña, Devon Gerardo. 1997. *The Terror of the Machine: Technology, Work, Gender, and Ecology on the U.S.-Mexico Border.* Austin: Center for Mexican American Studies, University of Texas at Austin.

Péristiany, John George, ed. 1966. *Honour and Shame: the Values of Mediterranean Society.* Chicago: University of Chicago Press.

Poniatowska, Elena. 1996. *Tinísima*, trans. Katherine Silver. New York: Farrar, Strauss, Giroux.

Portelli, Alessandro. 1991. *The Death of Luigi Trastulli and Other Stories: Form and Meaning in Oral History.* Albany: State University of New York Press.

Reddy, William. 1987. *Money and Liberty in Modern Europe: A Critique of Historical Understanding.* New York: Cambridge University Press.

Restrepo, Manuel. 1988. "Historia de la Industria." In *Historia de Antioquia*, ed. Jorge Orlando Melo. Medellín: Suramericana de Seguros.

Reyes, Catalina. 1993. "¿Fueron los viejos tiempos tan maravillosos?: Aspectos de la vida social y cotidiana de Medellín, 1890–1930." Master's thesis, Universidad Nacional, sede Medellín.

Roldán, Mary. 1991. "Purifying the Factory, Demonizing the 'Public Service Sector': The Role of Ethnic and Cultural Difference in Determining Perceptions of Working Class Militancy in Colombia, 1940–1955." Eighth Latin American Labor History Conference, Princeton University, April 1991.

——. 1992. "Genesis and evolution of *La Violencia* in Antioquia, Colombia (1900–1953)," Ph.D. dissertation, Harvard University.

Rose, Sonya. 1992. *Limited Livelihoods: Gender and Class in Nineteenth-Century England.* Berkeley: University of California Press.

Rubin, Gayle. 1975. "The Traffic in Women: Notes on the 'Political Economy' of Sex." In *Toward an Anthropology of Women*, ed. Rayna Rapp Reiter. New York: Monthly Review. Reprinted (1996) in *Feminism and History*, ed. Joan Scott, New York: Oxford University Press.

Sáenz Rovner, Eduardo. 1992. *La ofensiva empresarial: Industriales, políticos y violencia en los años 40 en Colombia*. Bogotá: Tercer Mundo.

Safa, Helen. 1995. *The Myth of the Male Breadwinner: Women and Industrialization in the Caribbean*. Boulder, Colo.: Westview Press.

Saffiotti, Heleieth. 1987. *Women in Class Society*. New York: Monthly Review.

Safford, Frank. 1965. "Significación de los Antioqueños en el desarrollo económico colombiano, un examen crítico de las tésis de Everett Hagen." *Anuario colombiano de historia social y de la cultura* 3: 49–69.

Samuel, Raphael. 1994. *Theatres of Memory*. New York: Verso.

Sánchez, Gonzalo. 1985. *Ensayos de historia social y política del siglo veinte*. Bogotá: Áncora.

——. 1985. "*La Violencia* in Colombia: New Research, New Questions." *Hispanic American Historical Review* 65, no. 4: 789–807.

Sánchez, Gonzalo, and Donny Meertens. 1983. *Bandoleros, gamonales, y campesinos: El caso de la violencia en Colombia*. Bogotá: El Áncora.

Sanín Echeverri, Jaime. 1980. *Una mujer de cuatro en conducta*. 5th ed. Medellín: Editorial Bedout.

——. 1998. *Obispo Builes*. Bogotá: El Áncora.

——. n.d. [1987]. *Crónicas de Medellín*. Bogotá: Banco Central Hipotecario.

Savage, Charles H., and George Lombard. 1986. *Sons of the Machine: Case Studies of Social Change in the Workplace*. Cambridge: MIT Press.

Scott, James. 1990. *Domination and the Arts of Resistance*. New Haven: Yale University Press.

Scott, Joan Wallach. 1988. *Gender and the Politics of History*. New York: Columbia University Press.

——. 1991. "The Evidence of Experience." *Critical Inquiry* 17 (summer): 793–97.

Segura, Nora. 1995. "Prostitución, género, y violencia." In *Género e identidad: Ensayos sobre lo femenino y lo masculino*, ed. Luz Gabriela Arango, Magdalena León, and Mara Viveros. Bogotá: Tercer Mundo Editores.

Sennett, Richard, and Jonathan Cobb. 1973. *The Hidden Injuries of Class*. New York: Vintage Books.

Sewell, William. 1993. "Toward a Post-Materialist Rhetoric for Labor History." In Lenard Berlanstein, ed., *Rethinking Labor History: Essays on Discourse and Class Analysis*. Urbana: University of Illinois Press.

Shaw, Christopher, and Malcolm Chase. 1989. *The Imagined Past: History and Nostalgia*. Manchester: Manchester University Press.

Somers, Margaret. 1992. "Narrativity, Narrative Identity, and Social Action: Rethinking English Working-Class Formation." *Social Science History* 16, no. 1: 591–630.

——. 1994. "The Narrative Construction of Identity: A Relational and Network Approach." *Theory and Society* 23, no. 5: 605–49.

——. 1996. "Class Formation and Capitalism: A Second Look at a Classic." *European Journal of Sociology* 37, no. 1: 180–203.

Sommers, Doris. 1991. *Foundational Fictions: The National Romances of Latin America*. Berkeley: University of California Press.

Spivak, Gayatri. 1988. *In Other Worlds*. New York: Routledge.

Stansell, Cristine. 1987. *City of Women: Sex and Class in New York, 1789–1860*. Urbana: University of Illinois Press.

Stearns, Peter. 1993. "Interpreting the Industrial Revolution." In *Islamic and European Expansion*, ed. Michael Adas. Philadelphia: Temple University Press.

Steedman, Carolyn. 1987. *Landscape for a Good Woman: A Story of Two Lives*. New Brunswick, N.J.: Rutgers University Press.

Stolcke, Verena. 1988. *Coffee Planters, Workers, and Wives: Class Conflict and Gender Relations on São Paulo Plantations, 1850–1980*. New York: St. Martin's Press.

Stoler, Ann Laura. 1996. "Carnal Knowledge and Imperial Power: Gender, Race, and Morality in Colonial Asia." In *Feminism and History*, ed. Joan Wallach Scott. New York: Oxford University Press.

Stoller, Richard. 1995. "Alfonso López Pumarejo and Liberal Radicalism in 1930s Colombia." *Journal of Latin American Studies* 27, no. 2: 367–97.

Sunkel, Oswaldo. 1995. "From Inward-Looking Development to Development from Within." In *Latin America's Economic Development: Confronting Crisis*. 2d ed., ed. James Dietz. Boulder: Lynne Rienner.

Taylor, Frederick W. 1911. *Principles of Scientific Management*. New York: Harper and Brothers.

——. 1903. *Shop Management*. New York: American Society of Mechanical Engineers.

Thompson, Edward P. 1963. *The Making of the English Working Class*. London: Victor Gollancz.

Tiano, Susan. 1994. *Patriarchy on The Line: Labor, Gender, and Ideology in the Mexican Maquila Industry*. Philadelphia: Temple University Press.

Tilly, Louise. 1993. "Industrialization and Gender Inequality." In *Islamic and European Expansion*, ed. Michael Adas. Philadelphia: Temple University Press.

Tirado Mejía, Alvaro. 1981. "López Pumarejo: la revolución en marcha," In *Nueva Historia de Colombia*, 9 vols. Ed. Alvaro Tirado Mejía. Bogotá: Planeta. I: 305–48.

——. 1981. *Aspectos políticos del primer gobierno de Alfonso López Pumarejo, 1934–1938*. Bogotá: Procultura.

Toro, Constanza. 1988. "Medellín: Desarrollo urbano, 1880–1950." In *Historia de Antioquia*, ed. Jorge Orlando Melo. Medellín: Suramericana de Seguros.

Torres Giraldo, Ignacio. 1972. *María Cano, mujer rebelde*. Bogotá: Publicaciones de la Rosca.

——. 1976. *Huelga general en Medellín, 1934*. Medellín: Ediciones Vientos del Este.

Tovar Zambrano, Bernardo. 1981. "La economía colombiana, 1886–1922." In *Nueva Historia de Colombia*, 9 vols. Ed. Alvaro Tirado Mejía. Bogotá: Planeta. V: 9–50.

Troulliot, Michel-Rolph. 1995. *Silencing the Past: Power and the Production of History*. Boston: Beacon Press.

Tsurumi, E. Patricia. 1990. *Factory Girls: Women in the Thread Mills of Meiji Japan*. Princeton: Princeton University Press.

Twinam, Ann. 1980. "From Jew to Basque: Ethnic Myths and Antioqueño Entrepreneurship." *Journal of Interamerican Studies and World Affairs* 22 (Feb.): 81–107.

——. 1982. *Miners, Merchants, and Farmers in Colonial Colombia*. Latin American Monographs, vol. 57. Austin: University of Texas Press.

Walby, Silvia. 1986. *Patriarchy at Work*. Cambridge: Polity Press.

Weinstein, Barbara. 1996. *For Social Peace in Brazil: Industrialists and the Remaking of the Working Class in São Paulo, 1920–1964*. Chapel Hill: University of North Carolina Press.

Williams, Raymond. 1977. *Marxism and Literature*. New York: Oxford University Press.

——. 1983. *Keywords: a Vocabulary of Culture and Society*. New York: Oxford University Press.

Winn, Peter. 1986. *Weavers of Revolution: The Yarur Workers and Chile's Road to Socialism.* New York: Oxford University Press.

———. 1994. "A Worker's Nightmare: Taylorism and the 1962 Yarur Strike in Chile," *Radical History Review* 58: 3–34.

Wright, Chris. 1993. "Taylorism Reconsidered: The Impact of Scientific Management within the Australian Workplace." *Labour History* 64 (May): 35–53.

Yelvington, Kevin. 1995. *Producing Power: Ethnicity, Gender, and Class in a Caribbean Workplace.* Philadelphia: Temple University Press.

Zapata, Juan Gonzalo. 1990. "¿Es necesaria una reestructuración en la industria nacional?" In *Reflexiones sobre la industria colombiana,* ed. Juan Gonzalo Zapata. Bogotá: Fescol.

Zavella, Patricia. 1985. "'Abnormal Intimacy': The Varying Work Networks of Chicana Cannery Workers." *Feminist Studies* 11 (fall): 541–57.

INDEX

Montoya y Hermanos, 6, 56, 107–108
Motivational slogans, 270 n.25; and religion, 178
Movies, 171, 175, 273 n.77

National Front, 212
Neoliberalism, 3, 241 n.2
Neo-Taylorism, xiv, 6, 11, 35. *See also* Coltejer: neo-Taylorism at; Fabricato: neo-Taylorism at; Tejicondor: neo-Taylorism at
Nolan, Mary, 17
Nostalgia, 3–4, 105, 242 n.8, 262 n.29

Olaya Herrera, Enrique, 131–132, 265 n.27, 266 n.39
Oral history, 64, 195–199, 204, 236–237, 254 n.47; class dynamics and, 128; methodological problems of, 182, 200
Ordinance 25 of 1918, 82–84, 106–107, 230
Organizacion Católico-Social Arquidiocesana (OCSA), 162, 272 n.63
Ortner, Sherry, 88
Osorio, Susana (pseud.), 3, 64, 105, 202–203, 227
Ospina, Pedro Nel, 15, 90, 140, 244 n.19, 258 n.69
Ospina Pérez, Mariano, 211, 60. *See also* Conservative Party: Ospinista group within
Ospina Vásquez, Luis, 45, 252 nn. 22, 25

Palacios, Marco, 251 n.20, 254 n.57, 259 n.87, 265–266 n.38
Palacios de Montoya, Ana (pseud.), 1, 4, 22, 203–208, 224, 227
Paños Vicuña, 55
Pantex, 57, 151
Pareja, Carmen, 137–140
Parque de Berrío, 77, 39, 46, 126
Parque de Bolívar. *See* Bolívar Park
Parsons, James, 54
Partisan politics, 19, 58, 61, 82, 212, 230–231; meaning of, for workers, 128–130; in small towns, 132; women's participation in, 146
Paternalism, xiv, 4–6, 11, 14–16, 34, 53, 58, 61, 100, 102, 124, 139, 141, 145, 148–149, 152–155, 176, 180, 198, 225, 229–235, 243 n.14; as modeled on patriarchal household, 117, 144–146, 149; and small-town Antioquia, 253 n.46; transition to bureaucratic forms

of, 154. *See also* Catholicism; Coltejer: paternalism at; Fabricato: paternalism at; Tejicondor
Patriarchy: in family organization, 117, 144–146, 229; ideology of, 30–33, 165–171, 207, 233
Patronato de Obreras, 74, 77–83, 85–86, 88, 90–91, 99–100, 231; and formal politics, 82; as a model imitated by firms, 78; working women's boredom with, 17, 89
Patronato of Fabricato, 1, 3, 78, 154–155, 166–171, 179, 186, 225, 233, 270 n.34, 273 nn. 77, 78, 80
Pepalfa (knit goods), 51, 162
Pérez, Francisco de Paula, 83, 148
Personnel files, 66, 152, 166, 201
Phillips, Anne, 30
Piece-rates, 110–111, 270 n.24
Pineda, Antonio, 64
Posada, Jorge, 222
Posada, Otilia (pseud.), 116
Prayer, 3, 70–71, 183, 185, 207
Pregnancy, 176, 181, 196, 199–208; concealed, 199–208; as motive for dismissal, 165–166, 274 n.106, 274 n.3; out-of-wedlock, 22, 148, 199–206, 208, 274–275 n.3, 279 n.48
Pride in work, 204, 210, 215, 220, 227
Priests, 6, 15, 65, 70, 78, 108, 111, 162–164, 184, 190, 226, 272 n.63, 279 n.41
Progress: as a discourse valorizing the city, 72; used as a verb, 69–70, 163; as valorized term, 227, 229, 257 n.44
Proletarianization, 17, 26, 103, 242 n.9
Protectionism, 1, 3, 14, 16–20, 45, 210–213, 229

Quijote (Cervantes's character), xiv, 92, 95
Quitting, 111–114, 152, 262 n.32

Rabinovich, Bernardo and Samuel, 197
Rabinovich family, 56, 197
Race, 28–29, 67, 79, 81, 115; as linked to gender and sexuality, xv, 28–29, 235; and race mixing, 80; and racial composition of workforce, 66; and racialized language, 95, 256 n.25, 262 n.40
Racism, 28, 80–81; and workers' perceptions and self-perceptions of, 65–67; remembered as absent from work relations at Fabricato, 19

Railroad workers, 133, 155, 266 n.47
Ramírez, Damían (priest at Fabricato), 156, 161–163
Recreational activities, 53, 154–155, 162, 167, 174, 225, 268 n.11, 270 n.34
Recruitment strategies: shifts in, with respect to gender, 8, 10–16, 34
Reinados, 171–176, 225, 233, 274 n.95
Religiosity, 64, 70–72, 139, 161–163, 184–187; and baptism, 113, 163, 196, 205; and Communion, 69–70, 82, 163, 175–176, 184; and Easter, 71, 175; first Communion ceremonies, 71, 175, 184; and religious festivals, 225; and religious icons, 178, 189. *See also* Small-town Antioquia: religious practices in
Reporters, 98, 135–136, 146, 159, 231
Rerum novarum, 15, 255 n.5
Restrepo, Adolfo, 274 n.106
Restrepo, Emilio, 15, 41, 47, 52, 55, 64, 72, 90, 95–96, 99, 102, 106–111, 140, 152, 178, 210, 270 n.29
Restrepo, Eusebio, 108–111
Restrepo, María Cristina (pseud.), 64, 157, 165, 179–180, 189, 191, 114, 199–201, 203, 220
Rojas Pinilla (head of military government), 60, 212, 254 n.47
Roldán, Mary, 51, 58–59, 61
Rosellón, 1, 3, 6–7, 55–57, 59, 64, 87, 123, 150–151, 157, 175, 193, 203, 222, 267 n.69, 267 n.3; and Barrio Rosellón, 268 n.8; neo-Taylorism at, 219, 226; paternalism at, 78, 150, 171, 203; purchase of Tejidos Hernández by, 55; strike at, in 1929, 140; strike at, in 1936, 123, 125, 133, 137–141, 146, 231, 267 n.3
Rubin, Gayle, 28–29, 31
Rural-urban migration, 58, 61, 64–72, 103, 170–171

Sacred Heart of Jesus, 52, 163, 189
Saenz Rovner, Eduardo, 18
Saffioti, Heilieth, 29
Saint Vincente de Paul Society, 53; hospital of, 54
Salas-cunas, 176, 274 nn. 102, 103
Sampling method, 242 n.10
Sanín Echeverri, Jaime, 77, 280 n.53
Santos, Eduardo, 211
Savage, Charles, 223–224, 233
Schools, for male workers' children, 149–150, 159

Scott, Joan, 31–33
Sedeco, xiv, 58, 226
Severance pay, 166, 204, 243 n.13
Sewell, William, 26
Shoes, 66, 68–69, 74, 96, 149, 260 n.99, 271 n.52
Silence, 187, 231; as a goal of factory inspector, 85–86; as a requirement ignored by workers, 87, 187–190
Sindicato de Trabajadores de Hilados y Tejidos de Antioquia, 134
Sindicato Textil del Hato, 158
Skirts: and hemlines, 169, 273 n.86; used to ridicule male strikebreakers, 90, 97–99
Small-town Antioquia, 60, 68, 71, 103; religious practices in, 184, 207. *See also* Rural-urban migration
Soccer (football), 150, 154, 254 n.59, 268 n.11
Sociability, 116–117, 124, 184, 187–199, 231. *See also* Co-workers
Social Catholicism, 14, 17. *See also* Catholic social action
Socialism, 61, 75–76, 110, 129, 130, 133, 173–174; and Socialist Liberals, 127; and Socialist press, 76, 90
Sociedad de mejoras públicas (SMP), 46, 49, 53
Solvés, Miguel, 109, 110–111, 210
Spiritual exercises, 78, 82, 159, 161, 184, 272 n.56
Sports teams, 150, 155, 225. *See also* Basketball; Soccer
Stedman Jones, Gareth, 25, 32
Stoler, Ann, 28
Stolke, Verena (formerly Martínez-Alier), 28
Stoller, Richard, 132, 211
Street rallies, 125–126, 129–130. *See also* Urban space
Strikes, 91, 109, 123–147, 224, 259 n.71; of banana workers, 125–126, 131; cooperation between women and men in, 98, 137; in Europe and the United States, 75; in 1935–1936, 5, 102, 123–147, 231–232; and strikebreakers, 125, 127, 135, 143; workers' ambivalence toward, 123, 141, 144. *See also* Fábrica de Bello
Supervisors, 79, 89, 90, 93, 136, 198–199, 223; anti-union activity of, 156; attacked by workers, 115; as a friendly presence, 191–192; as mediators be-

Ann Farnsworth-Alvear is Assistant Professor of History
at the University of Pennsylvania.

Library of Congress Cataloging-in-Publication Data
Farnsworth-Alvear, Ann.
Dulcinea in the factory : myths, morals, men, and women in Colombia's
industrial experiment, 1905–1960 / Ann Farnsworth-Alvear.
p.cm. — (Comparative and international working-class history)
Includes bibliographical references and index.
ISBN 0-8223-2461-x (cloth : alk. paper)
ISBN 0-8223-2497-0 (pbk. alk. paper)
1. Women textile workers—Colombia—Medellín—History—20th century.
I. Title. II. Series HD6073.T42 C854 2000 99-044769